The Pacific Muse

The Pacific Muse

EXOTIC FEMININITY

AND THE COLONIAL PACIFIC

PATTY O'BRIEN

A McLellan Book

University of Washington Press

Seattle and London

This book is published with the assistance of a grant from the
McLellan Endowed Series Fund, established through the generosity
of Martha McCleary McLellan and Mary McLellan Williams.

University of Washington Press
PO Box 50096, Seattle, WA 98145
www.washington.edu/uwpress

Library of Congress Cataloging-in-Publication Data

O'Brien, Patty.
The Pacific muse : exotic femininity and the colonial Pacific / Patty O'Brien.
p. cm.
"A McLellan book."
Includes bibliographical references and index.
ISBN 0-295-98609-3 (alk. paper)
1. Indigenous women — Pacific Islands — History.   2. Indigenous women —
Pacific Islands — Public opinion.   3. Women in popular culture —
Pacific Islands.   4. Indigenous peoples in popular culture — Pacific Islands.
5. Stereotype (Psychology) — Pacific Islands.   6. Pacific Islands — Colonization.
7. Europe — Colonies — Pacific Islands.   8. Public opinion — Europe.   I. Title.
GN662.O24   2006
305.48'8009965 — dc22
2005031050

The paper used in this publication is acid-free and 90 percent recycled from
at least 50 percent post-consumer waste. It meets the minimum requirements
of American National Standard for Information Sciences — Permanence of
Paper for Printed Library Materials, ANSI Z39.48–1984. ♾♻

Cover: *Amusemens des Otahitiens et des Anglais*, 1789

To Carmel O'Brien, who loved history

Contents

Acknowledgments / ix

Introduction / 3

I   *From Antiquity to the Discovery of Tahiti* / 17

II   *Colonizing Masculinities, 1767–1860* / 68

III   *Nature's Resources and the Forging of Empire, 1788–1890* / 115

IV   *Gender, Race, and the Body Politic in the Pacific and Europe* / 165

V   *From the 1890s to the Present* / 213

Epilogue / 263

Abbreviations / 271

Notes / 273

Bibliography / 307

Index / 333

Acknowledgments

As anyone who has lived with an intellectual project from research project to a book will be able to tell you, an entire story lies beyond these pages. That story is about the people who have lent their intellectual, moral, and material support to the writer throughout the many stages of this long process. In this case, *The Pacific Muse* began its life in 1992 in the Department of History, University of Sydney. *The Pacific Muse* was completed at Georgetown University, where I teach history through the Center for Australian and New Studies in the Edmund A. Walsh School of Foreign Service.

I need to thank the many people who have given me ballast during the life of this book. A number of them have seen this book through from its inception and I thank them for everything they have done for me over this time. They are my family: Sandra, John, Helen, and Maria O'Brien and Irene O'Neil. I also especially thank Ana Carden-Coyne for her friendship and intellectual generosity since 1992. From the University of Sydney, I thank the many people who assisted me, especially Richard White, Shane White, Richard Waterhouse, Jan Kociumbas, Penny Russell, Jim Masselos, Carole Adams, Wendy Brady, and Bettina Cass. In addition I wish to thank

Patricia Grimshaw, Margaret Jolly, Donald Denoon, Tim Rowse, Mary Spongberg, Sean Brawely, Mina Roces, John Gascoigne, Ian Tyrrell, Rae Frances, Bruce Scates, Grace Karskens, Deborah Oxley, Michael Pearson, and Alison Holland. At Georgetown University I am very indebted to Richard Stites, Peter Dunkley, Amy Leonard, Howard Spendelow, Kathy and Henry Nowik, Jane Ingham, James Collins, John Tutino, John McNeill, Bob Gallucci, Brendan Hill, Richard Teare, Ann Curthoys, Michael and Ros Crommelin, Tracey Macintosh, Cassandra Pybus, Kati Ferris, and John Corcoran. Thanks also to Witi Ihimaera. I am especially grateful to Grace and Tain Tompkins for all the assistance they have given me. In the greater Washington, D.C., Australian community, I thank Diane Bell and Kim McKay. I am also very appreciative of the friendship and support of Ray Hanna, Sarah Ross-Smith, Russell Cheek, Jude Clough, Lisa Doust, Pearl Grayson, Paul Maddock, Robert Lake, Maud Page, Jenny Hitchcock, Penny Hayes, Liz and Bill Laukka, Kate Mitchell, Anton James, Vida Carden-Coyne, Virginia Munro, Catherine Munro, the Davis family of Auckland, and the late great Philip Juster. And last, but by no means least, I thank Bruce Vaughn, and my new family, for everything.

I received financial support to conduct various stages of research from an Australian Postgraduate Award; the Farrington-Thorpe Scholarship; Frazer Traveling Scholarship; the Nancy Keesing Fellowship from Mitchell Library, Sydney; the Tempe Mann Fellowship from the NSW Federation of University Women; and a Summer Research Grant, School of Foreign Service, Georgetown University. I thank Peter Lowy and the Westfield Corporation for their generous support for Australian studies at Georgetown University. I also acknowledge the generous assistance I received from librarians at the many libraries and archives that I used to research this book. Finally, I extend my thanks to Lorri Hagman and Mary Ribesky of the University of Washington Press for their hard work on and support of this book, and to Stacey Lynn for her editing.

Thanks to you all.

The Pacific Muse

Introduction

In spite of the Pacific region's great mythological dimensions, knowledge about it remains minute in the West. Clichés tied loosely to fragmentary knowledge of the islands, their peoples, and the history of Western colonization in the region often alone constitute the Pacific in popular culture. The basis, if not the extent, of the popular lexicon of the Pacific is formed through the voyages of Captain Cook, the *Bounty* mutiny, the fiction of Herman Melville, South Sea stories by Robert Louis Stevenson and James A. Michener, the artworks of Paul Gauguin, and the anthropological writings of Margaret Mead, among others, as well as Hollywood films. These famous events, epics, adventurers, and admirers have cemented visual and literary visions that blend into tourist images of palm-fringed beaches and the promise of the Pacific paradise: intoxicating color, movement, and hospitality without peer. All of these disparate threads of Western conceptions of the region are persistently embodied in that immense emblem of exotic primitivism that I have named the Pacific muse.

The Pacific muse continues to be thought of as a natural and accurate portrayal of Pacific women, as benignly exotic and free of complications. This book contests this assumption. In this book, the stereotype of exotic femininity is the portal into the Pacific past. As we shall see, this effigy of exotic femininity is replete with historical myths and understandings. We shall explore what these myths and meanings were, and how they have constituted the Pacific muse stereotype. We shall look at alternate ways of viewing the Pacific past that eschew mythmaking. By taking this alternate historical path, we shall see a more nuanced and complicated history of colonial relations in the Pacific that lead us to rethink its most familiar remnant. We shall also move beyond the bounds of Pacific history to place the Pacific muse within the context of a broader history of exotic femininity forged in classical myth and thought that was shaped by colonial experiences and ideologies predating the mythologized 1760s' voyages to Tahiti, the historical moment in which many histories of Pacific colonial contact commence.

The stereotype of the island girl appears to be unchanging and timeless. For many this stereotype is anchored in a historical vision of early colonial contact in the 1760s, and has retained remnants from this capsule of myth and history ever since. The contact history of the 1760s is the reference point conjured up time and again, the authentic moment when Tahitian women were seemingly pure embodiments of women from classical myths. The stereotype harks back to these formative encounters constantly. Although the stereotype is anchored in classicism and the 1760s' voyages, it has not been static since this time. Aspects have been exaggerated, diminished, and changed. We shall see that the reasons for these alterations were bound up in the fusion of colonial desire, imperial agendas, and interactions with indigenous cultures in the Pacific. The island girl stereotype represents feminine primitivism, but it is intimately bound with ideas of whiteness and civilization. This book argues that the Pacific muse reflected concerns about colonial masculinity and white femininity, both contrasting them and at times absorbing them. Also, the complexities of the indigenous Pacific and the Pacific women supposedly represented were in constant interaction with the stereotype, challenging its narrowness. Far from being fixed, this icon of Pacific imperialism is as unstable and fluid as are notions of whiteness, gen-

der, and sexuality. By placing the Pacific muse at the epicenter of
this history, the cultivation of race and gender constructions that
are an integral part of this historical narrative will come to light. In
short, this is a history of colonial representations. But that is not the
only purpose of this book. It also asks how representations fed the
making of Pacific history and, conversely, how this history fed colonial representations.

Let us begin unraveling this stereotype by examining three postwar images. In the first, "Raire," an unself-consciously naked
woman adorns a postcard describing her as "a Polynesian Beauty"
(fig. a). The smiling Raire is captured in a delicate dance pose. Raire
embodies the colonial fetish of the "little brown gal" who has
retained the fabled Pacific sexual expertise despite exposure to
Christian morality. Her youthfulness and "exciting vitality" render
her a "typical Polynesian beauty." In "Sunkissed," we see a white
woman dressed as a Pacific exotic (fig. b). The woman in "Sunkissed" has imbibed the desired characteristics of Polynesian
women: she is physically perfect, passive, and pleasing. White
women continually encountered this colonial fetish as an ideal of
femininity because it stood in direct opposition to the sexless
Victorian model of white womanhood gradually eroded during the
twentieth century. The colonial artifact that "Sunkissed" emulates
became an aesthetic championed by white women living on Pacific
coasts, such as the "bronzed" Australian or Californian beach girl
or by an ever-increasing number of tourists, the leisured classes,
vacationing in the islands. "Sunkissed" embodies a childlike, nubile
ideal of womanhood, as the moniker the "little brown gal" celebrates.

With the rise of Pacific beach culture after World War II, white
women interacted with the icon of the South Seas woman in varying degrees. Grass skirts, frangipanis, and hula dancing became
central in the fantasy worlds of postwar suburban girlhoods, when
little girls mimicked the messages of feminine desirability received
from many fronts. In a photograph taken in 1949 of five girls dressed
up for the occasion of the Freshwater Swimming Club's gala day,
these little girls innocently partook in a colonial ritual that naturalized
their presence on the Pacific coast, specifically on Sydney's northern

a. "Raire: A Polynesian Beauty," 1960s postcard.

beaches (fig. c). By imitating stereotyped Pacific indigenes — significantly not the indigenous peoples of the Warringah area but of Hawai'i — these descendants of Europeans legitimate their presence in the region as "new natives" of a Pacific paradise. The appropriation of indigenous culture in this way signified a new era in colonial relations in which settler and indigenous cultures were seemingly fused and harmonized. Such an interpretation belies the complex web of ideas and historical processes that will be explored in this book.

This book is historical but reflects the era in which it is written. A resurgence of the Pacific muse stereotype is detectable in numerous guises: tourist images, clothing lines, and health products, as well as in books and other media. This resurgence highlights the persistence of romanticized views of Pacific peoples. The Pacific muse

b. "Sunkissed," 1950s postcard.

has enduring cultural cachet, although it is not accompanied by deeper and more complex understandings of the history of colonialism in the region.

Perhaps not coincidentally, the resuscitation of this stereotype comes after the paradigmatic shift in ideas about the West and race following the events of September 11, 2001. It is undeniable that "the West" and "its others" have undergone rapid and far-reaching redefinition in recent years. The benign stereotypes of the feminized Pacific jar with the menacing, masculine face of Islamic terrorism inhabiting the Middle East, North Africa, and South and Southeast Asia. What this new era in race politics does to conceptions of the Pacific and its people, which are still encapsulated in the Pacific muse stereotype, is to simplify Pacific peoples and trivialize them. The current messages that the stereotype conveys are ones lauding

c. "Freshwater Amateur Swimming Club Gala 1949." With permission of the Local Studies Collection Warringah Library Services, Australia.

Pacific peoples as blessed by nature's bounty, living healthy, natural lives in addition to being leisured, beautiful, and sexually alluring. Yet the contemporary Pacific is a troubled region, marred by poverty, environmental problems, poor health, and instability in indigenous politics across the region. The West still needs a new way to envision the Pacific that extends beyond the empty exoticism of stereotypes.

Also of interest is how contemporary indigenous cultural producers from the Pacific are engaging the stereotype. Artists and scholars of indigenous heritage have grappled with the stereotype and attempted to fracture the links between exoticism, eroticism, and racism inherent in it. Their work highlights the essence of this archetype: that it is familiar, but the Pacific, her peoples, and Pacific colonial history are not. Collectively these cultural producers stress how exotic femininity has corrupted and trivialized indigenous cultures. Their work informs this book throughout and will be discussed in chapter 5.

This book explores the history of exotic primitivism and how it has related to the peoples, cultures, and geography of the Pacific. It argues that the antecedents of Pacific exoticism can be traced from the evolution of female primitivism beginning with Odyssean temptresses. We shall see how these mythic figures served as blueprints for subsequent constructs of exotic primitivism. In addition we shall contemplate how classical ideas about gender, sexuality, and the environment also were factored into ideas of exotic femininity and trace their impact upon observations of Pacific women. This book also argues that the imperial precedents of colonization in the Middle East, Asia, Africa, and the Americas were profoundly important as a context to Pacific colonization. These historical precedents assist in understanding the cultural lexicon of Pacific colonization; they also demonstrate the gendered dynamics of imperialism and the patterns of behavior and treatment of indigenous women that Pacific colonizers carried with them across the seas.

The Pacific muse has been present in colonial representations of the Pacific since the sixteenth century, when colonial contact commenced. Not long after 1521, when the ill-fated Magellan voyage first sailed the Pacific, a new addition was made to the atlas of womankind, the South Seas woman. However, it was the discovery of Tahiti by the British mariner Samuel Wallis on his voyage in 1767 that marked the beginning of sustained colonization in the South Pacific region and the exponential increase in the cultural currency of the Pacific muse stereotype. From this historical juncture Pacific cultures influenced colonial traditions, producing a new dimension of exotic femininity.

By tracking the long history of exotic femininity, this book offers an explanation of how and why it has persisted throughout Western history. It assesses how female primitivism has altered over the expanse of time, particularly in response to the ideological watersheds of Christianity, Enlightenment scientific and racial theories, the Pacific labor trade, the imperial grab for territory, eugenics, the Pacific war, the nuclear Pacific, decolonization, and the twenty-first century. This book is concerned not only with monitoring changes in constructs of primitivism but also with ideals of civilization and whiteness from the classical tradition and beyond as these notions are profoundly interlinked.

Another purpose of this study is to explain the role of representations within the history of colonization in the Pacific. Representations of colonized people were distillations of both imperial ideologies and motives. Such representations reflected indigenous people's value within colonial cultural and economic systems and informed how they should be treated. This does not mean that colonial power was absolute. The ability of colonizers to act upon their ideas was often limited by the degree to which indigenous women remained part of their own societies. The diverse forms of colonial contact across the Pacific region entailed different experiences and responses from Pacific people. Since indigenous women were at the forefront of contact, they were also at the forefront of negotiating with colonizers and their expectations.

Pacific history cannot be conflated into one all-encompassing analytic model. Nowhere is this more apparent than in a study of intimate contact and colonial culture. It is indisputable that indigenous women were present on Pacific colonial frontiers, and many were there by choice. But this does not apply to all. Colonialism delivered unprecedented opportunities for women, but also exposure to unprecedented levels and new forms of exploitation. As the Pacific region encompassed different climatic zones, colonization differed markedly from temperate and tropical Pacific littorals to the pastoral frontiers of Australia, and women's experiences of it corresponded with differing colonial purposes.

The quest to uncover the historical experience of indigenous women in the colonial context offers interesting methodological opportunities. Owing to the extant historical sources, their silences, their fragmentary nature, and the fact that almost without exception colonizers produced these sources, only threads of the experience of indigenous women can be garnered. The evidence that does exist offers insights into women's lives. We shall see in this book how resourceful women often became, even in unenviable situations. We can see glimpses of the complexity of historical experience and the challenges that Pacific women made to the predominating stereotypes of them as one-dimensional historical figures.

In the same way that Pacific women cannot be combined into a monolithic historic category, so too we need to rethink the category of "colonizers." The nonindigenous people who came to the Pacific for the myriad reasons and quests that colonial economies and cultures supplied divided sharply along lines of gender, race, class, and nationality. Their interactions with Pacific women and the ways they represented them were shaped by their social position, their education, and their moral persuasion. Numerous colonial cultures coexisted that both intersected and opposed each other. Images of women in the Pacific resonate and amplify their authors' concerns and cultures, but the intent and outcome of representations differed markedly. There is no precise term to encompass the complexity of incoming peoples to the Pacific. European, Occidental, colonial, Atlantic, incoming — terms used in this book — fall short in conveying the cultural complexity inherent within this historical category. This is particularly so when one factors in the presence of African Americans in the sealing and whaling industries. Likewise, the categorizations of Polynesia, Melanesia, Micronesia, and Aboriginal Australia, similarly obscure greater demographic complexities. The limits of language are acknowledged, but these terms need to be employed.

As we shall see, numerous commentators on and creators of representations of Pacific women operated in the belief that the stereotype reflected a reality, while others knowingly dabbled in mythmaking and embellishment. The results also vary in their significance and potency. The widely publicized late-eighteenth-century voyage accounts of Pacific sexual escapades, for instance, entrenched expectations of freedoms for those who came after them that regularly fell short of the mark. Some visitors recorded Pacific women from firsthand experience; others imagined them from their armchairs or easels in Europe or newer European societies. The former did not necessarily carry more authority than the latter. The greater resonance of particular versions of Pacific exoticism related more to the skill of representers in embroidering existing tropes with layers that reflected the concerns and desires of their own time.

Enlightenment voyages and the sustained colonization that followed brought with them ideologies of male and female sexuality, gender, and race. These were not stable constructions, but ones debated and contested against the background of vastly different Pacific cultures. The stereotype of the Pacific muse was regularly a point of comparison in these debates. As in many stereotypes, there was a kernel of truth to them. Pacific cultures, like other cultures outside the Judeo-Christian or Islamic traditions, did not problematize sexuality but rather celebrated it and viewed it as a positive life force. Women's sexuality, the site of such great contention within Western cultures, was likewise celebrated. Pacific cultures revered beauty, though what constituted "beauty" extended well beyond the narrow definition explicit in the stereotype. What stereotypes of Pacific women did, and still do, is reduce women to one dimension: a passive sexuality that revolved around pleasing white men.

This book interrogates colonial culture in its many manifestations—from pictorial art, literature, and film to the journals of explorers and missionaries. It offers a reinterpretation of both the more familiar, canonical texts of Pacific imperialism and other not-so-well-known remnants of this cultural heritage. I have read these texts with an eye for revealing insights on gender, sexuality, race, femininity, and beauty and their wider historical implications. I concentrate upon exotic femininity typically associated with Polynesia, and contrast these exotic stereotypes with constructs of female primitivism that predominate in colonial representations of Aboriginal women in Australia and the western Pacific islands. Aboriginal women were initially viewed with the same exoticized gaze cast upon their islander counterparts, but this did not persist. Micronesian women, though the first encountered by Europeans, were often conflated with ideas about Pacific women derived from Polynesian and Asian contact, as they were not considered as distinct as Melanesian or Aboriginal women. Further work on comparative representations of Micronesian women is needed, though it is beyond the scope of this present book. Fleeting voyagers in the late eighteenth century and first half of the nineteenth delineated Melanesian women in the western Pacific. As Margaret Jolly has shown, these representations were characterized by the "jealousy" of men and the treatment of women as "beasts of burden."[1] But it was not until the second half of the nineteenth century that colonialism in that part of the Pacific altered with the advent of plantation economies. It is from this time that the history of contact in Melanesia is drawn into this narrative.

By the middle of the nineteenth century, the differentiations between ethnically different Pacific women were clearly enunciated. This was due to their seeming compatibility with classically derived notions of exotic beauty, as well as with colonial politics and agendas. I investigate why this diverse representative culture eventuated and examine the implications of this upon various women's experience of colonization across the Pacific region. Through the use of this methodology, the links between representations of colonized women, colonial agendas, differences in colonial economies, and experiences of colonization become more pronounced. Polynesian women are often cited as a neat fit with exotic feminine ideals, but this was not the case. We shall see that age, body type, maternity, and initiative all had an impact on the assessments of Polynesian women, which had implications in colonial history.

This book does not claim to be exhaustive. As colonialism in the Pacific was a global phenomenon, it is a diffuse historical subject. A history that places colonial constructions of gender, sexuality, and race at the center of analysis is necessarily complex. While this book is focused on the Pacific, it has implications that reach beyond the region as it engages with historical issues that resonate in numerous fields —intellectual history, art history, anthropology, gender studies, the history of sexuality, and colonial studies. The colonial Pacific was literally and metaphorically linked to old and newer Europes, most notably America and its Atlantic world and the European societies of Australia and New Zealand. All these historical facets have been drawn into this synthetic history that fuses literatures and different approaches to historical questions, periods, and regions.

As this book is a gender-focused world history, it has eclectic intellectual antecedents. My largest intellectual debts are to scholars who have explored Pacific, Australian, and New Zealand histories, the history of colonial representations of the Pacific, and gendered colonial histories in regions beyond the Pacific. I am indebted to historians who have illuminated the gendered history of the Pacific in ways germane to this study, particularly the work of Caroline Ralston, Patricia Grimshaw, Greg Dening, and Ann McGrath.[2] Regarding the history of Pacific representations I am indebted to the work of Bernard Smith, whose books, *European Vision and the South Pacific* and *Imagining the Pacific*, gave this field considerable scope and texture. Following Smith there have been a number of scholars who have extended his intellectual project by delving into various aspects of the heritage of colonial art and culture of the Pacific. Many of these scholars have adapted ideas and insights from the field commenced by Edward Said's *Orientalism* of 1978, which explored the power inherent in feminized representations of the colonial other.[3]

Since I commenced researching and writing on this topic in 1992, a vibrant field on representations of Pacific women has evolved.[4] The most important works for this study are those by Margaret Jolly, Haunani-Kay and Mililani Trask, Tereisa Teaiwa, Harriet Guest, Nicholas Thomas, Roy Porter, and Jane Desmond.[5] These authors have infused colonial representations of Pacific women with readings that illuminate their power, function, and ideological basis in colonial thought. Jolly, Guest, Teaiwa, Desmond, and Haunani-Kay and Mililani Trask have also interrogated the dual meanings of the female and the racialized body in colonial cultural production from eighteenth-century voyage artists and writers, film, hula shows, photography, and ethnohistorical constructions. Other scholars, particularly Neil Rennie, Rod Edmond, Bronwen Douglas, and Robert Nicole, have investigated the discursive creation of the Pacific in which the Pacific muse icon is present though not the central focus of their investigations.[6] These scholars have examined aspects of the heritage of colonial constructions of the Pacific in literature, art, and anthropological discourses in ways that have enriched the field. This book expands upon the parameters of these studies. Michael Sturma's work is a curious addition to this historiography in that he suggests that sexualized stereotypes of Pacific women have been empower- ing for them. While our works share a seemingly similar focus, my approach differs markedly from Sturma's in that considerations of imperial power, conceptions of race and gender, and their function within the machinations of Pacific colonial history figure prominently in this book. More recently, studies by Kathleen Wilson and Lee Wallace have interrogated the supposedly stable construct of white masculinity, a position shared by this study. Wilson was interested in how Cook's Pacific voyages assisted the forging of English iden- tity. Wallace argues that it is not the Pacific muse stereotype that is the "most sexually resonant figure" in the representational archive of Pacific colonization but rather that of the male body.[7] While there is a prominent homoerotic colonial vision of the Pacific, it does not eclipse that of women. These two visions of the Pacific are nonethe- less consistently connected, as this book argues.

In addition to this field of scholars who have studied repre- sentations of the Pacific, this book has benefited from a number of feminist and postcolonial studies in Asian, American, and African colonial history and cultural heritage. Of particular note is the work of Anne McClintock, Mary Louise Pratt, Londa Schiebinger, Sander L. Gilman, Ann Stoler, and Lenore Manderson, who have made invaluable insights for this book through their delineation of the connections between colonialism, the construction of colonial ide- ologies, and their gendered implications.[8]

The book's five chapters trace the development of the Pacific muse stereotype across time. The first chapter investigates the ante- cedents of the late-eighteenth-century representations of Pacific exotic femininity from classical constructions of exotic femininity to colonial precedents and the discovery of Tahiti. Chapter 2 explores the role of sex in the politics of empire building and how it influenced the creation of sexualized stereotypes of Pacific women. The myth of unfettered sexual freedom is tempered here by an examination of the realpolitik of colonization as well as the varied constructions of masculinity that had a cultural and political impact upon Pacific empires from the first voyages on. The third chapter focuses on the connection between racial and sexual stereotypes and the economies of empire. Ideology reduced women to natural resources for many colonizing men and, to a lesser extent, women. Chapter 4 examines how stereotypes of the Pacific were factored into debates about European women's social and political role and position. The relationship between ideas on the body and debates about women and politics are examined here with attention to the fortunes of women rulers in the Pacific within the era of colonial annexation. The final chapter explores the previous themes within the twentieth-century historical context. It examines the role the stereotype has played across a century in which colonization supposedly ended but the trivializing portrayal of the Pacific predominated and continues to do so. I will explain why this was so and how Pacific people are answering back and reclaiming their cultural heritage in the face of an increased visibility of the archetype in the twenty-first century.

I

From Antiquity to the
Discovery of Tahiti

If history were simple, this narrative of exotic femininity in the Pacific would commence in June 1767. In that year Tahiti was "discovered" by British voyagers under the command of Captain Samuel Wallis. Nine months later, French sailors on the Bougainville voyage discovered it too, naming the island New Cythera. Within a year Captain Cook, on his *Endeavour* voyage, arrived to observe the transit of Venus from the vantage point of the South Seas. From this time the Pacific was swept up into the rapidly changing world of modernizing Europe. Late-eighteenth-century British and French voyagers saw the Pacific and its peoples in unprecedented ways as they viewed this newest part of the New World through Enlightenment eyes. They saw new revelations about nature, race, gender, and sexuality in Pacific people. They also infused this latest imperial frontier with contemporary meanings that simplified and rendered it comprehensible. The stereotyping of Pacific peoples began after these first encounters. Women were the particular focus of Pacific voyagers. With the assistance of artists, writers, and theorists in Europe, these voyagers generated the popular conception of the Pacific as a sexually alluring woman, and the myth was launched with Oberea, the Tahitian queen crowned by Wallis, as its first figurehead.[1]

History, however, is not so neat. Thus the beginnings of this story extend back well beyond the late eighteenth century. British and French Enlightenment voyagers inherited a tradition of Pacific colonialism from their imperial predecessors. The Pacific had existed as part of the New World since Magellan's ill-fated voyage struggled around Tierra del Fuego and entered the Pacific in 1520. Magellan's voyage commenced two centuries of sporadic contact with Pacific Ocean peoples, by Spaniards searching for El Dorado. The Dutch sought commercial gold, as they had struck in the East Indies, and the Portuguese coveted more of the enrichment that East Indies spices had delivered them. These powers had carved out their empires along the eastern seaboard of the Americas, the western islands of the Pacific, and the Southeast Asian archipelago, supplanting Arab trading networks in a number of instances. Spanish dominance of the Philippine archipelago and Guam commenced in 1564. Portuguese economic dominance in Melaka and the Maluka islands was secured by the early sixteenth century, Timor by 1512, and a powerful trading presence in Canton from 1557. Dutch imperial domination of Java was achieved by 1618, the island thus forming the epicenter of the Dutch East Indies empire.[2]

The voyages that scouted for new frontiers of influence in the seas between the Americas and the East Asian empires had intermittent contact with Pacific peoples in the sixteenth, seventeenth, and eighteenth centuries. The experiences and myths of exotic femininity from the Americas, Africa, and the Orient had an immeasurable impact upon how these newer New World women were viewed. These imperial precedents and traditions were central to the eighteenth-century construct of the Pacific muse. Imperial experience was not the only factor that shaped ways of seeing and treating Pacific women. Notions of class and gender from within European societies profoundly influenced ideas of sexual accessibility, beauty, and value that were projected onto all exotic women.

This history of exotic femininity does not begin with Renaissance voyages to the Pacific or the other parts of the New World. The history of exotic femininity is substantially older, as old as Western culture itself. Many of the underlying ideas about women, female sexuality, and colonizing masculinity that informed ideas about Pacific women stemmed from classical Greek myth, science, and philosophy. These ideas have had remarkable stamina throughout the centuries and were of even greater consequence from the eighteenth century owing to the importance placed upon classical thought in the Enlightenment and Romantic movements. The interest by early explorers in the relationship between climate and women's sexual characteristics, directly derived from classical scientific ideas, was one significant instance of the application of antique ideas in the theater of modern colonialism.

Likewise, the eighteenth-century grand tour tradition was steeped in the Enlightenment fascination with the classical past. Travel allowed firsthand observation of foreign locales, classical ruins, and experience. Sexual experience was a central, albeit illicit, facet of this eighteenth-century travel culture that reputedly "'finished'" aristocratic youths before they assumed their positions of power at home. English visitors to the Pacific applied this grand tour culture, as Bernard Smith has shown, resulting in the classical rendering of Pacific peoples in art and understanding. The sexualized dimension of this culture had discernible effects in the Pacific through comparisons with accessible continental women and, moreover, the conflation of Pacific women with mythologized women of antiquity. Queen Oberea, the first popular female figure in Pacific imperial narratives, encapsulated the intersecting influences that fed into constructions of Pacific women, as we shall see in the chapter's final section. She not only embodied the preexisting ideas; she was transformed by European colonial culture into the figurehead of a new genus of exotic femininity, one resident and in this case reigning over the South Seas island of Tahiti, or so the new myths would have it.[3] This chapter weaves colonial history with extant notions about exotic femininity and searches for origins of these persistent ideas and practices that shaped the Pacific colonial culture immeasurably.

Renaissance Indians of the Pacific

Renaissance voyages unveiled the Americas and the Pacific concurrently. The American colonial experience was reflected frequently in the early images of the Pacific, and the two colonial episodes shared many characteristics. This similarity was due to a number of factors, not the least of which was that these regions, now considered separate, were conflated. Renaissance voyagers did not readily differentiate between non-European peoples, as later voyagers would do according to cultural and racial differences spurred by Enlightenment classificatory thinking. Yet Renaissance voyagers readily distinguished between themselves, the Europeans, and the inhabitants of the New World, who were most commonly described as "Indians." The Renaissance need to define "Europe" and "Europeans" featured commonly in colonial culture. Colonization was a fundamental part of the process of creating a shared cultural identity. Europeans needed their *others* in order to define themselves as well as to impose a rationale for colonization by configuring colonized peoples as weak, primitive, feminized, inferior, and disempowered and themselves as dominant, civilized, masculine, and technologically advanced. That need only increased with time.[4]

As with Pacific colonization, the bodies of women were often used as allegorical figures for the American continent. The enactment of colonial conquest was regularly configured as a dominating and forced sexualized assault upon feminized "virgin" land. This exaggerated the underlying power imbalance between the colonizing man and the colonized. This pattern of representing colonial subjugation was a hallmark of the occupation of the Americas and was both a symbolic and recognized means to express and gain power over indigenous societies. That is, colonization was normalized through being likened to a sexual act, as Anne McClintock has shown. The trope of American colonization as an eroticized encounter, with America depicted as the naked, vulnerable woman and Europe as a clothed, technologically advanced man, was famously depicted in Jan van der Straet's drawing *Americen Americus retexit* of 1575 (fig. 1.1).

Such images were powerful propaganda accompanying the actions of colonization.[5]

The naturalness of van der Straet's drawing belied the harsher consequences of the mapping of America as a sexually available woman. The philosophic license to colonize had a very real and brutal impact upon American women's experience of the invasion. So endemic was the sexual violence perpetrated upon Carib women by the men on the seventeen plus ships that sailed to the Caribbean on the second Columbus voyage of October 1493 to June 1496 that historian Tzventan Todorov described this particular episode as "one story in a thousand."[6]

In this "one story," Michele de Cuneo, a nobleman from Savona,

1.1 Jan van der Straet, *Americen Americus retexit*, 1575.

AMERICA.

Americen Americus retexit. *Semel vocauit inde semper excitam.*

displayed the attitude that Carib women were no more than bodies existing to provide him with sexual pleasure. De Cuneo's description of events displays the culture of male sexual rites that existed in Europe, where rape of unguarded women was acceptable practice. He had "captured a very beautiful Carib woman," whom he brought to his cabin, "and she being quite naked as is their custom, I conceived the desire to take my pleasure." As he attempted "to put my desire to execution," the woman fought back, treating him "with her nails in such wise that I would have preferred never to have begun." De Cuneo took a rope, "thrash[ing] her well, following which she produced such screaming and wailing as would cause you not to believe your ears." At this point the woman succumbed. De Cuneo finished his tale, informing his readers "that, I can tell you, she seemed to have been raised in a veritable school of harlots."[7]

The anonymous woman's challenge to his rape made this incident notable to De Cuneo and Todorov. His "thrashing" achieved an end beyond his expectations, confirming his initial assumption about the sexual skill of primitive women. This tale of sexual conquest is an illustration of the enactment of the imperial manifesto in which conquest, dispossession, and sexual violence were interlocking practices supported by authoritative concepts of race, gender, and class superiority.

One century after this Caribbean incident, Spaniard Don Alvaro de Mendaña "discovered" the Marquesas Islands in 1595 on his second Pacific voyage. A century after the Columbus voyages to the Americas, the Spaniards were looking for the fabled land and wealth of Solomon. Instead they stumbled upon the southern islands of Te Henua Enata and named the group the Marquesas and the islands St. Christina, St. Pedro, Dominica, and Magdalena. The records of this voyage reveal a similar combination of power, violence, and sexual access to women that was present in the Americas.

The voyage began in Callao, Peru, and consisted of four vessels holding nearly four hundred people. The voyagers included Mendaña's wife, Donna Ysabel Barretos; three brothers-in-law; "respectable married couples, unemployed adventurers and some prostitutes," all of whom were prospective settlers for a new colony in the west-

ern Pacific.[8] The Spanish first landed on St. Christina to hear Mass.
This gave them the opportunity to assess the merits of these curious "new" people, at close proximity. The pilot and future commander, Pedro Fernandez de Quiros, noted that this new genus of
woman was as "beautiful as the women of Lima," though whiter and
"not so rosy." Not only were they remarkable for their "delicate
hands, genteel bodies and waists," but also for their "sufficiently
white" countenances. De Quiros did not see these women himself
but reiterated the accounts of other witnesses. As well as the Spanish
men, Ysabel Barretos was taken with the beauty of the women.
Barretos, desiring to cut some of the hair of a "beautiful Indian"
woman who sat beside her and fanned her while she was ashore,
sought a souvenir of this "so very fine" hair. However the Marquesan
woman expressed displeasure at such a violation, the head and hair
being *tapu*, sacred.[9]

This idyllic encounter did not last long. Tensions mounted
between the St. Christina islanders and the Spanish who brought
with them one hundred years of colonial experience in the Americas.
The Spanish asserted brutal imperial mastery over these new
"Indians," killing at least two hundred. It was not until after this mer-
ciless spectacle of military might that the women came "lovingly" to
the Spanish. Historical accounts imply that women offered "bunches
of plantains and other fruit" and also acquiesced their bodies.[10]

As more islands were "discovered" by the intermittent Dutch
and Spanish voyages after 1595, increasing numbers Pacific islanders
were added to the human landscape of Indians of the region. One
of the first visual representations of Pacific women and men derives
from Oliver van Noort's expedition of 1598–1600 (fig. 1.2).[11] This
image attributed to the Dutchman van Noort reveals the place of
the imaginary in generating images of exotic peoples. The island
woman has been Europeanized and is heavily reminiscent of Eve,
complete with a fig leaf, unlike her exposed male companions. The
allusion to Eve carries with it dense layers of meaning, particularly
about sexual allure, temptation, and shame, that will be further expli-
cated below. This image reveals the dominance of Christianity as
the prism through which women were viewed and represented, a

factor in the representative tradition that would persist albeit with varying influence.

Owing to the brevity of early encounters, sexual contact between imperialists and the indigenes was infrequent. The Dutch Roggewein voyage, on which Rapa Nui was discovered on Easter Sunday in 1722, was a notable exception. This first encounter reflected the same interplay of colonial politics evident in the Mendaña massacre on St. Christina, although fewer islanders were killed on this occasion. When the Dutch landed on April 10, 1722, they became intimidated by a crowd of physically powerful, curious, and predominantly male islanders, and opened fire. Roggewein estimated that they killed "10

1.2 "Les Habitans de Lylle de la Droues" in Oliver van Noort, *Description du pénible voyage fait entour de l'univers ou globe terrestre,* Amsterdam, Cornille Claeffz, 1602.

or 12 besides the wounded." After the killings, the islanders brought
great amounts of food to the foreigners amid "doleful cries and lamen-
tation," so "that they might get the dead bodies." The Dutchmen's
curiosity was eventually sated when "at last they shewed [*sic*] their
women, intimating to us that we might dispose of them and carry
any of them aboard." The Dutch were "affected with all these
demonstrations of humility and the most perfect submission." The
women "would often sit down near to us and undress themselves,
smiling and enticing us to familiarities with them with every sort of
gestures," while "others, who remained in their houses, called us and
made signs for us to come and make free with them." Displaying
"perfect submission," the women's sexual invitations were seen as
the most definitive and pleasing sign of the islanders' defeat. There
was, therefore, no need to punish them further.[12]

The Mendaña, van Noort, and Roggewein voyages were part
of the European maritime expansion of the fifteenth and sixteenth
centuries, which brought the Atlantic, Indian, and fragments of the
Pacific oceans into the European imperial realms. A network of
entrepôts was established along the coastlines of Europe, Africa,
India, America, the East Indies, the western Pacific rim, and China.
The international trading networks created a socially dislocated
group of men, including itinerant workers who manned the merchant navies and trading vessels traversing the known world.
Imperial economies disrupted preexisting trade and production
networks, and forced dependence upon foreign goods. Servicing the
sexual desires of seafarers was one of the few ways that colonized
people could participate in these new economies. Access to the bodies of local women was an expectation of seafarers, and ports were
graded according to the plenitude of available women as well as food,
water, and alcohol.[13]

British buccaneer William Dampier mapped out the seafaring
sexual culture of the late seventeenth century. Prostitution, or "being
free with their women," was deemed by Dampier as a "custom" of
the peoples of "Pegu, Siam, Cochinchina and Cambodia," as well as
in "Tunquin." He found this out through experience, "for I did . . .
make a voyage thither, and most of our men had women aboard all

the time of our abode there." Similarly, he noted that on "the Coast of Guinea, our Merchants, Factors, and Seamen who reside there, have their black misses." According to Dampier, sexual contact with local women not only met the corporeal needs of men, but it was also considered a "piece of Policy." He claimed that "great men" of the empire sometimes offered their daughters, and in Guinea, the king offered his wives to help forge an "alliance" between "the chief Factors and Captains of Ships." Not only did this increase pecuniary opportunities, but also, according to Dampier, it made the empire safe and sustaining for European men. He argued that if "any difference about Trade, or anything else, which might provoke the Natives to seek treacherous Revenge (to which these heathen nations are very prone)" the female lovers or "these Darians" as he named them, "would certainly declare it to their Friends, and hinder their countrymen's design."[14]

Exotic Femininity and the Americas

William Dampier's reference to "Darians" evoked women of the Darien range of mountains that runs through present-day Panama and Columbia. It also evoked two exemplars of exotic femininity of the American imperial experience: Malintzin and Pocahontas. Malintzin, who was known to the Spanish as Doña Marina, was a woman of Aztec parentage who was instrumental in shifting the balance of power in favor of the *conquistadors* in their maneuvers to break the strength of Montezuma and create the imperial territory of New Spain from 1518 on. Stephen Greenblatt has argued that Malintzin played a pivotal role in the Spanish conquest of the Aztec and Mayan empires. Her role was further exalted by Bernal Diaz del Castillo in his *Conquest of New Spain*, which was a key historical source, Greenblatt argued. As she spoke the native tongues and rapidly gained proficiency in Spanish, she became indispensable to Hernando Cortés as an intermediary between two vying cultures, and forged her own base of power. Greenblatt suggested that she not only made the conquest of New Spain possible by applying her knowledge and her political cunning, but she also embodied the transition of power within the region. Malintzin, who gained notice for being "good look-ing and intelligent," became Cortés's mistress and bore him a son, Don Martin Cortés, a prominent member of the new hybrid Spanish-American people. She was a legendary figure within her own time and, according to Greenblatt, continues to function as "a resonant, deeply ambivalent symbol, half-divinity, half-whore, the saviour and betrayer." Malintzin was indicative of what was most desirable in a colonized woman, though she was not unique, Susan Midgen Socolow, has argued. Her conduct accommodated the colonizers while her appearance fulfilled an aesthetic ideal of exotic feminine beauty that would become the basis of the stereotype of the Pacific muse.[15]

The second American legend was Pocahontas, the reified "mother of America." Her myth emerged out of the nascent Jamestown set-tlement on Chesapeake Bay almost one century after Doña Marina. Pocahontas has been appropriated as an imperial trophy for four main reasons. She personifies, first, the commingling of American and English "blood"; second, the Christian "salvation" of the American heathen; third, the "colonial appropriation of American abundance"; and fourth, consensual colonization. She is a pliant his-torical figure, as the details about her are clouded by centuries of mythmaking.[16]

The Pocahontas myth has been the source of many misconcep-tions about the integration of British settlers with local peoples at the Jamestown settlement. Accounts of the Jamestown settlement suggest that a sexual economy was operating between English men and the local Algonquian women. In 1607 one chronicler of the set-tlement, believed to be Captain Gabriel Archer, wrote that "they [the Algonquian men] have many wives . . . these they abide not to be toucht [*sic*] before their face." The Pocahontas myth suggests that racial anxieties did not feature in this new colony. This was not the case. Pocahontas was exceptional in a number of instances. She was the daughter of Powhatan, "king" of the eastern seaboard region where the first colonies were established, and thus she was accorded the title of "princess." Her noble status within Algonquian society gilded her legend in American colonial culture. She was kidnapped by the colonists and held captive for a year. During her captivity she became the first convert to Christianity and was christened Rebecca after the Biblical mother of two nations. She married a Virginian planter, John Rolfe, in 1614, and a year later gave birth to the first child of a "new people," Thomas. According to legend she also brokered a peace between her people and the colonists, which was dubbed the "Peace of Pocahontas." In 1616, she traveled to England and was presented to the court of King James and Queen Anne. On her return voyage, she caught a cold and died at the age of twenty-two.[17]

Pocahontas's fame in American national legend is based on spurious evidence. It is claimed that she had a romance with John Smith, a settler and journal-keeper of the voyages and early settlement. Moreover, it was Smith who disseminated the story in his *The Generalle Historie of Virginia* of 1624. Published after Pocahontas's death, this account claimed that she effected his stay of execution when he was the prisoner of her father in 1607, and that she warned the colonists of an intended attack upon them by her people. This one story forged her mythic status and propelled her to the greatest heights in United States iconography.[18]

Her legend is founded in her aberration from frontier realities. Despite there having been a "scattering" of marriages between settlers and local indigenes in the early years of settlement, intermarriage did not become a widespread practice, as David Fowler and Robert Tilton have shown. Before departing England, colonists were discouraged from marrying New World people because of biblical law that stated "they may not marry nor give in marriage to the heathen." Not content with discouraging this practice through evoking Christian doctrine, authorities enacted legislation in various colonies from 1630, making marriage between whites and Indians or black slaves unlawful. Even though the most intense anxiety and harshest penalties were directed at sexual liaisons between black slaves and lower classes of whites, particularly when the woman was white, marriages between whites and Indians were not condoned. There were instances in which laws banning intermarriage between whites and Indians were eased in some colonies. Apart from the paganism of Indians, the negligible number of marriages between white men and Indian women was assured, Fowler argued, by the large numbers of white women from the early years in the colonies, the reduced populations of Indians, and the relative separateness of the two societies except on the frontiers.[19]

By the eighteenth century some colonists saw this enforced culture of division between white and Indian people as a lost opportunity to have avoided the years of conflict between whites and indigenes of America. Peter Fontaine, writing from Virginia in 1757 to his brother, lamented widespread illicit sexual relations: "many base wretches amongst us take-up with negro women," propagating a population of "black bastards" in the American colonies. The "blood" of white America and the mistreatment of native peoples might have been avoided, in his assessment, "if instead of this abominable practice . . . we had taken Indian wives in the first place" as it "would have made them some compensation for their lands." The prevention of legitimate relations also ensured that when there were relationships, colonial traders "leave their off-spring like bulls or bears to be provided at random by their mothers," furthering the immorality that Fontaine perceived as implicit in colonial relations, fracturing any possible cohesion between indigenes and newcomers.[20]

With the rise of Enlightenment race theories, the dream of an American utopia, peopled by a blend of indigenous and white races, faded even further, Tilton has contended. While horror at mixed-race people grew, by the 1820s paradoxically the popularity in American culture of Pocahontas and other "good Indians" such as Squanto, whose generosity to the starving colonists began the annual Thanksgiving tradition, rose to great heights. Such figures assuaged guilt for the contemporaneous dispossession of Native Americans as their assistance to colonizers made them complicit in settler success and the demise of their own people.[21]

The legends of Pocahontas, Doña Marina, and later Sacagawea so overwhelmed the stories of the American frontiers that they drowned out the broader reality of colonization. These women were supreme objects of imperial desire due to their perceived willingness to facilitate and lend legitimacy to colonial activity and their safeguarding of imperial endeavors even at their own people's expense. The myths surrounding these American women illustrate what was valued most in colonized women: exotic beauty and a sexual availability that signified compliance with the colonial project. As Raymond Stedman suggests, these legendary Indian women formed a colonial trope that he called *la belle sauvage*, that would be transferred to the Pacific in later times.[22]

Endearing images of early Central American frontier figures like Doña Marina competed with the overridingly negative stereotypes of Native Americans evident in the debates surrounding the first appearance of syphilis in Italy in 1494, which quickly spread across Europe. In attempting to locate a cause for the contagion, doctors oscillated for thirty years between blaming the new disease upon moral depravity, the "polluting" effects of Jews, or the newly discovered peoples from America. The "few Indians" who had been brought to Europe by Columbus as a souvenir for the Spanish king were the particular target of attention. Anna Foa has argued that by 1530, roughly thirty years after colonization of America commenced, the indecision in assigning the blame for syphilis had ceased and it was widely accepted that American Indians were the source of this blight upon Europe. Foa has argued further that an expository stereotype was therefore needed, one that focused upon the lasciviousness, immorality, and unnatural sexual practices of "American Indians."[23]

Amerigo Vespucci, the Italian voyager after whom this New World would be named, wrote of the Indians that "without regard to blood relations . . . they satisfy their desires as they occur to their libidos as beasts do." Another, Fernandez de Oviedo, concentrated upon the alleged libidinous habits of Indian women. He described them as so contaminating that "few Christians who carnally lie with Indian women of these places are saved from this disgraceful sickness." The link between the creation of the negative stereotype and the accompanying intense scrutiny of Native Americans had an obvious imperial design. The perception that colonized or primitive women were licentious and willing to enter into this relationship was central to colonial stereotypes of them. Not only did colonial stereotypes accommodate sexual exploitation; they dehumanized indigenes, providing justification for massacre, enslavement, dispossession, and sexual violence. The articulation of a heavily sexualized and pathologized discourse on Native Americans occurred simultaneously with their incorporation into a colonial economy of domination and power.[24]

Indigenous Americans were increasingly represented and treated as commodities, like their land. Such representative patterns can be traced from the south to the very north of the continent. The politics of race and marriage in early colonial settings were elaborate, however. In the early-seventeenth-century New France settlements of St. Lawrence River and Arcadia, it was official French policy for French men to take native wives. This deliberate encouragement of *métissage* was due, first, to the shortage of French women willing to occupy this difficult frontier. Second, the French at this stage considered it good colonial practice, having used the policy in Brazil. The intimate entwining of French men into New World societies was thought to ensure the survival of fledgling colonial enterprises and to solidify trade alliances for the French at the expense of competitors. By the early eighteenth century, France's liberal stance on interracial marriage was eroding, Olive Dickason has argued. The pragmatic beliefs that underlay the policy were not being realized, as the growing *métis* population was failing to demonstrate desired levels of loyalty to France. Regulations restricting American Indian women from inheriting their French husband's property were imposed, and by 1735, all mixed marriages required the consent of the governor or commanding officer, at which point the "ideal of 'one nation' foundered."[25]

When the English entered the Hudson Bay region from 1670, the practice of taking native wives was also adopted despite "determined efforts from London to prevent it" as in southern settlements. Apart from the harshness of this frontier and the imperative for ties with local indigenes to ensure commercial success, the other factor that ensured intermarriages took place despite the misgivings in London was that there were "virtually no white women" in this northern region until the early nineteenth century. This circumstance followed a deliberate decision in the mid-1680s to ban white women from immigrating, as their presence, deduced by the Hudson Bay Company's London Committee from the experience of one hapless wife, "constituted a burdensome nuisance" that hampered business, according to Sylvia Van Kirk. The consequence of this policy was the common practice of "double families," in which company men left wives and families in England and then started new families with local women in Rupert's Land, causing immeasurable economic, social, and emotional hardships for women on both sides of the Atlantic.[26]

The story of Cree woman Jane Taylor and her daughters illustrates how company men negotiated intimate relationships in the context of the northern fur trade. She married George Taylor, the sloop master at York Factory, and had eight children by him. Taylor took pains to instruct his brood in "clean and industrious habits" before he retired and returned to England in 1815. His daughters Margaret and Mary in turn became country wives of company men. These men in turn left their Cree wives, although they made some provisions for them, as the expectation was that the women would return to their relatives or were free to marry other men. Margaret Taylor's husband, however, took advantage of the changing culture and attitude to the presence of white women in the region in the nineteenth century. He later returned with an English bride, leaving Margaret economically and emotionally destitute. Indigenous women did seek out company men for husbands, yet the advantages of such unions were strongly weighted in favor of the Englishmen and increasingly so, as racial attitudes became more pointed in the nineteenth century, as Jennifer Brown has shown.[27]

This pattern of colonial relations was repeated regularly in the Pacific, particularly in connection with resource-getting industries that dominated the regional economy until the mid-nineteenth century. The difference in both colonial regions is that race was always a component in the Pacific. Race was not the only determining factor in women's disposability in sexual relationships. The practice of having country wives was well established in Europe. Working-class women in the metropolitan and rural areas functioned in a sexual economy in similar ways to indigenous women in the colonies. Yet indigenous women had less practicable recourse owing to the racial dynamics of colonization. The implementation of laws preventing the legalization of such unions in the American colonies worked in unison with growing cultural beliefs espousing native women's inferiority. Such attitudinal currency was carried to the ends of the earth with the expansion of empire into the Pacific from the late eighteenth century.[28]

The Black Body, Africa, and the Orient

The far-reaching effects of colonization in the Americas developed concurrently with the African slave trade that commenced in the Spanish colony of Santo Domingo in 1501. Interchangeable notions of blackness and primitivism had a powerful cultural currency from the twelfth century. The commencement of slavery intensified pre-existing cultural traditions exponentially. The discourses in relation to American indigenous women were applied with little variation to Africans. From the sixteenth century on, the increasingly prominent stereotype of Native American women as sexually promiscuous was applied to African women. Stereotypes of black women's hypersexuality were formulated to justify not only their enslavement and transportation to the American slave colonies, but also the inveterate sexual violence and abuses of white men, as Sander L. Gilman has argued.[29]

The increasing centrality of slavery to Western economies was accompanied by the development of strident race theories. Eighteenth-century American colonies and the Caribbean islands increasingly transformed themselves from "societies with slaves," wherein slaves were marginal to the economic core, to "slave societies," in which slavery was central to economic and therefore social and political structures, according to Ira Berlin. This shift was staggered according to the development of lucrative plantation crops, notably sugar, tobacco, and later cotton across the region. Race theories provided a logic that dehumanized dark-skinned peoples and made blackness synonymous with slavery and slavery synonymous with blackness. From the late eighteenth century, race theories became shriller, particularly with the formation of the development of liberal social theory and abolitionist movements that questioned the morality of slavery. One central plank of Enlightenment race theories was that primitive women's sexual behavior was based in immutable, scientific "fact," justifying the particular violations women suffered with the slave regimes.[30]

Preeminent men in the Enlightenment race field, such as Johann Blumenbach, Jacob Bontius, and the Comte de Buffon, made the female the icon of black sexuality in general by associating their supposed sexual proclivities with those of apes. While Buffon argued that black women were regularly the object of the oversexed attentions of orangutans, Bontius and Blumenbach suggested that the women were the instigators of such base sexual liaisons. As Londa Schiebinger has shown, this scientific gaze created a new representative discourse in both visual and written media that exaggerated the sexual characteristics in black women, principally grossly enlarged buttocks, labia (known as the Hottentot apron), and breasts. The belief that black women experienced easy childbirths suggested a wide vaginal canal. These were the most common traits of a stereotype that had been in circulation for some time, and they directly related to the slave economy. Beliefs that black women did not have difficult births justified working them hard while they were heavily pregnant and immediately after parturition.[31]

Within the category of "black women," gradations of animality existed. The majority of race and sex theorists held Hottentot women as the group of "black women" who possessed the most exaggerated physical and moral characteristics. According to Ann Fausto-Sterling, "a woman of colour . . . served as a primitive; she was both a female and a racial link to nature." Significantly located within the highly contested imperial domain of South Africa, the Hottentot woman was the subject of mythmaking and was transformed into the most extreme version of monstrous female sexuality.[32]

The story of Sarah Bartmaan, the woman who became known as the Hottentot Venus, exemplifies the prurient curiosity about black women's sexual difference in the early nineteenth century. Taken to Europe in her early twenties, Bartmaan was displayed across the continent for more than five years. Her buttocks were displayed to the paying public, and for an extra payment they could be felt. Cuvier's colleague Henri de Blainville examined Bartmaan's body and wrote on the significance of her cranium, ears, and eyes; other aspects of her face, especially her nose, lips, and teeth; her neck, trunk, and breasts; and her arms, legs, and joints, with a detailed summation, complete with measurements of her buttocks. Bartmaan modestly denied de Blainville the opportunity to examine her most intriguing physical characteristic, her genitalia. Nevertheless, he still wrote about it in detail.[33]

Her five years of public display ended when she died in Paris in 1816 at the age of twenty-eight. Georges Cuvier then dissected her body. He removed her "apron" and presented it to the Academy. Not surprisingly, Cuvier found that Bartmaan's removed sexual organs confirmed the suspicions of science that the Hottentot woman was hypersexual and therefore an inveterate primitive. Other less interesting organs also confirmed the scientific view that Hottentot women were the link between man and his simian ancestors: Cuvier argued that Bartmaan's pelvis and heart resembled those of an ape. His zeal at carving up this woman's body and exposing its secrets to the scientific gaze was directly related to the need to uncover the secrets of gender, race, class, and colonial order that followed the French Revolution. Penetrating the mysteries of the primitive woman was essential to the maintenance of the human order and the power relationships dependent on that order. [34]

Unlike African or Native American women, who were literally, scientifically, and theoretically exposed to the imperial gaze, those of the Islamic Orient remained veiled and largely hidden from view. The veiled Oriental woman signified the softer, desirable aspect of the East, a stark counterpoint to images of troublesome Islamic men. The omnipresent figure of the odalisque was the embodiment of ultimate imperial fantasy. The commercial relationship between the Ottoman Empire and Britain had been established during the reign of Elizabeth I. France became a presence in the Middle

Eastern region in the late eighteenth century. The East was part of the cultural colonialism of the West but was not affected by practical application of colonial ideas until late in the nineteenth century. Both the Orient as a setting and odalisques as literary and visual figures became more prominent throughout the nineteenth century, with increasing colonial contact with the region. In the travel literature of the time that formed the basis of popular information about Turkey in Occidental culture, the harem figured prominently. The harem captured the Occidental imagination, as it blended "conquest and enjoyment . . . power and pleasure . . . desire and domination," according to Joanna De Groot. Presided over by an all-powerful patriarchal figure, the harem represented the harnessing of voracious female sexuality. [35]

For most of the writers of such travel literature, the harem was largely an imagined place constructed around anecdote and male fantasy. Some travel writers, such as Robert Withers in his 1650 work, *A Description of the Grand Signor's Seraglio*, claimed to have gained entry to the famed harem despite admitting elsewhere in his book that "no white man can visit amongst the women." For this reason, European women made significant contributions to this imperial culture, as Renia Lewis has demonstrated. Among this group of European women, the figure of Lady Mary Wortley Montagu predominates. Wife of the British envoy to the Ottoman empire from 1716 to 1718, she gained access to the sequestered society of beautiful women. Her *Turkish Embassy Letters*, published a year after her death in 1763, became the authoritative text on harems, providing Orientalist artists with descriptions of the aesthetics and erotic rituals. These were transformed into rich canvases that became the visual summation of Orientalist desire. The artist Jean-Auguste Dominque Ingres painted some of the most renowned renditions of the harem, such as *The Bath*, circa 1865. He used Montagu's accounts as the source for his bathing scenes, which became the central focus of Orientalist vision, with their celebration of female sexuality, racial hierarchy, and the exoticism of place.[36]

In her writings, Montagu imputed a culture of sapphism not previously part of the mythology of the harem. Montagu's reports of

bathing rituals were of particular interest and figured most prominently in the art and literature succeeding her writings. She related
erotically charged scenes of black women tending the every whim
of naked odalisques with "skins shiningly white, only adorned by
their beautiful hair divided into many tresses," lounging on rich car-
pets and cushions or bathing in the many pools. Montagu's reports
resonated with colonial fantasy. In the colonial hierarchy of female
desirability, harem women were elevated, having been schooled
in the rites of primitive sexuality without possessing the negating
aspects of racial inferiority. Women were depicted within the Occidental aesthetic tradition of feminine beauty—whiteness, luxuriant
hair, and statuesque bodies. Lady Montagu perceived the harem and
the veil as providing the anonymity necessary to attain sexual and
social license.[37]

However, the harem also attracted Christian moral outrage as
the emblematic site of the perceived Islamic trait of enslaving and
degrading women. Critiques of the Orient stressed the cultural and
moral superiority of Occidental men. This perception of the harem,
common as it was, did not negate the sexual titillation Occidental
culture found in it, but rather enhanced it. Brutal treatment of womenfolk was a standard stereotype of savage masculinity, an archetype regularly activated in colonial representations for pragmatic
imperial purposes.[38]

Africa and the Orient were so deeply inscribed into the Occidental colonial lexicon before Pacific colonization commenced in
earnest in the 1760s that these ideas were bound to be overlaid onto
Pacific women. Africa, with its associations of excessive racial characteristics and human bondage, had its greatest application in the
Pacific when explorers saw Aboriginal and Melanesian women. The
myth of the Orient, with its close relationship to classical notions of
beauty embodied by Aphrodite and Venus, had greater resonance
when explorers looked at the eastern Pacific islands of Polynesia,
though these luxuriant tropes were also applied to women in other
regions as we shall see.

The imperial precedents from pre-1767 voyages, as well as the
experiences and culture generated from other imperial regions that

were shaped by class relations within European societies, all fed into the stereotype of Pacific women that evolved out of this new phase of colonial endeavor. We have seen what attributes were valued and venerated in exotic women and which ones had negative connotations. Yet these imperial encounters from continental America, Africa, the Caribbean, the Orient, and pre-Enlightenment discoveries in the island Pacific do not sufficiently explain the components of exotic femininity that fed into the Pacific muse. Techniques of representing colonized women established in these theaters of colonial engagement were enmeshed with another powerful stream of influential ideas derived from classicism.

Classical Myth and Colonialism

The Enlightenment voyagers came to the Pacific schooled in classical art, science, and literature. Much of what they rendered and described resonated with this classical education. We can discern this through examining an iconic image of luxuriant Tahitian women painted by William Hodges, the artist on Cook's second voyage in 1776. *Tahiti Revisited*, also known as *Vaitepiha Bay*, is imbued with the symbolism of water, heat, and their effects upon primitive female sexuality (fig. 1.3). Juxtaposed with the eroticized sublime landscape of dense tropical vegetation and soaring mountains, the three Tahitian women in the foreground serve as exotic fauna. In this rendition of Tahiti, the island is "unmanned," and the naked women allow the indulgence of the male fantasy of gazing upon women unobserved—a fantasy redolent of the bathing odalisque. While the women are portrayed as totally given over to sensual pleasures, they are not depicted as threatening, but rather as benign nymphs. The implied heat, nakedness, and languor combine to suggest that these women have no other raison d'être than to be sexual. These women are what Lord Byron termed "summer women." His poem *The Island* was based upon events and the aftermath of the mutiny on *H.M.S. Bounty* in 1789, when British sailors rebelled supposedly so they could return to the arms of their Tahitian lovers rather than to England. This event would draw Occidental attention closer to the "Circean

1.3 William Hodges, *Tahiti Revisited* or *Vaitepiha Bay*, 1776.
Copyright National Maritime Museum, London.

blandishments" of Tahitian women that some commentators claimed
were the sole cause of this infamous naval mutiny. Yet Hodges's early
images of Tahiti, the voyage literature, and the fictional accounts that
were inspired by this wondrous episode of European discovery of
uncharted territories and peoples reflected deep cultural traditions
from classicism.[39]

Late eighteenth- and early-nineteenth-century colonization in
the Pacific was steeped in classical preoccupations, allusions, and
ways of imagining. The tendency to look to classical Greece, and to
a lesser extent Rome, as a golden age of Occidental culture, was a

hallmark of the Enlightenment era. In the wake of the French Revolution, the Romantic movement also absorbed classical tropes. Romantics looked to the imagined classical past in their quest for personal freedoms untouched by the restrictions of Christianity and modern society. The resurrection of numerous classical preoccupations had a profound impact upon representations of the Pacific, as Bernard Smith and successive scholars have shown. Less well understood are the implications that this revival in classical thought had upon ideas of gender, sexuality, and female primitivism. Christianity, that other great ideological juggernaut in Occidental culture, interacted with these constructions, both challenging and reappropriating these pagan concepts of women and sexuality for its own purposes, which in turn also impacted representations of women in the Pacific, as we shall see.[40]

Concepts of female sexuality, beauty, and bodies that originated in classical science and mythology had a powerful effect on the way Pacific women were incorporated into the known Occidental world and remained dominant tropes in Pacific colonial culture. Constructs of sexuality and gender were axiomatic to Greek social organization and power. When Greeks looked beyond their borders, their visions of the outside world were preoccupied with the sexual and gendered organization of barbarian realms, imagined or real. *The Odyssey* provided the provenance for many metaphors utilized to incorporate Pacific peoples into Occidental culture. Yet these metaphors of gender, race, and primitivism became more reductive from the Enlightenment era on owing to the influence of contemporary gender and race theories, Christianity, and the need for a rationalized colonial ethos.

The Odyssey resonates in Pacific colonization, as it does in Occidental culture, on many levels. Numerous early voyagers felt that their travels repeated this fabled voyage, chronicling the tale of imperial warfare in the Aegean Sea. Similarly, the Pacific was dotted with mysterious islands, affording encounters with strange, enticing, and dangerous incarnations. *The Odyssey* described sea voyaging as a male activity and asserted a definitive hierarchy of power based upon designations of gender. The narrative operated on the gendered dualisms fundamental to classical philosophy. Water, for instance, one of the four elements that composed the universe, was gendered feminine. It was feminine in that it was a component of nature, and nature was posited as oppositional and inferior to man. Implicit in the man/nature dualism is the relationship of domination and subordination, specifically man's domination over all that falls into the amorphous category of "nature"—women, men of race and lower classes, animals, plants, land, and the seas. This dualism provided the logic for the subordination of the feminine realm by the masculine. It was also the crux of the distinction between civilization and primitivism. The struggle to maintain this hierarchical order was the definitive test of frontier masculinity in colonial narratives.[41]

The Odyssey had a profound influence on representations of the "female primitive," particularly in evocations of the Pacific muse. Encounters with female primitives of *The Odyssey* revealed different aspects of Odysseus's masculinity. A central theme of the Odyssean myth, which became core to Occidental colonization, is the traveling man's exposure to sexual danger. Odysseus's sexual adventures are telling tales that elucidate the persistent dualisms outlined above and that are axiomatic to understanding the construction of female primitivism.[42]

The female characters from the world outside of Ithaca collectively reveal the generic features of the "primitive woman." All were juxtaposed against the figure of Odysseus's wife, Penelope, the embodiment of chaste, civilized womanhood. Penelope's virtue was founded first in her fidelity, then in her nobility and beauty. Moreover, she was elevated above the other female characters by her ability to outwit her many suitors, who were often assisted by malevolent goddesses, and remain loyal to her husband.

In contrast, the uncivilized, primitive women were foreign to Ithaca. The most famous of these "super natural" barbarians were the enchantress Circe, the nymph-goddess Calypso, and the sirens. Their dangerous, unbridled passion and their attempts to lure Odysseus and his men away from their duty toward languid erotic encounters and oblivion characterized these versions of female primitives. These primitive women were by definition temptresses.

Calypso and Circe were self-determined, husbandless women and rulers of their respective domains. They also possessed magical powers that they used to enhance their sexual allure over Odysseus and his men, making them helpless and unable to resist the women's sexual wiles. Circe administered potions to Odysseus's men and turned them into swine with her wand with the purpose of ensnaring Odysseus in her "sumptuous bed." The disrupted and inverted gender order in *The Odyssey*'s foreign realms allowed these women's sexuality to run rampant. Extravagant, dangerous sexuality and beauty were hallmarks of exotic femininity from this seminal story on.[43]

Herodotus, writing circa 450 B.C., similarly followed a gender and sexual ordering in describing exotic, barbarian societies in his history. Herodotus often cited the different rituals regarding women as the factor that made those peoples distinct from Greeks. Lydians, for instance, "have very nearly the same customs as Greeks, with the exception that these do not bring up their girls in the same way." Lydians "differ from every other nation in the world" as "they take the mother's name and not the father's name."

For Herodotus, Babylonians likewise had curious customs in relation to women. The outmoded Babylonian marriage market was particularly fascinating, as it systematized the pairing of all eligible girls with a husband. The girls were ranked in order of beauty. The most beautiful girls were selected first in exchange for payments. These payments were amassed and used as an economic incentive for poorer men to choose the uglier girls as a wife. "This was the best of all their customs," claimed Herodotus, "but it has now fallen into disuse." The Babylonians had devised another curious plan "to save their maidens from violence and prevent their being torn from them . . . which is to bring up their daughters as courtesans." One ritual that Herodotus recounted was that all women born in the country "must once in her life go and sit down in the precinct of Venus and there consort with a stranger." She cannot refuse the first man who throws her money "so as to satisfy the goddess Venus." Herodotus thought this forced prostitution of all Babylonian women "shameful." The virtue of some women had to be retained in order for societies as a whole to retain their integrity.[44]

Herodotus's tendency to remark upon gender disorder in cultures beyond his own, thereby accenting the women in those cultures, was a tradition commenced by Aeschylus's play *Persians*. First performed in 472 B.C., this play is recognized as the first Greek tragedy and, more recently, as the first representation of the exterior Asiatic *other*. Edward Said cited this play as the beginning of the immensely powerful cultural tradition of Orientalism. Others, notably Edith Hall, have concurred with Said on this point. Hall argues that the "dangerous myth of the Orient as decadent, effeminate, luxurious and materialistic, which remains to this day a cornerstone of western ideology" originated with the Persian wars and therefore in this play that encapsulated this cultural development. Classicists debate whether Aeschylus's intention was to record Athenian victories over the Persians that carved out the Aegean empire, commencing the great Classical Age with historical accuracy, or with dramatic license. Hall argues that the importance of the play is as "a document of Athenian collective imagination." What is of greatest significance here is that Aeschylus constructed the defeated Persia as "essentially feminized," by making the aging queen of Persia an emblematic figure for her country. The defeat of the Persians was portrayed as license for sexual union imbued with imperial mastery. Hall highlighted the consequence of the portrayal of Persia as governed by a queen, that is a country "unmanned," without male leadership, and therefore incapable of repelling invaders. The queen mourns the actions of her son, Xerxes, who led the Persians to defeat, and her dead husband, who appears in the play as a ghost. Aeschylus's Asia was "emptied out of all its men" leaving only the softly grieving Persian women, who all ached "with desire for her man."[45]

Water and Mythic Women

Various colonizers applied the classical tropes of exotic women, Circe, Calypso, and versions of the Persian queen to Pacific women in order to illuminate them to a European audience. A more prevalent colonial trope from *The Odyssey* was that of the sirens. Pacific women, the vast majority of whom were not political rulers, were constructed with a similar primitivism as that of sirens. In this dominating stereotype they possessed a voracious and threatening sexuality, lacked individuality, lacked political power, and inhabited an environment that exaggerated these primitive characteristics.

Homeric sirens were bird-maids of Cyrene who attempted to seduce Odysseus with their song. Odysseus was warned of the sirens' power to "bewitch any mortal who approaches them" and destroy his life through attacking his familial relations: "if a man in ignorance draws too close and catches their music, he will never return to find his wife and little children near him." To survive his encounter, Odysseus instructed his crew to stopper their ears and tie him to the ship's mast so that he could hear but be restrained from physically falling prey to the sirens' song, the metaphor for their sexual potency. Odysseus's male ingenuity ensured that he was charmed by the power of the sirens, though not destroyed by it as was their aim. In classical legend, the sirens devoured the boatmen who came to grief upon the rocks after hearing their song. After failing to lure Odysseus to them, the sirens threw themselves into the sea and drowned.[46]

Although they were depicted as bird-maids in *The Odyssey*, sirens became increasingly, if not exclusively, portrayed as mermaids: half-woman and half-fish. They embodied the mystery and the moodiness of water. The sea perpetually threatens man's mortality by engorging him in watery depths, a metaphor for the perilous powers of women's bodies. The figure of the siren, a hybrid monster that conflates woman with animal, was a literal exposition of the belief that women were closer to nature, more animalistic, and therefore more dangerous than men.[47]

The motif of the siren as mermaid dates from antiquity. The Christian tradition readily embraced this image of the mermaid, which symbolized "the dangers of worldly pleasures, lust, and heresy" in the Romanesque period of Christian art of the tenth to twelfth centuries. Such a stance demonstrated the gynophobic tradition upon which Christianity was based. In medieval thought, nature was held to possess demonic powers. The mermaid represented the deceiving "barren lures of the flesh" in that her body was not procreative as it was wombless, though bared in carnal invitation. Her long, free-flowing hair denoted moral looseness. It enhanced her association with the aquatic environment by replicating the flowing motion of water with its seductive, treacherous qualities. Both hair and watery depths might entangle and overpower men's bodies.[48]

By the thirteenth century, the mermaid/siren had acquired a satanic symbolism, embodying all the activities and attitudes that the Church deemed heretical. Despite being the symbol of sexual temptation, the siren also embodied a punitive function that made her powerful, rather than merely an object of lust. Sirens as femmes fatales have been a constant in European lore, sometimes appearing in myths associated with rivers and seas, such as the nineteenth-century creation Lorelei, who supposedly sat on a rock beside the Rhine and lured boatmen to her and the rocks with her song. In the nineteenth and twentieth centuries, sirens were depicted with greater currency, reflecting fears about women's sexuality. Such fear particularly related to prostitutes, who were likened to sirens. They were pathologized by the medical profession as carriers of venereal diseases and therefore destroyers of society.[49]

Sirens have taken on other more benign forms that diverge from the woman-monster. In 1718, a natural scientist, Louis Renard, claimed that a "monster representing a Siren . . . [measuring] 59 inches long and of eel-like proportion" was captured off the coast of the Malukas and Terra Australis. It was reported that it "occasionally uttered cries like those of a mouse" and after its death, following a four-day and seven-hour captivity, left "feces," "similar to those of a cat." In this pictorial representation, the typical siren is a mermaid. Its diminutive size, its "mouse-like" song, and its curious taxonomic categorization as a crustacean diffused the sexual potency of this siren. Yet, that this siren so strongly resembled the mythic figure suggests the strength of the belief in this creature. It is an example of the infusion of sexuality, gender, and myth onto such taxonomical systems. In the nineteenth century a number of "mermaids" of similar proportions but of grotesque features appeared in Europe and America. That such fantastic creatures were reported as extant in the Pacific region reflects that this was the imaginative frontier of the globe at this time. When America was the imperial frontier for fifteenth-century Europe, journal writers of the Columbus voyages reported seeing sirens. In the journal of his first voyage, Columbus speaks of the "sirens" he saw off the Rio del Oro, but remarked that "they were not as beautiful as they are depicted, for somehow their faces had the appearance of a man."[50]

Along with the sirens, nymphs were other classical figures commonly alluded to in images of Pacific women. Nymphs, like sirens, did not have a fixed bodily form, though they were often portrayed as less dangerous than sirens. In Homeric epics, nymphs were often daughters of secondary deities who lived in the countryside, the woods (meliads or dryads), streams (naiads), and calm seas (neriads) and generally personified the fecundity and gracefulness of nature. They appeared often in myths, frequently in those with an erotic theme. In the myth of Hylas and the water nymphs of the pool of Pegae, the nymphs took on a sirenlike sinisterness by enticing or pulling Hylas into the pool when they were enamored with his youthful beauty. A similar fate was met by Bormus, a youth of extraordinary beauty who, like Hylas, went to draw water from the pool but was never seen again. When associated with water, nymphs were ascribed a predatory character.[51]

In classical thought there was the foundational belief that water compounded the power of women over men as it exaggerated the sexual and corporeal difference between the two sexes. Water emphasized the female body's lack of containment, its permeability. Classical physiological models, while not uniform in their theorization of sexual difference, yoked women with water, wetness, and coldness. Women's physical and psychological characteristics were defined by the predominance of water as classical historians Leslie Dean-Jones and Anne Carson have shown. Hippocrates differentiated the sexes through the characteristics of feminine water as opposed to masculine dryness and heat. He posited that "the female flourishes more in an environment of water, from things cold and wet and soft, whether food or drink or activities." In contrast, "the male flourishes more in an environment of fire, from dry, hot foods and mode of life." Wetness and dryness shaped all human characteristics, from the quality of the soul to the intellect and sexual propensity. Dryness was the soundest condition for human beings. "A dry soul is wisest and best," claimed philosopher Heraklitos, whereas wetness of mind denoted an intellectually deficient condition.[52]

Women were not able to transcend their wetness and thus were perpetually prone to instability, softness of the body and mind, fluctuating emotion, and sexual desire. Menstrual cycles, tears, sexual fluids, the waters of childbirth, and breast milk were all outward signs of woman's entrapment within the sexualized domestic realm. Greek philosophers interpreted woman's excessive wetness as a signal for their continual readiness and desire for sexual intercourse. Owing to their wetness, woman by nature lacked *sophrosyne* — soundness of mind and self-control. This was an added justification for the withholding of citizenship from the female sex and the social, political, and economic infantilization that stemmed from that exclusion.[53]

The assigned properties of water and wetness were therefore axiomatic in defining the female gender and in imposing restrictions on them in the classical Greek period. The multifarious associations of women and water that have continually featured in Occidental culture have taken on almost a subliminal symbolism, remaining eminently powerful in representations of women to the point of being indispensable clichés. In the case of representations of women who exist in a watery environment, on the littoral or on islands, the external, quotidian association with water exaggerated the effects of "wetness" upon these women. The watery environment signified a greater diminution of intellectual ability and powers of reason and the overwhelming predominance of emotion, instinct, and voracious sexuality. This of course had great consequences in ways of seeing Pacific women.

The myth of Aphrodite, or Venus, as the goddess became known during the Roman period and into the modern period, is the superlative example of the supposed influence of water upon women. In Cyprian lore, Aphrodite was originally Atargatis of Askalon. Her bodily form fused woman and fish, her body having a fish tail like a mermaid. Fishes and dolphins were sacred to her and symbolized

1.4 The Aphrodite of Rhodes. Marble, Hellenistic
period, first century B.C. With permission from
the Hellenic Democracy Ministry of Culture.

her power over fertility, her power over the sea, and her ability to provide safe sailing, a domain of the goddess's influence that extended beyond Cyprus. Later Aphrodite was venerated as the mother of Rome's founder, Aeneas. As Venus, "Queen of the Sea," she was the mother of Venetii, whose capital city, Venice, was named after her. She was more than the "Goddess of Love," as contemporary popular culture would have it, as she embodied the power over life itself: to give birth, to protect and nurture life, and to destroy it. She was a highly popular deity, evidenced by the fact that "more ancient statues survive of the nude Aphrodite than any other Greek divinity."[54]

Stories of the birth of Aphrodite, though varied across time and region, typically center on her as being born from the sea a fully grown, perfect woman, though not a virgin. The Aegean Sea was her matrix. Once born, Aphrodite stepped ashore on the island of Cythera as a goddess. Other stories have her being born out of a scallop shell, *kteis*. In Greek, *kteis* also means female genitalia, reflecting the connection between the sea and female sexuality. This version of her birth was depicted in Greek art. It is this version of the goddess's birth that resonates most in Occidental culture, owing to Sandro Botticelli's *Birth of Venus* of 1485.

An alternate representation of Aphrodite's birth was the *Aphrodite Anadyomene* tradition, or Aphrodite rising from the sea. There are numerous examples of this depiction of the goddess, with the *Aphrodite of Rhodes* arguably being the best known (fig. 1.4). This version of the goddess was incorporated into the Renaissance lexicon by Titian in his *Venus Anadyomene* (fig. 1.5). In both the classical and Renaissance images this superlative version of female sexuality is delineated by her nakedness, her long flowing hair, and her association with water. The associations of water in these statues reflect the Greek ritual of bathing before sex, a ritual important for men as well as women, but one particularly associated with Aphrodite owing to her sea birth.[55]

The young beautiful Venus wringing water from her tresses was a configuration of exotic femininity that was absorbed into the Christian tradition in a number of forms, as sirens and also as Eve, the paramount encapsulation of Christian fears of female sexuality.

1.5 Titian, *Venus Anadyomene*, c. 1520–22. With
permission of the National Gallery of Scotland.

Many a Pacific voyager alluded to the Edenic paradise they observed
in the Pacific. The romanticized existence of Pacific women and men
mirrored the descriptions of paradise from Genesis. Many an
observer saw these women as prelapsarian owing to their nudity,
their apparent lack of shame about their bodies and sexual desires,
and their environment of beautiful and bountiful islands that conjured "Eden." The evolving figure of Eve, like the siren, has been a
villain in Christianity as well as "a palimpsest upon which attitudes
towards bodies, sexuality and women were inscribed." Created in
Paradise as a woman, like Aphrodite, and unstained by sin, Eve was
initially a pure incarnation of woman. Yet the metaphor of Eve

instructs us to view the Christian prototype of woman as weak, corruptible and corrupting and, therefore, destined to fall, taking man with her. In appropriating this metaphor to describe Pacific women, Europeans were both evoking a sentimental vision of the state of woman prior to original sin, and prophesying and equating colonization with the inevitable Fall. Christian myth made the demise of colonized people seem inevitable.[56]

The figure of Eve has been an icon in Western art and literature. She does not negate other stock female figures but rather incorporates them in different incarnations. For example, she is present in the iconography of the siren as a mermaid, which interfused the sexually deleterious woman with the Satanic serpent. In the famous seventeenth-century Miltonian reincarnation of Eve, the resonance of classical female figures is apparent. Milton emphasizes her "wanton" entangling hair and her nakedness, "nor, those mysterious parts were then conceal'd," though she had not yet experienced "guilty shame." According to Milton's description of Eve, her highly charged erotic appeal would not long remain without the eternal burden of shame and the destruction of man's happiness, themes of Pacific colonial culture that became increasingly apparent with the intervention of eugenic ideas in the early twentieth century. The politics of race and sex would alter the once esteemed fantasy of South Seas love into one that contained the essence of the calamitous decline of the colonizing, white races from the second half of the nineteenth century. Early voyagers such as Johann Reinholdt Forster, who left a legacy of some of the most fascinating representations of Pacific women, thought Milton's Eve was the "inimitable masterpiece" of female beauty. For Forster, Milton's Eve was the template by which to assess real women, and as we shall see, others would evoke this Eve when alluding to Pacific women, though this allusion carried negative connotations, metaphors for the impact of colonial contact.[57]

This survey of Milton's Eve, sirens, nymphs, and goddesses shows how every feature of woman and her environs determined her erotic potential. This cultural proclivity to enmesh environment, bodies, and eroticism had profound repercussions in representations of Pacific women and the entire region as colonial representations intensified the construction of this genus of woman as essentially sexual. Representations of Occidental upper-class women served to shore up the female body by disguising orifices in clothing, posture, and restricted activity. Conversely, the imperial male gaze widened and exaggerated those of racialized women, who embodied female primitivism in both its excessive and unruly ways and its classically derived manifestations.[58]

Although representations of the Pacific Islands and their women have predominantly been associated with water and fecundity, in the Australian scenario the contrast between wet and dry land was axiomatic to representations of Aboriginal women. The fertile, heavily wooded and watered landscapes along the vast coastline compared with the immense tracts of desert and drought-prone country inland. George Worgan, surgeon on the First Fleet vessel *Sirius*, employed common female primitivist tropes to describe the Eora women of Port Jackson. These descriptions feature in his account of the early interactions between the invaders and the indigenous custodians of the Sydney region. Worgan's polarized perception of the Eora people oscillated between damnation and admiration. They "appear to be an Active, Volatile, Unoffending, Happy, Merry, Funny, Laughing, Good-Natured, Nasty, Dirty, Race of human Creatures as ever lived in a State of Savageness" he wrote of these New World people who would be now sharing the site of British settlement. He described the women as prelapsarian "Evites" and "wood-nymphs" and used the detestable category of working-class women, "Covent-Garden Strumpets." One woman he described as "practiced in all the Siren's Arts." Despite the repellent smell of fish oil that the women used to ward off insects, some of their bodies appealed to him like tempting fruit. There was "in some of them a Proportion, a Softness, a roundness, and Plumpness in their Limbs and Bodies" that could "excite tender and amorous Sensations, even in the frigid Breast of a Philosopher."[59]

The importance of watered environments within Occidental representations of female sexuality can be adduced most clearly by examining descriptions of surroundings wherein the element was lacking. Want of water was equated with barrenness and lifelessness, which had an immeasurable impact upon the constructed desirability of women living in desert regions. Edward Eyre's description of a young woman in the Flinders Ranges in the early 1840s elucidates this. As an explorer, Eyre was an imperial agent, although he argued that Aboriginal people had been "constantly misrepresented and traduced . . . by the world at large." In contrast to his somewhat liberal race politics, Eyre maintained the imperial tradition of using the bodies of Aboriginal women to read the land, in this case equating the scarcity of water with the supposed sterile womb of a young woman. He wrote that "we came upon a single native, a female, young but miserably thin and squalid, a fit emblem of the sterility of the country." They "could gain no information from her, she was so much alarmed, but not long after parting with her we came to a puddle of water in the plains, where we camped for the night." The Australian inland country in the midst of the crippling drought of the early 1840s was arid and a metaphor for death; the desert in the Orientalist representations of the Near East occupied an imaginary terrain similar to that of islands. Near East pockets of civilization, situated with ample supplies of water, have typically been portrayed as sexually and morally isolated by the parched desert surrounds, which heighten the luxuriance of the oasis, as the earlier discussion of the harem shows.[60]

Heat, Exoticism, and "the South"

The fusions of hot climates and water have had a cumulative impact upon representations of female sexuality. In Pacific voyaging, journalists often made reference to this belief. Romantic Russian explorer George Von Langsdorff likened the Marquesan women of Nuku Hiva to "the Medicean Venus" rising out of the water "with all their charms exposed," although with the pleasing modesty to vainly attempt to cover their nakedness with their hands. Langsdorff, a self-proclaimed "philosophic observer," pondered the reasons why "girls who seemed not more than eight or nine years old . . . [were] no less desirous of making a market of their charms than their older companions." After discussing the matter with Edward Robarts, the resident English beachcomber on the island, Langsdorff accounted for this perceived sexualized childhood, or "precocity of nature" as he phrased it, by the climate. "In comparison with what is to be seen in colder climates" he opined, "these children were now as forward as girls of the north of Europe are at nearly twice their age."[61]

Langsdorff's assessment of this gross discrepancy between the sexual propensity of European girls, presumably ones of his own class, and those of the South Sea islands, reveals a core element of the stereotype of female primitivism. That is, sexual activity and desire were not limited to postpubescent girls. The stereotype of primitive female sexuality held that young girls were sexually mature. In the context of colonialism, as well as in Occidental regions where poverty propelled many young girls into the sexual economies of cities, such a perception provided a scientific basis for the sexual exploitation of children. The age of consent in Britain was twelve; therefore the sexual exploitation of young girls was protected by law and in turn supported by scientific reasoning with a long heritage.[62]

Hot climates were the determining factor in the formulation of the racialized (as opposed to the classed) version of female primitivism. The provenance of this belief that tropical climates magnified women's sexual potency extends back to antiquity. Hot climates and weather, according to Aristotle, increased the wetness of women, thereby invigorating women's sexual desire, while hot weather had the opposite effect on men, rendering them sexually incapacitated. He reasoned that "hot natures collapse in summer by excess of heat, while cold ones flourish." As "a man is hot and dry but a woman is cold and moist . . . so the power of a man is diminished [in hot climates] . . . but a woman's power flourishes."[63]

Hot weather was viewed as having a similar effect on women as on plants and animals: it caused them to thrive. Consistently warm weather had the effect of "ripening" girls like fruit. Menarche was accelerated and libido was heightened. Hot weather, Aristotle argued, increased the animality of women, and once initiated in sex, these women reveled in it and did not possess the capacity of reason to stop. In this classical construction of women's sexuality are the seeds for the later theories of black and indigenous women's hypersexuality, as well as the justification of the ill treatment of non-Occidental women by their men, particularly in the practice of polygamy.[64]

These age-old ideas about gender, sexuality, and the environment were highly influential in the eighteenth-century era of colonization. The environment was believed to determine the moral as well as physical behavior of people, according to Enlightenment thinkers. Charles de Secondat, baron de Montesquieu in *L'Espirit des Lois* of 1748, espoused that hot climates expanded the nerve fibers. As tropical nature was bountiful and supplied its inhabitants amply with the fruits of the earth, this "made them indolent, more passive and more inclined to despotism and thus Catholicism." Montesquieu's associations of climate, intellectual capacity, work ethics, and religious persuasions are relevant to the colonies and also to the idea of "the South" that was warmer and closer to the equator from the western European center of comparison. Montesquieu was not alone in this revival of classical ideas about the effect of heat upon physical and moral characteristics. Adam Ferguson in *Essay on the History of Civil Society* (1767), John Millar in *Origins of the Distinction of Ranks* (first published in 1771), and David Hume, among others, adapted this classical science for eighteenth-century purposes. Their purpose was to explain the formation of immutable race distinctions as well as immutable class distinctions. Such a quest had infinite application in industrializing and imperial Europe. Heat arrested mental development thereby justifying rigid gradations of society and the exploitation of people lower down the human scale.[65]

Built into this idea was the justification of sexual exploitation of youthful girls and boys of the empire and the lower classes. The Scottish physician William Alexander expounded this belief in 1782. "In climates moderately warm, women acquire sense and experience, as their charms and beauties expand," he opined. In contrast, "in hoter [*sic*] climates, the body ripens long before the mind; and if they ever become sensible and intelligent, it is at an age when their short and fleeting beauty either begins to fade, or is irrecoverably lost." Similarly Comte de Buffon in 1797 argued that "in hot climates of Asia, Africa and America, girls are generally mature at ten years of age, and often at nine; though the menstrual discharge is less copious in warm countries." Buffon's determination relied directly upon Montesquieu's 1748 wisdom that Eastern girls reach sexual maturity far earlier than their Western counterparts "at eight, nine and ten years of age." Buffon, however, made this maxim apply to girls of additional, specific imperial regions. [66]

It is perhaps not coincidental that there was a resurrection of the idea of nymphomania or womb fury — the excess of sexual desire in women — not long after the "discovery" of Tahiti. Dr. Bienville's *La Nymphomanie, ou Traité de la fureur utérine*, published in 1771 in Amsterdam, with successive editions in French and English, reinvigorated the debate about climate and women's sexuality. An anonymous reviewer in the *Critical Review* derided Bienville for his obeisance to ancient medical theories, denouncing the "idea of a geographical determination of illness, in this case the notion that nymphomania is influenced by warm climates where women bask in luxury." Bienville had, however, influential brothers in this respect who articulated the links between hot climates and darkness of skin color, thereby transforming the argument to one that linked race, degrees of blackness, and degrees of temperature. Buffon claimed that "I have seen a girl at the age of 12, of a brown but lively and florid complexion, small in size, yet strong and plump, commit the most indecent actions at the very sight of a man, from whence nothing could divert her." Buffon professed to knowledge of instances where the *fureur utérus* had taken such a hold upon a woman that it had proved fatal. Two biographers of the revered eighteenth-century scientist have claimed that Buffon took an active interest in this aspect of his research, instructing his servants to procure girls for him of "extremely tender years."[67]

Nymphomania was likewise an interest for the Cook voyagers. Cook's earliest account of Tahiti in 1769 suggested another deleterious effect of precocious sexual behavior. He perceived that the "inferior sort" of Tahitian girl was physically stunted "owing possibly to their early amours that they are more addicted to than their superiors." Feeble-minded and feeble-bodied girls, a stereotype entrenched in representations of the working class, were commonly associated with early sexual activity. Cook's observation that sexual activity at a "premature" age stunted the growth of Tahitian girls coalesced with stereotypes of exotic female primitives that conflated childishness and a childlike body with sexual "ripeness." Apart from the causal arguments or the different moral stances upon these manifestations of Pacific women and girl's sexuality, what is universally apparent is how influential classical constructions of sexuality were upon these late-eighteenth-century figurations of exotic femininity.[68]

Environmental tropes impacted representations of Pacific women's sexuality and also fed into Occidental discourses on geography, in particular the concepts of *north* and *south*. The Pacific has always been bound up with notions of the South in the European imagination since it was first encountered by a notable Spaniard, Vasco Nuñez de Balboa, who crossed the Isthmus of Panama in 1513 and named the ocean "the South Sea." Geographically, the region opposed Europe, and functioned as the globe's underside, its lower stratum and the farthest extreme from the Occident. Classical geographers had imagined the Antipodes as the ulterior underbelly of the northern world. It was where monsters dwelt and established laws of nature were inverted, as well as being the location of the underworld.[69]

The designation of a region as South was more than a geographical imperative. In the eighteenth century the South personified racial, gendered, and sexed meaning in the northern European cultural imagination. If the globe was a body, the North represented the head and therefore embodied reason, genius, rationality, culture, individuality, consciousness, and high evolution, while the South represented the erogenous zones and so was corporeal, sexual, emotive, and natural. Southernness denoted regions of darkness, instinct, and femininity, a "natural" polar opposite of the concept of *north* that had long symbolized masculinity, rationality, and light. North was Occidental Europe, opposed to the exoticized inhabitants of southern Europe, Africa, the Orient, the Americas, and lastly the Pacific. In light of these views, the South Pacific woman was the polar opposite to the Occidental man, as much as her region, the South Sea, was the polar opposite of northern Europe. If northern Europe represented the mind, the Pacific was the body.[70]

A prime example of this distinction between North and South can be found in Jonathan Swift's mythologization of the South Seas. His 1726 creation of the South Sea island of Houyhnhnms Land inverted the order of nature by making horses the embodiment of the north, while man was reduced to a bestial state representing the colonized southerners. Swift's description of the debased yahoos was reliant upon buccaneer William Dampier's infamous assessment of Australian Aborigines, first published in 1697. Swift highlighted their bodies, in particular their buttocks, anuses, "pudenda," and in the case of the female yahoos, their "dugs" that "hung between their forefeet, and often reached almost to the ground as they walked." Swift limited their life experience to one of bodily function: menial work, vomiting, excretion and disease, and criminal behavior.[71]

The severest indictment Swift made of the yahoos is of the women. All yahoos were governed by their revolting bodies but the females even more so. Swift emphasized their sexual function and potentially infectious bodies with a proportion of them being syphilitic "prostitutes." Swift's female yahoos were an embodiment of negative stereotypes of female primitivism. The similarities between Swift's images, subsequent images of Australian Aboriginal people, and stock English stereotypes of the Irish and other despised colonized peoples are striking. While colonial representations of Pacific women, with the exception of Aboriginal women, did not often reach the depths of vitriol and revulsion that Swift plumbed, the imperial gaze was still often fixated on their bodies and their stereotyped aberrant sexuality.[72]

Notions of North and South were being strengthened at the time of Tahiti's "discovery" by the Occidental world owing to the Enlightenment and the fashion of the grand tour. The grand tour made by upper-class British men (and to far a lesser extent women) entailed travel to the Continent, especially Paris and Italy, to learn of the fine arts and the classics. For male grand tourists, their explorations of Europe's south also involved heterosexual and homosexual sensual liberation; they were "generally young, healthy, wealthy and poorly, if at all, supervised." Women on the Continent were "sites of enthrallment" whom roving young British men perceived as easy game. Sex with these foreign women was seen to "preserve the chastity of women at home." Despite the widespread practice of sexual adventure on the continent, the "public attitude to sexual adventure was generally unfavorable." Apart from issues of morality that gained importance across the century, the burning issue, as would be the case in the Pacific, was venereal disease. Although condoms were widely used, to protect British men from infection rather than women from pregnancy, numbers of the nation's most favored sons contracted fatal cases of syphilis.[73]

The influence of this sexual culture upon representations of continental women in the eighteenth century replicated the representations of Native American women some centuries earlier as the carriers of disease. Continental, and mainly Catholic, women were increasingly viewed as a danger to virtuous Britannia by threatening to seduce and infect her young men. In the burgeoning nationalist movement, British upper-class women, like a nation of Homeric Penelopes, stood alone among Europe's women of questionable virtue and primitive tendencies of overt sexual activity. Popular depictions of a young, beautiful, virtuous, and classically robed Britannia were emblematic of British aristocratic feminine virtue and therefore of the virtuous British nation itself.[74]

The grand tour experience generated a genre of travel literature centered on defining the Protestant north against the lascivious Catholic south. One such work was Germaine de Staël's Romantic classic, *Corinne or Italy* of 1807, which ranked among the three most popular books of the French Romantic movement. The novel comprises a constant dialogue between the two main characters concerning the antithetical North and South. The plot centered on the tragic heroine, the crowned southern "queen of letters," Corinne, who showed Italy to her British lover, Oswald, "the child of the northern cold and the mists," the rational man. De Staël delineated contemporaneous understandings of the North, the South, and its comparative region, the Orient, constantly reinforcing the unbridgeable opposition between the characters and the regions they represent. The gulf between the male self and the exotic, feminized *other* has been a standard literary device that "dramatizes the essential difference — of body and mind — that hinders all efforts at heterosexual union," as Julia Douthwaite has argued. In the travel literature generated from Pacific colonization, this trope was regularly employed from the time of Joseph Banks and Oberea, Fletcher Christian and Mauatua, and by Herman Melville in his construction of Tommo and Fayaway.[75]

De Staël made a seemingly neat differentiation between the civilized and the primitive according to female morality, gender status, and environmental influences upon the two oppositional cultures. Oswald's opinion that there are effectively two races, the Northern and the Southern, was supported by German Charles Meiners, whose ideas were representative of the contemporary theories on race and the South. In his *History of the Female Sex* of 1808, Meiners posited that there were two broad racial categories of origin, the Caucasian and the Mongol, which correlated with the Northern and Southern distinction. This was the basis for the strong commonalities between Europe's internal *others* — rural people, Gypsies, Jews, "Latin," Celtic, and Slavic peoples — and external *others*. Meiners made this determination on the basis of varying treatment of women within these societies. The Mongol, or "inferior nations," included the "heathen nations of Siberia," the aborigines of America, Negro Nations of Africa, the inhabitants of Mongolia, South Asia, the East Indies, and the South Sea, particularly Tahiti. Within Europe, the Mongols were the "Slavon nations," the Celtic nations, and the Greeks and Romans. The latter, he argued, had only partially advanced since ancient times. Instead, Caucasian peoples continued the tradition of great civilization from the Greek Golden Age. The Mongols, Meiners argued, "may be regarded as intermediate beings between the European and the irrational animals," and therefore these peoples were innately primitive, albeit in varying degrees. Southernness, therefore, also conveyed meanings about gender and race characteristics. It influenced ideas about primitivism and maintained particular potency in stereotypes of South Seas women, the exotic inhabitants of that illusive chimera, earthly paradise.[76]

The First Pacific Muse

From the 1760s, Enlightenment voyagers transcribed to the Pacific ideas on exotic femininity that had been circulating for centuries. These voyagers deployed classical tropes as well as those derived from earlier imperial legend and experiences. The extent to which these preexisting ideas bore influence can be measured through looking at the figure who would become the first Pacific muse, Oberea, queen of Tahiti. Oberea came to represent a genus of womankind "immersed in sensuality" symbolizing both her island of Tahiti and the concupiscent South Seas itself.[77] Oberea was composed of many parts fantasy and smaller measures of truth. She was loosely based upon the chiefly woman Captain Wallis mistook for the island's queen in 1767, Purea, as Greg Dening has shown.

The Queen Oberea who returned to England in various renditions, sparking a sensation in the European imagination, bore little resemblance to the woman Wallis encountered. After the Tahitians had suffered bloody military defeat by the British and the trade in sex and nails commenced, a "tall woman . . . of majestic deportment" came aboard the *Dolphin*. From the outset, Wallis treated her with deference, draping her in a blue mantel, which he "threw over her and tied with ribands," and presenting her with the mandatory imperial gifts of a "looking glass," beads, and other trinkets. At the time, Wallis was suffering from what is thought to have been scurvy. Oberea gave wifely care to the ailing Wallis, his first lieutenant, and the purser. Oberea assisted in undressing the three men for a massage in her home. After the treatment was completed, she took Wallis by the arm and aided his return to the ship. She ensured that "whenever we came to a plash of water or dirt, she lifted me over with as little trouble as would have cost me to have lifted over a child if I had been well." When the *Dolphin* departed, Oberea displayed "inconsolable sorrow" and "tenderness of affection." The intimate attention, kindness, and regenerative qualities of Tahiti, administered by the Tahitian queen herself and her subjects to their new colonial masters became incorporated consistently in images of Pacific women.

Yet Wallis's vision of the island queen conveyed her physical strength, agency, and resolve, facets of her character that would be leached away in subsequent, more fantastic representations that were compiled with preexisting traditions of portrayals of colonized women.[78] The one visual image created for the Wallis voyage depicted Oberea "in conversation" with Wallis (fig. 1.6). This illustration, from John Hawkesworth's edition of Britain's early Pacific voyages that first appeared in 1773, had several titles, including *The Interview between Capt. Wallis and Oberea after Peace being established with the Natives* and *Queen of Tahiti surrendering that is to Captain Wallis*. In this image, Oberea and her minions kowtow to Wallis and his men, the vanquished and the vanquisher coming together in a moment of island diplomacy with only an implication of sex.

Other versions of the Wallis and Oberea encounter were more explicit in their claim that "the interview" preceded sexual intercourse between the queen and the captain. The 1779 poem by Gerald Fitzgerald, *The Injured Islanders*, is a case in point. Oberea is depicted in terms that resonate with Aeschylus's *Persians* in that Oberea was portrayed as mourning the loss of her supposed lover and military conqueror, Captain Wallis, a love that surpassed her love of country. Oberea laments the loss of her wealth and power after military defeat by invaders from neighboring islands. This resulted in the loss of peace for her people as the invaders learned the avaricious ways of the Europeans and she was unable to offer resistance to the new threat without her British protector. Fitzgerald claimed he sought to redress the widespread mockery of the Tahitian people that stemmed from the scandalized reception of Hawkesworth's journals owing to their explicit sexual content. Fitzgerald stated that he was attempting in his poem to shift the popular focus of Tahiti from a site of "ridicule" to one of "Panegyrick." He also succeeded in perpetuating some long-held colonial tropes of feminizing and sexualizing the conquered in a similar vein to *Persians*, thus

1.6 Wallis in Conversation with Oberea. Illustration from J. Hawkesworth,
An Account of the Voyages of Discovery Undertaken in the Southern Hemisphere,
vol. 1, London, W. Strathan and T. Caddell, 1773.

naturalizing colonial defeat. The desired island woman nourishing
the Occidental man physically and spiritually was an allegorical figure, reappearing in many different personae in the narratives of Pacific
imperialism. The eager to please, docile figure of the island woman
resonated with its predecessor Aphrodite, particularly as Oberea was
described as the "*Dolphin*'s Queen." Representations of Oberea such
as that rendered by Fitzgerald also evoked harem women and the
Americas' imperial trophies, Malintzin and Pocahontas.[79]

It was the Queen Oberea of the *Endeavour* journals who launched
the myth of Pacific women. This Oberea had a sexual liaison with

Joseph Banks, presided over a public copulation, instructed young girls in lewd dances, and had a "tataowed breech," fueling her construction as the mistress of a South Sea seraglio. After the publication of Hawkesworth's journals, Oberea became the conduit of new and ancient fantasies of exotic femininity. The satirists of London delighted in the union of the ultimate symbol of the North—highly evolved Enlightenment man, young and virile, reputedly handsome, wealthy, and moreover educated (in botany no less)—and the diametric opposite on the compass of human difference, the savage, lascivious queen "from the Southern Main." In accepting Banks as a lover, it was presumed Oberea simultaneously ceded sovereignty of her island to the British. Oberea described Banks in one of her poetic voices, created by John Scott-Waring, as "my conq'ror and my King."[80]

In the bawdy theater and satirical poetry inspired by this encounter, known as the "Oberea Cycle," the fantasy-filled gulf of difference between Britain and the South Sea island was explored. The Joseph Banks of the anonymous poem *An Epistle from Mr Banks, Voyager, Monster-Hunter and Amoroso to Oberea, Queen of Otaheite* of 1773 is laced with vulgarities playing upon Banks's profession as a botanist and thinly disguised references to his erect penis: "but what a plant I did produce to thee." This Joseph Banks described Oberea as both a queen and "a common whore." The poems not only explored the abyss between Banks and Oberea; the character of Banks's jilted fiancée, Harriet Blossett, who embodied British upper-class feminine virtue, was juxtaposed against that of Oberea. The fictionalized Blossett lampooned Oberea as "a wanton Gypsy, Dirty Queen." In the poem *Otaheite*, which appeared in the *Monthly Review* in April 1774, Oberea was portrayed as presiding over a culture of women who were likened to Medea. Continuing in this vein, the poem *Transmigration* of 1778 reduced Oberea and her womenfolk to fornicating "wanton dames" and "demireps" and Drury Lane prostitutes whose genitalia were highlighted for the educated reader by the coded reference in "botanists . . . who scientifically tell/the wonders of each cockle-shell."[81]

Interest in Tahiti and Oberea was spurred by the arrival of Omai, the Raiatean native brought back to England by Tobias Furneaux, who captained the *Adventure* on Cook's second Pacific voyage. Omai resided in England for two years, providing endless interest for scientists, royalty, artists, and the press as Eric McCormack has shown.[82] Omai was immortalized in many artworks and also in the highly successful pantomime by John O'Keefe, *Omai: Or a Trip Around the World*, first performed in 1785. In this play Oberea was transformed again into the "Regent, Protectress of Oedeiddee (Pretender to the Tahitian Throne), An Enchantress."[83] In the premier production, the role of the Tahitian enchantress was played by Mrs. Martyr, and Britannia was played by Elizabeth Inchbald, who, apart from acting, also turned her hand to writing plays with a primitivist theme. The plot had Britannia, "The Queen of the [Pacific] Isles," attempting to arrange Londonia's marriage to the heir to the Tahitian throne, Omai. The character based on Oberea was first met in the Sandwich Isles, not Tahiti, where she intervenes in the match and instead attempts to have Londonia marry her charge, Oedeiddee. In the Circean side to her character, Oberea casts a spell over the two betrothed lovers, but her wrongdoing is unsuccessful. Omai is crowned, and visitors from all over the "Pacific main" attend the ceremony to honor the new ruler and to remember the "Genius of Britain" or the "Caesar of Britain," Cook. The costume Mrs. Martyr wore for the performance of Oberea reveals the cultural layers inscribed upon the mythic colonial figure. Most apparent were the quotations from classicism and America signified in the drapery, sandals, and the feathered headdress (fig. 1.7).[84]

Oberea still enjoyed Europe-wide fame in the early nineteenth century. Charles Meiners in 1808 summarized the reputation of the "queen of Otahetie, whose name is so well known even in Europe" by stating that she "had not only a multitude of lovers among her own countrymen, but made no scruple to grant her favours to the English, which gave not the slightest offence to her subjects." Oberea was described as a woman in her forties by the *Endeavour* journalists. As she was not of tender years, as the stereotype of exotic femininity required, she was increasingly portrayed as corrupting the younger women of Tahiti as well as imperial men like Banks, and

n°2

obereyau Enchantresse

1.7 Phillippe Jacques de Loutherbourg, "Obereyau (Oberea)—Enchantress."
Watercolor design for the pantomime *Omai: Or a Trip around the World*, 1785.
With permission from the National Library of Australia.

therefore an unworthy ruler of the island. This corrupting Oberea—the Pacific procuress—is best represented with her appropriation by at least one London brothel keeper, a Mrs. Hayes. Hayes advertised in the *Whoremongers Guide to London* that "at 7 o'clock precisely 12 beautiful nymphs, spotless virgins, will carry out the famous feast of Venus, as it is celebrated in Tahiti, under the instruction and leadership of Queen Oberea." Mrs. Hayes would take the role of Oberea for herself. As we shall see, displays of female sexuality and older age were incompatible in colonizers' eyes. Thus, although Oberea was the first Pacific muse, she was not a perfect fit for the archetype that would evolve in the years after she was first encountered.[85]

Oberea's place in Pacific cultural history replicates that of Malintzin or Pocahontas in the American context, as she was the first individuated woman of a new people. She was not considered merely "Indian" but rather an emblematic part of a new culturally distinct population who, paradoxically, fascinated Europeans with both their cultural difference and resemblance to Europe's classical past. Oberea was a pliant figure, a mélange of different voyage accounts and cultural misunderstandings infused with the long heritage of constructing exotic femininity from classical narratives that would become a foundation for future colonial representations of Pacific peoples.

In this chapter we have explored the a priori ideas about exotic femininity that would be expressed in the Pacific muse. In the following chapter we will look at Pacific colonialism and the culture that arose out of it in more depth. We shall return to the Wallis voyage and examine the formulation of stereotypes of Pacific women from the Bougainville and Cook voyages and beyond. We shall see how contemporary debates about male sexuality, race, and national character were affected by Pacific imperialism to 1860 and in turn how Pacific peoples were changed by the early decades of sustained contact.

I I

Colonizing Masculinities,
1767–1860

Unfettered sexual freedom for voyaging men was, and perhaps remains, the foremost myth of South Seas colonization. The fantasy of islands populated by classically beautiful and sensual women seeking sexual liaisons with foreign men stemmed from the early voyage accounts of British and French visits to Tahiti. These new women awakened visions of a lost classical past wherein sexuality was untouched by the corrupting hand of Christianity or other negative effects of modern civilization.

Here we shall begin with the Wallis voyage but view it through a lens other than the one focused on its role in creating the myth of Oberea. Instead we shall examine how this voyage established the initial sexual commerce with the islanders using the long-standing colonial practice of coercion. This sexual commerce shaped the myths of Tahitian women but also revealed anxieties and tensions about colonial male sexuality. These tensions and anxieties were constantly present in this era of Pacific imperialism, whereas they had not been in earlier imperial episodes.

Why was this so? We shall see that the influence of British and American missionaries who desired to shroud the Pacific in middle-class Christian values, the process of forging of distinct national characters, and the realities of empire building that increasingly featured violent retaliation by indigenes often sparked by sexual misunderstandings all contributed to an unease about imperial male sexuality in the Pacific. The bodies of Pacific women were sites of contestation within these debates about imperial male sexuality. The prevailing stereotypes of Pacific women consistently accommodated constructions of colonizing masculinities, to the point that they existed in a symbiotic relationship to each other. It is these tensions between colonial cultural myths, preconceptions, desires, and the realpolitik of empire that will be explored in this chapter.

Representing Seminal Events

At his first sight of Tahitian women, George Robertson noted their distracting sexuality. He felt nervous and vulnerable in the waters of this new island that the British vessel *Dolphin* had happened upon in late June 1767, particularly so in the presence of its people, "espetially as I hade now killd two of them." As the *Dolphin*'s second master, he was also under pressures of command as Captain Wallis was too ill to officiate. Yet Robertson was struck by the "good many fine young Girls . . . of different colours" that came down to the shore and stripped naked. Seeing the effect the women had upon the Englishmen, "attract[ing] our mens fance a good dale," Robertson reported that the Tahitian men made "them play a great many droll and wanting tricks and the men made signs of friendship to entice our people ashore."[1]

The following day at sunrise, three hundred canoes approached the *Dolphin*. By eight o'clock Robertson estimated five hundred canoes had surrounded the ship, with the "trading canoes" lying in close, most of which had on board "a fair young Girl . . . which drew all our people upon the Gunwells to see them." These women and the men in the canoes appeared "hearty and merry." The shore was lined with men, women, and children. The English took this as a sign that the Tahitians meant no harm.[2]

If the Tahitians' intentions were to distract these alien men, as

Robertson interpreted the situation, the plan worked. Before the English knew it, they had been attacked by stones, which cut and bruised several men. The English retaliated for the next five days in a bloody display of the capabilities of their weaponry, killing many Tahitians. On the third day of the bombardment, June 26, 1767, a party landed "to take possesion of this Beautyfull Island" in the name of King George. On the fifth day, the islanders were made sensible that "they were in danger of being shot any where in sight of the ship" after the English fired upon a hill. From that point on "they neaver Attempted to Molest us any more."[3]

Instead of combating the English, the islanders then warily began to establish cordial relations that, Robertson surmised, included the possibility of sex. Prospective sex and with such "handsome" women prompted a commotion among the men, who begged and pleaded for access to the girls, who, although seeming "afraid," were viewed as willing. Wallis restricted contact between his crew and the Tahitians once a daily shore station was established. To maintain control over his men, the potentially belligerent natives, and commercial transactions, Wallis allowed only minimal trade in food and pearls to take place. When potential intimacy was perceived, the men were ordered back aboard the vessel. It was in this context that Queen Oberea appeared on the *Dolphin*, supposedly ceding her island to King George.[4]

It was not until the morning of July 6, some thirteen days after initial contact, when Robertson was told by a member of the returned shore party that "a new sort of trade took up the most of their attention this day." It was reported to Robertson that "a Dear Irish boy one of our Marins was the first that began the trade." He received a "severe cobing" from "the Liberty men for not beginning in a more decent manner, in some house or at the back of some bush or tree." "Padys Excuse," Robertson noted with a degree of affectionate admiration, was his "fear of losing the Honour of having the first." His offence, in Robertson's view, was not that he had sex with the Tahitian woman but that he had abandoned basic standards of civilized behavior.[5]

Both Robertson and Wallis perceived the Tahitians' desire for

acquiring European goods, especially nails, as the main motivation
for the women "granting . . . personal favours." That nails were the
primary object the women would accept provided a source of bawdy
humor arising out of their phallic suggestiveness. Additionally Wallis
reported that Tahitian women of greater beauty demanded nails of
greater length, "as were proportional to [their] charms." The demand
for sex, and therefore for nails, caused Wallis concern as men began
dismantling the ship when the source of nails set aside for trade had
been exhausted. The connection between the breakdown of discipline and sex was most apparent to Wallis, who reported that this
"commerce . . . rendered them much less obedient to the orders that
had been given."[6]

The violation of authority in the quest for sexual contact with
local women would feature in Pacific imperial narratives from this
time on, as would another momentous consequence of this "commerce": venereal disease. The British were conscious from the outset that sex and imperialism in the Pacific were polemical. This
acknowledgment however, was not apparent or not considered consequential to the next voyagers to Tahiti.[7]

Nine months after the *Dolphin* sailed from Tahiti, the two ships
of the Bougainville voyage, *L'Etoile* and *La Boudeuse*, arrived. As the
French were ignorant of the earlier events, they interpreted the
women's bold enthusiasm for sexual relations as innate rather than
a result of recent violence and subsequent machinations of imperial
commerce. In the eyes of Louis Antoine de Bougainville, the vision
of a young, unashamedly naked Tahitian woman standing alone
among four hundred Frenchmen who had been at sea for six months
awakened in his imagination deeply embedded myths of exotic femininity. She had "negligently allowed her loincloth to fall to the
ground and appeared to all eyes as Venus showed herself to the
Phrygian shepherd. She had the Goddess's celestial form." When
recording his general impressions of other women of the island, he
embellished upon this classic myth of female salaciousness. "A gen-
tle indolence falls to the share of the women," with "endeavours" to
please men "their most serious occupation," he observed. The unmarried woman in particular, he deemed, suffered no constraint upon

her sexual passions. "Everything" invited "her to follow the incli-
nation of her heart or the instinct of her sensuality." These were
female noble savages who both resembled classical statuary and
possessed a pure and innocent sexual allure that matched their
physical perfection.[8]

Bougainville, seeing Tahiti through the prism of the French
Enlightenment, created for Europe a new embodiment of exotic femininity, *les tahitiennes*. His vision of the Tahitian woman was formulated by myriad tropes and experiences. This fund of ideas and images
formed the apparatus of colonial discourse that informed both the
representation and treatment of Pacific women. Bougainville had personally experienced the connection between imperialism and sexual access to colonized women when defending France's imperial
possessions against the British in Quebec in the late 1750s, having
had an affair with the daughter of an Iroquois chief.[9]

The French, despite their religiousness, did not adopt the British
equation of sexual prudery with virtue. Although a more sexually
tolerant culture existed in France, the empire provided even greater
license and opportunity for the fullest expression of French sexual
prowess. The equation of Tahiti as New Cythera was intrinsic to this
license, as it rendered sex free from the polemics that plagued it elsewhere. This weight of fantasy obscured the less attractive origins of
the first encounter, the *Dolphin*'s bloody bombardment, which invari-
ably influenced the Frenchmen's extraordinary reception.[10]

Bougainville's grandiloquent portrayal of Tahitian women
sharply contrasted with the views of Captain Cook one year later.
When the *Endeavour* left Tahitian waters to explore the Pacific after
its protracted stay of several months, Cook complained that the
ship's company was in a worse state of health than before they had
arrived. Not only was this due to the "constant hard duty that they
had had at this place." The "too free use of the women," resulting
in about half the men contracting "the venereal disease," was also
to blame.[11]

On this first sojourn at Tahiti, Cook had not attempted to hinder sexual contact between Tahitian women and his crew. The inex-
perienced Cook did not have any objections other than the morality

that determined his own sexual restraint. This set him apart from many of his officers, most notably Joseph Banks. It was not so much the activities of his men that he censured in his journals, but rather the shocking details of the sexual customs of these islanders. Cook often expressed his astonishment at practices he witnessed, or was told about, particularly public displays of women's sexuality and the *arioi*. His journal, that of Joseph Banks, and others featured details of the dances of naked young women and the public disrobing of a young woman before Banks. The most scandalous incident was the public copulation between a young girl and an older man when the girl was given sexual instruction from female bystanders, one of whom was Oberea. Cook was also shocked by the expression of "indecent ideas" in conversation by "both sexes" and the sleeping arrangements that allowed married and unmarried people to lie proximate to each other. Cook's interest was in conveying information about the Tahitians among whom, he declared, "chastity is indeed but little valued." The conspicuous lack of chastity among his men mattered little to him at this stage of his Pacific career, as he did not yet understand the problems caused by sex in the colonial process.[12]

The representations of exaggerated sexuality of Tahitian women, particularly those garnered from the Cook voyages, created the first scandal of Pacific voyaging. After the *Endeavour* returned to England, the accounts of these women were further embellished by John Hawkesworth in his edited volumes of the four British principals of Pacific voyaging: Byron, Carteret, Wallis, and Cook. Not surprisingly, the public attention homed in on these women.[13] The opprobrium that erupted after the Hawkesworth publication was a reaction to the author's celebration of the discovery of this new embodiment of primitive female sexuality. In some of the most vituperative attacks against him, Hawkesworth was accused of gross "violations against taste, morality and religion." His work was derided by one critic, who signed a letter, "A Christian." This critic charged that his voyage accounts were more deleterious to the morals of British youth than "the most intriguing French novel." It was even more notorious than Britain's infamous version of this literary genre, Cleland's *Fanny Hill or A Woman of Pleasure*, perhaps the "sin-

gle most read pornographic novel of all time." Hawkesworth's rendition of these great British feats of exploration were no more than
"Poison on every page."[14]

As it was first presented to a European audience, Tahiti was synonymous with sexuality. This island was personified by its "queen,"
Oberea, who took on numerous guises in the subsequent cultural
production, as we have seen. At the time that Tahiti entered the
European sphere of knowledge, ideas about sexuality were being
transformed along with the economic, ideological, political, and social
terrains of an industrializing and urbanizing world. The frankness
and ease with which the Tahitians treated sexuality heightened the
complexity, uncertainty, and hypocrisy that governed debates about
sexualities in the European world with varying degrees of intensity
according to national differences.[15]

One dimension of the attack on Hawkesworth was the fear that
young English women from the literate classes would be "corrupted"
by the evidence of Tahitian women's alleged unfettered sexual
expression. Some feared the English nation as a whole would decline
if its women slid from the pinnacle of feminine virtue by exposure
to such indecency. Some supposed experts on female sexuality, such
as the Comte de Buffon, believed that chaste young girls might be
corrupted by having their imaginations "inflamed by licentious conversation and obscene representations," thus precipitating disorders
such as the condition of nymphomania, a resurgent idea in scientific
discourses from 1771.[16]

Representations of exotic femininity were not only deleterious
to English ladies. Hawkesworth's representation of Pacific women
fed into existing debates about English masculinity. Catherine Hall
has argued that by the 1760s unchecked male sexual culture, which
was indicative of aristocratic privilege, was being challenged by the
emerging middle-classes whose "political freedom and power became
dependent on a prudish and rigid sexual ethic" based on Christian
sexual mores. Additionally, this change in attitude to male licentiousness was due to nationalistic sentiment and the need to define
English masculinity as controlled and elevated above carnal lusts.
This was particularly in opposition to perceived French debauch-

ery, Gerald Newman has shown, especially after the Seven Years War ended in 1763.[17]

These debates about male sexuality prompted related debates about female sexuality. Female sexuality, according to class and race, had been structured to accommodate upper-class male sexual pleasure. White women with class status were for marriage and producing heirs. For these women, unlike for their comparable men, sexual purity was imperative. As we have seen in relation to the grand tour, women of the lower classes and foreign women were typically perceived as available for casual, clandestine sexual encounters. Stereotypes of them represented them as a useful, naturally occurring population of "carnal magdalens" tempting men into sexual abandon. Male sexual privilege, enshrined in cultural practice, allowed men to move among the atlas of womankind and establish sexual relationships with them, usually in strict accordance with class and racial hierarchies. When male sexual privileges were challenged, stereotypes of sexually available women became increasingly visible, suggesting the naturalness of the status quo as well as women's ability to corrupt men.[18]

While some attention was paid to the behavior of men, women remained the key subjects of scrutiny in the debates about male sexual license. Both advocates for male sexual restraint and those who celebrated male sexual freedom believed that the morals of women determined the morality of men. Women of loose morals, whether they were prostitutes in England, on the Continent, or in Tahiti, had sirenlike powers to make men succumb to their invitation and lead them astray from their families. This supposed inability to withstand temptation was the great paradox within constructions of upper-class civilized, Occidental masculinity. Although men in this category considered themselves superior to all other people, evident in the power they wielded economically, militarily, and socially, they did not have control over their own sexual behavior. This widely held belief lay at the core of the sexual double standard.[19]

In the empire, this double standard was exaggerated, as the seductive powers of the empire's women were portrayed as far greater than women of the home regions. This was supposed to account for, or excuse, men falling prey to these women's wiles. Images of the empire's women portrayed them as indiscriminate in choosing sexual partners, a belief that was central to the stereotype of the Pacific muse that caused numerous tense and dangerous situations in the Pacific empire.

Female sexuality in Pacific societies was indeed viewed in ways anathema to the vast majority of Occidental traditions. In regard to Polynesia, women's sexuality was "not so much 'free' as celebrated and sacralised," as Margaret Jolly has argued. Colonialism, with its rapidly imposed economic, environmental, and social changes, in conjunction with military coercion on numerous occasions, affected Occidental men's incorporation into indigenous sexual cultures. It is often impossible to determine what motivated individual women to engage in sex with colonizing men given the extant historical evidence. Cultural codes, duress, and personal desire were ever-present factors governing women's actions. Despite the varying degrees of sexual agency exhibited by indigenous women, the colonial stereotype portrayed all women as willing participants in sexual interactions with colonial men.[20]

Pacific Women and the Cook Voyages

After the publication of Hawkesworth's book, aspersions were so thoroughly cast upon Tahitian women that they were portrayed in popular culture as nymphomaniacs and prostitutes from their "queen," Oberea, down to the "inferior sort" of young girl. Recall that Cook had portrayed this last category of Tahitian women as physically stunted, "owing possibly to their early amours which they are more addicted to than their superiors." So exaggerated were the myths applied to Pacific women from the *Endeavour* voyage that Cook felt obliged to qualify his remarks when he arrived at Tahiti the second time in 1772. Not all Tahitian women were prostitutes, he argued, but there was a proportion of the female population who were, as was the case "in other Countrys." According to Cook, the Tahitian prostitutes were not shunned by the higher-ranked peoples, and they did not express the sense of shame that Cook thought women in such a state should. These women were available to European men according to Cook's revised assessment of Tahitian women's sexuality, while those of the higher orders were not. Cook's assertions about high-ranking Pacific women were undercut by others. John Williamson, the third lieutenant on *Resolution*'s final voyage, wrote "Cook was mistaken" on this point. He could "positively assert" that the higher-born women of Ra'iatea were "comeatable." Cook modified his perceptions of women's sexual availability to foreign men according to an Occidental class model. However, this qualification arguably had little impact upon the images of Pacific women that were already entrenched after his debut voyage.[21]

Overall, Cook was confused about Polynesian women's sexuality as much as he was unsure about whether women were prostitutes "naturally" or whether economics played a critical part in forcing women to enter the trade. He argued both ways. By his final voyage, Cook seemed to think that the economies established by his voyages drastically affected women's decisions to become what he perceived as sexual commodities, either of their own volition or from coercion within their own societies. Regardless of Cook's attempts to rationalize the decisions of women, the economic conditions of imperialism gave even greater impetus to the stereotype, which he tried to nuance by comparing the situation in the Pacific to that in Britain. The increasing imbalance of economic and military power meant that more and more indigenous women would replicate the colonial stereotype in the eyes of voyagers.

The connection between the stereotype and male sexual license in the empire was not lost on Sidney Parkinson, the artist on the *Endeavour* voyage. In reporting upon the behavior of the crew at Tahiti, Parkinson revealed how empire operated in relationship to male sexual freedom. He revealed that "most of our ship's company procured temporary wives amongst the natives, with whom they occasionally cohabited." More telling was his observation that "in uncivilised parts of the world . . . reputed virtuous Europeans" allowed themselves "indulgences . . . with impunity as if a change of place altered the moral turpitude of fornication." He went on to articulate the pragmatic moral rational used by voyagers as "what is a sin in Europe is only a simple innocent gratification in America; which is to suppose that the obligation of chastity is local and restricted only to particular parts of the world." From the *Endeavour* accounts it is clear that perceptions of Polynesian women's sexual proclivity, and the understandings about the freedoms of the "uncivilized realms," were elemental in determining when sex was a "sin" or merely an "innocent gratification."[22]

For many an Occidental voyager who came to the Pacific in the succeeding years, God did not exist past Cape Horn, and so Christian consciences were metaphorically hung on that landmark to be retrieved on their return. Not only did this landmark denote for some men an ability to radically alter their sexual behavior, but such a landmark also designated the diametrically opposed sexual functions, which women in the differing regions could provide for the male voyager.[23]

Nowhere were the dichotomized representations of women according to their erotic or procreative function more clearly artic-ulated than in the *Endeavour* journal of Joseph Banks. Banks, who bragged elsewhere that "he had tasted Womans flesh in almost every part of the Known habitable World," portrayed himself as the object of many Tahitian women's sexual attentions. These women he rep-resented as the perfect complement to the brand of male sexuality he embodied in which "pleasure was the central business of life."[24] For Banks, Tahiti was a place for transient and highly spiced sexual encounters. Women for opposing, wifely purposes could be found among the Dutch of Cape Colony. If he had "been inclined for a wife" Banks wrote, "I think this is the place of all others I have seen where I could have best suited myself." While Banks devoted so much energy to Tahitian women, the superior wifely qualities of the Dutch women were summed up as "in general they are hansome with clear skins and high complexions and when married (no reflextions upon my countrey women) are the best housekeepers imaginable and great childbearers."[25]

Visual imagery played a significant role in perpetuating the stereotype of unproblematic sexual accessibility to Pacific women. Although a visual tradition of Pacific empire had existed since the sixteenth century, as we have seen, it was not until the *Endeavour* voyage that the first trained artists saw and represented the Pacific and its peoples. These artists produced a rich aesthetic product, such as William Hodges's *Tahiti Revisited*, that encapsulated the Pacific and sexual fantasy in high artistic style from the second Cook voyage (see fig. 1.3). In another artistic league, fantasy-filled illustrations of Pacific peoples published in voyage accounts offered the opportunity to embellish details of lascivious events and customs brought to light in the text. A case in point is the frontispiece to the seventh volume of Jean Pierre Bérenger's *Collection de Tous les Voyages faits Autour du Monde*, which paraphrased the Cook voyages. Titled *Amusemens des Otahitiens et des Anglais*, this image is saturated with sexual references, from the phallic mast that the sailor straddles to the naked, beckoning women frolicking in the water (fig. 2.1). The placing of the Tahitian women in water was an allusion to the voracious sexual figures of Venus and the sirens. This image is brimming with lewd connotation, giving weight to the fantasies of unfettered sexual freedoms on the South Seas island.[26]

The illustration *Representation of the Heiva at Otaheite*, which appeared in John Rickman's journal of the third Cook voyage, also delineated the unproblematic Pacific muse stereotype (fig. 2.2). At one level, this illustration appears ethnographically informative. It can also be read as an implicit commentary on triangular relations between the three groups of players in the colonial equation — Tahitian women, Tahitian men, and the British officers. The state of dishabille of the Tahitian women compared to the two groups of men is the most striking feature of this image. In the early imperial context, Pacific women's lack of clothing represented to adherents of the noble savage philosophy a virtuous lack of shame about sexuality that was revered for its naiveté and also because it "reminded" the Occident of their own classical past. An alternative cultural tradition of female nudity suggested readiness for sex. Half-undressed women also signified sexual availability and often poverty as well, two states regularly conflated in the stereotype of working-class women as prostitutes. In this image, the women's nudity connects their "primitivism" with the classical nobility of the Tahitian women.[27]

Amusemens des Otahitiens et des Anglais.

2.1 *Amusemens des Otahitiens et des Anglais*, frontispiece
of J. P. Bérenger, *Collection de Tous les Voyages faits Autour du
Monde par les Differentes Nations de L'Europe*, vol. 7, Lausanne, 1789.

Representation of the Heiva at Otaheite

2.2 *Representation of the Heiva at Otaheite* after Daniel Dodd
by Royce in J. Rickman, *Journal of Captain Cook's Last
Voyage to the Pacific Ocean,* London, E. Newbery, 1781.

The sexual connotations of the image are heightened by its wider
subject matter. It depicts the performance of the *heiva,* one of the
"indecent" dances that the Cook voyagers brought to fame in Europe.
Occidental culture was, and has remained, fascinated by the dance
of "savage" women. In the early phase of colonization the heiva was
the best known of these Pacific dances, although it was superseded
by the Hawaiian *hula.* The indecency of these dances stemmed
from the reading of them by Occidental observers as simulations of
sex. The performers' dress, or lack of, in combination with bodily
movements, compounded this belief. In stark contrast to upper-class
Occidental dances at the time, "savage" dances were structured
around a center of gravity in the pelvis, as opposed to the uplifted
chest that elevated the body toward the heavens. "Savage" dances,

in contrast, were directed downward and symbolized to foreigners "such indecency, such unbridled sensuality that they could only imagine them resulting from 'primitive' inferiority."

The public spectacle of watching the eroticized motions of colonized women was a culminating moment for the Occidental man in the empire. In the evolving stereotype, dance was the supreme expression of indigenous women's eroticism, "just as violence was that of black male eroticism." Many of the women's dances were related to sexuality, but the expressions of sexuality, their meaning, and purpose extended well beyond male sexual gratification, as they were almost exclusively interpreted by Occidental viewers. Instead they expressed the profundity of life, linking sexuality, spirituality, and cosmology.[28]

I have suggested earlier that Oberea was the first Pacific muse, yet she was problematic owing to her age and the disjuncture between her assertiveness, as recorded by firsthand observers, and her popular construction in poems and plays. Visually, the first summation of the Pacific muse is John Webber's *Poedua* (fig. 2.3). She is the epitome of the imagined Pacific, being "young, feminine, desirable and vulnerable." According to John Williamson, third lieutenant on the *Resolution*, she was painted with this intent, as Cook was "so very partial to the Society Isles, that the two or three portraits that have been made, are of women (one in particular)." By Thomas Edgar's reckoning, the women were deserving of this symbolic status as they "make amends for any thing deficient on the side of the Men, they are in fact Angels." Although Edgar personally preferred the women of Amsterdam, "2 or 3" young women who had remained on board the ships during their time in the islands favored him with their company. "I can without vanity affirm it was the happiest 3 Months I ever spent," he reminisced.[29]

In Webber's homage to this much admired genus of womankind, the high-born and half-undressed Raiatean female subject looks back at the viewer calmly and knowingly, inviting further fantasy. Standing among verdant foliage, proudly displaying her sexual confidence, she is portrayed in prelapsarian perfection. Her fine facial features, fair skin, youthful breasts, and long, loosely arranged hair

2.3 John Webber, *Poedua, Daughter of Oree, Chief of Ulietea.*
Copyright National Maritime Museum, London, c. 1780.

incorporate this young Pacific woman into the Occidental visual tradition of fetishized female icons. The harmonious image of tropical tranquility displayed in this canvas masked the violent circumstances in which it was initially created, circumstances that arose as a consequence of the stereotype, sex, and colonial power.[30]

When the two vessels were anchored off Ra'iatea in November 1777, two men deserted the *Discovery* to savor the fabled luxurious ease of the South Sea isles. One was Mr. Mouat, the son of naval captain Patrick Mouat, who also had been to Tahiti on the *Dolphin*, and the other was the gunner's mate, Thomas Shaw. Cook was approached by Mouat a few days prior to his desertion, when he "had expressed a desire to remain at these isles." Cook did not entertain the request. The rationale behind this desire, according to William Bayly, was that Mouat was in love with a young girl from Huahine. This love may well have been unrequited, as the woman in question "absolutely refused to marry him if he stayed" according to Bayly, "which seemed to hurt the Young Gentleman's pride."[31]

The lure of "engaging females" was the reason proffered for these desertions, a theme that would gain greater currency with the *Bounty* mutiny twelve years later. In William Bligh's thesis accounting for the *H.M.S. Bounty*'s loss, it is Tahiti, embodied by its women, that he held responsible for the grave act of mutiny. Bligh articulated this view in a letter to Joseph Banks. "It may be asked what could be the cause of such a revolution," Bligh wrote, deflecting blame from himself. "In answer to which I have only to give a description of Otaheite, which has every allurement of both luxury and ease, and is the Paradise of the world." "The women," Bligh further explained to Banks, who would no doubt have been receptive to his thinking, "are handsome and mild in their manners and conversation, with sufficient delicacy to make them admired and beloved."[32]

Whether it was wounded pride or infatuation with a Polynesian woman that motivated a privileged man such as Mouat to abandon ship at Ra'iatea in 1777, the consequences of his actions were considerable. As the British were unable to locate the men by their own means, Poedua, her father, the local ruler Orio, and his son, Taeura, were enticed aboard the *Discovery* and made hostages until Orio's influence secured the deserters' return. The three were held for five days, causing great distress among the captives and islanders who gathered onto the ship. It was during this time that Poedua was immortalized by John Webber as the superlative visual embodiment of the South Sea muse for the late eighteenth century. According to David Samwell, Mouat was found enjoying the paradisiacal company he had sought with an older woman and a younger one "he admired." Meanwhile, the fallout from his desertion continued. In retaliation for incarcerating Orio, Poedua, and Taeura, a plot was hatched to kidnap Captain Clerke, commander of the *Discovery*, the second vessel on this voyage. The plan was foiled by "a girl belonging to a Person on board the *Discovery*" who made it known to the British.[33]

Beneath the peaceful facade of Webber's *Poedua* were tense undertones arising from the machinations of the stereotype with sex and colonial power. These tensions were highlighted by the writings of Cook. He displayed a greater consciousness than most in recording the obviously negative effects that the trade in sex was having upon the indigenes and the responsibility that Europe had to bear for it. This was particularly so for the men under his command who had spent the greatest amount of time in the region.

Disobedience and desertion were one facet of the problem. Transmission of venereal diseases and the threat of violence from indigenous men were two other dimensions. Cook had permitted sex between his crew and the Tahitian women to take place during the *Endeavour* voyage. Yet this was the last time he was not attempting to keep his men away from the indigenous women, or lamenting his inability to effect separation. In his journals, however, he professed to be most concerned to prevent his men contaminating newly detected peoples in the ocean, particularly at the Friendly Islands, New Zealand, and Hawai'i. This ambition he resoundingly failed to achieve. The evidence casts doubt on the force of Cook's convictions in this matter on his third voyage. During his second voyage when he first visited Nomuka Island in the Tonga group, Cook wrote that "as our People had not quite got clear of the disease communicated to them by the women of Otahiete, I took all imaginable care to prevent its being communicated to these people." He went on to claim "that my endeavours succeeded." When he returned on his third voyage, he realized that he had been mistaken. He wrote that "this commerce has unhappily entailed upon them the Venereal Deasease." They had not "been long at Anamocka before some of our people were affected with it, and I had the Mortification to find that all our care I took when I first Visited these islands to prevent this dreadfull deasease from being communicated to them, prove enefectual."[34]

When the *Resolution* and *Discovery* arrived in Hawai'i in 1778, the first European ships to do so, Cook emphatically ordered his men not to engage in sexual activity with the Hawaiians. He did not want to pollute these islanders with venereal diseases in the same way the Tongans had been harmed. T. Bayly reported that Cook's decision, motivated by the "number of our people not being free from the fowl disease, they got at the Society Islands," was a "great disappointment to the Girls." Thomas Edgar expanded upon this by recording that "none of them [Hawaiian women] were permitted to come on board the Ships & every precaution was taken to prevent the Men from medling with them on Shore." No one exhibiting "the dreadful distemper" or those recently off the surgeon's list "were suffered to set foot on Shore." Ultimately it was "the great eagerness of the Women concurring with the Desires of the Men" that made it "impossible to keep them from each other & we had reason to believe that some of them had Connections with these Women both on board our Ships and on Shore."[35]

David Samwell confirmed this. He reported that Cook made a "severe injunction against us having any intercourse with the Women of these Islands." Yet when the *Resolution* was anchored off Ni'ihau, he wrote that "girls sleep aboard every night." Hawaiian women were left diseased like the other women around the ocean visited by Cook's crews. The flagrant disobedience of his crews (or perhaps his tolerance) notwithstanding, Cook's procedures to prevent transmission of venereal diseases were in any case fundamentally flawed because of the incorrect information about infection propounded by consensus on contagions and treatment. If a man did not display visible signs of infection through chancres he was deemed "clean," although he was probably still contagious.[36]

Maori women of Queen Charlotte's Sound were particular objects of study for Cook to gauge the impact of his men's presence, as the sound was used as operational base in all three Cook voyages. As the five ships under Cook's command were the only European vessels to make contact with the people of this district, beginning with the *Endeavour* in 1769, the indigenes were a good sample group in which to observe the effects of Cook's colonization.

During a stay in June 1773 in the course of the second voyage, Cook observed a marked change, since his previous visit, in the sexual culture and commerce between his men and the Maori. Cook wrote that Maori women "who I had always looked upon to be more chaste than the generality of Indian women" were readily engaging in a sex trade with strong persuasion from their men, for "a spike nail or any other thing of value" and carrying out sexual acts "not with the privacy decency seems to require." In a strong rebuke of the processes of colonization that were axiomatically based around sex, Cook noted that "the consequences of a commerce with Europeans" was that "we debauch their Morals already prone to vice." "We . . . [more to our shame civilized Christians] interduce among them wants and perhaps diseases which they never before knew & which serves only to disturb that happy tranquility they and their fore Fathers had injoy'd." "If anyone denies the truth of this assertion" he challenged, "let him tell me what the Natives of the whole extent of America have gained by the commerce they have had with Europeans."[37]

Cook's deliberations on the peoples of Queen Charlotte's Sound and interracial sex took on a greater importance after ten men of the *Adventure*, under the command of Tobias Furneaux, were killed there following the *Resolution*'s departure in 1773. The killings were a cautionary tale of the complexity of imperial diplomacy and the potential danger that indigenous men posed to European voyagers when they were antagonized. While this violent incident was not solely the result of the crew's sexual contact with women, it contributed to the tensions between the two groups of men. On other occasions sexual misunderstandings contributed significantly to increasing tensions between the two groups of men, as members of Marion Du Frense's ill-fated voyage discovered the previous year in New Zealand's Bay of Islands.[38]

For the most part, travelers operated upon assumptions based on their own simplistic conclusions about indigenous women and sexuality perpetuated in the stereotype, which proved inadequate. They had overlooked what was generally termed the "jealousy" of the indigenous men, a stereotypic trait of "primitive" man. In January 1777, this weak understanding of indigenous women's sexuality, stemming from the circulating stereotype, and its link to potential violence became apparent again when the third Cook voyage harbored in Adventure Bay, Van Diemen's Land. Cook reported that "some of the Gentlemen belonging to the Discovery I was told, paid their addresses [to the women] and made them large offers which were rejected with disdain." Whether this occurred "from a sence of Verture or for fear of displeasing the Men," Cook conceded, "I shall not pretend to determine." A male elder observed this exchange and "ordered the women and children" away, although some of the recalcitrant women, Cook wrote, showed "a little reluctancy," escalating tension between the two groups of men. He went on to censure the Tasmanian women and to formulate a code of behavior for future dealings in the South Seas and a philosophy about the availability of women's sexual favors:

> This conduct in Indian Women is highly blameable,
> as it creates a jealousy in the men that may be attended
> with fatal consequences, without answering any one
> purpose whatever, not even that of the lover obtaining
> the object of his wishes. I believe it has generally been
> found amongst uncivilised people that where the women
> are of easy access, the Men are the first who offer them
> to strangers, and where this is not the case they are not
> easily come at . . . why then should men risk their own
> safety where nothing is to be obtained?[39]

Another version of this event gives further dimension to the Occidental male gaze and the extent to which it was misinformed by a priori cultural assumptions about women, race, and sexuality. According to Bayly, the women's lack of clothing signaled sexual availability. The men were therefore baffled by the refusal of their advances, "tho all parts of the body is exposed, the Women refused to cohabit with our people on any Account." "The Old Chief suffered the women to stay with us about an hour & then sent them away," reflecting Cook's observation about the "jealousy" of indigenous men and its relation to accessibility of women.[40]

On his next sojourn in Queen Charlotte Sound, the first following the killing of the ten Britons by Maori, Cook reflected upon the issue of sex with the local women once more. On this occasion Cook's theory on sexual relations was colored by the preceding events that severely challenged the peaceable relations Cook had enjoyed with the Maori of Queen Charlotte Sound. Male sexual freedom was deleterious for more than health reasons, as it could inflame the vengeful "primitive" emotions of women and the fickle nature of the male savage, as the incident in Van Diemen's Land revealed. In a commentary on the polemics of sexual contact and diplomacy, Cook questioned the school of thought espoused by the likes of Dampier. "A connection with Women I allow because I cannot prevent it, but never encourage tho many Men are of the opinion it is one of the greatest securities amongst Indians," he reasoned. This rationale "may hold good when you intend to settle amongst them; but with travelers and strangers, it is generally otherwise and more men are betrayed than saved by having connection with their women." "How could it be otherwise," Cook concluded, since itinerant men "are selfish without the least mixture of regard or attachment whatevere." His observations, of many years standing, "have not pointed out to me one instance to the contrary."[41]

Desire, Danger, and the Pacific Muse

Cook's unprecedented experience in the Pacific led him to understand how Pacific colonization impacted indigenous sexual cultures and the sexual proclivities of women. He complicated the sexual culture of Pacific colonization in two ways. First, he admitted that this culture was exploitative in favor of the "selfish" men under his command who treated these women as commodities. The complexity of women's lives had been restructured to accommodate the sexual "needs" of his men. These "needs" were based upon male sexual gratification. An effect of the sex trade was that indigenous women's sexuality, which was viewed as positive within indigenous societies, was also dramatically altered to accommodate this aspect of colonial culture. Women's sexual needs, expectations, and desires were subordinated to those of the colonizing men, who did not bring with them a sexual culture that considered women's pleasure. This change made female sexual pleasure expendable in all sexual interactions by being equated with her ability to satisfy her partner. A sexual "revolution," as described by a number of historians, that had been occurring across the eighteenth century in Europe was rapidly imposed upon the Pacific.[42]

Missionaries have traditionally been the scapegoats for the much-lamented demise of Pacific women's fabled sexual prowess. Christian teachings did indeed promote a passive female sexuality organized around reproduction and male dominance. Before missionaries arrived, however, Cook realized that the colonial sexual culture forged by his voyages was responsible for altering manifestations of female sexuality. The stereotype of the Pacific muse held that island women were willing to provide sexual pleasure for men without demanding anything beyond trinkets in return. It was their ability to please white men that was portrayed as the pleasure women gained from the encounter.[43]

Cook's second important observation on the sexual culture in the Pacific added a devious layer to the stereotype of indigenous women. His warning to future voyagers not to put trust in "Indian women," was a caution drawing on stereotypes of female unpredictability exacerbated by primitivism. Pacific women were perceived by European men to be the chattels of their menfolk. European men consequently viewed sexual access to indigenous women's bodies as being at the discretion of indigenous men. Cook castigated women's usurpation of this male license that he and others perceived in the Van Diemen's Land incident. In a similar vein, when La Pérouse was at Port Jackson, he warned Captain Phillip to beware of the "perfidious caresses" of Samoan women following the attack upon his crew at Fagasa Bay in 1787. In the pantomimes and plays based upon this event that Jocelyn Linnekin has discussed, the character of the native woman was represented as "volatile and mercurial." Thus an element of danger in Pacific women's sexuality was also incorporated into the stereotype.[44]

Other tales of emasculation surfaced occasionally in Pacific voyage literature, drawing upon the underlying fears in Occidental culture of women's voracious sexuality that were intensified by racial traits. Charles Bishop, who captained a vessel engaging in the fur trade on the Northwest Coast of America in the 1790s declared that the women of the region were "Genereally Ladies of Easy access" but gave an alarming account of the fate of one unspecified crew. All the crew, bar one survivor who told the apocryphal story, were beheaded by the local men while "the savage North-West American women [cut] off their privities and thr[ew] them in wantonness at each other." The stereotype was not without ambiguity; although the women's sexual prowess was fetishized, Occidental culture had a long-standing tradition of fearing sexually active women. As the stereotype of the Pacific evolved, it combined passivity and meekness with a willingness to sexually please white men. However, the dangerous aspect of the stereotype remained a constant presence enforcing greater colonial power, as colonizers could readily reshape the stereotype into a denigrating representation when the occasion required.[45]

This operation of the stereotype is displayed in images of Pacific women who were infected with venereal diseases. Representations of Pacific women became increasingly layered with the contemptuous imagery of polluting Occidental prostitutes once it was widely understood that the sexual paradise of the Pacific was diseased. This imagery depicted the women's bodies as infected vessels and Occidental men as victims of their deadly allure.[46]

Cook's belief that men were the sources of venereal infection rapidly dissipated in the years succeeding his voyages. When Russia's imperial navy traversed the Pacific in the *Neva* and the *Nadeshda* from 1803 to 1806 under the command of Adam von Krusenstern, the current attitudes to "ladies of pleasure" were announced in assessments of Pacific women. At Nuku Hiva, Krusenstern reluctantly allowed women to come aboard on the first day, a decision he made knowing that "I had not a single venereal patient on board" and following reassurances from Edward Robarts, the beachcomber, that "this disease was hitherto unknown in the island." Krusenstern nevertheless "set bounds to this favour, and after the second day no females were admitted to the ship," an action that may also have been taken to prevent too strong attachments that might result in desertions. The economic importance of sex in the colonial Nuku Hivan economy, as Krusenstern saw it, meant that women still swam out to his ship and "would not go away until a few shots were fired over their heads."[47]

The Russian's military-style solution to these women's alleged insistence on sex in Nuku Hiva was given further currency when the expedition reached Hawai'i in June 1804. Here Urey Lisiansky couched sexual commerce in the language of war. He described the "company of about a hundred young women," who swam to his ship "not doubting of admittance," whom he forced to return ashore with an "affront offered to their charms, which they had never experienced before, perhaps, from any European ship." Lisiansky was adamant "not to permit licentious intercourse on board" between his men and "this troop of nymphs," not for moralistic reasons, but because he viewed these women as polluting. "The cause of my peremptoriness as to these female visitors, was the fear of their introducing to my crew a certain disease," he reasoned. "I had been given to understand [venereal disease] was very prevalent in the Sandwich Islands." He observed what he took to be "evident marks of its ravages" on "the persons of several of its inhabitants, of both sexes."[48]

The colloquial names assigned to generic "venereal disease" in the seafarers' idiom reinforced ideas that the source of contagion was not Occidental men. Terms such as the "Ladies fever" or localized adaptations such as the "Sandwich Island itch" and "New Zealand fever" were commonly used for venereal diseases across the nineteenth century. This cultural tendency to reproach indigenes for contamination had a long-standing tradition, as discussed earlier, stretching back to 1530, when the newly colonized Americans were condemned as the origin of the first wave of syphilis then sweeping Europe.[49]

The specter of venereal disease in the Pacific's sexual economy would become a concern for those controlling the commercial shipping and resource extraction industries. These industries inundated the region with thousands of men, especially in the first half of the nineteenth century. Many owners of whaling ships issued strict instructions to captains forbidding sexual fraternization with indigenous women, for one significant reason: it did not make good commercial practice. In 1850 the seaman William Wilson, aboard the Connecticut whaler *Cavalier*, recorded that information about the debauched behavior of the crew, particularly that of Captain Dexter at Ponape in the Caroline Islands, had to be treated with the strictest discretion. Wilson recorded that "the old man told us not to blab and tell that females had been aboard the ship . . . He was afraid of talk — that it would reach the ears of the owners." According to the delinquent Captain Dexter, the crew was in a dire state owing to the effects of copious alcohol and venereal diseases. He conceded that "we are half drunk the other half fucked to death."[50]

The dangerous ulterior to the stereotype of Pacific women, based in racism, negative constructions of female "primitivism," and fears about women and their polluting bodies, was an ever-present facet of the stereotype. Yet it was articulated with varying intensities at different times and according to regional disparities and colonial agendas. This aspect of the stereotype encapsulated the unpleasant aspects of the sex trade. Disease, disobedience among crews, and the danger posed by indigenous men all threatened the well-being of the Occidental man and the imperial mission in its many dimensions.

Imperial and Savage Masculinities

The great problems of venereal diseases and the possibility of violence and desertion stemming from sexual contact with indigenous
women had to be weighed up against the other potentially dangerous scenarios. It was thought that denying opportunities for heterosexual sex to large groups of men could have harmful effects upon
Occidental masculinity. The direst consequences of a lack of access
to female sexual partners were masturbation and homosexuality.
"Unnatural acts," especially buggery, were being viewed with ever
increasing concern at the time of early Pacific colonization. The
British Navy increased punishments for sodomy, especially during
the Napoleonic wars. Voyaging in the Pacific required prodigiously
long periods of absence from wives. While the sexual "needs" of voyagers had a scientific basis that promoted frequent sexual emissions,
it is unlikely that this rationale was applied by the common sailor to
justify his sexual pursuits. The engineers of the Port Jackson colony
explored the social and scientific issues of sexuality. They fretted
over the outcome of large numbers of working-class men being
removed to the other side of the world without sexual access to
women. Plans to import indigenous women from neighboring islands
were not realized. Instead convict women were used as sexual out-
lets for men. The vulnerability of the fledgling colony, combined with
American imperial experience and the warnings of men such as Cook
and La Pérouse, made Aboriginal women unsuitable for the colony's
engineers.[51]

As long distance voyaging offered a window onto working-class
men's sexuality, indigenous societies, with their relative openness
about sexual matters, provided a frontier for social scientists to make
comparative studies of the male gender across racial lines. Observations of this nature were a constant feature of the voyagers' gaze,
sublimated within colonial representations. Part of the stereotype
of Pacific women was that they were used to rough handling by their
men, who were prone to violence and irrationality, according to ignoble stereotypes of indigenous men that stressed their brutality
toward women.

David Collins, judge advocate and secretary to the New South Wales colony, created the basis for this stereotype as it related to Aboriginal men by describing the rough marriage ritual of Aboriginal society "observed" in the early years of the colony. The result was akin to the stereotype of a caveman seeking out the object of his lust, clubbing her over the head, and taking possession of her as a wife. While Collins described Aboriginal men as "ravishers," Aboriginal women's noble qualities were enhanced by the depravity of their menfolk, as they possessed a passivity and servitude to men that was greatly admired. Collins's account of savage male "love rituals" influenced Thomas Malthus's theory on population control in which he argued that the Aboriginal man's "barbarous mode of courtship" was an effective means of population control. His account also influenced subsequent descriptions of Aboriginal people, such as that of George Barrington, who turned marriage by capture into a romantic, "sentimental love tale." Although the Aboriginal men were brutish and exercised "absolute power" over women, all worked out well in the end, as the women, after being carried off and ravished, "seem contented, and seldom leave their husbands or his tribe for another." Aboriginal society around the settlement of Port Jackson was characterized as exhibiting a form of primitivism from prehistoric times, so-called hard primitivism, as Smith termed this concept.[52]

The French Baudin voyage of 1802 attempted to locate the essence of race by comparing the erotic power of Frenchmen with Aboriginal men of Maria Island, off the southwest coast of Van Diemen's Land. On this voyage, this most curious and most controversial aspect of colonialism was delved into with unbridled candor, revealing a decidedly clinical and interested anthropological gaze. Francois Péron, the naturalist on the voyage, in aiming to test the sensuality of Occidental men versus that of "primitive" man, posed such questions as "like most animals, do they [primitive men] only experience the need for love at fixed and intermittent periods?" Also, was the "continuity of desire and consequently that of sensual enjoyment therefore . . . one of the benefits of civilisation?"[53]

Working against the sexually insatiable stereotype of "primitive man," Péron wished to prove that Occidental men possessed ultimate sexual prowess. The nakedness of women was crucial in his formulation. The acceptance of such nakedness by "primitive" men supposedly denoted a lack of male pleasure at viewing of the female form and therefore indicated a severely depleted sexual drive in these men.

The French observations were no doubt influenced by the writings of Comte de Buffon, which were influential in the formulation of theories of race and sex, as we have previously seen. In Buffon's universal order there was certainly no entertainment of the idea of noble savagery of either the male or female variety. For Buffon, man living in the savage state, in this particular instance "the American savage," was "nothing more than a species of animal," who was denied the "sentiment of love" that was his sole means to relate to the female sex. He wrote that "Nature has withheld from them the most precious spark of her torch; they have no ardour for the female and consequently no love for their fellow-creatures." Without any capacity for love or sexual desire they treated their women "as drudges . . . or rather as beasts of burthen . . . whom they oblige, without pity or gratitude, to perform offices repugnant to their natures, and frequently beyond their strength." These men also did not value offspring; Buffon argued that "they have few children, and to those they pay little attention."[54]

In this French tradition natural man lacked sensual pleasure in viewing a woman's breasts and was "indifferent" to female nudity. This was a marker of his lethargic sexual desire that contrasted poorly with "civilized man." Péron noted that the Frenchmen aboard his expedition were constantly aroused by the sight of young naked Tasmanian women, while the Tasmanian men appeared unmoved by such erotic delights. Women's bodies were not eroticized by their men; also they seemed to know nothing of the sensual arts of kissing and caressing, Péron decided, after women he tried to kiss "all had that look of surprise and uneasiness."[55]

Much of Péron's data was garnered from one highly symbolic theatrical moment when the two categories of men compared "sense organs." He wrote that the Aboriginal men "showed an extreme desire to examine our genital organs." The French were most unwilling to acquiesce, though after the Tasmanian men insisted, it fell to the young sailor Citizen Michel, with his "slight build and lack of beard," to "set their minds at rest" about the Frenchmen's sex. Unexpectedly, Citizen Michel "suddenly exhibited such a striking proof of his virility that they all uttered loud cries of surprise mingled with loud roars of laughter which were repeated again and again." "This condition of strength and vigour in the one among us who seemed the least likely, surprised them extremely," Peron mused, as "they had the air of applauding the condition as if they were men in whom it was not very common." "Several of them showed with a sort of scorn their soft and flaccid organs," shaking "them briskly with an expression of regret and desire which seemed to indicate that they did not experience it as often as we did."[56]

The mandatory use of clothing in civilized nations aided men's sensual development, as such customs protected the "cutaneous organ" from "continuity of sensation which is alone sufficient to deaden sensibility." Penises of "natural men" were, ironically, "hardened" by exposure to "the inclemency of the weather," the cruel necessity of sleeping naked on the ground," and the "painful lacerations" from walking naked. Clothing also increased the "sweet and voluptuous sensations" sparked by women whose bodies were provocatively packaged in clothes. Citizen Péron's conclusions undermined Enlightenment and Romantic configurations of natural man and gave great support to the colonial mind-set that was so fundamentally based upon competing masculinities and sexualized expressions of power. That Frenchmen were capable of expressing "love" toward women while savage men engaged in animal-like fornication was graphically expressed by two voyeuristic images by Nicholas Petit, one of the voyage artists.[57]

The Russians of the Krusenstern voyage likewise took advantage of the nudity of the Nuku Hivan men to ponder the "sense organ" and how cultural and racial differences affected this all-important signifier of masculinity. Krusenstern noted that "the men are not circumcised, but some of them had the foreskin cut straight down . . . and like the inhabitants of St Christina, they tie the extremity with a knot." Krusenstern noted that there was a reciprocal interest in Russian penises from "modest beauties" of Nuku Hiva who swam out to their ship and "expressed a great degree of horror" at the sight of the penis of one of the Russian crewmen. Robarts confirmed that the women of Nuku Hiva "are quite obdurate towards those, who do not observe this fashion of [penile treatment]." This observation casts doubts upon the belief that indigenous women inveterately viewed Occidental men as the preferred sexual choice to their own men, as the stereotype suggested.[58]

Reading indigenous sexual cultures through the bodily exposure of women was part of French naturalist René Lesson's ethnographic method when he was at the Bay of Islands on the Duperry voyage in 1824. Lesson observed that although most of the young Maori women aboard *La Coquille* were "diametrically opposed to our ideas of beauty," some of the women exhibited enviable classic loveliness with their "dazzling white teeth and black eyes, full of fire and expression." This was "greatly enhanced by an advantage which is very rare among civilised women" as "the young New Zealand women, who in their happy ignorance know nothing of the use of bodices, have breasts which rival marble in their firmness, and which remain elastic and firm despite their fullness." Most telling was Lesson's conclusion that "these organs have no effect on men's feelings, in their eyes they are only reservoirs from which their children draw life."[59]

The notion that Occidental men were sexually superior to their indigenous counterparts was an essential component of the imperial stereotype. Stereotypes of sexually available colonized women were premised upon archetypes of primitive men that stressed their dilapidated sexuality and brutality toward women. The predominating stereotype of Pacific women always had her seeking out the white man above men of her own race.

The Missionary Position

The dominating images of Pacific women in the wake of the Enlightenment voyages fueled fantasies that they would indiscriminately service the needs of Occidental men. For those of a proselytizing persuasion, representations of women so abandoned to sensuality, and so unchecked in their interaction with low-ranking Occidental men, evoked a sense of alarm. The British Evangelical campaign to transform national morality that was under way by the 1760s sought to bring even the furthest flung people within the realm of Christian light. One of the foremost objectives of the missionary endeavor was the elevation of women from their savage state to wifely virtue. Targeting women was the means missionaries used to make permanent inroads into indigenous societies. As women were perceived as weaker and "softer" in the mind, missionaries considered them as more malleable, with greater potential to be corrected but greater potential to fall. Men were viewed as more attached to tradition, being the custodians of custom. The measure of missionary success was the degree to which women resembled the ideals of Occidental middle-class femininity, that is, "faithful wives, tender mothers and useful members of society" as Dandeson Coates of the London Missionary Society (LMS) stated that group's aims in the Pacific world.[60]

Reports of the existence of peoples living in moral abandonment, as well as their corruption from contact with European sailors, prompted the burgeoning Evangelical movement in Britain to act.[61] Missionaries ventured into the Pacific believing that it was the soft feminine paradise that predominating voyage images conveyed. It was not. Many islands, especially after European contact, were drawn into martial conflict in which both men and women participated. The missionaries were caught in the crossfire. It was only with indigenous patronage that they were able to effect any change to sexual customs, as they learned through trying experiences.

The first LMS assault on the Pacific began with the purchase of the vessel *Duff*, which was manned and cast forth into the godless region in 1796. The vessel stopped first at Tahiti, where eighteen missionaries were disgorged and two Tahitians, Haraway and Tanno Manoo, who were to act as language teachers in the maiden attempts at Christian conversion, were collected. The *Duff* sailed on, dispersing missionaries around the eastern Polynesian islands, ten on Tongatapu and two on Tahuata in the Marquesas. James Wilson was pleased with Tanno Manoo of whom he wrote, "she was . . . of a good natural understanding, evidently susceptible to improvement." She had conducted herself in an "affable," "obliging," and "useful" manner and had taken readily to wearing clothes, a matter of pivotal importance to the project. Wilson wrote of his pride at teaching the women a sense of shame about their bodies. The captain gave Tanno Manoo "a warm week-day dress, and a shewy morning gown and petticoat for Sundays." From then "she always kept herself clean" and "when dressed she made a very decent appearance; taking more pains to cover her breasts and even to keep her feet from being seen, than most of the ladies of England have of late done."[62]

The women of the Marquesas were not so worthy of praise and displayed to the people on board the *Duff* the essence of female degradation and therefore the size of the task ahead of them. Yet even Wilson was captivated by the figure of the first young woman who climbed aboard the boat, although he described her beauty in the more detached terms of an aesthete "that as models for the statuary and painter their equal can seldom be found." In Wilson's eyes, Tanno Manoo again proved how rapidly she had imbibed the European mores concerning the female body. Although he supposed that she "felt her inferiority in no small degree" to this Marquesan woman, despite having a "comely person" herself "she was ashamed to see a woman upon the deck quite naked." She duly "supplied her with a complete dress of new Otahietan cloth, which set her off to great advantage."[63]

The sexual temptation was palpable among the crew when the association with the young Marquesan women became more frequent. On one occasion the "mischievous goats" on board ate away the only covering of leaves some of the young women wore, leaving them "completely stripped naked." On another, Wilson found it "not a little affecting" to see "the most beautiful females" helping the sailors with shipboard duties "with the greatest assiduity." "No ship's company without great restraints from God's grace, could ever have resisted such temptations" if "they had not been overawed by the jealousy of the officers and the good conduct of the messmates."[64]

At the center of all missionary aims was the sexual constraint of indigenous women that was to be effected through reeducation and the shining example of male missionaries and their wives. The diametrically opposing ideas of female sexuality in the indigenous and European societies regularly caused alarm. John Harris of the *Duff* was perhaps the first to experience just how wide the gulf was. He was alone on the Marquesan island of Tahuata and the chief, Tenae, had left Harris his wife "to be treated as his own till the chief came back again." Wilson reported that Tenae's wife and friends attempted to "satisf[y] themselves" of Mr. Harris's sex while he was asleep, yet they did so in "not in such a peaceable way . . . that they awooke him." Mr. Harris on "discovering so many strangers . . . was greatly terrifid." He was so alarmed by "what they had been doing" that he was "determined to leave the place where the people were so abandoned and given up to wickedness." Wilson, however, thought that this incident "should have excited a contrary resolution" and prompt Harris to continue his mission, regardless of its unusual dangers.[65]

Despite the great hopes and investment that the LMS had made in the closing years of the eighteenth century to be a moral presence in the region, this venture, like its Spanish predecessor, failed, with the missions all but dissipated by 1808. The realities of indigenous politics, which were in a great state of flux, put the missionaries in grave danger, with some being killed. Also, a number of individuals were unable to cope with the practicalities of missionary life in the Pacific (of which Mr. Harris was all too well acquainted). William Puckey dwelt at length upon the extent of the problems in Tahiti, remonstrating that "the natives are so bent to the gratification of their lustful appetites that they have been guilty of [m]any obscene actions in our presence." Infanticide and female licentiousness rated highly in his journal, as did the overt presence of a homosexual population, the *mahu*. He wrote in shock that these people seemed to be given up to "vile affection for the men burn in their lust one towards the other, men with men working that which is unseemly." Puckey accounted for the presence of a homosexual culture by casting it as a consequence of poverty. He argued that it was common among men who "cannot afford to supply the women with extravagant Articles of dress," though this was not the case.[66]

The surprise at the sexual behavior of each race was mutual. "Some of them would not believe that we were English men," Puckey wrote, "because our practices are different from those of our country men who have visited the island." At least three of the LMS flock proved Puckey wrong on this count in the early years of the mission. John Cock "quickly succumbed to carnal delights" on Tahiti. Another who arrived with the *Duff* in 1797, Mr. Lewis, labored usefully for the missionary cause until he went to live with a Tahitian woman in 1799. He "intimated to his companions his intention of uniting in marriage with [her] solemnly proposing to abide faithful towards her until death." The other missionaries refused his request as they considered the woman an "idolatress" and marriage to her an "unlawful act." When Lewis did not relinquish his wicked lifestyle, his fellow missionaries "discontinued all Christian and social intercourse with him." His violent death some weeks later was an ominous warning to men with similar failings. Witnesses claimed that he had beaten his head against stones in front of the house where he had lived in sin, as if he was insane or possessed by an evil spirit. The missionaries surmised that he had been murdered.

Another missionary among the original party who landed on Tahiti in 1797, the twenty-four-year-old Mr. Broomhall, had also lived "some time with a native female, as his wife," but she left him. Broomhall asked to be removed from the island when the *Duff* returned in 1801. He moved to Calcutta and "made himself known to the Baptist Missionary Society," who accepted him to preach to the "heathen," but again "he fell into open iniquity and embraced a gloomy state of infidelity, the frequent consequence of backsliding from God." Like Lewis, Broomhall's sexual sins were succeeded by great misfortune—"a broken thigh at Madras and a severe illness in Calcutta" and then an untimely death when he perished in a shipwreck.[67]

Lessons were learned in England and later in the United States from these early "backsliders." The numerous missionary societies insisted upon men going to the region with wives—white wives—as assurance against the temptations of Pacific women, as Patricia Grimshaw has shown. This measure appeared to work, but the problem of sexual infidelity of missionary men persisted despite the presence of white wives and children. These families often helped conceal wrongdoing of such a dire nature.[68]

The sexual freedoms taken by the missionaries in the Pacific, albeit inviting both human and divine retribution, according to missionary William Ellis, were governed by personal convictions. Where indigenous communities had established sexual economies around the shipping, there was little constraint upon frontier man, excepting his own conscience, captain's edicts, and his possession of suitable material items for the sexual exchange. However, missionary influence began to alter the sexual culture in key areas of the Pacific, especially in Hawai'i and Tahiti, from the 1820s, as we shall see.[69]

National Types and Contested Masculinities

We have seen that ideas about male sexuality in Britain and the United States were undergoing a change at the time of the late-eighteenth-century voyages owing to the rise of Christian middle-class morality as the dominant cultural force. This moral middle class attempted to change aristocratic and working-class sexual cultures, creating tension between the classes. In addition, in the Pacific empire tensions also became apparent because of differing national codes of masculinities. British, French, and American masculine conduct was clarified in the colonies, especially through sexual relations with indigenous women. We can see how the stereotype of the Pacific muse operated with national constructions of masculinity by examining the controversy surrounding Captain David Porter's attempt to take possession of Nuku Hiva in the Marquesas for the United States in November 1813. The incident is also notable as the first attempt by a United States' agent to enter into the Pacific imperial game and displays once again the patterns of conquest and sexual access established from the first encounters in the sixteenth century.

In late 1813, Porter was brimming with praise for the peoples of Madisonville on Massachusetts Bay, whom he claimed along with their island, Nuku Hiva, renamed Madison Island. Their physiques and countenances were so beautiful that Porter claimed they had been "stigmatized by the name savages," for they "rank high in the scale of humanity, whether we consider them morally or physically." The laws of conquest, however, dictated that the submission of the indigenes, no matter how aesthetically pleasing, was imperative to agendas of imperialism. After a display of military might against the recalcitrant Happah, which made all the peoples of the island sensible that they too risked "destruction," Porter assured these beautiful islanders that "so long as they treated us as friends" and were "faithful to the American flag," further hostilities would be abated. "Our rights to this island," he declared, were "founded on priority of discovery, conquest and possession," which "could not be disputed." This indisputable right to the island was sealed by the Nuku Hivans' perceived request "to be admitted to the great American family." It was further legitimated by what Porter portrayed as the joyous and harmless union between his crew and the Nuku Hivan women that succeeded the defeat of the Happahs.[70]

Porter had ignited his crew's desires with the prospect of free sex before entering the Pacific, promising his crew that "the girls of the Sandwich islands will reward you for your sufferings during the passage around Cape Horn." The Nuku Hivan women instead bestowed this "reward" in an amorous atmosphere that was not, according to Porter, induced by the preceding bloodshed. Conveniently, his stereotyped perception of the women's sexuality suited such a promise. Porter reported that "virtue among them in the light which we view it was unknown, and they attached no shame to a proceeding which they not only considered natural, but an innocent and harmless amusement, by which no one was injured." This lack of virtue led to "helter skelter" between "the common sailors and their girls," and with "every girl the wife of every man in the mess, and frequently of every man in the ship."[71]

Porter himself may not have been as lucky as the rest of his crew. The object of his attentions, Piteenee, the granddaughter of the chief Keatonui, "repelled every thing like familiarity with a sternness that astonished me," reported the jilted Porter, although she "formed a connexion with one of the officers." Piteenee contradicted the prevailing stereotype of the young and nubile South Seas woman as indiscriminate in her choice of partner, by exercising personal choice and thereby frustrating Porter's plans to establish "the most friendly intercourse." The inducement of economic advantage had a marked impact upon Nuku Hivan women's choices in the establishment of a sexual economy with the Yankee men according to Porter. He wrote that "no jewel, however valuable is half so esteemed in Europe or America, as is a whale's tooth here," and Porter claimed "the charm of the whale's tooth . . . could purchase the favors of the best of them." Yet Piteenee's favors were beyond his purchasing power.[72]

Porter presumed that as the myths of Pacific women's embrace of European men had enjoyed such great publicity over the four previous decades, his continued celebration of them in his voyage journal would be palatable. In another trans-Atlantic context his frank descriptions of his men's "promiscuous intercourse" with the island women in combination with his brutal methods of securing "Madison Island" as United States territory may not have raised an indignant eyebrow. We have seen that armed coercions followed by fabled sexual escapades were all too common themes running through imperial narratives of the Pacific. But both Porter and the British publication *Quarterly Review*, which denounced him as "rapacious" and the "meanest buccaneer" for the activities recounted in his journal, were on a war footing. In retaliation to Porter's fervent nationalism and no doubt to ease the smarting wounds of military defeat by the United States in 1815, the *Quarterly Review* cut down this aspiring, though unsuccessful, imperial agent (his annexation of Nuku Hiva was never ratified by the U.S. Congress) to little more than a peddler of "pernicious trash." Also they described him as a perpetrator of unbridled cruelty in his methods of securing the "subservience" of the Nuku Hivans.[73]

The *Quarterly Review* articulated in the strongest terms the competing interpretations of male sexual license in the Pacific and desirable masculinity extant by this time. It charged Porter with being a vulgar churl for taking advantage of the "moral depravity of ignorant savages," and in committing to print particulars of the information too indecent for the *Quarterly Review* to "pollute our pages with the description which Porter gives of his transactions with these people." In the most strident section of the diatribe against Porter, the reviewer introduced the virility of the male national type as an issue. The reviewer drew a distinction between the two warring parties on the basis of male sexual restraint in the empire. This he connected to degrees of civilization and the "reputations of nations," a shift from nationalistic discourses that emphasized the link between potency and imperial power. The reviewer remonstrated that Porter's "language and his ideas are so gross and indelicate, so utterly unfit for this hemisphere, that we must leave the undivided enjoyment of this part of the book to his own countrymen." The magazine's editors were "at a loss to determine which is more disgusting and offensive—his nauseous ribaldry, or his impudent avowal of improper conduct." Porter admitted that the Marquesans acted according to custom, but "we departed from those principles of virtue and morality, which are so highly esteemed in civilization." The editors scoffed that he thought it enough "that each confined himself to one object, and she of the best family and rank," which, he says, "was as much as the most zealous *celebiate* could require."[74]

Porter's journal was considered so obscene and anti-British that the first British edition was censored. In the preface to the second edition of his journal, the publisher conceded that Porter had omitted "a few passages that might possibly admit of some objections," but attempted to disarm the British critic of the greater charges. Porter and his publisher looked back at the history of Pacific imperialism to support Porter's understanding of how Occidental men could behave in the Pacific and what could be reported of it to an Occidental readership without attracting censure. Porter's publisher defied the critic to "produce any passage from the first or present edition of this Journal, conveying a picture of voluptuous sensuality, and indiscriminate, vulgar licentiousness equal to that poutrayed" by British Pacific voyagers, namely Wallis, Cook, and his fellow voyage journalists, and even by missionary James Wilson. The publisher maintained that the British were largely, if not entirely, responsible for the initial and sustained "moral corruption" of the Pacific peoples. Further, it was pointed out that Britain and the

United States shared a common culture of male sexual permissiveness in the Pacific. So any claims to greater national virtue owing to male sexual restraint that the *Quarterly*'s reviewer suggested were nonsense.[75]

Porter's publisher had a point. Yet attitudes to imperial masculinity were shifting both in the metropolitan centers of empire and also in the Pacific. Within a few years of this exchange, missionary influence was beginning to have a marked impact. A change in the culture was achieved in some ports owing to the powerful patronage of the ruling indigenes in Papeete, Lahaina, and Honolulu. Following the Cook voyages, Tahiti grew as an important Pacific port, conveniently situated between New South Wales and Valparaiso, where it served as a center for sandalwood trade and then increasingly as a station for whalers. As in New Zealand and Hawai'i, the chiefs who controlled this trade grew rich through taxation and port charges and powerful through their access to guns. LMS missionaries played a pivotal role in both New Zealand and Tahiti in the rise of indigenous chiefs.[76] Pomare II, who succeeded in defeating his traditional foe by 1815 and uniting the Tahitian islands under his rule, declared that he had converted to Christianity in 1819. Part of his conversion involved the imposition of a new sexual order restricting the trade in sex, laws made at the behest of his LMS supporters.[77]

In 1823 Frenchman Thomas Pierre Rolland, not a good student of Pacific history, lamented the loss of the fabled days of sensual abandon that had formed the modern myth, synonymous with Tahiti. He wrote that Tahitian women were "no longer what they were in the days of Quiros and Bougainville when they used to swim from the shore to come on board in the hope that they might bestow their favours on a kind traveler." Missionaries had effected this change, he argued, by imposing harsh penalties upon women who defied moral ordinances in order to satisfy their instinctual sexuality. Regardless of this castigation, Rolland noted that in spite of punishment "some are not deterred from coming aboard at night between 10 and 11 p.m.," and "after having satisfied their desires, they swim back to shore." "In my opinion, there is no point in inflicting on them such harsh penalties" as "one can see their passionate nature" in "their features and eyes." In the end, Rolland thought it came down to power: "the missionaries simply want to be dictatorial."[78]

The French lament for the fabled days of Bougainville would become a constant refrain for years to come. When French naval commanders began displaying imperial interest in Tahiti after 1836, they did so on the premise of opening Tahiti to French Jesuit influence, a premise that had implications for the changed sexual culture, as it was cast as an issue of French citizens' rights in the island kingdom. In 1839, in one of a succession of French naval visits designed to force Queen Pomare to permit French priests on Tahiti, Captain Laplace arrived in the vessel *Artémise*. He insisted that "French Catholics should possess every privilege allowed to Protestants; that land should be appropriated for the erection of a Catholic church, and that French priests have full liberty to exercise their ministry."[79]

As his vessel was badly damaged, Laplace also landed his entire crew, a practice disallowed under the port regulations. One of them, M. Reybauld, wrote an account of this shore leave in which he evoked the elusive golden age of Tahitian contact. Unlike more recent visitors to the islands, Reybauld was not disappointed. This island that "Bougainville called the New Cythera did not belie its name. The whole of Papeete was one seraglio without restraint."[80] When night fell "every tree along the coast shaded an impassioned pair, the waters of the river offered an asylum to a swarm of copper-coloured nymphs who came to enjoy themselves with the young midshipmen." "Wherever you walked," he continued, "you might hear their oui! oui! oui! The word that all the women have learnt . . . and it is the only one." Reybauld's equation of the Tahitian women's sexual alacrity with their innate nature, which was so integral to Bougainville myth, was here reiterated and reified. The French had not only ensured freedom for Catholics, Reybauld argued, but also they had freed the Tahitians from a religion that professed to "save the soul" but "killed the body." The sailors, far from despoiling this paradise had, in Reybauld's view, revived it. The natives, he claimed, sought in the sailors "protection from the oppression of the sombre missionaries."[81] Reybauld epito-

mized the French ability to wed sexual liberty, Catholicism, and political discourses of freedom. As French power grew, so too did the erosion of the LMS missionaries' moral control. It was all but diffused
in the early 1850s following the establishment of France's protectorate
over the island, though Catholic priests began restoring a form of
moral order in subsequent years.[82]

In the Hawaiian ports of Honolulu and Lahaina the sexual
restrictions on visiting voyagers were condemned in a variety of ways,
from writings in journals to defiance and, in the most extreme case,
murderous rage. This time the anger was directed against Protestant
missionaries from New England. In 1825, the captain and crew of
the British whaler *Daniel* were so incensed by the ban on women going
to the ships in Lahaina that they threatened to kill Mr. Richards, the
American missionary whom they held responsible. In reality the missionaries did not have such power, but they pragmatically encouraged the reenactment of the *kapu* laws by the local chiefs, preventing
women from going near the foreign shipping. In evidence before the
Select Committee on Aborigines in British Settlements some twelve years
after the fact in 1837, William Ellis testified that a mob of men surrounded the home of Mr. and Mrs. Richards and declared "that they
would have his life or they would have females on board." In his
assessment of the incident, a fellow American missionary, C. S.
Stewart, wrote that the men were "exasperated at the restraints laid
upon their licentiousness through the influence of the mission."[83]

A similar prohibition on Hawaiian women going to ships in
Honolulu was effected four years later, according to Stephen
Reynolds, the American whaler who became a resident of Honolulu
from 1822. He reported in his journal on October 7, 1829, "Girls
prohibited from sleeping with anyone on board Ships." In 1839, John
Wilson, the surgeon on the British whaler *Gypsy*, was incredulous
that laws existed in Honolulu that restrained the sexual activities of
foreign men, placing them in the same infantalized category as "half-
civilised Kanaka females." "There is a law in force here," he wrote,
"which purports to have for its object, the suppression of lewdness
and sensuality not only on the part of the female portion of the population . . . but has the audacity and absurdity of extending the pro-

hibition to foreigners!" A skipper of a French whaler who was caught on two successive nights "cohabiting with a native woman . . . had to pay the penalty $15 each or be confined to the Fort for six months!" "Of course the fine was paid," Wilson indignantly remarked.[84]

The knowledge of the "closure" of these ports to the sex trade meant that a proportion of shipping began stopping at alternative Hawaiian ports such as Hilo on the west coast of Hawai'i. Despite the presence of the missionary Mr. Lynam and his wife, a covert sex trade still operated, according to "VC," a whaler who kept a journal on the *Achusnet*'s Pacific voyage in the mid-1840s. The *Achusnet* anchored at Hilo in March 1846, and at the conclusion of his entry for March 27 he wrote, "God Bless the Hilo Ladies Amen." Although the women "all seem to attend church," "VC" noted a duplicity that he named "Polynesian morality." "Lord only knows where their religion is," he wrote. "Money is their God." According to "VC," the stereotyped Hawaiian woman did not engage in sex with whaling crews to satiate innate sexual desires, as earlier observers of Hawaiian women would have it, but they entered into this exchange for overt pecuniary reasons.[85]

For the missionaries, sequestering young women had a twofold advantage. First, it protected the women from the physical and moral contamination of frontier men. Sexual intercourse with the "dregs of our countrymen"—seamen and pastoral workers from the ranks of the working and convict classes—degraded indigenous women further in missionary eyes. When intimately aligned with these men, indigenous women more closely resembled stereotyped working-class prostitutes, as their innate sexual immorality was combined with drunkenness, disease, and slovenliness. In addition, the alteration to indigenous women's environments, from untampered landscapes to towns with European houses and streets, transfered the sexualized spatial geography of Occidental cities and towns onto the budding imperial nodes. The shifting ideal of virtuous womanhood in the nineteenth century to middle-class standards of sexless, housebound mothers also exacerbated the gulf between the most immediate exemplars of good, civilized women—missionary wives—and "primitive" women.[86]

The moral agenda was a strong motivation for missionary interest in indigenous women's sexuality. This high missionary priority was constantly thwarted in all regions of the Pacific by the effects of colonial economics, which profoundly influenced manifestations of indigenous women's sexuality. Missionaries often acknowledged that one of the few (if only) ways women could participate in the new economies was as sexual commodities and that this imperative overrode the influence of Christianity in many cases. James Belich has noted in relation to New Zealand that there were two facets to the famed sex trade of the Bay of Islands. There was the woman-controlled sex trade, in which women participated in order to get access to highly valued commodities such as guns and clothes. There was also the man-controlled dimension that utilized slave women, captives of tribal wars, as sexual slaves for the sailors. Unlike in Tahiti and Hawai'i, the LMS missionaries were not able to curtail this trade in New Zealand as it was such an important conduit for trade goods and power for indigenes.[87]

In the Australian context, one of the Aboriginal Protectors appointed to oversee the pastoral invasion of the Port Phillip region around present-day Melbourne, William Thomas, wrote in November 1839 of his frustration at this sexual and economic nexus. He was approached one night by an "apparent gentleman" who said, "I want a lubra, here's white money!" Thomas dispatched him, but the man retorted "that a black lubra had a right to be a whore as well as a white one." Thomas conceded that he was sorry to "state that the blacks were willing to accommodate him. What can be done with these people under such circumstances and what power have I? None." E. S. Parker, another Protector, commiserated to his superior George Augustus Robinson in April 1840 about the lack of options he could offer the women of the Loddon Region. He wrote that "I cannot persuade the younger females to resist the importunities of the white man, while I am unable to offer a counter-inducement in the shape of food, clothing or shelter."[88]

The sexual demands and economic power of colonizing men therefore increasingly made the stereotype of sexually available indigenous women a reality on every new frontier, as the Cook voy-

ages had done. The stereotype of the Pacific muse was not a naturally occurring phenomenon that existed before a colonial presence
and that resembled the Occidental classical past. The muse was the
result of the intersection of male-driven colonial culture, Occidental
male identity, and colonial commerce, which was never far removed
from the body and sexuality, particularly in the case of indigenous
women.

Colonial Families

Colonial stereotypes have complicated sexual histories. In illumi-
nating the different arguments about sexuality, race and class, and
typecast categories of masculinity, a moral distinction seemed to exist
between whalers and missionaries. Yet these categories were his-
torically blurred. Notions of male sexual privilege championed by
some whalers were not necessarily incommensurate with prevailing
Christian ideology. The case of a New England whaling captain,
Icabod Handy, and his Maori daughter, Alice, demonstrates the complexity of morality, sex, and Pacific empire.

In the 1850s Captain Handy brought Alice back to America. He
placed her in the care of his two childless and widowed sisters after
his wife refused to have the eleven-year-old product of her husband's
relationship with a Pacific woman live with her in Boston (fig. 2.4).
In 1888, Alice's young daughter, also named Alice, wrote to one of
these aunts in an effort to uncover the secret of her mother's origins,
which had been a tabooed subject. The great-aunt revealed that her
mother was born on "Fiordland Island some where in the Pacific
Ocean" (possibly the South Island of New Zealand) and that her
grandfather was "never marrid to your Mothers mother." The great-
aunt explained, for "when seaman are away from home A long time
and go into port they will go after women." Christian devotion and
acceptance of male rights to sexual release in the empire were
rationalized in her aunt's view, albeit with an uneasy tension. When
Handy returned to New Zealand and found the girl living with an
aunt, he felt that as "he profests to be [a] Christian man it was his
duty to take your mother home with him" and raise her as a

Christian. The aunt assured her great-niece that her mother had been "baptised in her infantsy" by the resident "Inglish Mishionary." When she was placed in her New England school she "was an excellent scholar and was allways very much respected by schoolmates and all that new [*sic*] her."[89]

Pacific women did move across seemingly impassable social and racial barriers while Occidental men espoused opinions that to our sensibilities were in gross contradiction to their lives. In this instance, Alice Henrietta Handy transcended the stereotype of a Pacific island woman and become an upstanding example of New England, middle-class virtue. Her father was most keen to ensure that this transformation occurred, as were many other Occidental fathers who acknowledged and assumed a paternal role toward their Pacific daughters and sons. For instance, the previously mentioned American whaler turned Honolulu resident, Stephen Reynolds, who lived the

2.4 Alice Henriette Handy,
photograph from private collection.

dissolute life of a beachcomber, later in life ran a home and school for "half-caste" Hawaiian girls. This venture was an extension of his concern for the moral upbringing of his own offspring, of which he had seven.[90]

The Pacific muse stereotype operated in constructions of Occidental masculine identities as well as in defining "civilized man" in opposition to "primitive man." Not only were the constructions of these colonized women influential; they were central to the tensions. The stereotype of Pacific women was not simply the reflection of naturally occurring circumstances. Rather it was the result of pressures from the imposed masculine and sexualized colonial culture, though indigenous women exercised some agency in this sexual economy depending on their particular circumstances at different times and places. Investigating the historical experience of the Pacific's indigenous women demonstrates how grossly inadequate reliance upon colonial stereotypes is to understanding the lives of real women. In the next chapter we shall see how representations interacted with the lives of Pacific women affected by the growth of the colonial economies of the region.

III

Nature's Resources and the
Forging of Empire, 1788–1890

The colonial structures of the Atlantic world were carried to the Pacific after Cook's voyages of exploration. As with that colonial precedent, the initial economies revolved around the harvest of the Pacific's various animal and plant resources, which were sold as commodities in the Chinese, American, and European markets. The establishment of settler societies that hungered for land accompanied these oceanic trades. These conditions created a range of contact relationships between incoming Atlantic visitors and the Pacific's indigenous peoples. The cultural and geographic peculiarities of the Pacific made this empire distinct from the history of the other ocean. Yet, the overwhelmingly male voyagers who came from both sides of the Atlantic brought ideas with them that also profoundly shaped this new region's history. Race, class, and gender were as powerful in delineating historical experience in the Pacific world as they had proved to be in the Atlantic. The traffic of ships and their personnel from the 1780s on reduced the preexisting divide between these two oceans drastically and rapidly, creating economic, cultural, and biological "webs" that bound this new "New World" to the old.[1]

We have seen how ideas and images of exotic femininity in the

Pacific were challenged and reordered by sustained contact. Pacific women's sexuality was commodified by the exploratory voyages. Whalers and missionaries, for divergent reasons, reinforced this perception and practice. Here, we delve further into the realignment of colonial fantasies with the continuation of contact in different, and sometimes more permanent, forms. In particular, this chapter illustrates how the concept of indigenous women as natural resources, available for the utility of colonists, operated in the Pacific setting. Beginning with the resource-harvesting industries, extending to Australian pastoralism, and in the latter half of the century, to plantations, this chapter examines how the fusion of colonial economics with ideas about race, class, and human bondage transformed relations on the Pacific's various frontiers. An outcome of this analysis is an attempt to uncover women's responses to the newly imposed conditions, where evidence makes it possible. The hybrid settlements that evolved in the region, from Pitcairn Island to Bass Strait and Micronesia, are instances that offer a distillation of colonial ideas and practices and how they affected women and ideas about exotic femininity in the Pacific. They also shed some light on indigenous women's responses to colonialism.

Gender and the Pacific Empire

At noon on February 5, 1788, somewhere on the newly established sea-lane between China and the Hawaiian islands, the body of a young Hawaiian woman was "committed to the deep." Before this watery burial, Captain John Meares had taken the liberty of bestowing a Christian blessing upon his ill-fated charge. The young woman was deserving of such an honor, Meares reasoned, because she possessed "virtues that are seldom to be found in the class of her countrywomen." Meares had hoped to return the young woman, Winee, to her native Hawai'i, from which she had been "removed" some months before. If she had not fallen gravely ill, her final destination would have been England. Her voyage to England was instigated by Mrs. Barclay, the wife of Captain Barclay, who commanded the British *Imperial Eagle* on its 1787 voyage along the northwest coast of America to collect otter furs for the China market. According to Meares, Mrs. Barclay had been "so pleased with the amiable manners of poor Winee" when the *Imperial Eagle* refreshed at Hawai'i, that she felt "a desire to take her to Europe," where Winee was to act as an exotic maid-servant and "object of curiosity" for the captain's wife.[2]

Meares was sorry that Winee had suffered so greatly for such a purpose and admonished Mrs. Barclay in his journal. For the commercially minded Meares, Winee's removal, along with that of three Hawaiian men on board, would have been justified if she had been taken with "the better motive of instruction" or to gain an "advantage to commerce." When Winee caught a fever on the voyage across the Pacific, Mrs. Barclay left her in China for Meares to convey her home, but owing to extreme distress at her circumstances, she rapidly declined. Although she had been a "living spectre" for most of the time she had been under Meares's care, Winee's memory was graced by an illustration in his journal that resonated the stylized noble savage Pacific muse promoted by armchair travelers and certain philosophers of the late eighteenth century (fig. 3.1). She was portrayed as youthful, sexually appealing, and unspoiled. It was her apparent ability to transcend the sexually profligate characteristics of Hawaiian women of her "class," a stereotype generated by the Cook voyages, that ennobled her in Meares's eyes, and made her worthy of Christian rites before her body was cast into the Pacific.[3]

Winee's case was unusual in the colonial history of the eighteenth-century Pacific. Owing to the small numbers of white women in the Pacific empire at this time, it was less likely for Pacific women to be desired for their value as a lady's servant. The overwhelming numbers of men manning the empire meant that it was more likely that Pacific women's sexual, and to a far lesser extent reproductive, capacities were of importance. Winee was coveted for her labor, a condition that impinged upon many Pacific women's lives in the nineteenth century. Her experience sheds light upon the nexus between stereotypes of indigenous women of the Pacific as commodities and the extension of the Occident's burgeoning global economy. This "modern colonization" was distinguished from earlier epochs not only

Wynee, a Native of Owyhee.
One of the Sandwich Islands.

3.1 Winee, a Native of Owyhee. Illustration in J. Meares, *Voyages Made in the Years 1788 and 1789 from China to the North-West Coast of America*, London, Logographic Press, 1790.

in its ideology, which stemmed from Enlightenment science and philosophy, but also in being profoundly structured around the ideological and practical operations of capitalism. Representations of class, race, and gender that proliferated at this time clearly delineated the social, political, and economic ordering of humankind and

therefore expressed reasons and rationale for a spectrum of differing forms of social and economic exploitation.[4]

Winee's experience displays her entanglement within the colonial ideologies and commercial networks that extended from the
Atlantic slave and plantation economies to the Pacific, where indigenes of Africa and America functioned as natural resources in colonial economies and their accompanying cultures. The stereotypes of
indigenous women in the Pacific provided a logic for exploitation
of Pacific women for personal or commercial gain, or both. In this
chapter we shall explore the effects of the intertwined constructs of
femininity, masculinity, race, and sexuality in the establishment of
Pacific colonial settlements and early resource-getting industries.
It shows how colonial stereotypes affected indigenous women's
experience of colonization and illustrates that women consistently
transcended the narrow confines of this colonial construct.

The seven decades of Pacific colonization from 1788 to 1860 were
dominated by ecologically exploitative trades, specifically whaling,
sealing, and harvesting otter furs, sandalwood, and bêche-de-mer, and
by the spread of pastoralism in Australia, Van Diemen's Land, and
New Zealand. The two intertwined frontiers, on land and ocean, that
were advanced through these trades drew an influx of men into the
Pacific region. This rapid transplantation of largely transient populations of Occidental men consolidated the economic and cultural
conditions resulting from Cook's second and third voyages that were
definitive in popularizing the perception of indigenous women as a
supply of sex for Occidental shipping.

As the story of Winee demonstrates, by 1788 Hawaiian ports
were already incorporated into the shipping highway linking America's Northwest Coast fur trade to the Chinese entrepôts. To the
south, the establishment of the penal settlement at Port Jackson in
the same year provided a springboard for the land and oceanic frontiers of the South Pacific. On these coexisting frontiers, there was
a diversity of attitudes to Pacific women, as those of Mrs. Barclay
and Captain Meares attest. There was conflict among imperial personnel about how to value Pacific women, and questioning about

whether their conditions and status were innate to their societies or whether a colonial presence transformed indigenous economies and sexual availability as Cook had conceded. In addition, experience of indigenous societies and personal politics complicated colonial perspectives and treatment of Pacific women.

This complex web of ideas was again evident in a vignette rendered four years after the demise of Winee. In October 1792, George Vancouver, like Meares, was charged with the duty of returning another two young Hawaiian women from Nootka Sound of far northwest America. They were Rahiena, who was fifteen, and Tymarow, "about four or five years older." Vancouver noted that a Mr. Baker of the Bristol ship *Jenny* had "kidnapped" the women a year before. While Vancouver discounted reports made by American traders that the two girls were sold in exchange for furs to Native Americans, he remonstrated that the conduct of Mr. Baker was "highly improper" and "inexcusable," although he could not find evidence that they were "ill-used." To Mr. Baker, Rahiena and Tymarow were seemingly viewed as a resource for the taking, while Vancouver viewed them differently, owing to their social status on their native island of Ni'ihau.[5]

That they were young women of "some consequence" was apparent to Vancouver from their "behaviour and amiable disposition," particularly in the higher-born Rahiena. According to Vancouver, she possessed "an elegant figure," "regularity and softness of her features," and "natural delicacy." This natural nobility of the girls, their standing within their own society, and the precarious state of diplomatic relations between the British and the Hawaiians influenced Vancouver's recognition and treatment of them. He afforded them his personal protection on their return voyage on the *Discovery*, though he delivered them to Hawai'i instead of to their own island some distance away.[6]

Impressed as he was with these two women, Vancouver contended that the "qualities of these two young women," who seemed "endued with much affection and tenderness," could not be taken as characteristics shared by all Hawaiian women. They were exceptional. The contemporary perception of Hawaiian women as deficient in feminine qualities, which in turn determined their worth and treatment from Occidental voyagers, should not be dismantled, Vancouver argued. Prevalent sexualized images of indigenous women were readily used to cast aspersions upon whole populations, yet images inconsistent with this stereotype were not used to question prevailing preconceptions. Vancouver's account of these women displays the tensions between a reductive colonial archetype and the women on whom it was imposed. Also, what Vancouver perceived as elevating behavior and beauty in the women did not apparently induce Mr. Baker to treat them with their due respect.

Colonial culture undoubtedly commodified and simplified indigenous people, but the application of ideas and ethics foundational to imperialism were dependent upon individual politics and conditions specific to historical episodes, periods, and regions. Indigenous people's capacity to limit the imposition of colonial commercial and labor practices was highly contingent upon the degree to which Pacific people were extracted from their own societies and absorbed into colonial ones. These three women, for instance, possessed little capacity to influence their treatment, being reliant solely upon the benevolence of sea captains. Stereotypes provided rationale to mistreat indigenous people, but the varied conditions of empire meant that this rationale could not always be applied in equal measure.[7]

Women and the Bounty Myth

The lives of these three Hawaiian women show how the gendered and sexualized colonial ideologies brought to the Pacific from Atlantic colonial economies were deployed and given added impetus from the voyages of discovery. In the other focal point of colonial fantasy, Tahiti, the material legacy of the representations of women was made clear by the events surrounding the mutiny aboard *H.M.S. Bounty*. What would become one of the great mythicized events of Pacific colonization began with an unsensational commercial and ecological objective. The aim of the voyage was to transplant breadfruit plants from Tahiti to Jamaica; these were to be cultivated as cheap food for slaves. When the crew of the British naval vessel mutinied in 1789, with some of the mutineers subsequently colonizing Pitcairn Island, this voyage was catapulted into legend. More so than any other event in the early years of imperialism in the Pacific, this event epitomized how perceptions of indigenous women as sexualized commodities informed their treatment by Occidental men.

The *Bounty* mutiny is also significant in the early contact history of the Pacific because Teehuteatuaonoa, or Jenny, the Tahitian woman who left the Pitcairn Island settlement in 1817 aboard the whale ship *Sultan*, is a direct and documented source for events that occurred on the island. Teehuteatuaonoa had shared an intimate relationship with John Adams, who would be the last surviving mutineer.[8] She later left Adams, possibly while on Tubuai, and formed a relationship with Isaac Martin, with whom she lived on Pitcairn, though she did not bear any children, unlike the other women who were healthy reproducers: twenty-three children were found there in 1808. Teehuteatuaonoa's account of events leading up to the settlement of Pitcairn first appeared in the *Sydney Gazette* on July 17, 1819. This and two subsequent versions provide compelling evidence regarding how deeply entrenched, if not paradigmatic, the image of Pacific women as sexual commodities was to the mutineers. The accounts of mutineers and interviews with John Adams confirm the prevalence of this ideology.[9]

It is overwhelmingly clear from the extant sources that the desire to gain women provided much of the intrigue and ructions among the mutinous crew. Women were viewed as imperative to a viable settlement for sexual purposes, their reproductive capacities, and their labor. In addition, women lent men power within the new society wherein European systems of deference and status were largely meaningless, although Fletcher Christian retained some authority as the highest-ranking officer and leader of the mutiny. When the crew of the *Bounty* made its first stop at Tubuai, they were the first Occidental men to do so. Greg Dening has argued that the "*Bounty* men had lost the capital of twenty years of European-Tahitian cultural exchange," and so the sequence of exercising military coercion to gain sexual access to women had to be played out. After massacring upwards of twelve Tubuains, the mutineers returned to Tahiti, a plan fraught with risk of capture for their capital crime of mutiny. In 1837 John Adams revealed that the motivation behind this strategy was that "we lacked women: and remembering Tahiti, where all of us had made intimate friendships, we decided to return there, so that we could obtain one each."[10]

The *Bounty* returned to Tahiti briefly, leaving for Tubuai again after nine days. On board were twenty-eight Tahitians, but only nine women, including Teehuteatuaonoa, for the twenty-five mutineers. Again on Tubuai, the mutineers built a fort, and some mutineers hatched plans to capture more women by force, producing a series of skirmishes that led to another, bloodier slaughter by the English on September 2, 1789, in which some one hundred islanders were killed. The mutineers remained on Tubuai, although according to James Morrison, the womanless men "began to Murmer." They "insisted that Mr Christian would heed them, and bring the Weomen in to live with them by force and refused to do any more work till evry man had a Wife." Christian believed it would be better to "perswade rather than force them" and so "he positively refused to have nothing to do with such an absurd demand." After three days, tensions escalated. The men debated, and "demanded more Grog," which Christian had denied them. The men openly rebelled against this decision and "broke the lock of the Spirit room and took it by force."[11]

A vote was taken on September 10 to decide how to break the impasse. It was decided by sixteen votes to nine that they should return to Tahiti "and there Separate, where they might get Weomen without force." This plan was put into effect. Sixteen men opted to remain at Tahiti, leaving nine mutineers aboard the *Bounty* when it left Tahiti for the final time. Accompanying the nine mutineers were six Polynesian men, nineteen women, and a girl. According to Teehuteatuaonoa, with the exception of herself and Christian's "wife," Mauatua, the rest were kidnapped. One woman jumped ship and swam back to shore even though the ship was a mile outside the reef. Six women who were too old or "too ugly for their tastes" according to Dening were "liberated" near Moorea. The others "much afflicted at being torn away from their friends and relatives" were divided up among the men, one for each of the mutineers and three between the six Polynesian men. In all, twelve women — Mauatua, Vahineatua, Teio, Sarah Teatuahitea, Faahotu, Teraura, Teehuteatuaonoa, Obuarei, Tevarua, Toafaiti, Mareva, Tinafernea, and the "little daughter" of Teio — arrived at Pitcairn Island.[12]

The death of Teraura, the wife of John Williams, of a "scrophulous disease in her neck," not long after Pitcairn Island was settled, triggered the first of many killings on the island. The mutineers decided that Toafaiti, the wife of one of the Tahitian men, Tararo, would be "given" to Williams. Three of the Polynesian men plotted revenge, although this was revealed to Williams. Two of the three were killed while one was allowed to live as Martin's serf. The four remaining Tahitian men "studied revenge" and killed Christian, Main, Brown, Williams, and Martin. In the succeeding decade, all the men were killed on the island with the exception of Young, who died in 1800 of natural causes, and Adams, who lived until 1829. In contrast, three women had died on the island; nine were living there in 1800, plus the eleven-year-old daughter of Teio along with the progeny of the women and the mutineers.[13]

If the expectation was that the Tahitian women would comply with the image of them as passive vassals, the reality of the Pitcairn settlement should have exploded these myths of Tahitian women. Teehuteatuaonoa, for instance, built a boat. The plan was that the women would escape, though this was foiled. From her evidence, women participated in the politics of the island, in the development of new traditions, and in adherence to the old.

The women of Pitcairn Island were much more than pawns between the men or one-dimensional historical figures. Yet in subsequent representations, the women of Pitcairn are portrayed in simplistic images commensurate with the dominant stereotypes of Pacific women. The tendency to replicate female fantasy figures can be found in the earliest commentaries. These tended to follow Bligh's reasoning for the mutiny, that is, that the minds of the mutineers, "unendowed with virtue" were overcome by the Tahitian women's "ruinous work of seduction." Romantic poets to twentieth-century filmmakers also employed this rationale.[14]

The 1811 poem written by poet and playwright Mary Russell Mitford, *Christina Maid of the South Seas*, is a case in point.[15] The heroine of the poem is the daughter of Fletcher Christian, whom Mitford described as "irresistibly attractive," "gallant and amiable," and a Tahitian woman, "Iddeah." Iddeah featured in Bligh's *Bounty* journal as well as in missionary James Wilson's *Duff* journal. In the latter, she was characterized as a woman abandoned to wickedness for supposedly performing infanticide in 1797. However, Mitford transformed her blurry persona into an exemplary one and transplanted her onto Pitcairn. "Christina" was characterized as the first-born in a superior new race, the result of the mixing of superlative gender and racial traits, the best of British in Christian and the best of Tahitian in her mother.[16]

Christina was an improvement upon the unrivaled beauty of the "black-ey'd girls of Paradise" whose "witching smiles the soul entice" as she appropriated the best feminine attributes of both worlds. Her Tahitian mother bestowed her native beauty, "so slender, tall and fair" with "so graceful form," and her submissiveness upon her. Her modesty, devotion, and moral rectitude, ironically, were her father's legacy to her. Unlike the other young girls of Pitcairn, whom Mitford characterized as "houri," that is nymphs of the Islamic paradise, Christina was "like [a] timorous fawn." Mitford's attempt to form an image of Christina as classically beautiful was reinforced by her attire, as Mitford had her in "flowing drapery array'd" as well as reclining over "urns."[17]

Besides capturing the attention of this poet, this new hybrid race in the Pacific was also intriguing to those with a scientific and social interest in this racial mixture. Given the currency of ideas about the effect of climate, particularly heat, upon women's sexuality and moral conduct, these women living in the tropics of part-European ancestry were fascinating as they tested the basis of race theories. When Captain Pipon encountered the island in 1814 on a Royal Navy expedition, he reported that "the young women are still more to be admired, wonderfully strong, most pleasing countenances, & a degree of modesty and bashfulness that would do honour to the most virtuous nation." Their bodies may well have displayed the physical attributes so admired in Polynesian women, but Pipon added that "both men and women bear strong resemblance to English faces." The corporeal improvements to the Pitcairn islanders owing to their British heritage paralleled their moral elevation to middle-class moral standards. Not only did John Adams assure Pipon that "there is not one instance of any young woman having proved unchaste," he could also report that "the men appear equally moral & well behaved."[18]

Pipon thought the prospects for this first hybrid settlement in the Pacific were most promising as the "greatest harmony now prevails" with the racial and gender hierarchy aligned with European conventions. Adams presided as the island's patriarch. With his influence and the mixing of bloodlines, Pitcairn women were elevated in degrees of modesty well above the women Pipon had observed in the Marquesas. "I am convinced" wrote Pipon, "our fashionable dress makers in London, would be delighted with the simplicity & yet elegant taste of these untaught females." Pipon was himself delighted with the women obediently tending to their traditional gender roles of nurturing and reproducing. The fecundity of the women was the crowning achievement of the new society. Despite the dark beginnings of the settlement, which were brutal and murderous, Pipon was overwhelmingly optimistic about its future, predicting that "it is natural to expect hereafter there will be a progeny of beautiful people upon the island."[19]

Similarly, Lieutenant Shillibeer on the same naval voyage remarked on the difference between Pitcairn's young women, raised under Christian principles, and those of the Marquesas. In the Marquesas, "chastity is so little esteemed," Shillibeer wrote in his journal. By comparison, he was pleased to note that the Pitcairn Island women retained their mothers' exotic beauty, but "their minds and manners were . . . pure and innocent." They did not display the "lascivious looks, or any loose, forward manners which so much distinguish the characters of the females of other islands." The influence of Christian morality imparted by Adams, a strong British patriarch, in conjunction with the island's economy not being geared around a sex trade, meant that Pitcairn women were afforded the respect of Occidental women with class status. Male voyagers, therefore, did not expect sexual access to women on Pitcairn Island unless they were selected to enter the island society permanently as a husband.[20]

The story of the *Bounty* and the wider story of Pacific voyaging also captured the imagination of the consummate romantic, Lord Byron. His poem *The Island, or Christian and his Comrades* was first published in 1823. Like Mitford, Byron stitched together locations and characters from different voyage accounts and incorporated an unsympathetic representation of Fletcher Christian into his fanciful version of the sensual Pacific. Byron's heroine, Nehua, with her "wild and warm yet faithful bosom" was, unlike Mitford's Christina, a "whole savage." Byron borrowed this name from William Mariner's account of his survival of a shipboard massacre in Tonga in 1806 and his subsequent four-year experience of life on the islands before his return to England. In Mariner's account, which Byron openly acknowledged as a source, along with Bligh's account of the mutiny, Nehua was an awesome Tongan chief. Blurring the distinction between fact and fiction, Byron transformed Nehua into the "softest" savage, endowing her with the complete colonial fantasy of the infantalized Pacific muse. In his first description of her, Byron drew upon all the current tropes and embellished these with overt allusion to her sexually available body, particularly her Platonic "crimson cave" that was emblematic of sexually alluring Pacific women and the Pacific itself:

> There sat the gentle savage of the wild,
> In growth a woman, though in years a child,
> As childhood dates within our colder clime,
> Where naught is ripen'd save crime;
> The infant of an infant world, as pure
> From nature—lovely, warm and premature;
> Dusky like night, but night with all her stars,
> Or cavern sparkling with its native spars;

With eyes that were a language and a spell,
With all her loves around her on the deep,
Voluptuous as the first approach of sleep;
Yet full of life —for through her tropic cheek,
The blush would make its way, and all but speak,
The sun-born blood suffused her neck, and threw
O'er her clear nut-brown skin a lucid hue,
Like coral reddening through the darken'd wave,
Which draws the diver to the crimson cave.
Such was the daughter of the southern seas.[21]

The object of Nehua's love, affection, and unwavering loyalty was "the blue-eyed northern child," Torquil, a ship's deserter originally from the Hebrides. Nehua protected her lover from the pursuit of the tormented Fletcher Christian by leading him into a secret and secluded cave through a hidden underwater entrance.

Byron's poem signaled the intensification of interest in the legend of the South Seas woman following the *Bounty* story. Byron was not concerned in the moral improvement of women through the influence of their Pitcairn fathers as some of his predecessors were. Rather he was captivated by the dream of women who were innately conditioned to give succor to lost Occidental men. He thus refracted the *Bounty* story through this prism, creating the archetypal Pacific exotic of the romantic period.[22]

Like Mitford, Pipon, and Shillibeer before him, Sir John Barrow, the second secretary of the British Navy, was fascinated by the "interesting offspring . . . now peopling Pitcairn Island." His contribution to mythmaking about the Pacific centered around women who were ennobled by the combination of native beauty, European modesty, and femininity and who lived in this tropical idyll. Barrow likewise conflated more serious scholarship with flights of colonial fantasy as he too adorned eyewitness accounts in his *The Eventful History of the Mutiny and Piratical Seizure of H.M.S. Bounty: Its Causes and Consequences*, first published in 1831, in addition to quoting Byron's vision of Pacific women. The frontispiece of his historical work, made after sketches by Lt. Smith on the voyage of *H.M.S.*

Blossom of 1831, depicted two of this "new breed," "George Young and His Wife (Hannah Adams)" (fig. 3.2). Although this is a crudely executed portrait of two examples of the new race, the baby conveys to the viewer the famed fecundity of these women who flourished in this healthy climate. Barrow accepted Bligh's causational thesis for the mutiny (that is, the sexual allure of the women), which he described in Byron's words as "the nymphs' seducements." Barrow was pleased to note, like Pipon, that the Pitcairn Island women appeared to have inherited "their mothers' virtues"; while under the influence of British men they were kept "from their vices." Among their imagined virtues, this armchair traveler listed the "comely" shape of their faces, their beautifully even and white teeth, their "delicate and cleanly" breath, the "melting" softness of their eyes, and their bodily cleanliness.[23] For Barrow, these women were ennobled by their British heritage as well as their protection from the sexual commerce that was drawing in other female populations in the Pacific.

The power of this romanticized vision of Pacific women following the *Bounty* mutiny is ubiquitous. Not only is it fabricated, but it distracts from the less attractive realities of the establishment of the Pitcairn settlement, where there were clear connections between stereotypes of Pacific people, women, and the inveterate exploitation of indigenous people inherent in colonial economies. Once settled on Pitcairn Island the women actively shaped that colony; thus, they were far from the passive figures depicted in the subsequent portrayals.

Race, Sexuality, and New Pacific Populations

Pitcairn Island was one of several new settlements created in the early years of sustained Pacific imperialism. The exploitation of the working-class peoples was also a necessary facet of Pacific colonialism. The settlement at Port Jackson, the springboard for British colonial influence in the South Pacific, was based upon what authorities viewed as the transference of human refuse from British society. Like colonized indigenes, working-class people were also

3.2 George Young and His Wife (Hannah Adams). Frontispiece in Sir John
Barrow, *The Eventful History of the Mutiny and Piratical Seizure of HMS
Bounty: Its Causes and Consequences,* London, John Murray, 1839.

perceived as commodities who could serve as indentured laborers in the same way that their forebears had been sent to the American colonies. In the population of convicts transported to the Australian colonies there was an "over-representation" of Irish; estimates of the percentage of Irish women comprising the total number of women transported ran as high as 56 percent. The Irish as a colonized group were habitually represented by stereotypes akin to those peoples considered at the lowest rungs of humanity. Therefore, a great many of the vitriolic remarks leveled at the convict population were based upon ideas about class difference, but also racial perceptions of Irish people. While male convicts were used for a wide variety of tasks, working-class women were predominantly used for their sexual and reproductive function and their labor. Stereotypes of convict women stressed their sexual availability, and therefore all of these women were defined as prostitutes and were treated as such.[24]

Unlike the Pitcairn settlement, which was created by escapees from British law, the Port Jackson settlement was a planned affair. Yet like Pitcairn it confronted problems of gender, sexuality, race, and labor. A dramatic gender imbalance in the proposed convict population was of particular concern; the fear was that if it were not addressed, it would lead to "gross irregularities and disorders" among the already dissolute working-class men. A plan was mooted in official circles to import indigenous women to the Port Jackson settlement from "contiguous" locales such as China and the islands, particularly the Friendly Islands (Tonga) and New Caledonia, as suitable "companions for the men." Again based largely upon the images created from the Cook voyages, the plans to "import" island women to meet the sexual needs of convict men were perceived as an antidote to homosexuality and the lesser evil of masturbation while providing the means to found a permanent, healthy settlement.[25]

American James Matra was a proponent of the sexualized stereotypes of Pacific women as well as an advocate for a new British settlement on the east coast of New Holland for American colonists who had remained loyal to Britain during the War of Independence. He proposed in 1783 that after landing Europeans at Port Jackson, a ship should be sent to the islands "to procure a few families and as many women as may serve for the men left behind." From his experience on Cook's first voyage, he further argued that "there is every reason to believe they may be obtained without difficulty." Matra added that Sir Joseph Banks felt that "we may draw any number of useful inhabitants from China." This plan was incorporated into the instructions given to Governor Phillip. Whenever the *Sirius* and other vessels linked to the settlement "shall touch at any of the islands in those seas," their commanders were to be instructed "to take on board any of the women who may be disposed to accompany them to the said settlement." However "special care" had to be taken by the officers to ensure that "compulsive measures" were not exercised or that women were not lured away "from the places of their present residence" by "fallacious pretences."[26]

Fears of feeding the discontent of the Aboriginal people of the region by using local women for such purposes also underlay this plan. In addition, officials were concerned that convicts might form an alliance with Aboriginal people against the colonial authorities. Phillip thought "the arms of the native will be very formidable in their hands." He was adamant that sexual relations would not be established with local women and threatened to punish offenders severely with exile and hard labor. He wished to keep the invasion of Aboriginal lands as nonviolent as possible and hoped that the "native inhabitants" of New South Wales would be brought into "voluntary subjection" or, failing this, that a "strict amity and alliance" might be established, until the troubled colony was able to defend itself. Not interfering with local women was a central plank of the strategy to avoid early conflict, one that was rapidly discarded by men of the colony despite the threatened harsh punishments.

Almost nine months to the day after the colony was established, Phillip wrote to Lord Sydney concerning the instructions to "procure women from the islands," stating that as the colony's resources were under such great strain, any women brought would "pine away a few years in misery." Instead of using island women in the formula for a sustainable colony, he wrote that "more women will be necessary when more convicts are sent out." Working-class English and Irish women were to be sent out for the purpose of providing sexual relief for convict men and to be the mothers of future generations from which the colony could draw its workers.[27]

On the First Fleet, the bodies of women convicts on the *Charlotte*, the *Lady Penrhyn*, the *Prince of Wales*, and the *Friendship* were a part of the shipboard economies, along with rum and inadequate provisions. The surgeon on the *Charlotte*, John White, painted a picture of a sex trade that resonated with the legendary sojourns in Tahiti, but the stereotypes of working-class women as degraded prostitutes disallowed any mythologizing in this instance. Instead, according to White, this display of female sexuality, exacerbated by tropical heat, produced a thoroughly sordid exhibition. "So predominant was the warmth in their constitutions, or the depravity of their hearts," he wrote of the women, that they could not quell their "desire" to be with the men, that even "shame" or "punishment" could not deter nighttime connections. Arthur Bowes Smyth, surgeon on the *Lady Penrhyn*, also reported what he perceived to be the innate depravity of women under his charge. He wrote that their landing in Port Jackson in early February 1788 was marked by a "scene . . . that beggars every description" for the rowdy behavior of drunken men "making merry" with the women, even though a violent "tempest" raged throughout the night. More women were sent on the Second Fleet, who endured compulsory sexual union with the men on vessels. The *Lady Juliana* became notorious for this reason, spurred by steward John Nichol's remark that "every man on board took a wife from among the convicts."[28]

Convict women were an integral part of the imperial culture devised by the British government. The level of contempt that colonial officials had for these women can be gauged by the detached remarks of David Collins, the colony's deputy judge advocate, after the trial of Henry Wright in 1789, who was charged and found guilty of raping an eight-year-old girl. Collins felt that the decision to mitigate Wright's sentence from death to removal to Norfolk Island "during the term of his natural life" was a correct one. "The chastity of the female part of the settlement had never been so rigid as to drive men to so desperate an act," inferring that, as sexual opportunities for Wright were available elsewhere, the girl must have brought his sexual attention upon herself.[29]

Harsh attitudes toward lower-class women and Irish women were readily transferred to the indigenous women drawn into the penal colony and the economic zone that spread inland from Port Jackson and fanned out across the South Pacific. While Pacific island women were not removed by official sanction to Port Jackson, on the continental frontier of the colony, sexual relations were established with Aboriginal women within three years of the initial invasion. The commencement of these relations followed patterns from other regions of the Pacific. The sexual incorporation of Occidental men into indigenous cultures was often preceded by massive disruptions to the symbiotic relationship between the environment and indigenous economies. Other forms of duress, such as acts of military suppression and introduced diseases, forced indigenous people to establish commercial relations with foreign men.[30]

The impact of colonialism on the Eora people of the Sydney Basin, the Darug, Dharwal, Guringai, and beyond, was of a particularly insidious nature. The rapid importation of alien people alone would have been sufficient to force a revolution within Aboriginal society in order to deal with the new external pressures. There were 1,030 people aboard the First Fleet. By November 26, 1791, after the arrivals of the Second Fleet and Third Fleet in 1790 and 1791, respectively, Watkin Tench, captain-lieutenant of the marines, estimated the white population of New South Wales to be 2,887. This figure increased dramatically by the end of the century, with the population of the settlement reaching 5,100. Half of this number resided at Port Jackson, almost one and a half thousand inland at Parramatta and Toongabbie, and the remainder on farms long the Hawkesbury River.

The importation of livestock on Eora lands, the basis for a pastoral industry, had a two-pronged impact. First, the animals' hard hooves quickly destroyed plants, scared away traditional game, and fouled precious water sources. Second, the industry required the removal of Aboriginal people from their lands. This was increasingly achieved through violence. Disease also took its toll on the indigenous population. In April 1789 the Aboriginal population of Sydney Cove and well beyond its boundaries was ravaged by small-pox. John Hunter, who would become the colony's second gover-nor after 1794, reported in his travels around Port Jackson and Pittwater that the coves and beaches were littered with the dead bodies of Aboriginal People.[31]

It is in this context of severe stress that Aboriginal women com-menced participating in the colonial economy, with prostitution having become "commonplace" by 1796, as Ann McGrath has argued. Collins reported in 1791 that venereal disease was evident among the Eora people. He wrote that he feared "our people have to answer for that for though I believe none of our women had con-nection with then [*sic*] yet there is no doubt but that several of the black women had not scrupled to connect themselves with white men." Collins also reported upon the surprise of a mother who gave birth to a "light coloured" baby. This was an event that Collins did not swathe in romantic rhetoric or perceive as a progressive impe-rial act. This child was the result of illicit relations between the two races, a situation that both sides wished to hide according to Collins, although for different reasons. The mother "endeavoured to supply by art what she found deficient in nature" and rubbed the baby's little body with ashes and held it over the fire to "restore it to the hue with which her other children had been born." Collins found the cuckolded husband's affection to the child curious and some-what emasculating: "he appeared as fond of it as if it had borne the undoubted signs of being his own."[32]

Conflagrations in the Hawkesbury District on the northern edge of the colony erupted in the mid-1790s and escalated swiftly to open warfare between Aboriginal people, pastoralists, and the military by 1796. The conflict stemmed from the practice of kidnapping, detain-ing, raping, and even murdering Aboriginal women and children. In 1800, five settlers in the region were put on trial for the murder of two Aboriginal boys, Little George, who was about eleven or twelve years old, and Jemmy, who was fifteen or sixteen. The five were found guilty, but no punishment was meted out. This outcome disturbed Governor Hunter, who wrote to the Duke of Portland that the murderers were "living upon their farms with as much ease as ever." In the same letter, Hunter argued that the latest spree of Aboriginal retaliation against the settlers and military "proceeded from a soldier having in a most shameful and wanton manner kill'd a native woman and child."[33]

Mistreatment of women was a major cause of unrest between the indigenes and imperialists as contemporary accounts consistently reiterate. The treatment of indigenous women was reliant upon imperial agendas, commercial considerations, representations of evolutionary advancement, and the skewed power relationships between the colonizers and the colonized. Also, whether a woman lived among her own people or was removed from the protection of her people and culture into a white dominated society had immeasurable effects upon the way she was perceived and treated. Economic interests had, arguably, the overriding power to cut through previous means of representing indigenous women in the Pacific, from noble savagery to feminine beauty, to the point that their humanity was called into question. The disjunction of colonial representations of Pacific women into positive and negative archetypes was precipitated by economic and colonial agendas, as the rapid decline in the trend of representing Aboriginal women as romantic and exoticized savages demonstrates. For instance, William Blake used New South Wales as the setting for the visual archetype of romanticized noble savages in his 1793 etching titled "Aboriginal Family of New South Wales" (fig. 3.3). The Aboriginal woman here is ennobled by her classically formed body and fine features, as well as by her position as a wife and nurturing mother in a self-sufficient family unit living in harmony with nature. Within a few years, images of Aboriginal people emanating from the colony projected an antithetical view, owing to the politics of imperialism that crushed the romantic tendency to ennoble nature and "primitive" peoples.[34]

Women and Island Frontiers

The commencement of seaborne resource rushes emanating from Port Jackson after 1791 created the oceanic frontier of the Australian

3.3 William Blake, "Aboriginal Family of New South Wales," 1793.

settlement and brought a variety of indigenous women within the economic reach of the settlement. Thousands of men roamed the Pacific in ships — naval vessels, whalers, varieties of traders — all carving out spheres of influence and developing a network of ports across the vast ocean, which rapidly consolidated imperial economic conditions that commodified the bodies of local women and men. Violence was a prominent feature in the establishment of these industries, a fact acknowledged by humanitarian sections of the colonizing culture, as we shall see. There were attempts to protect Pacific islanders from "the oppression, violence and murder of unprincipled and lawless Europeans" with declarations such as that issued by New South Wales's Governor Macquarie in December 1813. In his directive, Macquarie stated that shipping could "not take from the islands any male native without his own and his chief's and parents' consent; and shall not take from thence any female native, without like consent." The following year this order was reiterated with the threat that disobedience would be met with "the utmost vigour of the law." As could be expected, this second attempt to stem the bloody nature of colonization also proved futile. In 1817 the British parliament weighed in, passing *An Act of the 57th of the King, for the effectual punishment of Murders and Manslaughters committed in places within His Majesty's Dominions*. Like its predecessors, this act did not ameliorate the mistreatment of islanders.[35]

Governor Macquarie himself took up specific cases of mistreatment, such as that of the Maori woman Atahoe, or Mary Bruce. She was the daughter of Te Pahi, the Nga Puhi leader who traveled to Port Jackson from the Bay of Islands in 1805 with Reverend Samuel Marsden. Macquarie took up her cause because the wrongs committed against her by her white husband had in his opinion, "soured relations" between Sydney traders and her people of Kororareka, then the most important port in New Zealand. Atahoe's story, or what can be pieced together from extant evidence, highlights colonial attitudes to indigenous women who were detached from their familial sphere and absorbed into colonial society. In addition, it also displays the attitude that indigenous wives deserved different treatment from that of a white wife.

In this exceptional instance, Macquarie wrote of the reprehensible behavior of Atahoe's ex-convict husband, George Bruce, who "shamefully and cruelly neglected [Atahoe] in her last illness." Macquarie also criticized him for abandoning their daughter to be supported by the Sydney Female Orphan School when he returned to England in 1810, possibly because "he was greatly involved in debt here."[36]

Bruce was pardoned by Governor King some years earlier and left Sydney aboard the *Lady Nelson*, which he then deserted, according to Macquarie, at the Bay of Islands. Bruce countered Macquarie's accusation in his memoir, arguing that he did not desert the *Lady Nelson* but was asked to stop there by the captain until he was called for on the return voyage to Britain. Bruce wrote that after being among the Nga Puhi for seven months, "I consented to be marked in the face where I received my wife with all the power that country possessed." According to Bruce, not long after this event he and Atahoe were duped by a Captain Dalrymple, who carried them against their will to Melaka. In Melaka, Bruce claimed, he became separated from Atahoe, who was still aboard the ship when it weighed anchor for Penang. Bruce relied upon the mercy of the governor of Melaka in order to have his "consort" restored to him.

Bruce's account of his interaction with the governor of Melaka shows that Atahoe, owing to her race and gender, was commodified. Once the governor had written to Penang "respecting my consort . . . he found that she was bartered away by Captain Dalrymple to Captain Ross." "The governor wrote several times but receiving an impertinent answer every time he was fully determined to put the law in force against any person who should have detained her." Bruce had to personally travel to Penang armed with a letter to the governor from his Melakan counterpart.[37]

Upon arriving in Penang, the hapless Bruce was shunted about by the governor there, who supposedly cared little for his predicament, and so had to face Captain Ross himself, "who then had my wife in possession." Ross had bought her as a servant for himself and his wife, with her primary duties being the care of their child. Bruce had to "solict . . . him in a most humble manner" for her return. Ross "hesitated awhile asking me by what authority she was my wife." Bruce told him "by being ignorant enough by suffering the face which God had given me to be disfigured & loosing my blood & suffering pain according to the rules of her country she was mine." Ross informed Bruce that she was out with Mrs. Ross and her child and to return the next morning and "if she was willing to come with me I should have her." Bruce returned as requested and "he presented my wife to me." The reunion was heartfelt Bruce recalled: "after an absence of 3 months she was deeply affected which occasioned her a flood of tears."[38]

After Bruce and Atahoe were finally reunited, they traveled to Bengal before returning to Port Jackson supposedly en route to New Zealand with "express order" owing to Atahoe's advanced pregnancy. Yet Atahoe died in Sydney after giving birth to their daughter, who Bruce would abandon to the care of the orphan school. The epitaph on her Sydney tombstone began "Sacred to the memory of Mary Bruce, Princess of New Zealand who Departed this Life Feb 27 1810, Aged 18 years." Macquarie's motive in taking issue with the tribulations of Atahoe was to ensure that Bruce's claims of authority in New Zealand, marked as he was with a *moko* and owing to his marriage to a high-born woman, were shattered along with any pecuniary advantage. On the contrary, Macquarie stressed, Bruce was so badly thought of in Kororareka for his "ill-usage and neglect of this wife" and their daughter that he was "much despised and disliked."[39]

On the initial voyage that took Bruce and Atahoe away from New Zealand was another beachcomber, Edward Robarts. Accompanying him was his Marquesan wife, Ena-O-Ae-A-Ta. Like Atahoe, Ena was about eighteen years of age. Ena, described by the Russian Captain von Krusenstern, as "so handsome" that she "must have been allowed to be beautiful, even in Europe," had two little daughters with her. One child was born on her native Nuku Hiva and the second, Ellen, was born in Tahiti. Robarts, who had arrived in the islands in 1797, had removed a greatly distressed Ena from her home so he could escape the warring island. His timing was poor, as he just missed the sandalwood rush in the Marquesas that would have brought him, as the only white man on the island, great fortune. On Tahiti, Robarts raised the ire of missionaries as he had a still, and they insinuated that he beat Ena, who attempted suicide as a result of the mistreatment. In September 1806 the missionaries recorded that "the Marquesan woman . . . made some attempt to hang herself . . . She said her pity for her young infant was the only cause that prevented her from putting into execution the hasty resolution."[40]

Ena, like Atahoe, was a high-born woman, which entitled Robarts to land and thus a supply of food on Nuku Hiva. He also bragged for the rest of his days that he had married "royalty." Robarts referred to her mostly as "my consort" in his journal, although he wrote in a letter to a friend "king gave me his own sister Ena-O-Ae-A-Ta, to be my bride, as a small token of his esteem; I have ever since thought it a great one." The custom of offering useful castaways wives and land was a means of inducing them to stay, although this was often misinterpreted as a sign that women were considered chattels in their own societies. Marriages involved binding kinship duties and reciprocal gifts to the woman's family that often caused exasperation and some confusion for the unsuspecting husbands, as Caroline Ralston and Greg Dening have shown. Women were also often free to leave unsuitable marriages but when removed from their land, as Ena and Atahoe were, such options were eliminated.[41]

War on Tahiti prompted Robarts to move again, so Ena and her daughters were taken on a miserable and prolonged voyage around the Pacific. Their first stop was supposed to be Port Jackson, as Robarts had heard of the unequaled opportunities there, but they got only as far west as New Zealand, where they encountered Bruce and Atahoe. Robarts claimed that Bruce was hiding from authorities, and Ena concealed him under the cot on which her two daughters slept. As the ship left New Zealand, Atahoe and Ena were thrown together on the *General Wellesley*'s circuitous sandalwood-getting exercise that took them to Fiji, New Ireland, and Pelau before heading for Penang, where the food supplies were so low that Bruce claimed they were forced to eat the ship's rats. In Penang, Ena had a third child and the family enjoyed some prosperity before Robarts's employer died in 1810, forcing the family to move again to Calcutta. Here Ena died in 1813 of unknown causes, in poverty. Unlike with Atahoe, there was no official condemnation of her mistreatment by her husband excepting the missionaries' mention of it, although Robarts's actions and Ena-O-Ae-A-Ta's loss were no doubt long remembered on Nuku Hiva.[42]

Robarts had imbibed a sense of power and privilege over his spouse that was derived from a complex web of race and gender preconceptions. Although this was not always the case, there seems to have been a common thread through many of the interactions of incoming men and indigenous women from transient encounters to marriages. There were, no doubt, many genuinely affectionate unions, as Ralston found in her study, although the imperial mind-set of domination over those considered weaker persisted through to, and even culminated in, intimate relationships. The ethos of exploitation for economic gain lay at the heart of imperial endeavor. Through their labor or their land, or by aiding men's incorporation into the political life of communities, indigenous women could substantially increase these men's wealth and influence. The harsh reality of relationships in the Pacific empire between incoming men and indigenous women shatters the romantic illusion of the Pacific as paradise, which was so intimately bound up in the Pacific muse stereotype. The illusion of isles of loving women embracing Occidental men was just that, an illusion.[43]

Women and Whaling

Nowhere in the Pacific imperial narrative is the nexus of gender, power, and nature more pronounced than in the titanic battles between man and his ultimate adversaries, the sea and the leviathan. The whaling industry facilitated the interaction between colonial and colonized people on an unprecedented scale. The industry established global links between whaling men, indigenous women who populated "refreshment" ports across the Pacific region, and the women in home ports. If the early exploratory voyages had begun the widespread trade in sex, then the whaling voyagers, with the immense numbers of men that they brought to the Pacific, compounded exponentially the conditions that enticed women into prostitution. The lives of women living proximate to the major refreshment ports frequented by whaling vessels in the Hawaiian Islands, Tahiti, Kororareka, and Dusky Sound in New Zealand took on a seasonal pattern that in the pelagic phase of whaling revolved around the migratory habits of the sperm whale. Both shore-based and pelagic whaling peaked in the 1830s. This meant that the trade in sex was also at its most intense at this stage of colonization. At its zenith, there were thousands of men who roamed the ocean seeking out whales.[44] The currency of the stereotype of the Pacific woman as a sexually available "island girl" increased enormously due to this extensive commercial industry and the popular culture generated by it.[45]

When the French corvette *La Coquille* sailed into the port of Kororareka in March 1824, the men on board witnessed the effects of years of sustained contact between whalers and the local Maori women. For René Lesson, the thirty-year-old naturalist on the Duperry voyage, it was an ironic occasion. At one level the arrival seemed to replicate the hallowed days of Pacific voyages when the young women of the Pacific clambered aboard European vessels and unconsciously appeared to the men like Venuses born from the sea. The connection between this mythology and the Duperry voyage was emphasized, coincidentally, by the vessel's name, *La Coquille*, literally the seashell, and so evoked Sandro Botticelli's image of feminine beauty, sexual desire, and sexual purity. "Poets," Lesson rhapsodized, "represent the divine Venus on a chariot carved from a seashell, our *Coquille* throughout our stay at the Bay of Islands, became her temple, and her altars were raised on our orlop."[46]

On another level, Lesson was filled with repulsion at the sex trade. The Maori women who remained on board *La Coquille* were "at the disposal of the crew who used them to their hearts' content." Their "corrupt morals made us blush in spite of the fact that we were used to seeing them dispense their favours to all comers." They were like a "flock of ewes in search of buyer," he stated. The physical condition of the women he saw as primitive, although in some, he found their features erotic. In their "first bloom," the girls were "characterised by broad faces, masculine features, thick lips often black with tatooing, wide mouths, flat noses, badly arranged, untidy hair, general dirtiness, and bodies impregnated with stomach-turning odour of fish or seal."[47]

This "repellent picture" was "partly redeemed" according to Lesson by "some precious advantages given them by nature, and their dazzling white teeth and black eyes, full of fire and expression, are

in fact powerful attractions." Yet, their bodies were more than sites
of erotic pleasures; they were inscriptive surfaces, mapped terrain,
and quite literally bodies "totally imprinted with history" to be read
by Lesson and all else whose eyes fell upon their flesh. Lesson could
read the story of colonization from their skins; "their arms and breasts
were tatooed like those of the seamen with the names of their lovers,
the names of the ship, and the date of the visit to the Bay of Islands."
"By inspecting their bodies," he continued, "one could trace the itin-
erary of ships putting into port, of which these medallions kept a
record as long as they lived."[48]

The story he gleaned from the tattoos upheld the preconceptions
about the Pacific women as universally available to Occidental men.
One young Maori woman who was an exception to this rule and provided a site for a particularly ugly test of French virility intrigued
Lesson. He recorded as no more than an amusing sport, attempts
by a "large number of volunteers" from *La Coquille* to deflower a
"young New Zealand girl," which lasted for "three days." No man
was able to "conquer" her, as Lesson phrased it, as her "vagina was
blocked by a thick cartilaginous membrane." The intensely voyeuristic interest in this woman's body and her treatment by the crew of
La Coquille displays how much the sexualized stereotype of Pacific
women dehumanized women and the extent to which it justified men's
predacious behavior toward them in the process of colonization.
James Belich has suggested that this young girl was probably a slave
forced into the sex trade and that her vagina may have been blocked
owing to the effects of syphilis, "but she may have been very young,
and it is impossible to believe that she was willing."[49]

This sexualized stereotype had been strongly associated with the
Pacific by whaling crews since the industry began. However, it was
the whaler turned writer Herman Melville who changed the stereotypes of the bawdy whalers into something with greater cultural
appeal in his first and most popular novel, *Typee*, evoking classical,
biblical metaphors to describe Pacific whaling. Interestingly, during Melville's lifetime, this book enjoyed far greater popularity in
Britain than in the United States. Through his novels, Melville elevated whalers from one of the lowest-grade professions, "a butcher-

ing sort of business," manned by the lower rungs of the working classes and, in American fleets, by considerable numbers of African Americans, to supreme embodiments of the American national type. In his masterwork, *Moby Dick*, he wrote of the generic whaleship as a patriotic Yankee colonizing emissary. "Whaling is imperial!" he declared, and a "pioneer in ferreting out the remotest and least known parts of the earth," battling "virgin wonders and terrors." Whaling was also the "true mother" of "that great America on the other side of the sphere," Australia, and the "uncounted isles of all Polynesia confess the same truth." In Melville's eyes, whalers were colonial agents par excellence. This imperial dominance entailed a sexualized assertion of dominance over nature and indigenous peoples.[50]

Typee, first published in 1846, was based upon the whaler to beachcomber experience that would become such a popular genre in imaginings of the Pacific. Melville had lived out this fabled life himself for one month, four years earlier on Nuku Hiva, when he lived among the Taipi. In order to embellish his scant knowledge of Nuku Hiva, he borrowed heavily from the experiences of more seasoned castaways such as Edward Robarts. Melville merged titillating fantasy with such beachcomber accounts to create a literary version of the prevailing stereotype of Pacific women as sexually appealing, youthful objects of desire in the character Fayaway, his Pacific muse. When the book was published in New York, shortly after its initial publication in London, the American publisher thought it best to censor Melville's portrayal of "sea freedoms." What Melville had created was a fantastic hybrid that evoked many cultural currents of colonial desire. The narrator, Tommo, gave a description of "the beautious nymph Fayaway, who was my particular favourite," which distinguished her physically from the other Typee women. "Her free pliant figure was the perfection of female grace and beauty." Her face "was a rounded oval, and each feature as perfectly formed as the heart or imagination of man could desire." She had "full lips," "teeth of dazzling whiteness," and "her hair of the deepest brown flowed in natural ringlets over her shoulders and whenever she chanced to stoop, fell over and hid from view her lovely bosom." Her "strange blue eyes" seemed to resemble the Pacific itself, being "most placid, yet unfathomable; but when illuminated by some lively emotion, they beamed upon the beholder like stars."[51]

Melville's physical construction of Fayaway evoked the classical configuration of the colonial stereotype in all her prelapsarian perfection. The statuesque figures of Aphrodite and Venus and Milton's Eve resonate through this image, as does Byron's Nehua and Mitford's Christina. Her physical flawlessness, "each feature as perfectly formed as the heart or imagination of man could desire," also marked her out as a morally superior being. Despite the flagrant sexual fantasy here, the narrative is ambiguous as to whether this powerful sexual attraction was ever consummated. Melville relied upon prudish suggestion instead of overt confirmation of Fayaway's sexual inclinations, therefore leaving her morality intact. As the most coveted beauty on the island, her preference for the white man was also a sign of her superiority.[52]

The nourishing, sexually replenishing allegorical figure of Fayaway was the holy grail of whalers, the reward for the danger and loneliness of the trade. Melville married the bodies of the island woman and that of the whale as the two stylized bodies sought by the industry. They both stood as the feminine opposition to the Occidental man in what Melville painted as a glorious, natural congress. The colossal bodies of whales encased feminine nature in its most predatory and immense form. The language and symbolism of the hunt was overtly sexual, the execution of the kill a metaphorical sexual act. This aspect of the industry was heightened by the practice of targeting female whales. In the months of May to October pregnant and nursing whales migrated to spawning grounds in bays and harbors, rendering them slow and particularly vulnerable. John Wilson, surgeon on the British whaler *Gypsy*, recorded in 1840 that it was "usual" if no "better chance offers to fasten a calf having care not to kill it." It was expected that the cow "will come to its succor when she is quickly victimized." It was clearly evident, Wilson acknowledged, that "there is a strong affection shown by sperm whales for each other ... which is taken advantage of by the whaler."[53]

The commodities to which the whales' bodies were reduced —

whalebone or baleen primarily from right, blue, humpback, and fin whales; ambergris from the gut of sperm whales; and various oils — formed the basis for Occidental-based industries that beautified the bodies of upper-class women. Whalebone and baleen refigured the waists and exaggerated the bosoms of women to more aesthetic, "feminine" dimensions in corsetry, which were de rigueur throughout most of the nineteenth century, providing a hungry market for the skeletons of the thousands of whales killed in the Pacific.[54] Yet bones and baleen were not the most vital whale product. In the more industrial, urbanized nineteenth century, the "spiraling consumption" of whale oil for street lighting and multifarious other uses made the oil so crucial a commodity that the control of its supply was an international issue. Whale oil was the primary motivation for the Pacific rush, with fashion requirements being a significant secondary market.[55]

Women's fashions mirrored the fluctuations in Pacific whaling, with the massive supplies of whalebone having influenced fashion styles and thus the shape and health of generations of Occidental women across the century. Ambergris, a most rare spoil of the industry, was a source for perfumes, while oils were made into soaps and cosmetic creams. By 1817 corsets and tight lacing had returned to vogue, reaching their most extreme form in the 1840s. From the late 1850s the refuse of the whale cull was readily absorbed with the advent of the crinoline. This massive cagelike structure masked a woman's sexually suggestive legs and greatly inhibited her movement, giving a blooming, floral effect to a woman's form and mirroring the rise of the icon of the Victorian woman.[56]

Melville did not detract from the masculinity of whaling by portraying it as an industry geared around the beautification of women. However, he did make specific linkages, albeit with poetic license, between the bodies of whales and Occidental women in *Moby Dick*: "in New Bedford, fathers, they say, give whales for dowers to their daughters, and portion off their nieces with a few porpoises a-piece." Melville is likely to have contrived such rituals from the colonial Pacific, where sperm whale teeth, or *tabua*, directly influenced Occidental man's sexual access to island women, as David Porter reported of the Marquesas in 1814, as we have seen earlier.

Tabua were, and remain, highly prized objects used as gifts exchanged on important occasions, including marriages. Wealth was reliant upon tabua in the Marquesas, the Gilbert Islands, and Fiji. In Fiji, for instance, "the whale tooth stood for a woman." This circumstance was seized upon by early whalers and sandalwood traders. The possession of these prized objects drastically altered the social and political landscape of the island societies and greatly assisted incoming men in their endeavors to gain economic and sexual access to them.[57]

Sealing, Pastoralism, and Aboriginal Women

Sealing was the other major Pacific industry of the first half of the nineteenth century that drew indigenous labor into it. Like the whaling industry, sealing had a marked impact upon treatment and representations of indigenous women involved in this economy, who were predominantly Aboriginal and Maori, although women from further afield were also enmeshed in the operations of this trade. The nature of sealing, however, required different relationships between the men and women involved, as was also the case with the pastoral industry, and this difference influenced the dominant stereotype of women dramatically. The prevailing stereotype of women involved in these two industries was more akin to that of slaves than to the luxuriant fantasy figure of the "island girl" that occupied the minds of many a whaler.

Seals inhabited colder and more remote extremities of the Pacific, primarily the Bass Strait islands, Tasmania, southern New Zealand and the far-flung islands in the Southern Ocean: Macquarie, Auckland, Campbell Island, and the Antipodes Islands. The industry was at its most lucrative from 1790 until the 1830s, when numbers of fur seals became depleted to the point of extinction. Seals were sought for their furs and bodily oils for sale in China and Europe. Harvesting these commodities was labor intensive. Coupled with this need for labor and the isolation of many sealing settlements from indigenous communities and colonial ports with their portion of humanitarian voices, sealing, especially on the Bass Strait islands, produced one of the most infamous episodes of mistreatment of indigenous women in Pacific colonization. This injection of harsh economic exploitation into the relations with Aboriginal people of Van Diemen's Land rapidly dissolved the exoticized vision of Tasmanian Aboriginal people rendered by early transient observers such as Jacques-Julien La Billardière in 1792 and François Péron in 1802, as we shall see.[58]

Sealing in Bass Strait commenced after the first settlement at Port Jackson in the late 1790s. Enterprising colonist Charles Bishop was the first to go forth and capitalize upon reports of teeming populations of seals to the south of Port Jackson, returning with nine thousand skins in 1798. Following further exploration of the region and the establishment of a penal outpost on the island of Van Diemen's Land in 1803, the cull rapidly grew. In the first decade of the nineteenth century some ninety-eight thousand skins were exported from Sydney. Decimation of the seal populations most proximate to the British colonial outposts necessitated that the industry span out to more remote islands.

The penal settlement on the Van Diemen's Land was established concurrently with a pastoral frontier. The dispossession of the indigenous people on Van Diemen's Land to "free up" land for livestock was supported by military operations, as was the case on the Port Jackson frontier. The pastoral frontier was forged predominantly by men who operated either beyond the reaches of British law or in a legal climate skewed to accommodate, if not endorse, imperial enterprise regardless of accompanying violence. The remote and inhospitable locations for the sealing industry produced an even more lawless scenario. Sealers had intermittent contact with shipping and traders for almost thirty years until 1830. At this time, when the industry was already in decline, the conditions of women living on the islands became part of missionary George Augustus Robinson's so-called Friendly Mission under instruction from Governor Arthur. He attempted to stem the "dire atrocities" perpetrated by the sealers, many of whom were believed to be escaped convicts, against the Aboriginal people of Van Diemen's Land and New Holland, particularly against women. So great were the "cruelties exercised upon them [which] beggars all description," Robinson claimed, that "their sufferings hav[e] been far greater than those of the Indians at the hands of the Spaniards." Robinson directly linked the mistreatment of these people with popular conceptions of them. They had been "represented as only a link between the human and brute species," a notion that Robinson attacked as the antithesis of the truth, as "they are equal if not superior to ourselves."[59]

Robinson's belated observations upon the declining industry notwithstanding, there is scant information concerning the activities of Bass Strait sealers and the women who became entangled in the economy of the islands whether willingly or through force. Captain James Kelly observed in 1816 that "the custom of the sealers in the Straits was that everyman should have from 2 to 5 of these native women for their own benefit, and to select any of them they thought proper to cohabit with as their wives." Kelly's observations were supported by Mr. W. Stewart, who wrote in 1815 that the sealers obtained the women by force and kept them "as slaves or negroes." The "benefits" of having Aboriginal women were numerous. Sealer and mutton birder James Munro told Robinson that "when the black women were first brought over from the main, they were intended principally to gratify the sealers." It was soon apparent that the women had skills with monetary potential, particularly hunting seals, kangaroos, and mutton birds and preparing them as saleable commodities. The women gathered food from the oceans, tended crops and farm animals, and executed domestic chores and so were integral to the men's survival.[60]

Kelly argued that the women were obtained through barter with indigenes, a claim that Robinson emphatically refuted. Robinson was adamant that sealers abducted large numbers of women who were used in the industry. Robinson argued, with a more favorable view of Caribbean slave culture than was warranted, that once the sealers had captured women, they treated them worse than the slave proprietors in the West Indies, because they "subjected them to hard labour and cohabited with them." The Aboriginal people that Robinson encountered were so afraid of abductions and depredations that "they would approach the coast very cautiously, if at all." The striking gender imbalance in the Aboriginal communities was further evidence for Robinson that women were removed by force and in extensive numbers. Robinson also reported that there were "many instances" where sealers had cohabited with Aboriginal girls from when they were children. Charley Peterson of Gun Carriage Island lamented to Robinson that if More.ter.mor.rer.lune.ner, or Poll, was taken away from him "he did not know what he should do." He "said that he had the girl ever since she was eight years of age." Robinson concluded that "it appeared the man had cohabited with this female from her infancy." James Munroe had likewise "had Jumbo ever since she was a child, and several others the same."[61]

Town dwellers also had young women and girls in their "possession." Major Abbott compiled lists of the girls for the colonial secretary in 1827 and then again in February 1831. Seven young women or girls lived in Launceston at this time and there were three or four in similar circumstances in George Town, and Mary Reiby, the renowned ex-convict businesswoman, also "has one that she has had upwards of two years." The endemic colonial practice of using children for chattels and, moreover, sexual purposes displayed the influence of the stereotype based upon race and gender theories that stressed that "primitive" girls were "ripe" for sexual behavior much earlier than white girls, although working-class children were similarly configured, as we have seen in earlier chapters. In the Australian colonies it was clear that there was significant economic and social gain to be made from holding Aboriginal women captive. Once white women were ensconced within the new settlements, girls were sought out for easing their domestic duties, as was fitting for women of higher class status.[62]

The women drawn into the Bass Strait sealing trade were not only local women, but also women gathered from around the sealing economic zone that extended as far west as Mauritius and as far north as Hawai'i. In 1802 Nicholas Baudin reported that one man, Daniel Cooper (spelled "Cowper" by Baudin), who was then residing at Elephant Bay on King Island with seven other men had a Hawaiian woman, "whom he had brought from Mowee." She lived with Cooper in a "wretched hovel" and "took the place of wife and chief housekeeper." In 1830 there was also at least one Maori woman with John Taylor, whom Robinson described as a "mulatto" from Virginia. There were conceivably many more women who were not from the Australian mainland or Tasmania who came with their itinerant men to Bass Strait but had died or left before Robinson surveyed the population. At least seventy women were on the islands in 1830, most of them originally from Van Diemen's Land. A number had been taken to Mauritius and Sydney by sealing gangs, while others had been traded among the sealers. Dumont D'Urville recorded the presence of east coast and Van Diemen's Land women in King George's Sound on the southern tip of Western Australia among the newly arrived sealers and whalers in 1826. D'Urville surmised that these women "appear to have been abducted."[63]

Women of Bass Strait were viewed as contested property by both the sealers and the colonial government for which Robinson was an agent. Robinson wished to end the system of slavery and establish a mission where Aboriginal people could be protected from the impact of colonization and be converted to Christianity. Robinson reported that several sealers argued that they would not give up their women because "the government had no right to them and that they had as much right as the government to them." Robinson, however, secured government support for his plan. After posting a notice on Gun Carriage Island concerning the surrender of Aboriginal women and children to Robinson's care, he was moved to remark that "considering the previous character of these abandoned individuals it may appear a matter of surprise . . . that the women with whom they had so long cohabited and bought and sold and had exercised such lordly authority over, should be induced to deliver them up with so little resistance." The sealing industry was now in steep decline and so these women had outlived their economic utility.[64]

The characterization of Bass Strait sealing communities derived from numerous sources with their rough men and mistreated women contrasted starkly with the state of the industry across the Tasman Sea in the Foveaux Straits. The perceptions of this eastern outpost of the Australian industry differed for material reasons. The men involved in the industry here were derived from the same sources as the Bass Strait, emancipated and escaped convicts. However, these men were incorporated into Maori communities. Violence in the early years of contact was "initially quite frequent" according to Belich. However, by 1803 the Maori cooperated with sealers in the enterprise and capitalized upon this new industry to their advantage. Sealers were useful and so were permitted to live semipermanently among them. The sealers lived in these hybrid communities on Maori terms, the essential difference between their counterparts in Bass Strait, who had no restraints placed upon them. This had an immeasurable impact upon relations between Maori women and sealers.[65]

Removed from their own communities, Aboriginal women had little practical protection given the climate of antipathy against them that reigned in the Australian colonies. London Missionary Society missionary Lancelot Threlkeld reported the opinion of William Cox, "one of the largest holders of sheep in the colony" in Bathurst in 1824, the year martial law was proclaimed in the region owing to the undeclared war that raged there between pastoralists and the Aboriginal people. Cox had stated that "the best thing that could be done, would be to shoot all Blacks and manure the ground with their carcasses, which was all they were good for." He further "recommended . . . that the women and children should especially be shot as the most certain method of getting rid of the race."[66]

Violations of Aboriginal women were not viewed as a criminal offense, whether on the frontier or in the colonial centers. The pack rape of an Aboriginal woman in the center of Sydney at the "old race ground," now Hyde Park, in 1827 demonstrated the dominant ideas about the Aboriginal women as the *droit de seigneur* of white men. In this instance there was sufficient "suitable" evidence to prosecute the offenders, as there were white male civilian and police witnesses to the attack who tendered statements, Aboriginal evidence being inadmissible at this stage owing to perceived linguistic, religious, and conceptual deficiencies. The *Sydney Gazette* reported that the case was remanded "in order to take the opinion of the Acting Attorney General as to the mode of the procedure," but the case was not pursued. In glaring contrast to the rhetoric condemning violence against Aboriginal women in the early years of settlement, the mistreatment of them became an integral part of the culture of the pastoral frontier and went unpunished except in a few instances, notably in the 1838 Myall Creek Massacre Trial. "Gin busting" was a frontier custom in which European men "deliberately cheated, raped and abducted black women." This custom was premised upon a misreading of Aboriginal women's status within Aboriginal society and Aboriginal customs that involved "an intricate web" of reciprocal obligations and kinship.[67]

With the surrendering of warring Aboriginal tribes in Van Diemen's Land and the demise of the sealing industry from the 1830s, the next colonial front that occupied Robinson's attention was the new pastoral frontier of Port Phillip, the present-day state of Victoria. Some key figures in the Van Diemen's Land invasion moved to the Port Phillip colony, bringing with them their ideas about Aboriginal women as sexually available chattels. Two images of Aboriginal women produced by pastoralist John Herder Wedge in 1835 at Port Phillip illustrate this. Wedge was a surveyor and explorer and member of the first pastoralist group in the area, the Port Phillip Association. His prurient illustration titled *Native Woman Sitting Port Phillip 1835* conveys the notion that Aboriginal women were degraded and readily exploitable. The stereotypes of Aboriginal women as ugly, animalistic, and diseased provided men on the frontier "with an excuse for taking away their [Aboriginal people's] lives." With such attitudes having been held by armed and powerful men, the British government-sponsored protectorate, headed by Robinson with four other missionaries, could do little to stop a repetition of the brutal invasions from previous frontiers. Aboriginal vendettas from the Van Diemen's Land frontier resulted in the first hangings at the Melbourne Gaol. Two Aboriginal men who had accompanied George Augustus Robinson to the settlement in 1841 with Truganini, Fanny, and Matilda were hanged for the murders of whalers who Truganini claimed had pack-raped her as a girl on Bruny Island. The women were excused of the crime on account of their association with Robinson's good works. Robinson also vouched for their good characters.[68]

If squatter Neil Black is to be believed, the prevailing attitudes to Aboriginal women among the Port Phillip District pastoralists were extremely harsh. Black's journal of September 1839 to May 1840 recorded that shepherds and hutkeepers would "sleep all night with a lubra and if she poxes him or in any way offends him per-haps shoot her before 12 the next day." Melbourne police magistrate Foster Fyans estimated in 1840 that two-thirds of the Aboriginal pop-ulation of the district was infected with venereal diseases. Yet he refused to acknowledge that this reflected widespread sexual con-tact between European men and Aboriginal women. Asked in the 1845 *Select Committee on the Condition of Aborigines* conducted by the New South Wales legislature whether there was a flourishing pop-ulation of mixed descent children, Fyans replied, "Half castes I have never heard of in this country. I should not think any European would brutalise himself so much!" Others, however, connected endemic violence against women and children with Aboriginal retal-iation in Port Phillip. One of Robinson's Aboriginal protectors, E. S. Parker, stated in 1845 that the "vicious treatment of Aboriginal women was the origin of nearly every Aboriginal outrage which had occurred in my district."[69]

This state of affairs persisted despite the efforts of the evangel-ical movement to alter frontier culture. The wave of humanitarian-ism in the antipodean colony stemmed from the high point of the antislavery movement in Britain. After achieving their aim in 1832, abolitionists turned their attention to the moral issues of empire. A series of Select Committee hearings on Aborigines of British Settlements from 1835 to 1837 heard evidence on the conditions of "natives" in South and West Africa, the Canadas, Australia, the South Sea islands, New Zealand, and South American colonies. As was the case with the antislavery movement, Evangelicals had to battle virulent polygenic race theories that posited that racial difference was equivalent to the difference between species. Such race theo-ries justified not only the perception of native people as property and therefore their labor as a lucrative commercial resource, but also the worldwide dispossession of indigenous peoples. Evangelicals were particularly concerned in their Select Committee hearings with the condition of women, as representations of women were used as the measure to gauge the extent of suffering and level of degradation of a whole population. Indigenous women's health, fecundity, and morality were focal points in proffered evidence.

In the Australian colonies, the height of this Evangelical sentiment was marked in December 1838 with the retrial and hanging of seven men accused of the gruesome massacre of up to twenty-eight or more Aboriginal people, mainly women and children, at Myall Creek, near present-day Inverell. Evidence at the hearing reinforced the frontier attitudes to Aboriginal women as natural resources for the men's taking. Three people were spared from the massacre, a small boy and two young women, who were held hostage and raped by the men before they escaped from a hut they were confined in. One of the witnesses, Robert Sexton, said of this practice in his evidence that "one of the men had a black gin with him. She seemed to be a prisoner, he offered to give her to me . . . He asked if I would keep the gin 'till he came back again." Other witnesses expressed similar attitudes to these Aboriginal women. They viewed these women as currency among themselves. The mistreatment of these women was frowned upon but was not pursued as a criminal offence. Stereotypes of Aboriginal women portrayed them as so depraved that sexual abuse of them was considered impossible.[70]

The meting out of severe punishments in the Myall Creek trial was in spite of mainly malevolent newspapers that sided with pastoralist interests that stressed the victims were "a few black cannibals," not a peaceful group of women and children. The first trial saw the men acquitted of the offense, but after a direct order from the Colonial Office, the men were retried, subsequently found guilty, and hanged in one of the most socially divisive legal decisions in Australian history. The community was ideologically partitioned into primarily pastoralist sympathizers, who held that Aboriginal people were not human and murdering them did not constitute a crime, let alone one for which white men should be hanged. The stereotypes of Aboriginal women generated by pastoralist sympathizers during these show-trials avoided reference to the sex of the victims. Instead, the stereotypes exaggerated the lowly racial status of these women. Representations of Aboriginal people as rural pests attempted to justify the endemic violations of Aboriginal peoples in colonial society, from sexual defilement to murder.[71]

Opposing this construction was that promoted by those mainly of a humanitarian and missionary persuasion. Although this group still believed in a racial and gender hierarchy, they also believed in the capacity of British law to protect the indigenes and provide the means for "legitimate" colonization, that is, colonization effected through treaty rather than violence. Also, they held that all people possessed souls and were therefore deserving of exposure to the light of Christian teachings. The humanitarian representations of women emphasized their gender as well as race. The ideal scenario for missionaries was to see Aboriginal people off their lands and therefore abandoning their "primitive" ways in favor of a mission existence wherein their lives revolved around the Christian God and an accompanying work ethic.

As elsewhere in the Pacific, Aboriginal women were trained by missionaries and their wives to be good mothers and homemakers. The domestic skills, which were the focus of missionary instruction, were needed in the wider colonial economy, as they were in the rest of the Pacific, as a class of servants to ease the burdens of colonial women and men. That is, Aboriginal women would assist in upholding the status and comfort of colonial women and the maintenance of their middle-class femininity by relieving them of laborious "women's work." This rationale about race and femininity operated across the Pacific and was the central focus of missionary teachings that were also devised to "cure" the libidinous and dissolute nature of these women promoted by the colonial stereotype.[72]

Oceanic to Plantation Economies

A constant refrain throughout the evidence proffered in the 1830s *Select Committee on Aborigines in the British Settlements* held in London regarding the Australian and South Seas colonies was the adverse effect that large rogue populations of lower-class men were having upon indigenous peoples, particularly women. The perception that caused the greatest concern to many witnesses at the hearings was that large numbers of escaped convicts from the Australian colonies took up life as whalers and seamen and then roamed the Pacific, often as lawless bandits. One witness reported that "there is nothing more injurious to South Sea Islanders than seamen who have absconded from ships," as, according to another, they go and "live amongst the savages . . . with their low habits and all their vices."[73]

Reverend John Williams, who mainly focused upon Ra'iatea, where he had been stationed for eighteen years, told of an incident that had occurred about three years earlier when the whale ship *Oldham* was captured by the inhabitants of "Wallace's Island." Williams reported that "the captain was a man of exceedingly wicked habits." He was "not content with the poor unfortunate females that came on board the ship," so he got "most of his crew intoxicated, went ashore, and was in the act of dragging away the chief's wife and daughter . . . when they [the islanders] arose upon them and massacred them nearly all." "Some time" afterward a war ship went to the island and fired upon the people, killing more than sixty. Witnesses reported upon other notorious incidents that had occurred, many of them between whalers, traders, and Maori. As with the incident described above, many of these other skirmishes were related to men attempting to gain sexual access to indigenous women through a misguided reading of predominant stereotypes that stressed indigenous women's sexual availability.[74]

The final report from the Select Committee hearings proposed that the solution to avert the continuation of "disastrous calamities" stemming from the intercourse between South Sea islanders and "natives of Europe" was to extend the protective arm of British law beyond the eastern shorelines of the Australian continent. In order to overcome the logistical obstacles of policing the vast Pacific area and the unworkable system of trying to make perpetrators and witnesses against them come to Sydney for trial, it was suggested that some method of "trial on the spot" be devised. Although this method also had problems, something had to be done; otherwise "the South Sea Islands must be delivered over to the most degrading and intolerable of all forms of tyranny." Not only was the presence of lower-class men beyond the control of law seen as perpetrating great suffering upon indigenes on both the pastoral and oceanic frontiers of Australia. The Select Committee was also concerned that an entrenched culture of piracy, like the infamous Caribbean episode, might take hold in the western Pacific.[75]

Riding upon the crest of this Evangelical wave, Captain Blake was sent from Sydney in 1839 aboard *H.M.S. Larne* to the Bonin and Caroline islands to investigate "acts of violence committed on the Natives by British Subjects and particularly by the Master and Crew of the Cutter *Lambton* of Sydney." It became known that Captain Hart of the Sydney trader *Lambton* had committed atrocities on the tiny coral atoll of Ngatik in July 1837. The motivation for Hart and his crew was commercial avarice for tortoiseshell. What transpired according to men of the *Lambton* was that after trading had broken down between the Ngatik and Hart's crew over tortoiseshell, relations descended into hostilities, with the island men preventing the ship's crew from landing. The *Lambton* left, but returned, and in the succeeding days its crew systematically killed every man on the island, perhaps eighty-five men. One witness stated that then "the females were ravished, some before the blood of their husbands was cool, and many of the younger and best looking were distributed amongst the men and brought over to Ascension [Island]."[76]

After the atoll was "taken" by traders, European men began to settle there. James Hall was one of these settlers who did not partake in the massacre but who had earlier visited Ngatik in 1836. Captain Blake recorded Hall's impression "that the population is greatly reduced, as, on his first arrival there, he frequently knew of women destroying their young children and hanging themselves." Hall and other settlers "took each of them four or five children under their care, whose Mothers had destroyed themselves, and whose fathers had been killed." By 1840, Blake recorded that there were upward of thirty European and American men on Ngatik who had been involved in the whaling, tortoiseshell, or bêche-de-mer industries. Then domiciled on Ngatik, they were involved in making the atoll a viable refreshment port for whalers by raising animals for trade and no doubt continuing to harvest more turtles for the tortoiseshell trade using the skills of the women.[77]

The hybrid island settlement that arose out of the massacre on Ngatik was one among a number of scattered settlements across the Pacific islands since Pitcairn, though not all had such bloody beginnings as these and the Bass Strait communities. Yet all involved the transplanting of women from their native country to far-flung islands, and with the extant records it is difficult to determine how willing these women were to partake in establishing new, remote settlements.

When whale numbers had been depleted in the grounds off Australia and Hawai'i, one strategic location for a new society, which extended British influence from Hawai'i, was the Bonin Islands at the gateway to northern Asia and the favored whaling ground of the Okhotsk Sea. Discovered in 1827, the islands provided an enticing new frontier for colonists in Hawai'i, with five white men and a Tahitian man and "a party of natives [Hawaiians]" arriving in 1830 on Peel Island. In 1831, Captain Charlton, the English consul in Honolulu, sent six Hawaiian women from Oahu aboard the whaler *Kent*, "to assist in forming a new settlement there." The colonists also sought women from the more proximate European settlements such as Guam, including Maria de los Santos y Castro, the only woman about whom anything is known from the early years of the colony. She was brought from Guam at age fifteen and was first the wife of Matthew Mazarro, a Genoese four times her age. After he died in 1850, Maria became the wife of Massachusetts-born Nathaniel Savory, the appointed British consul of the island, to whom she bore ten children. Savory had had at least one other wife on the island, "a young girl" from Hawai'i who was taken away with other women in an act of piracy by Captain Barker aboard the *St. Andrew* in 1849. This woman and a number of others were supposedly so disenchanted by life on the Bonins that they revealed the location of valuables that were likewise duly removed from the islands.[78]

By the 1860s the economic and ideological conditions of empire had shifted. With the demise of the resource-getting trades that had dominated the Pacific economy for the first half of the nineteenth century, the emphasis changed to labor-intensive plantation economies. This was when the western Pacific islands of Melanesia commenced being an imperial frontier in earnest. Cotton was an important crop for a decade while American markets were disrupted by the Civil War. Later, sugar and copra dominated the late-nineteenth- and early-twentieth-century colonial economies of the Pacific. In this new era, Pacific peoples were regularly depicted and treated as expendable commodities in a harsh labor system. Many of the most vituperative colonial images of Western Pacific peoples who predominated in indentured laborer populations were heavily influenced by the long-standing perception that Melanesians embodied negative, "hard primitivism," as opposed to Polynesians, who resembled exoticized primitivism. Not only Melanesians were used for field labor. Hawaiians were utilized in sugar plantations on their islands until 1875, when Asian workers who would work for lower wages supplanted indigenous workers.[79]

The islanders sought after in the backbreaking work on tropical plantations were predominantly men. This exacerbated harsh attitudes and the characterization of these people as hard primitives. Women made up 6 to 8 percent of recruits in British colonies; their numbers may well have been higher in French-run plantations of New Caledonia. Although their numbers were small, women experienced plantation work as oppressive. For workers in the field, there was little accommodation in the regime for pregnancy and child care. Sexualized violence was endemic. There was also little regard for the needs of married couples; sexes were separated in their sleeping quarters. Women, like the men, resisted the excesses of the system with varying success.[80]

Enforcers of discipline and hard work were armed not only with canes and whips, and Master and Servant acts that supported physical upbraiding of workers, but also an intensified ideological armory to uphold the system. Throughout the eighteenth and early nineteenth centuries, race ideology had buttressed slavery and colonization by arguing that black and indigenous peoples were inferior beings. By the 1860s, the challenge to the slave economy of the United States, culminating in the Civil War, precipitated the most virulent phase of scientific race ideas, when polygenic and dying race theories predominated. These polygenic theories rejected the central Christian belief that all humans shared the same origin, instead arguing that different races were the equivalent of different species.[81]

The demographic effects of this phase of colonization, viewed through the lens of polygenic and Darwinian racial theories, became evidence for colonial officials and theorists alike that Pacific peoples were dying out. Ironically, it was argued that the labor system in itself was not harmful. When properly administered, it would prove uplifting to "the brown man." Fiji was often cited as the case study of what would follow when the "doomed old ways" of traditional society vanished and were not replaced by new ways. The 1893 *Report of the Commission on Fijian Depopulation* found Fijians had become "jaded, lazy [and] obsessed" with "the fashionable callousness or care-nothing spirit of the age." Fijians, in the twenty years since British annexation in 1874, were "drifting in a morass of uncertainty with nothing to cling to . . . no lodestone . . . and the result was death, both physical and racial for the will to live had gone." Colonists had to arrest this population decline by actively developing new regimes and social structures. Christianity was, of course, key. So too was what John Wear Burton, the Methodist missionary and critic of abusive labor practices in the early-nineteenth-century Pacific, termed the "Gospel of Work."[82]

In this stage of colonization, the need for an indigenous labor system was married with a supposed benevolent, preservationist colonial ideology. Colonial policies based on this philosophy would supposedly ameliorate the decline in birth rates as well as the lack of interest in life that precipitated the early demise of adults. This would prove to be a constant source of debate among colonial officials and scientific experts in the twentieth century, who watched population numbers in the Pacific with intense interest. This concern only increased after World War I owing to apprehensions about the territorial expansion of Japan in the region and the influenza epidemic of 1917, which decimated indigenous population numbers.[83]

Within Australia, representations of Aboriginal people in the wake of Darwinian race theories sank below the depths already plumbed. Aboriginal women were almost uniformly presented as the archetype of the "primitive primitive." This was a direct result of the project of dispossession in which land and sex were seen as intertwined commodities. Further, competitiveness over scarce resources and the knowledge that settlers could make enormous economic gains through the unmitigated exploitation of Aboriginal labor and lands lay beneath the shift in the representative tradition of Aboriginal women. Images of Aboriginal women who had resembled noble savages at the beginning of the nineteenth century, as we shall see in the following chapter, had sunk to a vituperative nadir by its end. The 1870 poem by J. Brunton Stephens *To a Black Gin*, as well as a number of visual images, typified this descent that was matched by a belief in Aboriginal people's inevitable disappearance.[84]

Yet, at the time that these images were being produced in the southern cities of Australia, Aboriginal labor was proving invaluable to the expanding cattle industry that had established itself in the tropical north of the continent. Unlike the southern pastoral industry, where white labor fulfilled the economic need, in the north, Aboriginal labor was fundamental to its function. Women's labor was particularly sought after. Women's skill as stockworkers elevated them to the highest status jobs in the territory, as Ann McGrath and others have shown. Also, they were desired as companions for white stockmen. So prevalent was the pairing of Aboriginal women with white stockmen on this frontier that it produced a series of racial purity laws in the twentieth century that attempted to define men's and women's work and to prevent the sexual companionship of white men with indigenous women. The entrenched culture persisted, in part by the practice of disguising Aboriginal women as men to prevent legal detection. The documentary record shows little trace of romantic attachment on this frontier. Those white men manning this newer Australian frontier imbibed the inherited culture that denigrated Aboriginal women, belying the fusion of colonial and indigenous societies that existed there.[85]

In the Polynesian context, the Pacific muse stereotype persisted as a widely used representative trope in spite of these economic and cultural shifts in the latter half of the nineteenth century. Now it functioned as a nostalgic aesthetic, depicting young Pacific women untraumatized by colonization. The women depicted were young and alluring, not Christians or laborers, but still languishing exotics. It was a popular trope for the burgeoning visual culture of photography and *cartes des vistes* in the closing decades of the nineteenth century. Yet South Seas mythology was not untouched by the rise of polygenic race ideas, as the final chapter shows.

This latest ideological development was incorporated into the Pacific muse stereotype as earlier preoccupations and anxieties about race, sexuality, and colonial power had likewise been articulated through the stereotype, as we shall see in the final chapter. We have seen how notions of imperial masculinity and the economies of empire affected the stereotype. In the following chapter we shall examine how anxieties about femininity and women's role in European society were mediated through images of natural women in the Pacific from the late eighteenth to the end of the nineteenth century.

IV

Gender, Race, and the Body Politic in the Pacific and Europe

Despite their physical and supposed historical distance from the eighteenth-century centers of civilization, Pacific women were drawn into the web of arguments, debates, and formulations about civilized societies and women's part in it. Pacific peoples supposedly lived in a world uncorrupted by the commercial and social ambitions or restrained by Christian beliefs. Instead they existed in the most harmonious relationship with nature. As pure embodiments of womankind, they served a multitude of purposes for those who theorized about society in this time from three interrelated disciplines: philosophy, science, and anthropology. The use of science to support conservative social agendas was not new in the eighteenth century. As we have seen, since the classical Greeks, science had in varying ways consistently matched arguments for women's inclusion in the public realm of political power, education, and commerce with evidence that reputedly proved the "unnaturalness" of such a social transformation. Scientific evidence concluded in varying ways that women's bodies determined their mental, physical, and emotional characteristics, rendering them unsuited for positions of power and personal autonomy.

Vigorous questioning of the status quo in the eighteenth and nineteenth centuries reinvigorated interest in the body politic and the
social and political meaning of human bodies. From the Enlightenment and French revolutionary period to the era of Queen
Victoria, questions about what constituted nobility in woman and
all social ranks descending from it were refracted through Pacific
women. Initially, maternity was the determining characteristic of
nobility in these new natural women, though this fell into disfavor
owing to politics of colonialism as well as the perceived physical
effects of maternity upon the body.

So far this book has shown how the dominant stereotype of
Pacific women evolved through the sexualized economies of empire.
In this chapter we examine the political potential images of natural
women in the Pacific had in debates about the roles of women in
society. By exploring constructions of female noble and ignoble savagery, we shall see how meditations on the female body fed into formulations of civil and primitive societies and debates about women's
political and social position. These debates had a marked effect in
the colonial realm. In the final part of the chapter, we will look at
how ruling women were drawn into these debates and conceptions
about women. In the heat of colonial politics, their legitimacy to rule
was read through formulations of femininity in which race, class,
and the body were paramount.

The Pacific Muse and the Age of Revolutions

After their "rediscovery" in 1767, Pacific peoples became highly useful for social scientists in the serious business of formulating theories of gender, race, and sexual difference. "Savages" supposedly held
the key to deciphering the mysteries of humanity. Since the Cook
voyages, personnel were sent with the specific purpose of making
professional assessments of Pacific peoples. Planners of these epic
voyages viewed the inclusion of such experts as an indispensable part
of scientific information gathering, a central aim of these voyages
emanating from an enlightened Europe.

It was believed that women living in nature furnished distinct opportunities to unravel the mysteries of mankind. French thinker Joseph Marie De Gérando espoused such a philosophy. He encouraged his observers, particularly those who manned the Baudin voyage sent forth from Napoleonic France in 1800 to observe the state of women. He wanted his voyager-philosophe to collect empirical data on such subjective questions as whether female savages were aware of the "laws of modesty" and if so, did they observe them, or are they so "brutish" that they "completely lack inhibitions" and "go before men without a blush"? Was the "emotional love of savages purely physical," and "does it fasten itself on an individual or indiscriminately on several?" he wondered. Observations made of savage women by explorers "will teach us what right a woman has on common property, what work she does, what protection she is given," and, most intriguing, "whether even in the most savage countries, the female sex preserves something of that sweet and secret power, rooted at once on her weakness, on her sensitivity, and on her charms."[1]

As women of the Pacific lived the furthest distance from modern Occidental civilization, studying them was particularly important for De Gérando and other like-minded exponents of the study of "primitives." He considered voyaging to the Pacific as tantamount to time travel, back to the childhood of Occidental culture, the mythic golden age, arguing that "each step" the voyageur-philosophe makes "is a century over which he leaps." Pacific peoples, therefore, offered the best opportunity for European scientists to "penetrate nature and determine its essential laws." This data was used as a "barometer" to assess the progress different genera of "primitive" men had made along the path to civilization. "The state of women" was considered a primary variable in equating racial hierarchies of men as "consideration of the female sex" seemed to De Gérando, among others, to be an "effect of civilization."[2]

Of the two nations pioneering Pacific exploration in the late eighteenth century, France was particularly interested in the accumulation of ethnographic knowledge. France shared this desire for knowledge with England, as it was directly linked to national prestige and power. The questioning about social order became more urgent in the wake of the French Revolution. A primary interest for both the men and women who pondered the universal condition of women was the relationship between the female sex and the body politic that was defined as a masculine realm. Tradition had been sufficient to exclude women from political participation until 1789. After the Revolution new reasons had to be found to maintain women's exclusion from the body politic in this unprecedented political order. Theorizing about the body politic reached a crescendo, with the outcome being the emphatic redefinition of the world of politics and power as exclusively male, as numerous scholars have shown. The small numbers of women who did seek entry into the political realm were subjected to disproportionate attack by revolutionary leaders. They were represented as having renounced their womanliness, femininity, and virtue. They were, in the words of Jacobin deputy Fabre d'Églantine, "adventuresses, knights-errant, emancipated women, amazons." Their aspirations were tantamount to not only a renouncement of their sex, but an invasion of a world to which they were by definition excluded.[3]

This demonization of "public" and politicized women was most dramatically evident in depictions of Marie Antoinette. Antoinette was accused of using her sexual wiles to exert indirect power through powerful men. She supposedly corrupted the body politic through grotesque sexual practices. The popular press represented her various monstrous incarnations even before the Revolution, though the events of 1789 propounded this existing practice. A more legitimate form of women's political action in the revolutionary years was their participation in the march on Versailles in October 1789 and riots, especially those of 1793, which brought the Jacobins to power in June. Women did hold special advantages however. They were immune as targets of military force, and different groups leveraged this principal to great effect.[4]

Proponents of the status quo argued that because of woman's sexual difference, she was incapable of participating in public life. This idea was pivotal in the construction of modern, democratizing nation states. Politically aspiring women had expected that political and social rights would be extended universally, regardless of sex. The language of the 1789 Declaration of the Rights of Man and the Citizen does not exclude women or men from the body politic because of their race. Yet, as the history of the French Republic demonstrated, with other nations following suit, democratic slogans of universal suffrage and citizenship tantalized women with the possibility of equal status with men, yet simultaneously trampled their hopes on the basis of sexual difference. In the debates about citizenry from 1789 to 1791, deputies were less ambiguous about to whom they thought citizenship rights should be extended. It was a male privilege. There were demonstrations against this exclusion. Most notable among these was Olympe de Gouges' Declaration of the Rights of Woman and the Citizen penned in 1790 and Pauline Léon's reading of a petition to the Legislative Assembly on March 6, 1972, which demanded women's "natural right" to organize themselves into a unit of the National Guard. Such audacity was ruthlessly punished. De Gouge and others were arrested and sent to the guillotine in November 1793 for their activities.[5]

To counter these women's arguments, "evidence" of their incapacity to share in political power had to be created by those determined to keep the patriarchal order intact. The Marquis de Condorcet, who perceived women's social condition as akin to "slavery," wrote "that if women were to be excluded from the polis, one must demonstrate a 'natural difference' between men and women to legitimate that exclusion." Eighteenth-century scientists were more than equal to the task of developing physical "evidence" propounding that the gender status quo be maintained despite alterations to the economic and political makeup of Occidental societies that was adjusting the number of men who shared power.[6]

One profoundly influential scientific school at the forefront of manufacturing indissoluble "evidence" of gendered and racial difference was the new science of craniology. Craniology was based upon the premise that the skull was molded upon the brain, and therefore the shape of the skull "could be read as an open book." Enlightenment scientist Lord Monboddo formulated this new branch of empirical research. He made extensive use of material that he found in accounts of Pacific voyages, as did J. F. Blumenbach and Georges Cuvier. Cuvier also instructed the Baudin voyage in the art of observation. Women's brains were generally considered to be smaller and "less firm" than men's, signifying that women had "less fortitude, were less reasonable, more emotional, had greater compassion and instinct for supporting offspring," attributes that were supposedly not exhibited in men's skulls. Women's skulls were also found to exhibit a larger moral faculty than men, indicating that women had a greater "feeling of duty, obligation, incumbency, right and wrong," all of which supported woman's confinement to the domestic, familial realm and denial of her educational and legal rights. Other physical characteristics exclusive to women, particularly breasts, were also taken to denote woman's mandatory familial, reproductive role. Racial differences were reaffirmed with this new science. It directly challenged the movement to abolish slavery, based upon Christian teachings of shared humanity, that was gaining momentum from the 1780s with the rise of Evangelicals in the English political system, while supporting other manifestations of colonization under way across the globe.[7]

New conceptualizations of sexed bodies and concomitant reassignment of social meaning to them were only a part of the response to the need to demonstrate the "natural difference" between men and women to legitimate women's exclusion from the polis as Condorcet prescribed. There was also the need to reinvigorate the stock of knowledge and evidence about the naturalness of separate spheres and the universal condition of women. For this reason, theorists, such as De Gérando, looked to "savage women" to revitalize this dimension of the armory of evidence. Proof of the patriarchal ordering of "natural societies" and women's "natural" placement in the domestic realm as nurturers and vassals to their husbands was a cornerstone of conservative arguments that sought women's continued relegation to secondary status in Occidental societies.[8]

Engendering Noble and Ignoble Savages

In the French Enlightenment, noble savagery, as it is commonly defined, operated as a mirror to European society, reflecting and magnifying its ills through the construction of man living in utopia. Ignoble savagery, in contrast, shed positive light upon civilization as it portrayed natural man as living in degraded condition. Both concepts were maps that charted the human condition and explored the relationship between environment, political structures, and the human character. A number of scholars have shown the links between observations of natural man in the Pacific, constructions of male noble and ignoble savagery, and its implications for Pacific colonization.[9]

Yet how did women function in this nexus of ideas, empire, and constructions of savagery? If we consider the questioning about the ordering of genders and women's social functions, these concepts of savagery assume another dimension from the masculine counterparts. Viewing Pacific women as noble or ignoble savages relied upon concepts of nature as well as more practical concerns of colonization. Nature was both venerated and devalued in Enlightenment thought. This affected representations of "primitive" women, whose embodiment of nature was twofold. These noble and ignoble images fed into the highly charged debates about women in the eighteenth and nineteenth centuries, combining data from science, philosophy, and anthropology. The images of Pacific women generated in this context distilled the questions about femininity, race, nation, and the gendering of power. Malleable images of Pacific women were used as female exemplars for white women and measures to assess the worth of Pacific women.[10]

The notion of noble savagery stemmed from the classical idea of "the Lost Golden race," described in one version as "they are communistic; they live in a juristic state of nature; their life is simple and virtuous." Within the atavistic intellectual movement of the Enlightenment and the modern culture that emerged from it, classicism itself was conflated with the lost "golden age." This meant that the imagined Classical Age was synonymous with forms of "primitivism" for those thinkers and artists who viewed natural man as sacrosanct. American peoples were unsuitable embodiments of noble savagery by the late eighteenth century owing to centuries of trade, warfare, competition for finite resources, and everyday interaction that both demystified and complicated the indigenes beyond the simplistic ideal. A fresh imaginative site was required, and the Pacific fulfilled that need.[11]

Native Americans were instead increasingly characterized as ignoble savages. This idea was aligned with burgeoning scientific disciplines and the Scottish Enlightenment movement. The ignoble savage provided an overt rationale for imperial and exploitative activities, whereas the noble savage was a more complex imperial device. The ignoble savage was likewise derived from classical writers who compared "primitivism" unfavorably with civilized societies.[12]

According to Ronald Meek, this idea of ignoble savagery had been revived in the seventeenth century by Hugo Grotius's *Law of War and Peace*, published in 1625, and, moreover, from Thomas Hobbes's *Leviathan* of 1651. Hobbes's equation in the *Leviathan* of a state of nature with a state of war and his verdict that a state of nature was a condition of constant insecurity, antagonism, and brutality were definitive in the subsequent formulation of the Enlightenment ignoble savage. In the context in which it was written, Hobbes's argument in the *Leviathan* that the laws of nature were based upon self-interest and self-preservation provided justification for colonization under way in the Atlantic.[13]

The ignoble savage was premised on a concept of man's progress that stressed technology and commerce as the criteria for advancement through four linear evolutionary stages. In this conception the lowest form of humanity, the first stage, were people who subsisted through "hunting animals and feeding on the spontaneous fruits of the earth." Man advanced in this scale through dominating animals in shepherding or pastoral activity, which marked the second stage. The third stage was marked by the mastery of land in agriculture. Finally, the highest stage was designated by commerce being the economic modus operandi. This entailed domination over not only animals and land, but over people who did not evolve: the lower classes; colonized peoples, and the female sex. As we have seen in relation to the construction of savage masculinity, the treatment of women in indigenous societies was a fundamental means to assess "evolutionary advancement" of men. This was true for those writers who denigrated savagery as it also was for those who venerated it.[14]

The writings of Jean-Jacques Rousseau were prodigiously influential in formulating the gender debate on the philosophic front in prerevolutionary France. Rousseau stridently argued that it was crucial that women not be given political rights, as society would disintegrate without their confinement to the domestic sphere. He appealed to the "natural order" and reason to support his societal model, which was based upon the subjugation of women in the private sphere by men in the public, political sphere. He argued in *Émile* that "women do wrong to complain of the inequality of man-made laws; this inequality is not of man's making, or at any rate it is not the result of mere prejudice, but of reason." According to Rousseau, the basic societal bond, the social contract, could be entered into exclusively by men, as only men possessed reason.[15]

Women however, could and must enter what has been termed by Carole Pateman as the "sexual contract," the lesser, private relationship based upon women's sexual subservience and reproduction. For Rousseau, woman's power lay in the imperative role of motherhood and in her beauty, that is, in her ability to incite passions in men. Beauty was the feminized indicator of racial advancement or the test to assess the value of individual women. Beauty denoted the physical and moral health of women. Northern European classically derived standards of feminine beauty, most notably fair skin, delicate features, certain types of hair, and the size and shape of their bodies, were the benchmarks of beauty used by Occidental observers. Rousseau believed that these two desired states of being for women could coexist: motherhood and nubility. Subsequent anthropological observations of Pacific women did not concur as we shall see.[16]

Rousseau's dogmatic message to his female readership, particularly in *Émile*, was grounded in the concept of "woman in nature." Although not named as such by Rousseau, "woman in nature" existed by implication as the complement, sexual partner, "helpmeet," and procreator to the antisocial subject he named the "savage man" or "man in nature." For instance, in *Discourse on the Origin of Inequality* Rousseau figured that "the only goods he [savage man] knows in the universe are nourishment, a woman and rest." "Woman in nature's" existence is further fleshed out in *Émile*: "there are countries, I grant you, where women bear and rear children with little or no difficulty." In such countries where women performed maternal feats, Rousseau's imagined men were likewise superlative physical specimens. It followed for him that "when women become strong, men become still stronger; when men become soft, women become softer."[17]

"Woman in nature" was the purest embodiment of nature because of her sex and her closeness to the environment. Rousseau took her supposed lack of shame in her nakedness as a sign of her heightened animality, and so he venerated her for instinctual obedience to the laws of nature. Paradoxically, woman in nature's closeness to nature meant that she was even less of a historical agent or sentient being than were other categories of woman and represented the furthest extreme from the venerated state of "reason." In *Émile*, "the Caribs," along with the "Redskins of Canada," American Indians, and European peasants, were upheld as the most virtuous "natural" people. Their noninterference in nature's preordained ways provided valuable wisdoms for the lost enlightened peoples whom Rousseau hoped to instruct. With his logic that all "natural people" lacked reason, it followed that certain racially inferior men were also unable to enter the social contract, although Rousseau did not pursue this implication, concentrating instead upon how this closeness to nature affected the female sex.[18]

Rousseau located the origin of sexual difference in the beginnings of families that succeeded "the first developments of the heart." In *Discourse on the Origin of Inequality*, he posited that "the habit of living together gave rise to sweetest sentiments known to men: conjugal love and paternal love. Each family became a little society all the better united because mutual attachment and liberty were its bonds." From the establishment of the family, "the first difference was established in the lifestyle of the two sexes. Women became more sedentary and grew accustomed to watch over the hut and the children, while the men went to seek their common subsistence."[19]

Pacific peoples did not "exist" in Rousseau's contemplative realm, as he was writing in the years prior to the new era of Pacific voyaging in the late 1760s. Nevertheless, his configuration of the first family, the savage family, reverberated subsequently in numerous images of Pacific peoples. Such influence is clear in the depiction of Nieuw Hollanders in the Dutch publication of 1802 *De Mensch: Zoo Als Hij Voorkomt op Den Bekenden Aardbol* (fig. 4.1). Here illustrator Jacques Kuyper fused Rousseau's vision of the savage family with an eyewitness representation of Aboriginal men, that of the *Endeavour's* artist, Sidney Parkinson, *Two Natives Advancing to Combat*, which became the blueprint for indigenous men of New Holland after it was published in 1784. The noble savage is stylized in all his classical perfection: muscular and sovereign, and therefore innately good. The female noble savage was consigned opposing characteristics: youthful elegance, fine features and skin, and virtuous sexual attractiveness in that her sexuality was geared toward reproduction as opposed to wanton desire. Rousseau's vision of the utopian "lost paradise" of a "beautiful coast, adorned only by the hands of nature" also echoes through this image. The male ideal embodies the affectations of primitive culture, being covered in body paint, clutching weapons, and standing in a defiant and protective posture. The woman, in contrast, embodies all that was considered noble for a woman. What is admired in this "natural woman" is antithetical to what is to be admired in her spouse. Her husband has freedom and sovereignty, while she is his willing vassal. There is no conflict between the natural man and the natural woman in this picturesque scene, as both have unquestionably assumed their naturally preordained roles.[20]

According to Rousseau, the virtues of "woman in nature" as mothers were numerous. They did not swaddle their newborns, and they did not have to endure the intervention in childbirth and mothering by midwives, doctors, or nurses, and they breast-fed without question. Environmental benefits of fresh air, the vegetarian diet of country mothers, and strengthening exercise also aided the health and well-being of children born to more "natural" women. Within this discourse on mothering, the issue of mothers breast-feeding their

NIEUW—HOLLANDERS.

4.1 Jacques Kuyper, "Nieuw-Hollanders," *De Mensch: Zoo Als Hij Voorkomt op Den Bekenden Aardbol,* Amsterdam, Johannes Allart, 1802.

own offspring was a cause célèbre for Rousseau. Breast-feeding made a brief return to fashion for upper-class Frenchwomen following *Émile*, coupled with campaigns of doctors, other moralists, and statesmen who were "scandalized by excessive infant mortality" and the various social implications from the widespread practice of wet-nursing. Upper-class women could afford to shift their practices. The women for whom this practice remained in place were artisan women who worked for their husbands and could not afford the time to care for infants. For these women, the choice was to send babies to rural wet nurses. George Sussman has found that despite the campaigns that accused women of neglecting their children for the purposes of preserving their beauty, there was no "wholesale return of urban mothers nursing their infants in late eighteenth century France."[21]

Medical professionals in France and Germany, convinced by Rousseau's argument for the moral and physical well-being of babies breast-fed by their own mothers, as well as the direct connection to the health of the state, were not willing to leave the matter to the discretion of women. They lobbied for laws that would make it illegal for healthy women not to breast-feed their own children. In 1793 the French National Convention determined that only women who breast-fed their own children would be eligible for state aid. Similar laws were instituted in Prussia the following year. The time and economic pressures that forced artisan women to persist with farming out babies outweighed the financial incentives provided by the state. In addition to feeling the pressures of the workplace, nursing mothers were also often forced to decide whether to care for infants or their husbands. Breast-feeding and sexual activity were deemed incompatible, as sex was thought to spoil or dry up milk. Husbands often decided in favor of their own interests over those of their children, and mothers acquiesced due to fears that their husbands would be tempted into adultery or unhealthy substitutes such as masturbation, Mary Sherif has argued. Authorities could not combat the combined forces of social, marital, and economic pressures for a large section of the urban female population.[22]

Ethnographic representations were another tool to persuade

women of their natural duties. A second image from Kuyper's publication purportedly representing a noble savage family of the Pelaw
Island, present-day Palau in Micronesia, captured a sexually alluring natural mother in the act of caring for her infant in ways that
reflected the Rousseauian ideal (fig. 4.2). This island was brought
to Europe's attention in 1779 with George Keate's publication of
accounts of the sailors from the East India Company vessel, the
Antelope, that was shipwrecked in the archipelago five years earlier.
This image of these islanders, as with the one of the New Hollanders,
is overwhelmed with romantic notions of noble savagery. The contemporary political dogma surrounding breast-feeding is flagrantly
on display for the consumption of women in Europe.[23]

The message from these images of Pacific women for a late-
eighteenth- and early-nineteenth-century European audience is
indubitable. Sexual difference was a natural fact, and women's confinement to the domestic, reproductive sphere was likewise "natural." A woman's sex determined her entire nature and role. It
therefore followed for Rousseau and many who predated and succeeded him, that "a different morality; a different education; a different level of access to knowledge and truth and . . . an entirely
different social and political function from that assigned to men" was
appropriate for women.[24]

Pacific Women and Gendered Debates

For philosophers who came after Rousseau who had the Pacific
within their sphere of contemplation, the voyage accounts of Wallis,
Bougainville, and Cook provided much food for thought. In these
writings, the Pacific woman was the site for debates about femininity as well as discourses on colonialism. The tension between sexual desirability of colonized women and the need for exemplars of
femininity for Occidental women were played out in representations
of Pacific women. As previously discussed, the early Pacific voyages
generated a great deal of literature and discussion in Europe, with
Tahiti in particular capturing the imaginations of many writers, poets,
and playwrights as well as philosophers. What titillated many

PELEW-EILANDERS.

4.2 Jacques Kuyper, "Pelew-Eilanders," *De Mensch: Zoo Als Hij Voorkomt op Den Bekenden Aardbol*, Amsterdam, Johannes Allart, 1802.

Europeans was the concupiscence of the Tahitian women as opposed to images of virtuous mothers. The account of Tahiti by Philibert Commerson, naturalist on the Bougainville voyage, in particular, propelled Tahitians to a stellar status in the European imagination. He famously launched the island to the French public with the quote that appeared in *Mercure de France* for November 1769, which began "ils ne connaissent d'autre Dieu que l'amour" (they know no other God but love).[25]

Voltaire, who read the accounts of Bougainville and Cook, was similarly captivated by the displays of sexual freedom on Tahiti and the publicly displayed sexual union between a young man and woman reported by Cook and others. Voltaire perceived sexuality in Tahiti to hold the status of religion, and described that renowned event as a "service divin." For Voltaire, Tahitian women were ennobled, above all, by their sexuality. Commerson's configuration of Tahitian women inspired Nicholas Bricaire de La Dixmerie to use the literary device of the exotic as a critic of French culture in his *Sauvage de Taïti aux Français* of 1770. In this instance his exotic critic was a male Tahitian sovereign who visited France and made statements, the most pronounced concerning the "woman question," "which he examines from all angles: aesthetic, moral and political," argues Julia Douthwaite. For La Dixmerie, clothing was axiomatic to understanding the social standing of the two opposing types of women, Tahitian and French. Tahitian women's transparent dress indicated their sexual freedom, which in turn marked the general health of the entire people: "Look at our beautiful Tahitian women! Their clothing floats in the wind. An ingenious gauze hides their nudity from sight, but lets one see their charms. Nothing fights against desire; everything excites it." To the Tahitian king, French women's confined, inaccessible bodies reflected their sexual repression and their "social vulnerability." Tahitian men were blessed by the "gifts" of women who were both beautiful and sexually free. La Dixmerie was arguing that social health could be gained from women's sexual freedom, as this assured the happiness of men.[26]

Denis Diderot expanded and altered the conditions of female nobility by positing fecundity as the primary determinant of femi-

nine goodness. Utilizing a scintilla of "evidence" from voyagers'
accounts, tinged with a far greater portion of fantasy, he concocted
a "Tahiti" through which he mirrored Europe's problems in his
Supplément au Voyage de Bougainville, written in 1772 though not published until 1796. Diderot lampooned many aspects of the European
established order, particularly religion, marriage for life, and European imperialism. He aired views on the valuation of women, sexual freedoms of both genders, male power over wives and children,
divorce, child custody, and incest, which he deemed "not against
nature," but rather an act of "love," "respect," and "generosity" of
fathers, sons, and brothers toward their daughters, mothers, and sisters. He advocated greater freedoms for women through arguing that
lifelong marriage without the option of divorce "violates the liberty
of male and female, by chaining them for ever one to the other."
Overall he evaluated women according to their fecundity, dismiss-
ing beauty as the primary indicator of a woman's worth that was
paramount to upper-class culture. Diderot's construction of the
European versus Tahitian measure of feminine value was obviously
inflected with the class concerns of his day. Aristocrats placed prestige in women's delicacy and demureness. The lower classes valued
the strength of women who could withstand numerous births and
remain useful as workers. It is the latter qualities that Diderot
endorsed through his invented Tahitians.[27]

In the *Supplément*, a French chaplain acted as the spokesman for
France and Christianity in dialogues with the wise Tahitian patriarch, Orou. Orou hit upon the essential, albeit imagined, differences
between Tahiti and modern France, arguing that in Tahiti female
nobility was measured by fecundity over physical beauty. "In order
to be beautiful" in Europe "a woman must have a brilliant complexion, a broad forehead, large eyes, refined and delicate features,
a slender waist, a small mouth, small hands, a small foot," Orou outlined. In direct contrast, "none of these qualities are considered" in
Tahiti. Here "the woman on whom glances fix and who is pursued
by lovers is the one who holds out the promise of a large family, at
once active, intelligent, brave, healthy and robust." He continued
that "there is practically nothing in common between the Venus of

Athens and that of Tahiti. One is the gallant, the other the fruitful Venus." Beauty of the imagined Tahitian mother was immaterial compared to the beauty of a woman's children: "a Tahitian woman once said with contempt to another native . . . 'You are beautiful, but your children are ugly. I am ugly, but my children are beautiful, and I am the one the men prefer.'"[28]

Diderot's representation of sex and imperialism was fraught with ambiguity. In the first instance he soundly condemned, via the ninety-year-old Orou, sexual relations between the men of the Bougainville voyage and Tahitian women, and their all too apparent results, miscegenation and, moreover, venereal disease. Through the unfolding farcical plot, Diderot went on to condone the sexual union of the chaplain and Orou's wife and three daughters, highlighting the unnaturalness of celibacy and the authority of the Church on sexual matters. The chaplain not only abandoned his vows of celibacy but submitted to all four "charming suppliants," the first being the youngest daughter, Thia. At nineteen and without a child, Thia implored the cleric to "honour me in the hut and among my people. Raise me to the rank of my sisters, who laugh at me." She beseeched him, "make me a mother. Give me a child that one day I may lead by the hand, beside me in Tahiti; who may be seen in nine months' time, hanging from my breast. Grant me this favour and I will never forget thee." Despite repeating "but my religion, but my calling," the French chaplain succeeded where "young Tahitians" had failed, transforming Thia into a "fruitful Venus." The obvious paradox here is that although the Tahitians are supposedly being upheld as the noble savages by Diderot, French men possessed supreme virility. Although Diderot deemed child care to be the preserve of women, it is interesting to note that Bougainville recorded in his voyage account that Tahitian children "are taken care of by both their mothers and their fathers."[29]

The conflicting perceptions of "men in nature" that were present in Diderot's text were symptomatic of the problems with the masculine dimension of the noble savage ideal as a whole. The concept of male noble savagery was as impractical as it was implausible, as few European observers would demote themselves down the evolutionary ladder below "savage men" regardless of philosophic beliefs. In the battles over land, resources, and political power, colonizers on most occasions viewed themselves as pitted against men, despite evidence that many Pacific women were not excluded from political power and land ownership. The female ideal was not as far-fetched as the male ideal, having been centered on "natural functions" of mothering, servitude, sexuality, and physical beauty.

Pacific women also provided anthropological evidence for the Scottish social scientist William Alexander. His two-volume study, *The History of Women from the Earliest Antiquity to the Present Time of 1782*, relied also upon "historical data" and was "composed solely for the amusement and instruction of the Fair Sex." Despite claims that this was a history of women, Alexander saw women's historical progress as determined by the different stages of evolution of man. As with the previously discussed social scientists, Alexander perceived the treatment of women as axiomatic to determining the progress of man.[30]

Beginning with natural men and civilized men, he argued that "man in his rude and uncivilized state forms his connection with woman from a regard to the beauty of her person only." When man progresses beyond this basic state, he chooses women with "regards to the qualities of her mind also." From this human genesis, Alexander then proceeded through a linear history of Occidental culture from the ancients to the Middle Ages to reach the highest point of regard and freedom of their sex anywhere in contemporary Occidental culture. Meanwhile the position of women's non-Occidental sisters had deteriorated markedly over time. The tenor of *The History of Women* is that women of the North should feel gratified that their men treat them with such dignity and respect. Moreover, women's lives cannot improve beyond the point reached in the sole civilized sphere of the European North.[31]

Tahiti provided a fascinating conundrum to Alexander's schema of the advancement of women through history and across different cultural spheres. With Tahiti in mind, he admitted that the condition of women "does not always proceed upon a uniform plan," echoing a similar philosophic mind-set as De Gérando that the "consideration of the female sex was an effect of civilisation." It was strange that the men of this island, "sons of our nature, and almost entirely fed and clothed by her hand . . . without the least knowledge of art, or glimmering of science," treated their women with "every rank and dignity, and even the supreme authority of the island," alluding to Queen Oberea. Alexander read this latter trait as a mark of the "weakness and softness" of Tahitian men as opposed to a mark of civilization.[32]

The sexuality of Tahitian women was also puzzling. They were sexually liberated but were still highly regarded by their men. Yet the freedoms enjoyed by Tahitian women, especially those of the arioi society, led to social discord. Women's hedonistic quest for sexual satisfaction meant that the family, the essential social unit, had no place within this society. He argued that when men and women of this group agreed to keep children and not smother them in the moment of birth and adopt the role of mothers and fathers, they are both "extruded from this hopeful society." Alexander's portrayal of women in nature and the family in nature diverged markedly from Rousseau's noble savage ideal. The weight of voyage evidence showed that the "flagitious" sexuality of Tahitian women and those of neighboring islands, in combination with a unique social arrangement, had dire consequences. The malleable object of the Tahitian woman was useful to Alexander, as he could apply his veiled political rhetoric for the "benefit" of his Occidental female readers. Tahitian women were interesting for Alexander, but they were not suitable prototypes: rather they were foreboding figures not to be imitated.[33]

Pacific women also captivated some of the isolated female voices of the Enlightenment. Marie-Josephine de Monbart's proto-feminist novel, *Lettres Taïtiennes*, of 1784, utilized Tahiti to contrast the conditions of women in nature and in civilized society, as well as pronounce her objections to French and, more stridently, British colonization of the island. As Douthwaite has shown, Monbart followed the lead of Charles Louis de Secondat, baron of Montesquieu, who penned the *Lettres Persanes* in 1721 about an exotic visitor to

Paris, as well as Françoise de Gaffigny's *Lettres d'une Péruvienne* of 1747. Monbart created a young Tahitian couple, Zeïr, a male who travels to France, and Zulica, the heroine, who acquired the skill of writing from French voyagers. Through this couple, Monbart articulated her agendas on female education, the freeing-up of French women's sexuality, and condemnation of European colonization, which makes Tahitian women, even Zulica herself, prostitutes. Unlike the male writers who fetishized the sexuality of Tahitian women, Monbart qualified the sexual customs of Tahiti by arguing, via the learned island woman, that sexual access to women was not indiscriminate but was governed by a series of codes. These codes that protected woman's body, an analogy for the political state, were corrupted by colonial penetration, which reduced Tahitian women to mere sexual commodities. Monbart construed the evidence of polygamy in Tahiti not as a sign of women's degradation but as a way of releasing the sexuality of women from the confines of life-long marriage. Douthwaite argues that Monbart debunked many of the evolving stereotypes of Tahitian women, by allowing the possibility that these women possessed intellectual capacity and the trait that was supposedly exclusive to northern men, reason.[34]

Similarly, Mary Wollstonecraft used "anthropological evidence" coupled with literary examples to support her call for the extension of rights to women. In *A Vindication of the Rights of Woman* of 1792, she made a fleeting reference to George Forster's (she named him "Foster") *Account of the Isles of the South Sea*, made after his Pacific tour on Cook's second voyage of 1772 to 1775. The state of Tahitian women therefore was included in her thinking upon the condition of woman in the non-Occidental realms. Forster's account would have provided much food for Wollstonecraft's thoughts on the condition of women. Ideas of feminine nobility and ignobility, as well as comparisons between civilized women and their amorphous, conglomerated counterparts, uncivilized women, permeated her thesis in *Vindication*. While she claimed that "I wish to see women as neither heroines nor brutes; but reasonable creatures," she implicitly concluded that civilized women are more capable than their savage sisters of attaining an enlightened state and of gaining personal liberties owing to the superior sensibilities of their men. Indeed, the state of uncivilized women served as a warning against the withholding of rights from civilized women. She argued that "liberty is the mother of virtue, and if women be, by their very constitution, slaves, and not allowed to breathe the sharp invigorating air of freedom, they must ever languish like exotics, and be reckoned beautiful flaws in nature."[35]

Wollstonecraft, a Rousseauian acolyte, accepted the colonial stereotype of the languishing exotic and the trivial, sexualized existence of women from the non-Occidental realms. Such a conclusion is not so surprising given that an authority on "exotics" like Forster perpetuated this reading of Pacific women. Forster argued that the "chief points of female education" in the "happy isles" of Tahiti, the Friendly Islands (Tonga), and the Marquesas "is to learn the great art to please." Girls "are instructed in all the means of gaining the affection of the males, of studying every winning art, and of habituating themselves to that sweetness of temper which never fails to merit the return of attachment." As attractive as this seemed to Forster, such a blueprint for women's education caused discomfort for Wollstonecraft, who wished to see civilized women's education extended beyond training in coquetry.[36]

Apart from these few commentaries by women, the development of stereotypes of noble savagery and the Pacific woman was the work of men. The eighteenth-century debates on gender roles generated by armchair travelers about women's place within society and the use of women's bodies for reproduction, the sexual pleasure of men, or their own sexual satisfaction display the tensions raised by viewing Pacific women as noble savages and therefore exemplars of femininity. The writings of these armchair commentators display the conflict between motherhood and concupiscence as well as motherhood and colonialism. Owing to colonization, European commentators shifted what they considered noble in Pacific women. Images generated by voyagers submerged philosophic images of natural mothers with young, beautiful, sexually available woman. Exotic nobility, therefore, became virtually synonymous with nubility.

Science, Femininity, and the Anthropological Field

This tension between nobility as motherhood or as youthful beauty is evident in the vignettes of Tasmanian Aboriginal people and other Pacific peoples brought back to Europe by Citizen Jacques-Julien La Billardière. La Billardière was the naturalist aboard the D'Entrecasteaux expedition that scoured the Pacific in search of the two lost vessels of the La Pérouse voyage, whose fate after leaving Botany Bay in March 1788 provided one of the great mysteries of Pacific voyaging. La Pérouse was a believer in the noble savage ideal prior to the attack upon his crew in Fagasa Bay, Samoa, in December 1787. La Pérouse's disappearance and speculation that he may have met the same end as Cook or his compatriot Marion du Fresne in New Zealand in 1772 dented the veneration of natural man considerably in the Occidental world. Although the D'Entrecasteaux crew was particularly wary of attack, La Billardière was seduced by the displays of happiness and tranquility of the Tasmanians and rendered glowing reports and images of the family groups that he encountered.[37]

The nobility of the women encountered in the summer of 1793 was assured by a number of characteristics for La Billardière, mainly by their trust of the Frenchmen, a trust that La Billardière found rather astonishing given the sexual reputation of lower-class sailors. Young women walked with the strangers, observed them, ran races with them along the beach, of which La Billardière reported with "pleasure" that some of the Frenchmen who attempted to catch them "could frequently run better than these savages." One "young girl" who possessed a kangaroo skin, which La Billardière wished to take as a specimen in exchange for a pair of pantaloons, also impressed him with her artlessness in allowing "us to put them on her for ourselves." "Desirous of avoiding every cause of offence," La Billardière continued, "we behaved with all the gravity we could on the occasion." In this instance the young woman's lack of awareness of her vulnerable nakedness and innocent sexuality elevated her. Her mind was obviously uncontaminated by lascivious thoughts unlike these visitors. When this unquestioning trust on the part of the Tasmanian women was breached by three sailors who "took the opportunity of one of the most retired places, to treat them with a degree of freedom which was received in a very different manner from what they had hoped," the women fled immediately. La Billardière reported with relief that the young women involved in this incident did not disclose what had transpired to their men-folk. The attack upon the La Pérouse crew in Fagasa Bay had been accounted for in some analyses as a result of unwanted sexual advances by the Frenchmen toward Samoan women.[38]

The harmonious family scene in *Savages of Van Diemen's Land, preparing their Repast*, which illustrated La Billardière's journal, dis-

4.3 *Savages of Van Diemen's Land, preparing their Repast*, 1800.
Plate in J. La Billardière, *Voyage in Search of La Perouse 1791–1794*,
London, John Stockdale, 1800.

Savages of Van Diemen's Land, preparing their Repast.

Pub.d by I.Stockdale, Piccadilly, 14 th April 1800.

plays the easy integration of the Frenchmen into the society and a highly romanticized view of savage life (fig. 4.3). La Billardière was also struck by the "greatest marks of affection" that the mothers "lavished" upon children. "Yet, their confidence in us was so great, that one of the women, who was suckling a child, was not afraid to entrust it to several of us," La Billardière marveled, and this was duly included in the family scene. The nobility of Tasmanian mothers was rendered in the image *Woman of Van Diemen's Land* (fig. 4.4). The depiction of the noble mother here is less stylized and fictitious than the Kuyper illustrations of noble savage women, as it contains ethnographic information in the appearance of the woman and child, as well as in the mother's curious manner of carrying the baby on her shoulders. Her posture and gesture toward the child convey both her vigilant attention toward her offspring and her natural grace and femininity. She could be ennobled and a mother.[39]

While La Billardière depicted the Tasmanian women's displayed trust, innocence, lively inquisitiveness, modesty, and maternity, he highlighted the inequality between the sexes by casting the Tasmanian men as brutish savages. Rather than detract from the women, La Billardière's conclusions about Tasmanian men undercut the already mortally wounded noble savage man. He reported that only the women searched for food and then waited upon the menfolk during repasts. There was seemingly a strict hierarchy of power within each family that "seemed to us to live in perfect independence." He wrote that "we observed in the children the greatest subordination to their parents, and in the women the same to their husbands."[40]

That the women took care not to upset their husbands or to challenge their subordinated status added to La Billardière's positive depiction of them. He saw this care that women took was "to avoid giving their husbands any occasion for jealousy." One sailor nevertheless boasted once back on board "of the favours he had received from one of the beauties of Cape Diemen." La Billardière remained skeptical, concluding that "it is difficult to say, how far his story was founded in truth." In his Pacific encounter, not even the much vaunted women of Tonga were represented in such a good light as

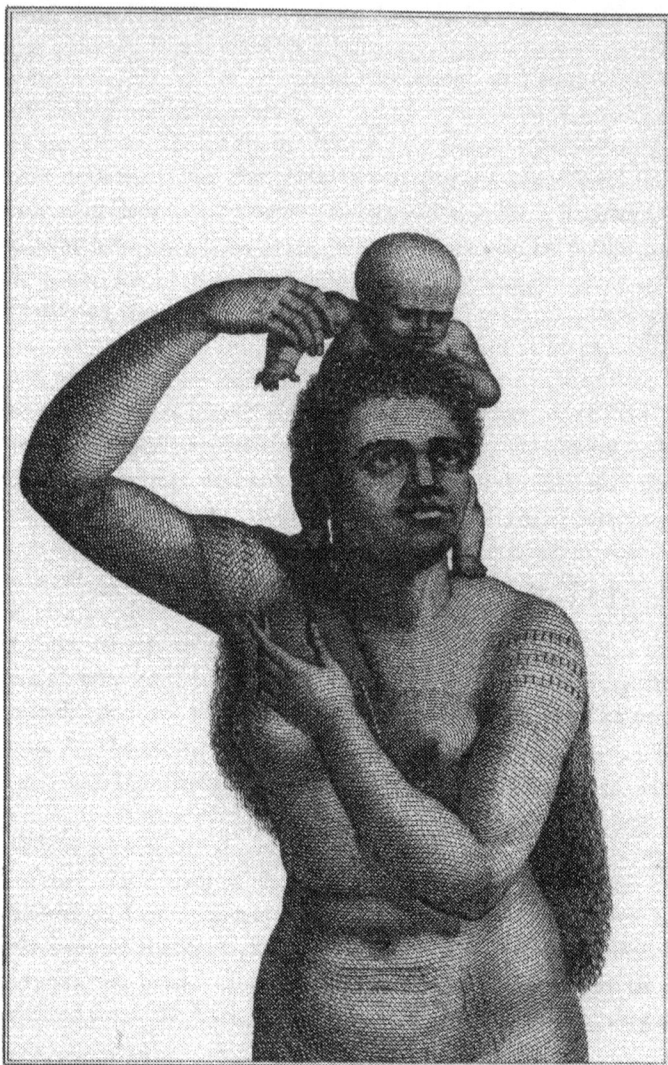

Woman of Van Diemens Land.

Pub.d by J.Stockdale, Piccadilly, 15.th April, 1800.

4.4 *Woman of Van Diemen's Land*, 1800.
Plate in J. J. La Billardière, *Voyage in Search of La Pérouse 1791–1794*,
London, John Stockdale, 1800.

the Tasmanian women by La Billardière, even though there were many captivating exemplars of femininity he encountered in Tonga, as we shall see.[41]

In 1802, Captain Nicholas Baudin chastised Citizen La Billardière for his "imperfect report" of the Tasmanians, who were not the "good and peaceful" savages that they had been led to expect. Baudin cited La Billardière's lack of professional qualification; he was after all "merely the botanist" on the D'Entrecasteaux voyage. Botany had been more than adequate to equip the likes of Joseph Banks and Philibert Commerson with an authoritative ethnographic voice in the late 1760s and early 1770s. In the ten-year period between the D'Entrecasteaux and Baudin voyages, studying "primitives" carried a higher cultural value and so had to be conducted with a professionally informed gaze, as outlined by De Gérando. It was in this period that the gender debates that had dominated the philosophic, scientific, and political discourses across the eighteenth century reached an unprecedented intensity.[42]

The often densely political images of Pacific women revealed gross contradictions in European feminine ideals as well as the core of attitudinal currency toward all women and then colonized women. The virility of savage man was measured by the degree of eroticization of woman's body by Occidental observers. As previously discussed, women's nakedness reflected badly upon their men. Women's casual nakedness signified sexual lethargy and effeminacy in men, a standard stereotype of colonized masculinity. However, these readings of women's bodies carried more valence than just assessing masculinity. Unlike European women, who wore garments to reshape and mask the effects of reproduction and breast-feeding on their bodies, Pacific women's near or complete nakedness, among many other things, facilitated a most telling commentary on the incompatibility of ennobling femininity and motherhood. It is clear that designations of nobility and ignobility in colonial images of Pacific women had everything to do with their bodies.

The volume of commentary on Pacific women's breasts reflects the intense interest in and symbolism of the female breast in Occidental culture, "representing both the sublime and the bestial in human nature."[43] Londa Schiebinger argues that "the grotesque, withered breasts on witches and devils represented temptations of wanton lust, sins of the flesh and humanity fallen from paradise," while the "firm spherical breasts of Aphrodite, the Greek ideal, represented an otherworldly beauty and virginity." Nineteenth-century medical textbooks described "virtuous," virgin breasts as "pert, small, conical and with tiny rose coloured nipples," Mary Spongberg has argued, while nonvirgin, depraved and "primitive" breasts were described as "elongated and pendulous, with large, hard nipples, dark in colour." Breasts were the keys to assigning value to women according to the dichotomies of young and old, beautiful and plain, sexually desirable and sexually repellent, civilized and primitive in the ignoble sense, and virtuous and depraved. In the course of Pacific colonization, some of the less prudish journalists conveyed details of the shapes of breasts, which would have been considered as "legitimate" comparative anatomy, although it was no more than thinly veiled voyeurism. William Wales, the astronomer on Cook's second voyage, did not skirt the ugliness that he perceived in the bodies of women who had suckled their children. Tahitian women, whose "personal beauties" he felt had been greatly exaggerated by the likes of Bougainville, were in his estimation lacking true beauty in many facets. However, he found that "the Breasts of the young ones before they have had Children are very round and beautifull, but those of the old ones hang down to their Navals."[44]

François Péron's account of the bodies of Aboriginal women of the west Australian coast and Van Diemen's Land elucidate the glaring contradictions in the ideals of womanhood that had such a great deal of currency in the Napoleonic France from which the Baudin voyage sailed in 1800. The myth of scientific detachment is more than evident in Péron's observations as these were determined by his own individual taste in female sexual attractiveness in addition to the current political and social discourses of his time. The image that so starkly conveys the enmity to women's bodies that obviously displayed the effects of reproduction is that of a lone, "heavily pregnant" woman observed on the west Australian coastline by a party of Frenchmen from the *Naturaliste*. Reports of pregnant women are rare in the surviving documentation of colonialism in the Pacific, although it is probable that the observation of pregnant women would have far exceeded the minimal reportage of them. This historical silence speaks volumes about the hostile contemporary attitudes to pregnancy that are manifest in Péron's account, which also may have been colored by Dampier's notorious judgment of west coast Aboriginal people. While the French perused this woman's body, she remained rigid with fear, squatting on her heels and hiding her face in her hands, escaping at the first opportunity and leaving behind a "spontaneous evacuation." Péron reduced her to an animalistic creature that by her physical form alone rendered her thoroughly ignoble. She was "horribly ugly and disgusting," and her body was "uncommonly lean and scraggy and her breasts hung almost to her thighs." "The most extreme dirtiness added to her natural deformity and was enough to disgust the most depraved of our sailors." The woman's "natural deformity" was perhaps her belly.[45]

Pregnancy was deemed anathema to ideals of beauty despite the unwavering hegemonic view that a woman's destiny was to procreate. The social rituals surrounding pregnancy in the eighteenth-century and nineteenth-century Occident are testament to the revulsion with which it was viewed. Concealment of the belly through copious clothing, a long confinement prior to birth, and the employment of a host of euphemisms were the main tactics used to shroud an event considered infra dig in polite society. Pregnancy, rather than being seen as the paragon of femininity, was instead seen as the strongest display of women's innate animality.[46]

The gaze of observers was not always positive when evaluating young women who might otherwise have complied with Occidental conventions of beauty. Captain von Krusenstern of the three-year Russian voyage of 1803 to 1806 strongly refuted previous claims that Marquesan women were among the most beautiful in the Pacific. With his disapproving eye, which he claimed was "impartial," Krusenstern demolished the longstanding reputation of Marquesan women that stemmed from Mendana's voyage in 1595. In addition to bodily shape, feminine beauty also depended upon deportment, as Krusenstern argued that "their form . . . is anything but beautiful." They were "generally short, and without carriage and this is the case with even girls of eighteen" and "their gait is likewise awkward and unsteady, and their lower stomach particularly large." He concluded that "their ideas of beauty must be very different from ours, otherwise they would take more pains to conceal their defects."[47]

Attractive body form determined the placement of women on the parallel hierarchical scale to that of man. Contemporary conventions of ideal beauty held that external appearance defined the internal moral constitution. When natural beauty was coupled with aristocratic deportment, it signified nobility. Watkin Tench, captain in the First Fleet Marines, immortalized Barangaroo, a woman of Sydney Cove, in a classic rendition of the female noble savage trope. Barangaroo was presented to Tench in September of 1790 in a petticoat that she was persuaded to wear for the occasion. Tench reported that "we soon laughed her out of it [the petticoat]" and she stood before them innocently naked. Her apparent physical beauty combined with her natural mastery of ladylike etiquette won Tench's admiration. He was amazed that "as much feminine innocence, softness and modesty . . . as the most finished system could bestow, or the most polished circle produce" could be found "amidst a horde of roaming savages, in the desert wastes of New South Wales." That such an image could be produced of an Aboriginal woman at this point in the invasion of Aboriginal lands reveals a great deal about the colonial attitudes to colonized women. Beautiful young women were not viewed as opponents of the invaders. Rather a different set of expectations and antagonisms were imposed upon them, determining the nature of imperial representations of them.[48]

The same ideas were at work with François Péron when the Baudin voyage reached the coast of Van Diemen's Land by the summer of 1802. Péron gave one effusive account of a young woman, Ourê-Ourê, of Maria Island. She captured the men's interest with her "winning gestures and gracious smiles." In many ways Ourê-Ourê complied with the criteria for nobility in her own person: young, sexually attractive, suitably admiring of the Frenchmen (particularly Henri Freycinet), and, importantly, she was part of a kind family group. Together this family softened Péron's harsh scientific eye and satisfied his Romantic yearning for the noble savage. He wrote that "with inexpressible delight I came to realise in them those brilliant descriptions of happiness and simplicity of the state of nature of which I had savoured the seductive charm many times in my reading."[49]

A few days later, a number of men from the *Naturaliste* landed on neighboring Bruny Island to gather wood, hunt, and fish. Péron reported that after rounding a point, he saw "about twenty savages coming towards me." "Being well aware from our previous mishaps of the danger of such encounters," Péron wanted to avert trouble and so retraced his steps. He met with the surgeon and an officer, who together decided to "try to obtain an interview with them." The Frenchmen felt assured that their number and weapons would "protect us from their evil designs." On their approach, the party of Tasmanians climbed over the sand hills, leaving the French to attract their attention "especially by waving our handkerchiefs." The party stopped and allowed the French to approach.[50]

Péron reported that "it was then we realized we were dealing with women, and that there was not a single man among them." The French were ordered to sit. Once the strangers were seated, the women squatted down on their heels and began to talk animatedly, laughing, questioning these strange people and "often seeming to criticize us and to laugh at our expense." At this point the surgeon, Monsieur Bellefin, began to sing, accompanied by "vivid and animated gestures," which silenced the women. When he finished, some responded with "peals of laughter" and "loud cries," while the girls "kept silent . . . showing nevertheless by their gestures and by the expressions on their faces their surprise and satisfaction." The women's vital sense of fun, at the Frenchmen's expense, did not sit well with the submissive and demure attitudes of "natural women" that the ideal, exemplified by Ourê-Ourê's family, had led them to expect.[51]

Meanwhile, Péron's anthropological eye roamed over these women's bodies laid bare to his scrutiny. Despite all their apparent vivacity, Péron concluded that most were ill-treated, degraded, and "ignoble" based upon a superficial examination of their body shape, skin, hair, clothing, and facial attitude. His assessment was loaded with detail of the attitudes to and connections between feminine appearance, societal status, visceral constitution, and worth. He found these women "repulsive," as "their build was generally thin and withered, their breasts pendulous and flabby." Some of the older women had "ignoble," "gross" faces, while others looked "fierce and sombre." His belief in the ignobility of Tasmanian men was also to blame for their state. He concluded that "in general one could see in all of them something of the apprehension and dejection which misfortune and slavery stamp on the faces of all those beings who wear the yoke." Their men also fitted with expectations as "nearly all were covered with scars, shameful evidence of the ill-treatment of their ferocious spouses." What Péron was seeing were not characteristics particular to this race of women, but rather universal features of the enslaved and the working classes.[52]

Two or three girls of fifteen or sixteen were exempted from Péron's condemnation. In these girls he could perceive the classical physique of "pleasant forms, lines of sufficient grace, and breasts which were firm and well placed," although "their nipples were a little too big and too long." This physical shape coupled with "something in their faces of much artlessness, more loving and softer" suggested to Péron that "the best qualities of the soul must be, even among the savage hordes of the human species, the particular prerogative of youth, grace and beauty."[53]

Age of women was a key determinant in their classification as noble or ignoble as Péron's account shows. Some of the most vituperative comments by European observers of Pacific peoples were leveled at old women. Peter Cunningham, an infamous voice of pastoralism in Australia, opined that old Aboriginal women "are absolute frights . . . and only require a tail to complete the identity." To adherents of polygenist race theories in vogue in the Australian colonies from the 1820s, especially among pastoralists like Cunningham, the alleged lack of sexual attractiveness in indigenous women negated their gender and humanity. The Occidental world assigned such little value to women whose sexual attractiveness and reproductive function was perceived as having "expired" that they were regularly deemed useless and represented as figures of fun when they were represented at all. This pattern of cultural treatment of older women still predominates in Occidental culture. Yet the devaluation of older women contrasted dramatically with the attitude in indigenous societies, where old age was respected and old people were considered powerful, as they were repositories of knowledge. Occidental culture, by contrast, valued nubility in women, especially in colonized women, above all else.[54]

The Enlightenment stereotype of the Pacific woman as a mother in nature was rapidly overshadowed by the fetishization of the sexually available indigenous woman. This eighteenth- and nineteenth-century Occidental culture, despite the pronatalist edicts of social theorists, valued youth, beauty, and sexual attractiveness in women and spurned those who exhibited the bodily effects of childbearing. The Pacific muse reflected these concerns as well as those of the imposed colonial economies in which women's bodies were viewed as items of trade.

Pacific Women, Power, and the Body Politic

Beauty in women in the late eighteenth and early nineteenth centuries, adduced by the representations of Pacific women, centered on the body, an obsession that has not waned with time. Beauty in the female body was an orderly body, a body that was minimalist, childlike, and "close to the bone." The female body represented disorder, as it was an aberration of the standard human form, the white male body. Yet a slim female body signified containment of this corporeal disorder. A contained female body, particularly with the aid of garments to refigure the body into more "aesthetic" shapes, was a mark of status for European women. Noble beauty was synonymous with bodily constraint. This notion of feminine beauty stood in diametric opposition to ideas of feminine beauty and female status within some Polynesian societies wherein corpulence signified status and power. Occidental representations of chiefly women of Polynesia, who were literally "noble" within their societies, were not represented within the female noble savage convention by Occidental observers owing to their body shape. Politically pow-

erful women in the Pacific embodied the perceived physical grotes-
querie of women in the public realm. Occidental discourses consistently held that only "unnatural," masculinized, and unvirtuous
women would enter the public realm. That is, political power could
not coexist with femininity.[55]

The contrast in representations of noble savage women and that
of chiefly women, often described as "queens," is demonstrated in
the illustration from the La Billardière account of this late-eighteenth-
century Pacific voyage titled *Dance of the Friendly Islands, in the presence of Queen Tiné* (fig. 4.5). The young Tongan dancers are depicted
in the classical tradition in their draped clothing and their distinguished, graceful postures and fine-limbed, shapely bodies. However,
Queen Tiné's "extraordinary" corpulent figure and age, "at least fifty
years of age," set her outside of the feminine ideal. Her maternal
bosom, heavy arms inelegantly arranged, and closely cropped hair
"cut to the length of about two inches and a half" designate this
"queen" as a parody of the regal refinement expected of Occidental
royal women. General D'Entrecasteaux's refusal to accept Tiné's invitation to sleep in her house, unlike Banks's famous dalliance with
Queen Oberea, prompted La Billardière to remark, "I do not imagine that the old lady had any other intention, than to procure him a
more pleasant and healthy residence." La Billardière's comments
were spiced with the amusing possibility of Tiné's unwanted sexual
advances toward the commander.[56]

Hawaiian queens and *kuhina-nui* likewise were often depicted
in a mocking tone, owing to their fleshy bodies and their perceived
comical adaptation of European women's clothing. This stood in
opposition to the power that these revered women had within their
own societies, as Hawaiian historian Lilikalā Kame'eleihiwa, has
shown.[57] The visit of King Kamehameha II and Queen Kamamalu
to England in 1824 evoked shrill expressions of white racial superiority. This was nowhere better exemplified than in the account of
courtier Mary Berry, who attended a function for their "savage
majesties" hosted by Secretary of State George Canning. Kamamalu
was the subject of the closest scrutiny and the strongest attacks by
her harsh observers. Miss Berry recounted of the May reception that

Dance of the Friendly Islands, in presence of the Queen, Tiné

Pub.^d by J. Stockdale, Piccadilly, 14.th April, 1800.

4.5 *Dance of the Friendly Islands, in the presence of the Queen Tiné*, 1800.
Frontispiece, Jacques-Julien La Billardière, *Voyage in Search
of La Perouse 1791–1794*, London, John Stockdale, 1800.

Mr. Canning entered, "giving his hand to a large black woman more
than six feet high, and broad in proportion, muffled up in a striped
gauze dress with short sleeves, leaving uncovered enormous black
arms, half covered again with white gloves." Kamamalu's clothes were
also a source of derision, as was her short, uncurled hair, for Miss
Berry. The queen and her lady in waiting, who had "a gayer and
more intelligent countenance," were soundly inspected, so much so
that Miss Berry was moved to remark that "one should have pitied
them for the way in which all eyes were turned upon them." She concluded, however, that such charity was unwarranted, as "it seemed

to me that their minds are not sufficiently opened, and that they are not civilized enough either to notice or to suffer from it." If this were the case it was fortunate, as Kamamalu and her female companion were slighted in every conceivable way that English good breeding would permit. The Hawaiian women's decision to remain apart on this occasion, however, suggests that they possibly were well aware of the ill will of their hosts. Another guest on this occasion, a Mrs. Arbuthnot, was no less scathing in her report of Kamamalu. She reported that "the King was nothing remarkable, but I feel convinced that the Queen is a man in woman's clothing. She is six feet & a half high, immensely broad, & thick about the waist; in short, shaped exactly like a man."[58]

George IV, who was not present on this occasion, reputedly reacted to the prospect of receiving Kamehameha and Kamamalu "as if I would sit at table with a pair of d—d cannibals." The English press were likewise hostile toward the Hawaiian party, "charging them with being gluttons and drunkards," and their visits to the British Museum and the Drury Lane's Royal Theatre were widely reported. The ridiculing representations of the Hawaiian royal visit to England were overshadowed by Kamamalu and Kamehameha both contracting measles and dying within two months of Canning's reception.[59]

Similarly, Russian Captain Otto von Kotzebue was not so critical in his remarks upon the body of aliʻi Nāmāhana, who was then governor of Oʻahu, appointed by her sister aliʻi nui Kaʻahumanu. Kotzebue found Nāmāhana's countenance "prepossessing and agreeable." He described her in 1824 as not older than forty, six feet two inches tall, and "rather more than two ells in circumference." The culturally relative notions of female beauty manifest in body shape provoked Kotzebue to comment that "Nāmāhana thought people too thin . . . On the Sandwich Islands a female figure . . . of immeasurable circumference is charming." Meanwhile, a European lady who wished to "touch" men's hearts had to undergo considerable discomfort as she "laces tightly and sometimes drinks vinegar" to achieve the desired aesthetic of physical fragility.[60]

The appropriation of European dress alone was by no means

sufficient to ennoble highborn indigenous women in the eyes of Occidental observers. Such status required strict adherence to the conventions of body reshaping and attention to other details of feminine appearance and deportment. Powerful Hawaiian women such as the kuhina-nui Kaʻahumanu and Kinaʻu, whose girth was often a point of interest, were revered and courted by the American missionaries in the islands, because their influence depended upon these women. Missionary power was greatly enhanced when Kaʻahumanu converted to Christianity in 1825. Transient observers had no need for such diplomacy.[61]

Jacques Arago, the artist on the second Freycinet voyage, which visited the Pacific in 1819, was not reticent in ridiculing highborn Hawaiian women. His first encounter with noble women was with the wife of the Honolulu governor and her sister, who "excited" his astonishment at their size but were "only miniatures." "Many instances were necessary" he wrote, "before I could be convinced that, in this country, such repulsive masses of fat could be regarded as the greatest beauties." These regal women did have some redeeming qualities for Arago. They were "familiar," though not with that "air of licentiousness which characterizes the women of the lower classes." They allowed themselves to be "freely handled" and they also had hands "so fine that it would be rare to meet with any better."[62]

Arago was far less generous in his descriptions of the five widows of Kamehameha I. He represented them as resembling a "hippopotamus," and more like "shapeless masses of flesh than human figures." He described Tammeamaroo (Kaʻahumanu) as the "smallest" of the five at "30 stone." Despite her "prodigious" fatness, Arago found her face "interesting" and her "manner very engaging." After "longer observation," he wrote, he could understand "the strong attachment that Tammeamah [Kamehameha] had for her." Arago's curiosity was aroused by her very elegantly tattooed "legs, the palm of her left hand and her tongue," and the self-inflicted marks of mourning for Kamehameha on her body. Russian voyager Louis Choris depicted a half-naked and amply proportioned Kaʻahumanu in 1820 (fig. 4.6). Choris drew attention to her size by placing a servant man beside her to fan her. The man's body is dwarfed by the magnitude of Ka'ahumanu. Apart from the presence of the servant in this image, there is no evidence of any devices from the Occident's visual lexicon to convey female nobility. While her face is serene, her bodily size was anathema to the ideal of delicacy that was desired in women. She appears a formidable figure of Pacific nobility, but not sexually attractive or available.[63]

Of all the highborn Hawaiian women that he encountered, Arago was most taken with Kaou-Onoé. He described her manners as "childish, soft and even simple; which in her is not unbecoming." Her

4.6 Jean-Pierre Norblin de La Gouraine d'apres Louis Choris, *Reine Cahoumanou (Ka'ahumanu)*. From *Voyage Pittoresque Autour du Monde*, Paris, De L'Imprimerie de Firmin Didot, 1822.

Reine Cahoumanou

greatest recommendation was that she had generous affection for those strangers who "pleased" her and "examined" them with "her pretty hands." In return, these strangers "were allowed to judge for themselves the elasticity of her bosom and the fineness of her skin." Regardless of her regal status in Hawai'i, Arago believed that Kaou-Onoé would have been willing to grant the "last favour" to European men. This perceived sexual accessibility to a royal woman and the deference she showed to Arago and his companions charmed him immensely. So great an impression did the young Kaou-Onoé make upon Arago that he wrote, "I would strongly recommend to strangers who go to Owhyee, and wish to pass some agreeable moments there, to get acquainted with this interesting female."[64]

As we have seen, missionaries began having a noticeable impact upon the cultures of Hawai'i and Tahiti in the 1820s, which was achieved through the conversion of chiefly men and women. The conversion of these chiefs was not an ideal arrangement for missionaries in many cases, as these rulers imposed regulations upon the lower orders of their populations but often did not observe new moral codes themselves. Also, many chiefs used the missionaries for their own pragmatic purposes. Ka'ahumanu, for instance, treated Sybil Bingham as one of her retinue of servants, calling upon her to make clothes and be available for other purposes upon demand.[65] Missionaries across the Pacific bemoaned this invidious situation they had to endure at this time when their continued presence in the islands relied upon the good graces of indigenous rulers. As the axis of power began to shift in the Pacific from the late 1830s, when Britain and France sought formalized imperial links through protectorates, indigenous chiefs met these colonial power challenges by imbibing European trappings of noble refinement that lent a modern and civilized face to indigenous rule. This evolution was most marked in Hawai'i and Tahiti.[66]

Natural Nobility in the Age of Victoria

As missionary contact began to have an impact on Pacific societies, with their emphasis on female morality coupled with British diplomatic and cultural allegiances, Pacific queens in Hawai'i and Tahiti increasingly fashioned themselves upon the young queen Victoria. The Victorian model of noble womanhood rejected the past aristocratic excesses and immoralities that were associated with European monarchies and embraced the middle-class ideal for women to be wives, mothers, and "angels of the house." While Victoria was a very powerful woman politically, her style of rule was portrayed as an extension of her "natural" domestic duties and not a corruption of her preordained womanly role. That is, she operated in a public world that was reconfigured as "a domestic nest." Victoria followed the lead of her uncle, William IV, and aunt, Queen Adelaide, who ascended to the throne in 1830 and were celebrated as "bright models" for the middle classes, as Lenore Davidoff and Catherine Hall have demonstrated. This gave her public power legitimacy, as it accorded with the dictates about how a woman could operate within the body politic while maintaining her virtue that were established by the political discourses of the French Revolution and were adopted in England and beyond.[67]

For Pacific queens, this adaptation to a Victorian appearance, which symbolized the transformation to Christianity, modernity, and virtue, also lent legitimacy to indigenous rule, which was being challenged by colonial powers. For Queen Pomare of Tahiti, her resemblance to Victoria was a factor in the Anglo-French controversy of the 1840s that became known as the "Tahiti Affair." A series of French naval officers began inveigling themselves into Tahitian politics from 1838 with the aim of dismantling the exclusive LMS missionary presence on the islands and supplanting British cultural, political, and diplomatic influences. In 1842 Queen Pomare was compelled to sign a document in dubious circumstances making Tahiti a French protectorate. Pomare was duped by leading chiefs, and the French admiral Abel Du Petit Thouars and Jacques Antoine Moerenhout, a Belgian "merchant adventurer" who acted as U.S. and then French consul on Tahiti. The circumstances surrounding Pomare's fateful signing of the document were made all the more outrageous, to her supporters, as she was heavily pregnant at the time and was sup-

posedly threatened with a French naval bombardment by Moerenhout if she did not comply.[68]

After this, successions of wrongs were perpetrated against the
young queen by the French in the eyes of her LMS missionary supporters and their numerous and politically active congregations in
England. These wrongs culminated in the queen's deposition in 1843
and the annexation of the island to France. This precipitated a colonial war lasting until 1847, when Pomare returned from exile, was
restored to her throne, and accepted the French protectorate. From
1843 to 1847 LMS supporters vigorously lobbied the British government to pressure King Louis Philippe to reverse the belligerent
actions of his agents in Tahiti.[69]

Within the LMS campaign the character of the young queen was
central. The LMS stressed that in the half century that they had been
active in Tahiti they had transformed the island from the idolatrous
place that scandalized Christians following the reports from the early
voyagers to an "improving" people "just adopting the forms and insti-
tutions of European civilization." Queen Pomare was emblematic
of this transformation in the same manner as Queen Oberea had epitomized its decadence in early contact history. A slew of publications
appeared during these years emphasizing the queen's similarities
to the young Victoria, to whom Pomare wrote often during the time
of political flux, appealing for the assistance of her "sister queen."
Pomare was whitened in these representations, literally and metaphorically, as her Christian virtue and maternity were used to legitimate her continued rule. Pomare also styled herself to comply with
a queenly image acceptable to Britain.[70]

The zenith of this campaign was marked by two visual images.
The first, which appeared in the *Illustrated News* in 1844, showed
Pomare as a churchgoing mother as "Queen Pomare with her husband
and children, going to church in Tahiti" (fig. 4.7). The second, and
widely disseminated, image by LMS artist George Baxter was titled
*Pomare, Queen of Tahiti, the Persecuted Christian Surrounded by Her Family
at the Afflictive Moment when the French Forces Were Landing* appeared in
1845 (fig. 4.8). In this portrayal, the crowned Pomare, baby in her

lap and surrounded by other children and her ennobled, anglicized husband, gazes heavenward while the French troops land on the beaches below. Baxter did not shy away from depicting Pomare as a South Seas Victoria or Madonna and child, endowing her with the ample bosom and majestic disposition akin to that epitome of feminine virtue. The LMS missionary malcontent John Orsmond claimed that this portrait was condemned by other missionaries for its lack of realism and being a too overt allusion to Victoria. He also claimed that even Pomare "scoffed" at the likeness.[71] Yet the LMS publication *Missionary Magazine* lauded this portrayal of "the exiled and homeless Sovereign of Tahiti . . . as a correct transcript of the original."[72]

4.7 "Queen Pomare with her husband and children, going to church in Tahiti." *Illustrated News*, 1844. With permission from the National Library of Australia.

4.8 George Baxter, *Pomare, Queen of Tahiti, the Persecuted Christian Surrounded by Her Family at the Afflictive Moment when the French Forces Were Landing*, 1845. With permission from the National Library of Australia.

In stark contrast to the image of Pomare promoted by the LMS, other sources cast dire aspersions upon her. As I have argued elsewhere, these negative portrayals derive from two missionaries, the aforementioned Orsmond and William Crook, and also the highly partisan Moerenhout, whose ethnographic writings had a disproportionate impact upon subsequent representers of Tahiti, especially those from France, such as Paul Gauguin.[73] These three put about rumors that Pomare was anything but a paragon of feminine virtue, claiming that she drank and, worse still, had syphilis. While Pomare did not comply with the narrow band of characteristics of feminine virtue put forward by the LMS, and in her youth she had indulged in the Tahitian cultural revival akin to the arioi, her story was far more complex than these sources and the many historians who have accepted their vision of Pomare will allow.[74]

Contemporary observers of Pomare read her body for clues to her character. Charles Darwin observed in 1835 that she, then aged twenty-two, was "a large awkward woman without any beauty, grace or dignity," and her only "royal attribute" was a "perfect immoveability [*sic*] of expression under all circumstances" that he thought "sullen." Walter Brodie, who observed Pomare while in the islands in 1841, thought that Pomare was "still good-looking" at age twenty-eight but was "rather stout." It was thought that she had given birth to five children by this time. Herman Melville, who claimed to have arrived at Tahiti at the time of Du Petit Thouars's protectorate in September 1842, portrayed Pomare in *Omoo: Adventures in the South Seas*. He introduces Pomare sympathetically, though in passing, as the victim of intimidation by the French following the declaration of the protectorate, but when he discusses her directly toward the book's conclusion, he relates scuttlebutt about her, declaring "the reputation of Pomare is not what it ought to be." She was "always given to display" and "previous to her misfortunes she spent the greater portion of her time sailing about from one island to another attended by a licentious court." The most lurid account of Pomare involves "a conjugal assault and battery" made upon Pomare by her husband Ari'ifa'a'ite a Hiro.[75]

This spectacle of the brawling royal couple was embellished with the claim that Pomare was "something of a Jezebel" in her private life, though in her public role she was supposedly "lenient and forbearing." The narrator, Paul, finally lays eyes on the queen after being permitted into her house. When she appears, she is barefoot and "not very handsome; her mouth, voluptuous; but there was a care-worn expression in her face, probably attributable to her late misfortunes."

When she caught sight of the unwelcome foreigners she "seemed surprised and offended and . . . waved us out of the room."[76] Melville's depiction of Pomare is probably drawn from his imagination, with details gleaned from other published accounts. His image of Tahiti's sovereign befits his overall portrayal of the island as one in decline owing to drunkenness, smallpox, elephantiasis, and the "virulent disease which now taints the blood of at least two-thirds of the common people of the island."[77] Some young women who complied with the myth of nymphlike Tahitian women were excepted from his melancholy representation of Tahitians at the time of French takeover.

For all the conflicting representations of Queen Pomare, the stress on her Christian virtue during the "Tahiti Affair" did not ameliorate her colonial predicament. Though she was restored to her throne in 1847, she complained in 1851 to the French president that she was "a stranger in my own land, my word is useless it is of no value."[78] LMS missionary Thomson concurred with this new status quo in the French protected Tahiti, writing that Pomare was now "a queen without power."[79] Though the tactic of appropriating a Victorian appearance and attitude did not yield the desired results for Pomare in Tahiti, Hawaiian queens increasingly adopted this queenly mode from 1854 when Queen Emma, wife of Kamehameha IV, came to the throne. Her choice to fashion herself on Victoria reflected her British education and heritage (her father was English) as much as the favorable treatment Britain received in political affairs.[80]

Queen Emma did not rule in her own right, so this "self-fashioning" in the image of Victoria, as Robert Bott described it, had limited political potential. This was not the case for her rival to the throne Liliuokalani, who came to the throne in 1891, succeeding her brother Kalakaua. Like Queen Pomare's colonial predicament fifty years earlier, Liliuokalani's short reign was fraught with problems of American disaffection for monarchy coupled with *haole* planter desire for power, which resulted in her overthrow in 1893.[81]

During the five-year period between her overthrow by the haole oligarchy and the annexation of Hawai'i to the United States

4.9 *Her Majesty Queen Liliuokalani*. Frontispiece, Liliuokalani,
Hawaiʻi's Story by Hawaiʻi's Queen, Boston, Lee and Shepard, 1898.

in 1898, Liliuokalani campaigned for her restoration. She combated images of her in the United States as a pagan and a "black savage." Liliuokalani also had to challenge the widely held belief that her people were dying out, while as a monarch she represented an outmoded and old world political order. As in numerous other colonial circumstances, colonists stressed that the passing of indigenous peoples along with their political and social arrangements was inevitable. An indigenous government led by a woman provided even further justification for the demise of a Hawaiian-ruled Hawai'i.[82]

Liliuokalani attempted to supplant these race-based images of her through emphasizing her cultivation, which included her "superior command of English," music, and letters. She was considered by some to be the "best educated woman in Hawaii" and possessed a regal serenity and appearance that was considered "handsome" in her fifties.[83] Her main vehicle for her political legitimacy, which was coupled with Hawaiian rights, was her book, *Hawaii's Story by Hawaii's Queen*, first published in 1898. The image of her in the frontispiece to the book shows how closely she styled herself upon Victoria in her jewelry, rich gown, and pose, but most important in terms of the iconography of Victoria was her maternal bosom and hips (fig. 4.9). Unlike her regal model, Liliuokalani did not have children, but she nevertheless conveyed maternal care over her Hawaiian people. Like Pomare, she pleaded for assistance from Victoria, her "sister sovereign," though Britain did not intervene on her behalf.[84]

The strategic importance of Hawai'i to the United States only grew after 1893 following the Spanish American War and the U.S. acquisition of the Philippines and Guam. Coupled with the haole political influence in Washington, Liliuokalani's best efforts to preserve the self-determination of Hawaiians came to nothing. As Jane Desmond shows, in the "new" American Hawai'i, the hula girl rapidly increased in prominence. Thus the depoliticized colonial stereotype of the Pacific muse supplanted politically powerful, older indigenous women as emblems of the Hawaiian islands.[85]

We have seen in this chapter how feminine ideals across the nineteenth century shifted from noble savage women in the Pacific to the white ideal of Victoria. Scientific race theories and Christian missions left little space in which indigenous peoples could be viewed as models of humanity. At the beginning of the century, Pacific women were admired for their skills as natural mothers by armchair travelers. By century's end, it was the colonial culture derived from actual voyaging that elevated the stereotype of the sexually accessible woman to the center of the colonial gaze. Through this transition of feminine ideals from natural mothers to replicas of Victoria to sexually accommodating island girls, we have tracked the shifts in ideas about women and the body politic, as well as the imperial politics related to ruling women in the Pacific. In the following chapter we shall see that with the erosion of Victorian moral values and race theories in the twentieth century, Pacific women returned as exemplars for white femininity, though more along the lines of the island girl, Pacific muse stereotype. Also, as the Pacific shifted from the periphery of the imperial gaze to its center, owing to economic, military, and cultural shifts, the Pacific muse became increasingly visible in colonial culture, though simultaneously more trivialized, as we shall see.

V

From the 1890s
to the Present

By the turn of the twentieth century, with only very few instances to the contrary, the world was carved into empires governed by a handful of imperial European nations. The effects of imperialism were evident globally. In the Pacific, only Tonga remained unannexed by a European power, although it became a British protectorate in 1900. Britain's strategic and commercial interest in the region had been increasing since 1788, when the Port Jackson colony was established, and fanning out to other points on the Australian mainland and Tasmania, ensuring her exclusive control of the massive continent and surrounding islands. From Australia, British annexation extended to New Zealand in 1840, Fiji in 1874, and the southeast quarter of New Guinea in 1884. In 1892, Britain declared a protectorate over the Gilbert and Ellice islands, and New Zealand acted as Britain's imperial agent and annexed the Cook islands and Nuie in 1899, bringing immense territorial control to Britain in the region.

Britain's imperial competitors in the Pacific came from traditional quarters: France, Germany, and the United States. France's formalization of interest increased from the 1840s, with the Marquesan and Tahitian islands being annexed and made a protectorate, respectively, in 1842, as we have seen. French interests in the western Pacific were solidified by the annexation of New Caledonia in 1853 and the Loyalty Islands in 1864, with both France and Britain establishing a joint condominium over the New Hebrides in 1887. German interests were relatively late but nevertheless extensive: the northeast quarter of New Guinea, the Marshall and Solomon Islands in 1885, the Northern Marianas and German Samoa, both in 1899. The United States, although it had rejected imperialism beyond the Americas for more than one hundred years and had upheld the Monroe Doctrine in an attempt to curb European imperialism in the Americas, became acquisitive in the Pacific with the annexation of Hawai'i in 1898. The one-sided Spanish-American War brought the Philippines and Guam as spoils of war to the United States in 1898, and the annexation of eastern Samoa followed in 1899.

Until the Japanese defeat of Russia in 1905, which shattered the "legend of white invincibility" and tore apart "the veil of prestige that draped white civilization," Pacific peoples were dominated by Europeans. As white nations grew in power, Pacific populations reached their lowest numbers for the colonial period, seemingly fulfilling predictions that they were dying races. After disease, the most pernicious effect of colonialism at this time was the labor trade. By the turn of the twentieth century, measures had been implemented, however uneven across the region, to regulate recruitment and lessen its worst excesses. These had been widely publicized, particularly in the British controlled regions in the 1870s and 1880s, by humanitarians concerned that a system of slavery was operating in the islands controlled by nationals of new liberal democracies. The plantation structure of the Pacific economy transformed islanders into laborers. Though men were more highly valued as workers, women were still drawn into the plantation machine and its culture. The plantation system had its most drastic impact on the western Pacific islands of Melanesia, but the need for labor transformed colonial relations throughout the region. Strategic imperatives replaced economic ones only with the territorial expansion of Japan following the redistribution of the German empire after the Treaty of Versailles. Japan's continued quest to expand erupted into the Pacific War in 1941 followed by its Cold War and atomic-testing aftermath.[1]

The sustained analysis of race in nineteenth-century social sciences increased the imagined divide between civilization and savagery. This divide was reinforced materially by imperialism at its zenith. Conceptions of gender and sexuality had likewise undergone closer definition bolstered by the late-nineteenth-century advents of psychology and sexology. These new paradigms for evaluating humanity solidified long-standing class and race constructions inherited from Christianity and Enlightenment sciences that were in turn heavily informed by the classical Greek tradition, as we have seen. These combined discourses had numerous consequences. For our purposes they exaggerated the gulf between white men and women and their exotic counterparts.

Paradoxically, while Pacific peoples endured the yolk of plantation-based colonialism, the Occidental quest for worlds untouched by the effects of modernity and civilization boosted the fantasy of a Pacific paradise. Like the explorers and romantic travelers to the Pacific we have already examined, a new generation of writers, artists, pleasure seekers, and investigators of the human condition looked to the Pacific for inspiration at the end of nineteenth century. Yet what they were seeking was now almost impossible to find, if indeed it ever existed. The stark contradictions between the imagined and the colonized Pacific seldom failed to jar those who made the journey to seek the Pacific firsthand. Some reworked the tradition of representing the Pacific accordingly. Others did not, instead rendering the most exotic images of the Pacific to date. Despite these conflicts within the cultural production of the Pacific, the stereotype of exotic femininity not only prevailed but reached new levels of visibility and potency. The various reasons for this outcome are outlined here, commencing with the artist Paul Gauguin, whose vision of the Pacific has cast an enduring shadow on all that followed.

An Artist in the Empire and His Muses

From his first view of Tahiti, Paul Gauguin was disappointed. The island he "burned" to reach failed to live up to its mythic reputation of ineffable grandeur, and the legendary women of Tahiti also left him underwhelmed. He wrote that "this small island" to a "man who has traveled much" was not a "magic sight." Not only was the island itself less than spectacular when compared to the bay of Rio de Janeiro, but the women of Papeete, renowned for their unfettered sexuality, were cloaked, literally and metaphorically, in the garb of Christianity. In the retrospective account of his early days in Tahiti, *Noa Noa*, Gauguin described a group of women in the funeral procession of King Pomare V. He died a few days after the impoverished artist reached the French-ruled kingdom in 1891. Gauguin attempted to undress the women of their impure trappings of imperialism, their clothing, to locate the sexually overwrought bodies that to him represented the essence of his imagined Tahiti. He wrote of "their breasts leading and the conical shells which tipped their nipples drawing the muslin of their dresses to a point." They possessed "all the suppleness and grace of a healthy animal" and spread around them a mixture of "of animal scent and of sandalwood and gardenias."[2]

Like so many Occidental voyagers before him, Gauguin lusted for the mythologized halcyon days of Tahiti encapsulated by Bougainville. At first he was lacking any substantial knowledge of Tahiti, but what loomed largest in his imagination was a place of tropical fecundity, feminine beauty, and sexual emancipation that waited for immortalization. Gauguin's Tahiti was confected by more than a century of Occidental travel literature, anthropology, and art and half a century of photography. From the 1880s, Gauguin's formative artistic years, the long-standing South Seas myths woven from the earlier phases of colonization were revived and embellished for a popular audience of readers with a fresh interest in the empire.

One Gauguin biographer, Bengt Danielsson, argued that Gauguin may well have gained his education in Pacific mythology from the Parisian Universal Exhibition in 1889. Yet Danielsson argued that

Gauguin would not have been satisfied with the women on display, as the "specimens of the celebrated *Vahines tahitienes*" were "married women of impeccable morals" and "not the young, beautiful and seductive naiads one would have expected." Rather, Danielsson continued, they were "middle-aged matrons more remarkable for corpulence and ugliness than anything else." Though this display left much to be desired, Danielsson contended that Gauguin could have seen official publications, produced by France's Colonial Department in the same year, that milked the myths in the hope of luring travelers and migrants to France's imperial outpost. These brochures noted that a "Tahitian woman is usually a perfect model for a sculptor." Although her "features can occasionally be a little too Malayan," these racial traits were negated by "her large, dark eyes, so wonderfully fine and clear, her almost excessively full lips, and her marvelously white teeth" that rendered her "so sweet and innocently voluptuous." Her physical embodiment was completed with a classic rendition of exotic noble savagery á la Voltaire: the handbook concluded that Tahitians only knew "life at its brightest" and "for them, to live is to sing and love."[3]

Though numerous scholars have speculated about the sources of Gauguin's interest in the Pacific, it is clear that he was seduced by the promise of an Arcadian paradise.[4] Before making the voyage to the South Seas, Gauguin wrote of his expectations to his Danish wife, Mette: "May the day come — perhaps soon — when I can flee to the woods of a South Sea island, and live there in ecstasy, in peace and for art." He dreamed that "there, in Tahiti, in the silence of the lovely tropical night, I can listen to the sweet murmuring music of the heart, beating in amorous harmony with the mysterious beings of my environment." His reverie was completed by his expectation that this new island life would also include "a new family" and the freedom from "this European struggle for money."[5]

Gauguin was one of a long line of artistic voyagers who used the colonized world to fire their imaginations and provide intrigue, inspiration, and interest for an Occidental audience. The final choices to locate Gauguin's "Studio of the Tropics" were either Tahiti or Madagascar, where he intended to develop his own distinct artistic style and subject matter in the tradition of recent compatriots such as Ingres, Gérôme, and Manet, whose work composed the core of late-nineteenth-century Orientalist art. In 1887 Gauguin visited Martinique, where he had produced art that evoked his overtly sexualized gaze upon the feminized dark races of "paradise" by aligning lush vegetation, tropical fruits, and naked, dark-skinned females with superstitious ways.[6]

Gauguin transposed this exotic vision to Tahiti and incorporated and embellished the disparate elements of the Occidental representative traditions of the Pacific with the concerns of modernism. Modernism's preoccupation with the primitive, on one level, reflected the influence of Freud, who stressed the need to study "savages" in order to locate "our untamed selves, our id forces—libidinous, irrational, violent, dangerous." On another level, the primitivist concerns resonated with the classical influence in the movement. The classical concept that particularly attracted modernists, as it had romantics a century before, was that of a pastoral idyll of a people existing in a childlike state of nature. The recently developed discipline of sexology questioned the nature of sexuality, asking whether it was innate or learned. This increased the demand for accurate, scientific studies of primitive or nonevolutionary peoples who served as the basic building blocks for these theories. In this climate, anthropology became professionalized and reified. Photography and the work of artists such as Gauguin gave a visual dimension to the circulating ideas at the end of the nineteenth century.[7]

As in earlier eras, the interest in primitivism in the late nineteenth century had not only a racial dimension but also a gendered one. The modernist movement was often described as "misogynistic," a term that Gauguin used himself when corresponding with friend and playwright August Strindberg. This stance clashed with the contemporaneous first wave of the feminist movement, with its concerted effort to end male privileges. The movement attempted to dismantle constrictive Victorian expectations upon women by fighting for suffrage, educational and professional opportunities, and economic independence from men. In these social and political struggles, the female body was strongly contested ground. The sexualized female body, a common subject for the modernist artists, was often portrayed as an object of fear, suspicion, and loathing, while simultaneously configured as an object of desire. This vision collided with the feminist quest to institute women's autonomy and independence from men at all levels, especially in the sexual realm, by challenging heterosexuality and marriage as compulsory destinies for women.[8]

In this context, representations of Pacific women in the fin de siècle of the nineteenth century acted as a conservative antidote for the first wave of feminism, just as they had one century earlier. Starkly opposing those who agitated for widespread restructuring of society along gendered lines, native women were characterized as given over to their natural domesticated roles, animalistic sexual drives, and subservience to the male sex. The intersection of race with gender seemingly diminished the danger indigenous women posed to white men. The colonial gaze was shaped by discourses that denigrated and infantilized those with brown skin. Brown skin signified sexual saturation without the same devouring and emasculating propensity of white women.

Gauguin revived early contact fantasies by breathing a modernist life into them. This struck a deep chord within popular Occidental culture, resulting in Gauguin becoming a supernal artist, albeit posthumously, and his Pacific images being revered. Gauguin was affected by modernist ideas about primitivism as much as he espoused the irreconcilable contradiction concerning women in that he simultaneously venerated and feared them. He wrote of his first encounter with his first Tahitian bride, Tehaurana, who became known as Teha'amana, "that girl . . . enchanted me and scared me . . . the mocking, though tender lip showed clearly that the danger was for me not her."[9]

In stark contrast to the perfect bodies of the young women who dominated his imagination then, Gauguin was a very sick man when he reached the Pacific. He was infected with syphilis so advanced that in November 1891 he began coughing blood and experiencing severe chest pains, an indication that he had entered the secondary stages of his affliction and was still highly infectious. Gauguin's illness plagued him all his time in the islands until syphilitic coronary

complications finally killed him in 1903. This condition did not temper his hunt for sexual adventure. *Noa Noa* is laden with Gauguin's
search for sexual partners whom he deemed the least civilized.
Finding a less civilized woman meant searching for partners with
less sexual experience; thus he conflated the "primitive" with "the
child." In his writings he revealed not only this desire but also his
hope that women he saw would be "willing to be, in a word, taken:
crude capture," that was a "longing to rape," but he was too timid
and lethargic to effect this craving.[10]

Gauguin's attitude to the Pacific women he intimately encountered has given rise to vibrant scholarly debates. These debates reflect
the gender and race politics of Gauguin's day as well as postcolonial and feminist concerns of the late twentieth century. Did Gauguin
consider the women, or more correctly girls, he encountered to be
"aesthetic commodities," as Griselda Pollack argued? Or did he in
fact "love" his muses in what Danielsson euphemistically termed
"anthropological" love, that is, love that could exist only in the empire
and was not transferable to Occidental realms? Was it sexual relations with men he sought over those of women? His art, his writings, and his history in the islands are so "richly contradictory" that
biographers who revere him, and postcolonial and feminist scholars
who attempt to modify his cultural stature, all find evidence supporting their positions.[11]

For the purposes of this study we are examining how Gauguin
aided the increasing prominence of the Pacific muse stereotype,
which he undoubtedly did. In terms of the history of this colonial
icon we have examined so far, what is inescapable with Gauguin is
how he legitimized his access to and portrayal of young girls through
his conceptions of race. His experiences were the epitome of the enviable "sexual tourist," who openly lived out the sexual fantasy of his
artistic images.[12] There were a number of Tahitian girls who were
Gauguin's muses during his Tahitian and Marquesan years. They
were Teha'amana, Pau'ura a Tai or Pahura, Marie-Rose Vaeoho, and
Tohotaua. Interactions between male artists and their muses often
involved a sexual relationship. This relationship was complicated in
the colonies. Gauguin intended his Tahitian muses to meet all his

needs — sexual, aesthetic, and domestic — while remaining pliant and undemanding of him. It was a relationship that was exploitative, reflecting colonial gender and racial status quo. Yet these girls associated themselves with him, at times "with some alacrity." On the islands, young women were permitted to be with Gauguin. Also, these young women did not always comply with his expectations that they would be passive and obedient, and left him when they so desired. Yet, his relationships were aligned in his favor, an impression he himself propagated as a man comfortable with his colonial privileges.[13]

Forty-three-year-old Gauguin described his first muse, Teha'amana, "a child of about 13," as his "little mistress with the instinctive ways and the golden body" and who was "docile and loving." He painted her in a number of works, most famously in *Spirit of the Dead Watching* (or *Manao tupapau*). As Griselda Pollack has shown, this painting was dubbed the "brown Olympia" when exhibited in Europe in 1893 (fig. 5.1). Like Olympia, Teha'amana was pubescent, but more shocking to conservatives and exhilarating to libertines was the overt suggestion that both women were sexually experienced. Gauguin inverted Edouard Manet's famous image circa 1863 in several ways apart from substituting Teha'amana's brown skin for Olympia's luminous white skin. First, the body is turned over, increasing the vulnerability of the posture by fully exposing the buttocks. The exposure of the buttocks signified the bestiality of the subject, signifying her primitiveness.[14]

Gauguin explained the positioning of Teha'amana in a matter-of-fact tone to Mette in 1892. He wrote that in this position she was "indecent." "Yet, I wanted her that way . . . one of our own young girls would be startled if surprised in such a posture. Not so a woman here." In a notebook he wrote for his daughter, Aline, he contradicted this reason for positioning his model this way. He knew how this image of "a nude Kanaka girl" would be interpreted, that she was either "preparing herself . . . for lovemaking" or "that she has had intercourse," both of which "answers well to her character." For his daughter, however, he claimed that these ideas were "indecent" and the decent explanation for her positioning was "fear." One may speculate on Gauguin's motivation in making such claims to his daugh-

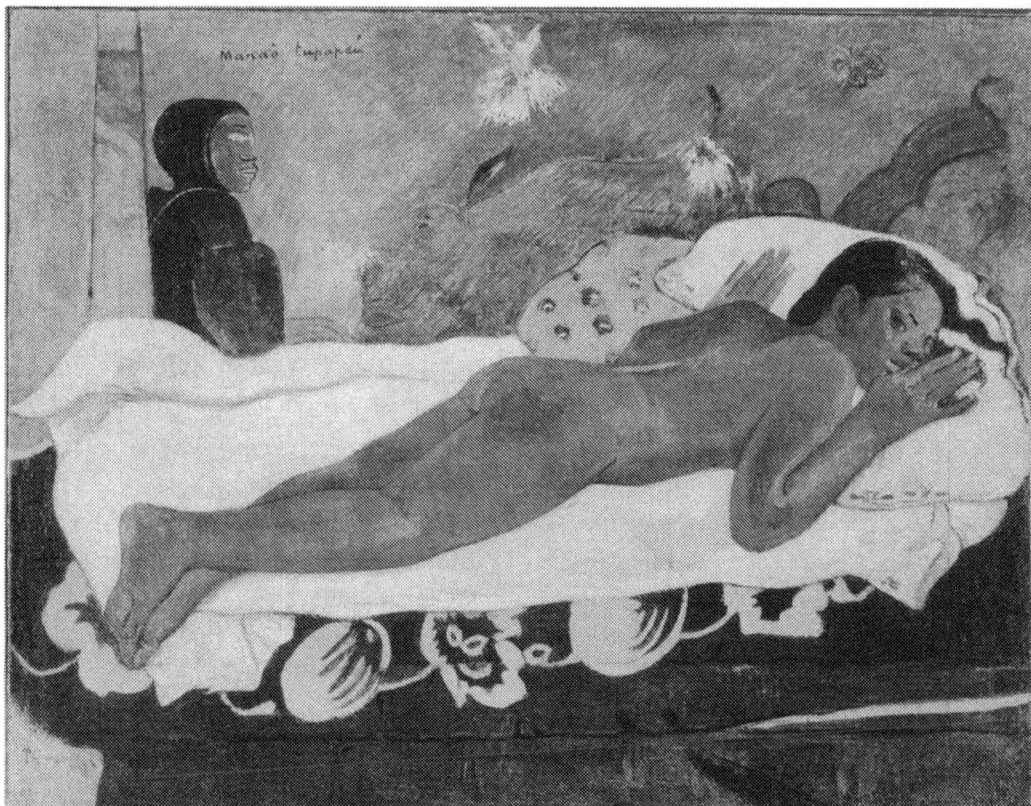

5.1 Paul Gauguin, *Spirit of the Dead Watching—Manao tupapau*, 1892, oil on canvas. With permission from Albright Knox Art Gallery, Buffalo, New York.

ter. His concern for "decency" in representing his naked subject was out of character for Gauguin, who flaunted his libertine lifestyle and his strenuous disregard for any moral dictates. For the historian however, his defense indicates he well understood what the manipulation of the female body and race indicated.[15]

After Gauguin returned to Tahiti in 1896 he married Pahura, then aged fourteen. Although older than Gauguin's so-called optimum age of thirteen, she was considered still "young enough to fulfill his long-held fantasy" for thirteen-year-olds, according to David Sweetman.[16] Their time together was marred by the now forty-seven-year-old Gauguin's medical condition, which saw him hospitalized midyear for "ulcerous legs and buttocks." For Pahura, Gauguin's disease touched her life through the death of their baby daughter, who lived for only a few days in December 1896. The baby's cause of death, though it cannot be confirmed, may have been congenital syphilis inherited from her French father. The birth and the aftermath of the death of the baby girl inspired two works, *The Birth of Christ* and *Nevermore*, the latter becoming another of Gauguin's famous Pacific nudes (fig. 5.2). In comparison, *Nevermore* is not the "deeply moving portrait" of the young mother in the grip of grief at the loss of her firstborn. Instead it resonates with the composition of *Manao tupapau*. The predominant figure is a young, supine naked female form laid across a bed, with ghostly spirits and "the bird of the devil" behind her, which she watches out of the corner of her eye. The bird is a direct reference to Edgar Allan Poe's raven in his poem of the same name. As with the portrait of Gauguin's former spouse, *Nevermore* is charged with sexuality from the very posture of the naked brown body, notably with pubic hair painted in, a rare addition in the tradition of the female nude, heightening the animal sensuality of the reclining subject.[17]

In spite of what these portraits suggest, Tahiti was unable to quench Gauguin's desire for unrefined savagery. Aware of his immi-nent death, he wrote to his friend Charles Morice in July 1901 informing him of his plans to move to the "cannibalistic island of the Marquisas." He hoped that once there "in savage surroundings, com-plete solitude will revive in me, before I die, a last spark of enthusi-asm which will kindle my imagination and form the culmination point of my talent." Leaving Pahura and their new son, who was named Emile (as was his son by Mette), Gauguin arrived in Hiva Oa in September 1901. Here he built his legendary house christened *Maison du Jouir*, "The House of Pleasure," or as Sweetman translated the name, "The House of Orgasm." He plastered the walls with pornographic images that were supposed to entice prospective sex-ual partners and models to enter. Gauguin's presence on the island incited the wrath of Monseigneur Martin, the Christian guardian of the island, who perceived the artist as a serious threat to the moral and physical hygiene of his flock. As had been the case on Tahiti,

5.2 Paul Gauguin, *Nevermore*, 1897, oil on canvas. The Samuel
Courtauld Trust, Courtauld Institute of Art Gallery, London.

Gauguin flaunted his amoral lifestyle, adamant that the local cler-
ics would not interfere with his right to unchecked sexual pleasure.
Gauguin focused his attentions upon the girls of the nearby convent
school and remained a menace despite marrying for the third time
in November 1901.[18]

His last wife, fifteen-year-old Marie-Rose Vaeoho, bore a daughter, Tahiatikaomata, in September 1902 but was not immortalized
by her spouse in any artistic works. She was given a sewing machine,
but her domestic duties were lightened by the employment of a cook
and gardener owing to the Hiva Oa economy making little demand
on Gauguin's meager funds. Gauguin's favored muse on Hiva Oa
was Tohotaua, a married young woman, who possessed a physical
curiosity — red hair — that fascinated the artist. Tohotaua featured in
a number of his Marquesan works, particularly the portrait *Woman
with a Fan*, which was painted from a photograph in which she wore
a dress. Gauguin's distortion of the original image of Tohotaua from
clothed to half naked reflected his desire and artistic prerogative to

portray her not as she was but rather how he wished her to be, that is, untouched by the moral weights of civilization.[19]

Like other leading men of culture of his time, including Oscar Wilde and his friend August Strindberg, Gauguin was a recalcitrant, antiestablishment figure, and not a person who fits easily into colonial categorizations. He was a contradictory figure. On the one hand, he was an authoritative voice for the imperial attitudes of the age, a quality gained from his life as an Occidental male on the frontier. On the other, when on Hiva Oa he was regularly locked in battle with the French authorities and championed indigenous people's rights. He celebrated his "going native" as an extension of libertinism, rather than as a sign of his degeneration into a "second rate white man" eschewing the growing discourse on the deleterious effects of the tropics on the white racial character. His lack of respect for authority and his wish for personal autonomy sat alongside his misogynistic and colonial attitudes.[20]

Gauguin's visual and written work reflects his adherence to a potent mix of race ideology and modernist gender politics. His portrayal of the eastern Pacific in the form of a languishing exotic body coincided with the ultimate age of imperial self-confidence when every island and continent was controlled by Occidental powers. This overriding imperial power fed into every interaction between colonizers and colonized and was evident in Gauguin's many intimate relationships while on Tahiti and Hiva Oa, where he died in 1903.

Arguably Gauguin's most significant legacy is what his experience on Tahiti and Hiva Oa and his vision of the Pacific came to represent after his death. His view of the South Pacific was more complex than just that of languishing exotics. However, it was his images of sexual young women that have become his most famous and the most clichéd images of the desired South Pacific since. Once Gauguin's art gained a reputation, his vision became a representative scorched earth, obscuring all that came before it and leaving a mark on all that succeeded it. Gauguin quickly became an icon of Occidental culture. His paintings reflect more upon the gender, race, and imperial politics of the Occidental world than they show the actions and works of one individual.

The Serpent in Paradise: Race Anxieties and the Pacific Muse

The height of imperialism, the labor trade, supporting race doctrines, and the growing strategic importance of the Pacific had immense implications for representation of the region, as we have seen through reviewing the work of Gauguin. He captured the essence of imperial desire in the Pacific. His work also marked the shift from the Pacific being at the periphery of the imperial gaze to being at its center. Combined with the beginnings of tourism and the rising popularity of beach culture after World War I, the Pacific appeared with more frequency in postcards, souvenirs, and advertising. It was the figure of the sexually accommodating island woman that was most often used to familiarize the Pacific to its new audiences. The pedigree of this leitmotif extended back to antiquity, as we have seen. Yet in the dramatically altered relationship between the Occident and this imperial zone in the twentieth century, the figure of the Pacific muse reigned as the voluptuary female figure of the century.[21]

We have seen that Gauguin did not encounter paradise, but he consistently presented as much on his canvases. Other artists who were lured to the ocean by expectations similar to Gauguin's were not able to ignore the lack of romanticism in the Pacific they encountered. Robert Louis Stevenson's descriptions of the islands became quotable quotes encapsulating the hackneyed myths. Yet his South Pacific stories published in the 1890s revealed the darker sides of colonization. The story *Beach of Falesá* added an element to the South Sea romance. It spoke of race politics and, like another of his short stories, *The Ebb-Tide*, portrayed the ugliness of imperialism in stark realism. Similarly, Jack London homed in on the proliferation of disease and the corruption of paradise in his stories. Louis Becke, the Australian supercargo turned writer, likewise portrayed the Pacific as a corrupted paradise. His 1895 novel, *His Native Wife*, explored the effects of the tropics upon whiteness, coupling island romance with degeneration, violence, and alcoholism, as did many of his other stories. Becke's Pacific was a deeply troubled one, replete with the contradictions of tropical beauty and the imposed labor culture that made savages of the white men who oversaw it.[22]

The serpent in paradise that these late nineteenth-century writers identified, miscegenation, affected subsequent portrayals of colonial relations in both Polynesia and the western Pacific islands of Melanesia. Colonialism in the western Pacific had been relatively limited, compared to the islands of Polynesia, until the close of the nineteenth century. The first wave of colonization in Melanesia was shaped by intense racial paranoia and the harsh indentured labor system. Coupled with these conditions, the colonial vision of the western Pacific had always differed from the east in that these inhabitants were categorized from the earliest encounters as "hard primitives," that is, having an excess of masculinity and "African" racial features. There had been no period of romanticization of cross-cultural sexual relations in this region of the Pacific. Many colonizers were confused about the cultural differences, imagined or actual, between these two Pacific groups, as Margaret Jolly has shown. Many thought the Polynesian-based colonial myths embodied in the Pacific muse related to all peoples of the region.[23]

One such mistaken colonist was Robert Fletcher. The Oxford-educated Fletcher had been lured to the Pacific in 1912 by Stevenson's letters, which praised Polynesia, particularly Samoa, only to find himself part of the brutal plantation system in the New Hebrides. He wrote two books about this experience. The first, *Isles of Illusion*, was a series of candid letters he wrote to a friend in England that were published in 1923. In *Isles of Illusion* he deplored his part in the brutalities of the plantation economy in which he worked as an overseer and lay doctor. Moreover, he expressed his self-loathing for succumbing to physical and moral degeneration when "he took himself a native woman," Onéla Kohkonne, whose age he estimated as "only about fifteen," in 1916. He proceeded to father children with her. Fletcher told his friend of the sexual permissiveness of the islands in classic South Sea terms and often conflated the Polynesian and Melanesian Pacific. However, his familiarity with contemporary race ideologies in all their harshness arose when he broached the subjects of the perceived childlike intellect of Onéla and his contempt for his own offspring. He estimated that "his little brown woman" and her peers had the mentality of "four year old white children."

He considered her body beautiful "in its doll-like tininess" and her devotion to him most affecting: "she behaves to me like a very nice Persian kitten or terrier pup."

Island life allowed Fletcher to adopt different standards, but, he asked his friend, "do you think I could tolerate her in civilisation? Not for a week." Fletcher, in spite of himself, had great affection for his firstborn child, yet, owing to his racial anxieties, expressed relief to his friend Bohun Lynch when the second child died. It is these anxieties that underlie the gruesome conclusion of *Gone Native*. In that story the central white male character, George Donaldson, rejects the opportunity to marry the daughter of a white mission-ary, whom he found sexless. Instead he "went native" and married an island woman, Ouéla Kokhon, whom he renames Topsy and with whom he had a child. At the story's conclusion he chooses to make himself a redemptive sacrifice to sharks, atoning for his wrongs to his race and in the process saving his island child. Miscegenation resulted in individual and racial death, according to the contempo-rary race politics, a view to which Fletcher subscribed. The dire results of white men living on islands was underlined in the fron-tispiece to the first edition of *Gone Native* (fig. 5.3).[24]

The rambling yarn of trader Tom Richards, *White Man Brown Woman*, first published in 1932, contained similar fears about the mix-ing of blood in the islands. Unlike Fletcher's experience and story, Richards lived in Mangareva in the Tuamotus, in the Polynesian Pacific. Richards relays his father's stern warning about giving in to the wiles of the island girls, which he subsequently ignored. His father asked him "to promise . . . that you will never marry a woman with dark blood in her veins." He has "seen too many cases where a young man has become infatuated with a pretty face and eventually mar-ried the girl" and then "realized she lives in another world to his." "She may be able to speak perfect English," he continued, "but her whole outlook is native, she cannot discuss the problems of her life with him or be anything more than a physical companion, her native blood will always predominate, she will seek the companionship of others of dark blood." Richards does ignore this dire warning and builds a life on the islands with his islander wife and family. Although

5.3 Frontispiece from *Gone Native* by Robert Fletcher,
Boston, Small, Maynard & Co., 1924.

he dedicates the book to "his native woman and children" and others, he apologizes for his decision. "Sheer force of circumstance has made me take a native woman for a companion" once his endeavor to "hold a white woman's love was a ghastly failure." "Now I am a human derelict, who has made an unholy mess of his life, the least I can do is to stay by the native woman who has mothered my children, and who adores me as an Island woman can."[25]

In contrast to this parallel tradition that was testing South Sea myths, the paradisiacal Pacific became more and more visible. The increasing popularity of Gauguin's art aided this change. He was not long dead long before the panegyrizing about his life commenced. His friend and constant correspondent, Charles Morice, published *Paul Gauguin* in 1903. While the works of Matisse and Picasso "shocked the viewers," Gauguin's Tahitian nudes struck an immediate chord with the popular audience.[26] In 1919 the British author Somerset Maugham published his novel *The Moon and the Sixpence*, which amplified the sexualized aspects of the Gauguin story into a popular legend. Maugham transformed Gauguin into the British bohemian artist Charles Strickland and forgave him all his less becoming personal traits, such as the abandonment of his European wife and family because of his artistic genius. Maugham indulged in the fantasy of the colonial man's sexual adventure on an island filled with mistresses with "little golden bodies." Tahiti was immediately appealing to the Gauguin character, for the island "is smiling and friendly . . . like a lovely woman graciously prodigal with her charm and beauty." In addition to the lusciously feminine landscape, he described the flora and buildings and the "flamboyants" as flaunting "their colour like a cry of passion," and "sensual with an unashamed violence that leaves you breathless."[27]

The generically luxurious Tahitian woman in this novel was directly juxtaposed against the impenetrable white woman, the wife of Captain Nichols. Maugham described Mrs. Nichols as "a woman of about twenty-eight," though she could have been forty. Unlike Tahitian women, "she gave me an impression of extraordinary tightness." Every feature suggested her sexual repression: "her plain face with its narrow lips was tight, her skin was stretched tightly over her bones, her smile was tight, her hair was tight, her clothes were tight." Strickland could not "imagine why Captain Nichols had married her, and having married her why he had not deserted her." Maugham grasped a central tenet of Gauguin's images of Tahitian women; their appeal stemmed from their difference from the Victorian white wife. Gauguin's images that gained the greatest currency in popular culture after his demise were the ones that fused ethnography, pornography, and art. These paintings, along with ethnographic photography, literature, and later cinema, fundamentally undercut Victorian sexual dictates and challenged young white women to shed the "tight" Victorian ideal and transform into a Pacific exotic.[28]

The Pacific Muse in Early Cinema

For all the power of Gauguin's frozen moments of colonial erotica, cinema eclipsed his work as a conduit of the Pacific muse, though his influence remained evident. Charles Chauvel, the preeminent Australian filmmaker from the 1930s to the 1950s, for instance, cited Gauguin as a foremost figure in the genealogy of representers of the Pacific along with the fabled eighteenth-century voyagers.[29] Cinema took the current ideology promoted by social scientists and artists and injected these ideas into popular culture, most often via Hollywood. Cinema was a particularly cogent vehicle for colonial discourses, because it was able to shift and emphasize aspects of the gaze. It could reflect stereotypes through living images and it created an illusion of intimate, "natural perception" in the viewer. Film was like a "magic carpet ride," as Robert Stam and Louise Spence described it, that could fly the viewer around the globe and imbue the viewer with a sense of mastery over the subject. The industry fed upon popular culture and reshaped popularized prejudice in order to create characters and scenarios with which the viewer could identify. Cinema relied upon extant colonial stereotypes but gave them, and their accompanying insidious ideas, attitudes, and interactions, a greater, normalized life.[30]

Cinema was a commercial industry based upon representation.

The product on the big screen was but one dimension of the industry. In its entirety, cinema distilled all the issues of race, gender, economics, imperial agendas, sexuality, and colonial fetishization as they related to the Pacific's indigenous women. These categorizations determined how on- and off-screen employment was allocated. Once in front of the camera, race and sex were again at work informing decisions about which bodies and which parts of bodies required focus, the extent of exposure, and in what ways characters should be portrayed that would ring true to a mass audience. The long-standing connections between race and representation of women flowed into the film industry, which adopted disparate codes of decency based upon the criterion of skin color. Through the lens of the film-camera, a whole new world of possibilities for presenting an old imperial gaze was now practicable.

The pioneers of this new medium were anthropologists who purported to have the "evidential gaze" of ethnography. Like Wallis, Bougainville, and Cook, these pioneers left their indelible mark on all that followed. Their vision of the Pacific was what their successors, in the majority of cases, would attempt to emulate.[31] The distinction between ethnographic documentaries and fictional films has never been clear cut. The structural anthropologist's supposedly clinical gaze was as wedded to race and gender ideologies and the yearning for peoples arrested in the childhood of humanity. Likewise, documentary filmmakers overtly indulged in the conflation of an imagined past and present for the sake of audience titillation. The overarching importance of commercial viability also shaped ethnographic films so that they would appeal to a popular audience.[32]

In 1926, the Canadian filmmaker Robert Flaherty, with the assistance of his wife, Frances, complied with similar forces in their representations of the Pacific. The Flahertys were fascinated with the notion of supposed purity of the "primitive" and prior to their foray into the Pacific had sought other indigenous subjects from all parts of the globe, such as the Inuit and Aran Islanders. Their 1926 film, *Moana: A Romance of the Golden Age*, set on the Samoan island of Savai'i, was, however, funded by Paramount Studios, which greatly influenced the end product. Flaherty's filmic Samoa was prefaced in the opening titles with the information that this was "British Samoa, the mandate of New Zealand." His aim, however, was to present an "authentic" precontact tableau, which required altering what he saw in favor of what complied with the modern romantic yearning for the lost golden age. The Flahertys totally obscured the all too apparent imperial presence with their lens, and instead filmed "the drama of Samoan life as it rolled itself naturally before us, as far as possible untouched by the hand of missionaries and the government."[33]

The writings and photographs of Robert Louis Stevenson, among the first to use photographic cameras to document his travels, formed the primary basis of the Flahertys' imagined Samoa. Stevenson's vision was introduced in the titles with his words "the first love, the first sunset, the first South Sea Isle," inviting the viewer back to an imagined past. A pivotal detail necessary in creating this illusion was that the film's participants had to reluctantly shed their European dress in favor of superseded island dress. For the majority of the cast this entailed wearing *tapa*. Portraying an "authentic" Fa'angase, the young lover of Moana, involved voyeuristic close-ups of her bared breasts. In one scene, strongly reminiscent of a Gauguin painting, she reaches up to a tree to pluck its fruit. In the closing scene, Moana and Fa'angase are depicted preening their bodies with oil and flowers for dancing. After this preparation, they dance. Paramount wished to capitalize upon the overt exoticism and eroticism of the portrayal of Samoa. The film was initially released as *Moana: The Love Life of a South Sea Siren*, ignoring the fact that Moana was male. For its subsequent screenings, the film was called *Moana: A Romance of the Golden Age*, a title laden with modernist yearning for a gilded classical past.[34]

Flaherty was associated with two other films that perpetuated similar visions of Polynesia: *White Shadows in the South Seas* (1929) and *Tabu* (1931), which he wrote, but which were directed by Fredrich Murnau. *White Shadows* was based on the 1919 novel of the same name by popular writer Fredrick O'Brien. This book was an indictment of the French imperial presence on Tahiti, à la Gauguin, but also served as a vehicle for colonial stereotypes. *Tabu*, like *Moana*, presented a South Sea romance between Matahi and Reri, played by "native born South Sea Islanders," although it was noted that some of the cast were "half-castes and Chinese." The Bora Bora society portrayed in *Tabu* differed markedly from the Savai'i depicted in *Moana*. Rather than a resounding endorsement of Samoan society, *Tabu* presented reservations about the primitive condition. The images of luxuriant, paradisiacal land and seascapes populated by naked, sporting youths were juxtaposed against cruel, malevolent chiefs who enforced superstitious laws and hierarchies. Reri was of royal blood and deemed *tabu*, or inaccessible, to Matahi. This ultimately led to the separation of the young lovers and the death of Matahi. This presentation of ignoble savagery embodied by male chiefs would feature in future films, carrying with it messages about the stark contrasts between civilization and savagery, as we shall see.[35]

At the time the Flahertys were making their pioneering ethnographic romances of the Pacific, Western culture was reeling from the horrors of World War I. The Pacific, with the exception of quick and contained naval actions against German imperial outposts in 1914, was protected from the apocalyptic events occurring on the other side of the world. The fallout from this epic event exacerbated existing fears about race, gender, and sexuality in three apparent ways. First, the cultural conditions that produced the yearning for untouched paradises, free from the ills of modernity, were now more urgent than before. In addition, the war induced questioning about who was savage and who was civilized after Europeans inflicted such horrors upon each other. And third, the war also unleashed serious fears that the white race was doomed and that "colored" people were on the verge of overrunning them.

In the Pacific region, these fears were directed at Asia. Unlike the Pacific islands, Asia was teeming with "effervescent" and industrial peoples. The Pacific islanders were not only far less numerous, particularly after the devastating influenza epidemic of 1918, but were considered "lethargic" and doomed. Nevertheless, they were still the source of growing racial anxieties. These were most strongly enunciated in eugenic science and in turn in popular culture, as Fletcher and Richards' autobiographical writings attest. These two effects of the war both strengthened the Pacific as the site of earthly paradise and corrupted it, especially in relation to sexual contact with indigenous women.[36]

Whitening the Pacific Muse

As distaste toward cross-cultural sexual relations was becoming more evident after WWI, white women began to appropriate what they considered desirable in the Pacific exotic. This trend echoed the fashion of the Pacific a century earlier in the Romantic era. Now it operated with far greater and long-lasting valence. In the late nineteenth century, and even more so in the post–WWI years, advertising companies entered the arena as arbiters of feminine ideals. Advertising worked in collusion with cinema to promote a fashionable, sexually liberated young woman. This further undermined Victorian morality in the interwar years. From the 1920s, fantasies of sexually knowing white women, embodied in the flapper, were conflated with colonial fantasies of Pacific women.[37]

Cinematic representations of Pacific women fed the escapist fantasies of Occidental audiences, imbuing them with current pedagogical and political agendas of the time. They conveyed not only cultural curio in a kinetic medium, but also didactic messages for spectators of both genders. As cinema has been overwhelmingly obsessed with youth and beauty, young women were required to play the narrow band of roles that could be categorized as the pretty love interest in the predominating genre of Pacific-based films, the South Sea romance. In the plethora of such films, white or South American actresses have been the preferred choice to portray the "Hollynesian," a Hollywood-styled Pacific muse of no consequential geographical location, as Richard Barsam described this figure. Yet the "Hollynesian" was whitened to ease race anxieties.[38]

From the beginnings of the Hawaiian film industry, the practice of casting white actors as indigenous women was evident. Actress Virginia Brissac imitated the colonial fantasy of a Hawaiian woman in two films in 1913: *The Shark God*, set in "pre-missionary

Hawaii," in which Brissac played the chief's daughter who was involved in a love affair; and *Hawaiian Love*. A reviewer wrote at the time, "Miss Brissac . . . portrays the Hawaiian character charmingly."[39] American Betty Compson played a "half-caste" Hawaiian in the 1923 film *The White Flower*. The publicity for the film teased that the swimsuit-clad Betty would be seen "riding the surf" and "shocking us all with her hula." This film was the subject of *Time*'s first film review. According to Robert Schmitt, the review displayed a distinct unease with the film's themes of race and sex, describing it as "another of those Hawaiian pictures concerning a beautiful half-caste with too many beaux of different shades of pigment."[40]

The exotic dances of the Pacific, which had figured so strongly in the colonial imagination since the Enlightenment, remained a fascination, as Jane Desmond has shown regarding the hula. Film provided the means to display indigenous dance, which has long been considered erotic and indecent, in motion, complete with bodily revelation, gyrating hips, and other sexually overloaded movements. The dance sequence became a principle scene that not only functioned as a central "geographical signifier" of the Pacific and savagery, but also allowed for exposure of the female body in the throes of an erotic dance disguised as being of legitimate anthropological interest, as in Flaherty's *Moana*.[41]

In Paris, Josephine Baker had made her debut in Paris at the Folies Bergère in 1925. Dancing topless in her famous banana skirt in the *Revue Négre*, which was supposed to represent "Negro" culture in America, Baker instead conjured up the fabled South Seas and the jungles of the Congo, as Phyllis Rose has argued. Baker's more explicit performance harked back to France's eighteenth-century mythologizers of the Pacific, Bougainville and La Pérouse, for the show's reviewers. It transported them on an imaginary sexualized exploration of the tropical empire, in the style of Gauguin, without the need to physically endure the rigors of travel. While Baker was initially a Paris-based phenomenon, her rapid rise to fame reflected the ardor across the colonial world for the exotic. Baker's show was the risqué end of the spectrum of fashionable theatrical presentations of the Pacific. Plays and musicals first appeared in the early years of the twentieth century. By Baker's time, musicals such as *Bird of Paradise* and *The Adorable Outcast* were enjoying long-standing popularity among audiences.[42] Also songs like *My Little Bimbo Down on the Bamboo Isle* of 1920 celebrated the fabled sexual ease of Pacific island girls, as did its cover design (fig. 5.4).

In representations of island culture, dance was the supreme moment of sexualized primitivism. Similarly, dance was the hallmark of sexually liberated white women in the 1920s. Conservatives viewed flappers as aping the "lascivious" dances of African Americans, though Polynesian cultures were also fused into this expression of women's sexual liberation. In the 1927 film *Hula*, Clara Bow starred as Hula Calhoun, the flapper who "went native," which meant she swam "in the altogether"; wore a grass skirt, a lei, and an exposing top; and, as would be expected, danced the hula. The film begins by setting the scene as "a Hawaiian isle — a land of singing seas and swinging hips where volcanoes are often active and maidens always are." Hula's permissive family of gamblers and drinkers allow her great freedom, which includes close relations with Hawaiians, especially the older male character of Kahana. In one character's estimation, Hula's contact with the Hawaiians made her "become as primitive as they are." In order to attract the attention of the stilted English engineer Anthony Haldane, with whom she falls in love, she upstages Hawaiian women at a lu'au and "shows them what my name means" and dances a caricature of the hula. Her methods work, and the enraged Haldane seizes her and declares, "I can't stand seeing the girl I love going to the devil." Hula then transforms into a delicate white woman to fit her relationship with Haldane, and her hula days are over. Although Clara Bow did not have the complete set of typical physical attributes of the Pacific muse — long hair and tanned skin are absent from the configuration — popular understandings about Hawaiian women's culture and sexual prowess were central to this film's narrative.[43]

The other highly significant innovation in the history of the Pacific muse in the 1920s was the publication of Margaret Mead's anthropological study of adolescent Samoan women's sexuality, *The Coming of Age in Samoa*, in 1928. The twenty-three-year-old Mead,

5.4 Cover illustration for the song and music for *My Little Bimbo Down on the Bamboo Isle*, 1920. Words by Grant Clarke. Music by Walter Donaldson. With permission from Rare Book, Manuscript and Special Collections Library, Duke University.

who had read stories by Maugham, based herself on the American Samoan island of Tau for her fieldwork. Mead, whose anthropological work was framed by psychology and sexology, aimed to investigate the "extent the storm and stress of adolescence in our kind of culture is biologically determined and to what extent it is modified by the culture within which adolescents are reared." Using her sex as a means to gain the confidence of young women, Mead claimed to have found a society in which young girls enjoyed secret sexual freedoms. She concluded that cultures, and not nature, shaped sexual behavior. She showed that it was possible to have a sexual utopia where freedom reigns for both men and young women and thus she wanted her book to serve as a blueprint for modern American society to rethink attitudes to adolescence and sexuality for girls.[44]

Despite its more complicated intents, *Coming of Age in Samoa* opened new realms of sexual fantasy for the Occidental readership. So too did Bronislaw Malinowski's *The Sexual Life of Savages*. Malinowski's ethnographic fieldwork in the Trobriand Islands was informed by sexology. In his preface to the book, leading sexologist Havelock Ellis highlighted how "sex and the Pacific have been a constant fascination since the Enlightenment voyagers but these Europeans were incapable of understanding them and they had no time to penetrate the surface." Ellis was partially right, as it was the eastern Pacific islands that had fascinated European voyagers, while the Trobriand Islanders in Melanesia had not, until this time in history. Meaningful investigations of sexual cultures were only now possible Ellis went on, owing to new understandings brought to light by modern social scientific inquiry, allowing the "right questions" to be posed.[45]

The fascination with sexual practices and social arrangements that undermined strict Victorian regulations only increased, finding its greatest expression in the mass youth movement promoting "free love" after World War II. Mead and Malinowksi's studies of Pacific cultures became benchmarks for alternatives to Victorian sexual organization. For some key writers of postwar feminism, such as Simone de Beauvoir and Germaine Greer, for whom the issue of female sexual liberation was paramount to social liberation, the representations derived from these ethnographers' work were of great interest. Mead's writings were crucial for supporting arguments for white women's sexual emancipation, causing her to be dubbed "the mother of the sexual revolution."[46]

Mead's work demonstrates that fetishization of Pacific women's sexuality was not the preserve of men. Women influenced by the feminist movement looked back both to classicism and to "primitives" for "naturally occurring" examples of female sexual emancipation, thereby constructing a counterdiscourse to the restrictive Victorian conceptions of femininity. Mead actively explored the possibilities of "going primitive" herself, transforming her appearance by wearing indigenous dress. Images of her posed as a "native" form part of the vast retinue of photographic images, numbered at fifty thousand, she made as part of her studies. White women were complicit in the processes of perpetuating colonial fantasy, albeit in greatly divergent degrees to men, as the notion of empire increasingly provided the means for liberated women to push the boundaries of discourses on femininity and forge modern identities.[47]

The Pacific Muse with Censorship and Speech

Two changes that altered the cinematic medium immeasurably, and directly influenced representations of indigenous women, were censorship and sound. The early years of film had been quite risqué, promoting the freer sexual culture of modernism. By the 1930s, U.S. authorities were making a concerted effort to curb this coercive medium by imposing censorship regulations. Sexual references, bodily revelation, and other profane subjects, such as miscegenation, were expurgated from the early 1930s to the mid-1950s. These laws affected decisions to set films in the non-Occidental world Ella Shohat has argued. An Oriental setting, albeit a studio replica of one, whether it be the Near East, Africa, or Latin America allowed a "narrative licence for exposing flesh without risking censorship" or less censorship, as often happened. White- or brown-skinned women of southern European or Latina descent playing exotic women neutralized the anxieties generated by the common narrative of love across racial divides.[48]

The advent of the talkie in 1929 added a new realm to assist in the development of racial and gender hierarchies already prevalent in cinematic portrayals of Pacific women — she would be allowed to speak after more than a century. It is a telling detail that Murnau's *Tabu* was a film kept silent at the time that sound technology was available. Giles Deleuze has contended that this decision was premised upon a desire to maintain the innocence of natives, who were often imagined in a prelinguistic state, communicating instead through movement and emotions. This had particularly been the case with imagining colonized women.[49]

Now that she could talk, what would a Hollynesian be allowed to say? Such a question, along with the issues of censorship, can be explored through the portrayal of Luana by Mexican Delores Del Rio in the 1932 film version of *Bird of Paradise*. The storyline is strikingly similar to that of *Tabu* as well as to the great tale of love across racial divides: Puccini's *Madame Butterfly* of 1905. Here the high-born Pacific princess falls in love with an American, Johnny Baker, who sails into the waters of Luana's island on a pleasure cruiser. This film begins with the all-important arrival scene that was a constant feature in this genre of films. This scene is so important because it acted as the cinematic device that immediately juxtaposed the two widely divergent cultures: the Americans with their trappings of civilization and the Pacific islanders arrested in their precontact state. Johnny's encounter with Luana begins when she saves him from a shark. She emerges from the waters and chatters animatedly to the American, like the exotic bird of paradise that she is, and the two fall instantly in love. Against the warnings of the malevolent medicine man, Luana pursues Johnny by swimming naked to his ship at night. Johnny joins her and with the help of strategic use of light and shadow to hide the most private bodily parts, the viewer sees the rest of her. The two emerge from the water and Johnny tackles her, but she resists until he gives Luana her first kiss. Luana points to her lips and begs for more. The suggestion here is that her previous experience of sex with island men is brutal and rapacious, a common element of primitive male stereotypes, as we have seen before with European assessments of "primitive love rituals" in the early 1800s.[50]

The contrasting sexuality of the American and island men is explicitly portrayed when Luana is presented to her betrothed island husband in a frenzied night ceremony. She is stripped to her skirt, with a only a lei attached to her breasts, and is forced to prostrate herself before him and then dances for him in tears. Johnny rescues Luana and they escape to a neighboring island, where he builds a house and, without instruction, she carries out the domestic, nutritive duties. Her other main occupation is watching the volcano, Pele. Her native superstitions are articulated in pidgin English: "Pele get angry," and "I must be here if Pele call." To these statements Johnny replies, "You belong to me now . . . I'll take you to civilization where we don't have crazy superstitious ideas, where people are accomplishing something."

After Luana and Johnny are captured by the island men, who intend to kill them, the American crew intervene just in time and take both to the ship. The sailors discuss whether Luana could "adapt" to life in the United States. One sailor opines that "if Johnny came home with a native wife it'd break his mother's heart." Luana is then shown in the ship's kitchen and is totally lost trying to find Johnny a glass of water. This scene suggests that in America she would only be able to perform her sexual functions: domesticity would be impossible and reproduction undesirable. The film ends with Luana giving herself up to face volcanic sacrifice in order to save Johnny from the death curse placed upon him. As in the opening scene, Luana, the pan-Polynesian girl, instinctively values the American man's life far more than she does her own. Also, the film carries the message that love across such a racial divide can only be fleeting and full of dire consequences.

In addition to the impact of speech and censorship through films, the demise of the flapper in the 1930s resulted in actresses being styled in what would become the classic Hollynesian configuration — young, slender, long lustrous hair, decorated with flowers, an inviting smile, and increasingly tanned skin. Actress Dorothy Lamour fit this character type and developed this role in the numerous films in which she starred, including *The Hurricane* of 1937, in which she played Marama.[51] Gene Tierney also fulfilled a classic rendition of the Pacific muse on film in the 1942 film *Son of Fury*. Beginning in "early nineteenth century" urban England, the film purported to retell the true story of Ben Blake, an illegitimate son of an aristocrat who is ill-treated by his avaricious uncle and deprived of his birthright among British nobility. Blake escapes by going to sea and deserts ship in the opposite world of Polynesia, with its palm-lined beaches and happy population. The crude comparison between the mean metropolis and the Pacific paradise was extended to the two female characters: a scheming aristocrat who feigns love in order to exploit Blake further, and the "beautiful Polynesian girl" played by Tierney. When Blake first sees her sitting on top of a rock in classic mermaid pose, and unable to make her say anything he can understand, he says "I think I'll call you Eve." After their first kiss, Eve moves into Blake's house and commences domestic chores of her own volition. When Blake expresses his surprise at his new acquisition to a fellow beachcomber, he receives the reply, "You looked at her; that's as good as asking."

Eve gives Blake herself in every feminine way, and in return Blake gives her and her people technological advancement. He teaches her English by scrawling words in the sand, beginning with "love." When the difference between earth and sky is too much for Eve, she exclaims, "Me stupid!" and when she struggles in vain to use a knife and fork, she again exclaims, "No, I'm too stupid." The fantasy of the docile, devoted Polynesian woman is summarized by Eve telling Blake to return to England and not worry about her: "I can only be happy if you are happy."[52]

Tierney's Eve drew upon the long-standing traditions of exotic femininity, incorporating all the tropes of female sexuality, paradise, and Milton's "masterpiece" of Eve, as described earlier. This Eve also embodied the particularly desirable traits of an exotic — docility and an innate knowledge of how to be domesticated as well as sexually alluring to her white man. She is classically perfect. She has long, flowing hair, smiles often, and is regularly adorned with flowers. Yet love does not last across racial divides; it is fleeting and cannot be sustained.

Casting, Race, and Romance

Occidental male and female fantasies of the *other* were realized time and again in film. Despite the prevalence of the stock figure of the Pacific muse in Occidental cinematic output across the twentieth century, very few indigenous actors played such roles after the early "ethnographic" films. There were notable exceptions before the shift in the 1960s toward employing indigenous actors who fitted the part. Australian filmmaker Charles Chauvel resisted the fashion of Hollywood of the time by employing Tahitian women to play the seductive women who lured the British sailors to mutiny in his *In the Wake of the Bounty* of 1933. This decision was not without its problems. Chauvel wished to promote the same thesis for the mutiny as that provided by Captain Bligh, writing that "I place the softness of Tahiti and its women first among the elements which caused the mutiny of the Bounty." In order to make this point quite plain to the viewer, Chauvel included explicit scenes of a smiling woman emerging from vegetation bare-chested and arms outstretched toward the newly arrived British vessel, women running sirenlike to the water, swimming and sitting on rocks, and a predatory, serpentlike woman sliding onto and, ultimately, seducing Christian (fig. 5.5). A promotional poster for the film encapsulated the drama of the mutiny by claiming that "each sailor kidnapped a South Sea Maiden and disappeared from civilization for over twenty years," therefore tingeing the seduction thesis with violence, an accurate portrayal of this historical event, as we have seen earlier. Along with depiction of the violence, the explicit sexual display, by the 1930s standards, caused problems with film censors, as Stuart Cunningham has shown. Chauvel attempted to sidestep the censorship regulations by making the film appear to be a documentary.[53]

Chauvel did not attempt to assign individuating characteristics to any of the "dusky maids"; he had no leading ladies or close-ups of faces, but presented images of bodies in grass skirts and leis, with

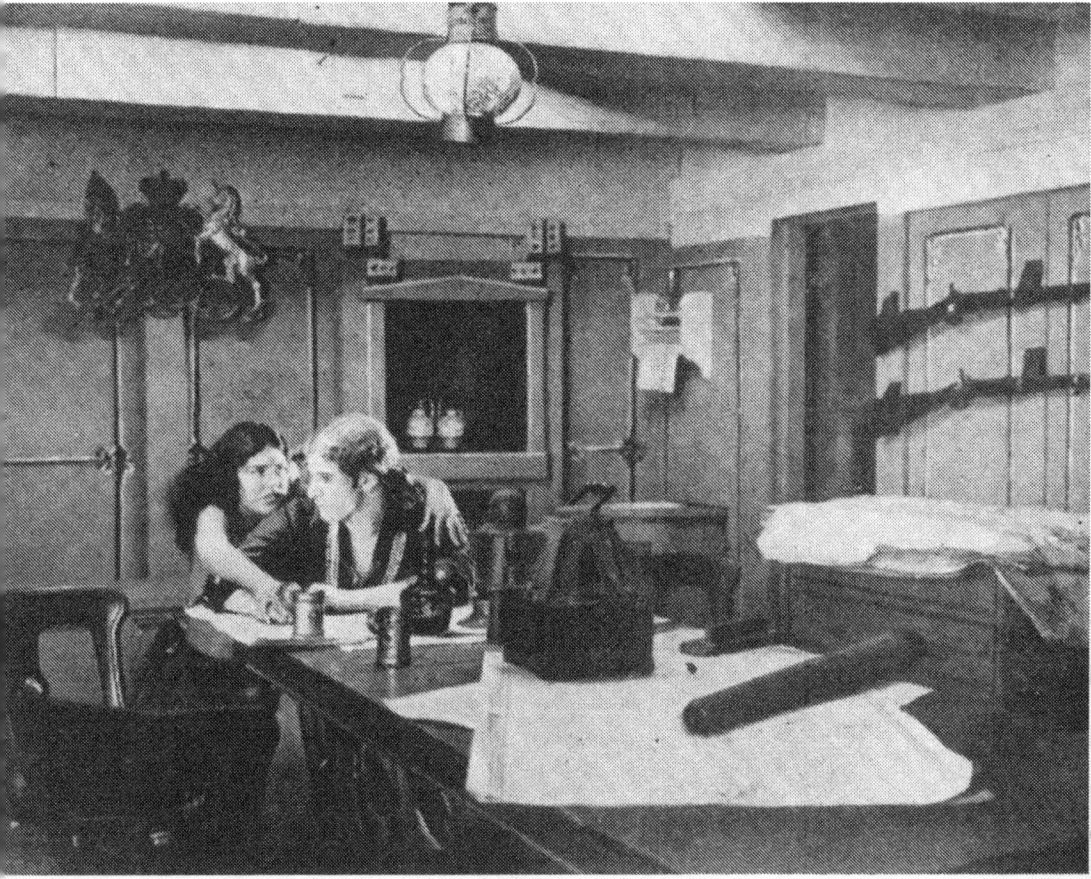

5.5 *After the Mutiny—Christian and His Isobel.* Still from *In the Wake of the Bounty*, reproduced in C. Chauvel, *In the Wake of the Bounty*, Sydney, Endeavour Press, 1933. Reproduced with permission from the Chauvel Estate, c/o Curtis Brown Australia Pty Ltd.

long hair and exposed breasts (fig. 5.6). He wrote of the tribulations of finding enough suitable women to form the "ballet of twenty beautiful Tahitians" that would satisfy his image of the Tahiti of 1789, when the *Bounty* first arrived. "It was impressed upon me by all that I would find it most difficult to secure a ballet of twenty beautiful Tahitians, as there were few pretty girls who were good dancers—

and not fat." He continued that by the age of sixteen "most Tahitian girls become corpulent . . . and, if quite healthy, were mountains of flesh at the age of forty." With the aid of a local man, Lulu, these problems were overcome and Chauvel could report that "within a week a sunripe ballet of beautiful girls was at our location . . . being led through primitive dances."[54]

5.6 *Filming the Tahitian Ballet*. Reproduced in C. Chauvel, *In the Wake of the Bounty*, Sydney, Endeavour Press, 1933. Reproduced with permission from the Chauvel Estate, c/o Curtis Brown Australia Pty Ltd.

During the filming of scenes "depicting" the *Bounty*'s arrival, Chauvel was delighted with the vision created for the cameras, evoking the quintessence of classical primitivism with the "lithe brown girls with bodies that swayed from the hips with a grace of movement which is the gift of the wild and untamed. They passed by with a regal tilt of the head and with peals of laughter . . . shining tresses of jet-black hair fell to their waists." This glorious display of the colonial fantasy of Tahiti through the bodies and movement of young women was as transient as it was highly stage-managed. After the filming was over, Chauvel's aide, Lulu, lamented that "only one year and some will be too fat [to dance]; some might die quickly like we do here; others will go with white men who will beat them if they dance."[55]

Despite these other serpents in paradise identified by Chauvel — body fat, dying races, and violent white husbands — Chauvel glossed over all the unseemly problems and opined in the opening narration that "Tahiti today is a beautiful dream of the past." The second half of the film was concerned with gathering footage of contemporary Tahiti and Pitcairn Island, to trace the remnants of the myths and examine the eugenic results of the colonial experiment. Chauvel approved of what he saw on Pitcairn, commenting on a formation of young men performing calisthenics, "given that the men are the product of over one hundred years of inbreeding their physiques and mental capabilities surprise one."[56]

Chauvel's use of Tahitian women, albeit in chorus-line roles, starkly contrasted with the Hollywood adaptation of the *Bounty* story released two years later in 1935, *Mutiny on the Bounty*. As this film focused on the reproductive romances between Fletcher Christian and his Tahitian counterpart, Maimiti (fig. 5.7), and Roger Byam's coupling with Tehanni, the filmmakers cast Mexican actresses Mamo Clark and Movita Casteneda in these parts. Greg Dening, who has provided an enlightening analysis of the successive *Bounty* films and the role they have played in creating the relationship between cultural literacy and history, though not with an eye to explaining their role in perpetuating stereotypes of Pacific women, showed that these actresses were cast as they were deemed "very much Polynesian in appearance." They exhibited the necessary attributes of long flowing hair and the adoring smile, though both had luminously white skin. Jane Desmond has argued that casting "near white" South American actresses was common practice during this phase of Hollywood, as Dolores Del Rio's casting as Luana also attests.[57]

Hollywood attempted to racially neutralize this celebrated story of the colonial man's sexual encounters with indigenous women; yet these relationships were portrayed. Contrast this with the contemporary colonial politics in Australia that obscured a similar history between colonial men and Aboriginal women. The endemic brand of racism that governed white relations toward Aboriginal peoples in Australia at the time prompted filmmakers to avoid portraying such relationships, regardless of how prominent they had been in

5.7 Clark Gable as Fletcher Christian and Mamo Clark as Maimiti in *Mutiny on the Bounty*, 1935. Getty Images.

colonization of the continent. Katherine Susannah Prichard's 1929 novel about love between a young Aboriginal woman and the son of a cattle-station owner, *Coonardoo*, broached this taboo subject. In the story, the weight of familial disapproval assures the failure of the romance. Beyond Prichard's novel, filmmakers avoided any portrayal of this forbidden coupling, despite its prevalence at the time in northern Australia, as we have seen.[58]

Even in films based upon the famous bushranger Thunderbolt, who, it was well known, had an Aboriginal partner and accomplice, Mary Anne Ward, this fact was tampered with to make the end product palatable to its audience. In the 1910 film *Thunderbolt*, the Aboriginal woman is included as the woman who rescues the bushranger from the police. In the 1953 version, *Captain Thunderbolt*, the relationship is present, although it was dealt with self-consciously and diminished to a "sexless affair" akin to mateship, as Andrew Pike argued.[59] Julie Janson's more recent play on this subject, *Black Mary*, has attempted to redress this cultural blindness toward white and Aboriginal relationships on the nineteenth-century frontiers.[60]

The Pacific Muse and the Pacific War's Aftermath

The Pacific War and its aftermath brought many changes, yet it also reinforced long-established traditions in colonial relations and representations of the region. The Allied military presence in the Pacific, which expanded exponentially with the outbreak of war in 1941, recapitulated the effects of nineteenth-century industries like whaling, with thousands of men being deployed upon islands across the Pacific. This new development was easily factored into the established race and gender structure in cinematic portrayals. The war seemingly provided a fresh set of story lines for filmmakers. However, the dichotomy of the masculine Occident and the feminine Pacific was exaggerated by the conflagration. The established themes of paradisiacal romance returned with new vigor as a mark of the repacification of the region by the Allies. Also the war precipitated a profound reevaluation of Occidental nationalisms that were premised upon the eugenic need to reassert domination by the white races over the "yellow peril" and politically motivated indigenes in the wake of the war. U.S. influence expanded after the war in the island Pacific, with Japan's extensive Pacific empire shifting under the American flag as the Trust Territories of the Pacific Islands and Hawai'i being made a state.

The deployment of more than a million U.S. servicemen to the Pacific islands, Australia, and New Zealand produced a common experience between white women and indigenous women. The war sexualized white women in these countries to unprecedented levels. Advertising and the cinema were the main vehicles promoting the transformation of the sexually pure, unerotic white woman into a sexually enticing object of male desire, as Marilyn Lake has argued. This drastically affected the Pacific muse stereotype.[61]

What altered markedly as a result of World War II was that the Pacific muse stereotype shifted away from a whitened ideal and back to one that embraced the exoticism of Polynesian "soft primitivism" as encapsulated in the paintings of Gauguin. For indigenous women, this change meant that they were even more determined by their race, gender, and sentimentalized conceptions of their culture. For white women, it entailed the mimicking of the Polynesian ideal epitomized by the image "Sunkissed" (see fig. 1.2). The prominence of this feminine ideal went hand in hand with beach culture and surfing. The Pacific islands, especially Hawai'i, were the readily acknowledged home of this new craze that involved the appropriation of appearance as much as it did cultural practice, and so the iconography of the islands reached a zenith in visibility through beach kitsch—hibiscus flowers, tikis, tans, leis, hula skirts, and hula-hoops.

Pacific tourism was revitalized after the cessation of hostilities. Though island tourism had commenced in the 1910s with cruise ships, postwar economic prosperity, and improvements in transport, especially in the 1960s with the introduction of air travel, more and more of the affluent classes from Europe, the United States, Canada, Australia, and New Zealand could experience the islands firsthand. These travelers wanted to see the imagined island idylls. As a result indigenous cultures were systematically diminished to a commercially packaged commodity so that the region appeared like a theme park offering indigenous experiences that complied with stereotypes and colonial hierarchies.

The young female body was once again the site through which this latest phase of colonial relations was mediated. This was particularly the case with Hawai'i as it was drawn further into American mainstream culture. As Haunani Kay and Mililani Trask have argued, "without beautiful Hawaiian women dancing, there would be no tourism." The bodies of these women performing the hula were the means for tourists to "ponder sexuality" and receive legitimate gratification under the guise of an educative ethnographic display. Desmond has shown how the postwar tourist industry in Hawai'i revolved around the sanitized sexual staging of the hula and other Polynesian dances that became *the* ethnographic event of island holidays.[62]

Cultural production in the form of Pacific-set novels and nonfiction added weight to the revived colonial stereotype. The writings of ethnographic adventurer Thor Heyerdahl from the publication of the *Kon-tiki* voyage in 1947 whetted the West's appetite for information about Polynesian history and culture. As Catherine Lutz and Jane Collins have shown, *National Geographic* magazine at this time was also integral to the conveyance of this Pacific ideal.[63] Charles Nordhoff and James Norman Hall's often reprinted *The Bounty Trilogy* of 1932 likewise continued to reshape popular conceptions of this myth and more closely define the Tahitian female characters of the story in the postwar era. Christian's love interest, Maimiti, was described as "slenderly and strongly made, in the first bloom of young womanhood . . . with her magnificent dark hair unbound . . . [she] made a picture worth traveling far to behold." Her temperament also fulfilled the fantasy as "she cast down her eyes while a blush suffused her clear olive cheeks." In narrator Roger Byam's assessment, "the young English seaman and the Indian girl . . . made a handsome couple."[64]

Film, as expected, was also a highly important and interconnected conduit of this reordered, postwar relationship between the Occidental world and the Pacific. Unlike the interwar films, young, nubile indigenous actresses were cast in sexualized roles, though they were few in number. The makers of the 1962 *Mutiny on the Bounty* version sought "authenticity" and so relied upon *National Geographic* and

5.8 Narla Kunoth as Jedda and Robert Tudwali as
Marbuk in *Jedda*, 1954. Reproduced with permission from
the Chauvel Estate, c/o Curtis Brown Australia Pty Ltd.

Bengt Danielsson, aforementioned biographer of Gauguin and
author of *Islands of Love* of 1966, as an adviser on Tahitian representation and culture. A central plank of this authentic representation
was casting the correct Tahitian female lead. Tarita Tumi Teriipaia
was chosen to play Maimiti, as she supposedly fulfilled the "vision

of voluptuous, innocent South Sea languor." She also entered legend for her off-screen romance with her leading man, Marlon Brando, pictured together in figure 5.8. The 1984 remake of *The Bounty* also had a Tahitian actor, Tevaite Vernette, in the role of Mauatua, playing opposite Mel Gibson's Fletcher Christian.[65]

Charles Chauvel's 1954 film, *Jedda*, also had an indigenous actress play the title role in this Northern Territory frontier drama. The Chauvels found a young Arunda woman called Rosalie in the Anglican Hostel for girls in Alice Springs and gave her the stage name Narla Kunoth and the role. In publicity Jedda was described as "Eve in ebony" (fig. 5.9). One of the great concerns in the film was about Jedda's appropriate partnering with a man. Her marriage choice was limited as she was "between" two cultures, and so the civilized "half-caste" Joe was the only one deemed fit by her white foster mother. Instead of following this path, Jedda succumbs to primitive forces that take control of her when she is seduced by the "wild" Marbuk, a "full-blooded" Aboriginal man living by traditional ways, who captures her and eventually kills her.[66]

Jedda and the 1962 *Mutiny on the Bounty* were still unusual for casting indigenous actresses in sexualized roles. It was more usual for older female actors to play Pacific island equivalents of the African American stock figure of Mammy. Hilo Hattie and Mamo Clark were among the handful of indigenous actresses, in this case Hawaiian, who developed careers in films playing postmaternal, jolly, and musical characters who sang, strummed ukuleles, and orchestrated love matches of the younger characters, as Schmitt demonstrates. In stark contrast to the bodily revelation that was standard in filming younger women, these women were dressed in baggy Mother Hubbards, which enabled only the form of the maternal bosom to be seen.

Two portrayals of older women, in films based upon novels by James A. Michener, diverged markedly from this pattern. In the 1958 hit *South Pacific*, Juanita Hall played Bloody Mary, who was supposed to be Tonkinese but was often interpreted as Polynesian. Tahitian Jocelyne LaGarde portrayed Queen Malama, who closely resembled Ka'ahumanu in the 1966 epic *Hawaii* depicting the arrival of American missionaries in 1820. For this role LaGarde received

5.9 Marlon Brando as Fletcher Christian and Tarita Tumi Teriipaia as Maimiti in *Mutiny on the Bounty*, 1962. Getty Images.

the rare honor for nonwhite actors of nominations for both a Golden Globe and an Academy Award for best supporting actress. The inversion of the benign, happy-go-lucky older woman figure to a sexed matriarch served particular narrative devices in these two films. These characters provided comic relief, especially in the case of Bloody Mary. Bloody Mary's observation that Lieutenant Joe Cable was "a saxy man" was the source of derisive humor from the onlooking men and was intended to operate in a similar way for the audience. The character's age and corpulence set her up as a figure of revulsion. The reception was ensured by her determination to prostitute her daughter Liat to Joe Cable, as Margaret Jolly has discussed. LaGarde's Queen Malama was more complex, empowered, and pivotal to the story of missionary success over repellent Hawaiian sexual and social practices. Yet in her first appearance she is hoisted, like a horse, onto the ship bearing the missionaries, thereby emphasizing the hefty weight that so fixated nineteenth-century observers of Polynesia's chiefly women prior to their adoption of Victorian style. The cinematic treatment of these older women clearly displays the links between nubility and sympathetic portrayals.[67]

Touristic images of health, happiness, and prosperity propelled by popular culture hid a new colonial agenda being enacted upon the Pacific region. With the development of atomic weapons, atolls in Micronesia and deserts in South Australia became sites to carry out testing programs, far away from Occidental metropolises in North America and Europe. Eroticized female bodies and nuclear testing are linked, as Teresia Teaiwa has shown, as both are symptomatic of postwar colonial relations in the Pacific that trivialized indigenous peoples in both drastic and more benign ways. French designer Louis Reard launched the daring two-piece swimsuit in 1946, naming it after the atoll he heard about in reports on Operation Crossroads. This U.S. operation launched a testing program on Bikini and Enewetak Atolls lasting until 1958 that cast radioactive waste across neighboring islands. The first tumors began appearing in exposed islanders in 1963. This was followed by decades of legal proceedings by the Marshall Islands government seeking disclosure of information, acknowledgment of responsibility, and compensation from the U.S. government. As a consequence, substantial payments continue to Marshall Islands up to the present.[68] In Australia, a Royal Commission sat in 1984 to inquire into British nuclear testing in South Australia. It recommended the British government pay for the extensive cleanup required after its 1950s testing program at the Australian sites of Emu Field and Maralinga, traditionally owned by the Maralinga Tjarutja people, whose health and culture also suffered immeasurably because of the tests.

As the United States and Britain wound down their Pacific-based testing programs, France commenced its program. In 1962, France announced its intention of shifting its nuclear testing program from Algeria, in the wake of the successful independence movement there, to Moruroa and Fangataufa atolls. Atmospheric testing commenced in 1966, with 41 tests carried out before international pressure forced the tests underground in 1974. When testing was halted temporarily in 1992, 134 underground tests had been carried out — 175 explosions in total. The most marked effects of nuclear contamination have been evident in Polynesian women's bodies, especially those women whose husbands worked on the atolls: the miscarriages and their babies that were so deformed they could not survive. Midwives of long standing in Tahiti attested that monstrous birth defects began occurring among the indigenous population from 1967 and were still occurring when they retired in the mid-1980s.[69]

When French president Jacques Chirac announced in 1995 that France would recommence its nuclear testing program on Moruroa and Fangataufa atolls, France was subject to worldwide condemnation. Protests against the French decision took many different forms. Two prominent antitesting campaigns run by Greenpeace (fig. 5.10) and Australian Westpac Bank with the Saatchi & Saatchi advertising company adopted Gauguin images to evoke sympathy for the plight of the peoples of eastern Polynesia. Both campaigns took Gauguin's *Women with Mango Blossoms*, a highly romanticized and feminine image of Tahiti by the French colonial artist, and juxtaposed this idyll against the violation of French nuclear testing. While their arguments against the resumption of French nuclear testing in the Pacific were intended to benefit indigenous peoples, the portrayal of Tahiti and the Pacific as a vulnerable woman harks back to narrow popular perceptions. In contrast, media images of the rioters in Papeete following the first test were overwhelming masculine (fig. 5.11). These men were portrayed as savages unleashing chaos.[70] Consciously or not, these 1995 portrayals of Tahiti kept alive the highly problematic stereotypes of Tahitian women and Tahiti as feminine that have had such great currency in the popular media across the twentieth century. They demonstrate that Occidental cultures had clearly not outgrown the Pacific muse, conveyed so cogently by Gauguin, film, and literature across the century.

The continued popular desire for the feminine Pacific belies many realities of the postwar Pacific. From the mid-1960s, many Pacific nations sought and gained independence, but others did not. The story of the Pacific in the last decades of the twentieth century is characterized by aid dependency, inadequate services, strained resources, and faltering governance. Independence from colonial powers has been a mixed blessing for Pacific island nations in economic terms. The disparity between the per capita incomes of islanders living in independent nations compared to those who remain under the umbrella of France and the United States as dependencies and territories is great. According to the *CIA World Factbook*, the GDP (gross domestic product) per capita income in $US for French Polynesia was $17,500 in 2001, while in the Cook Islands it was $5,000, and in Tuvalu, $1,100.[71] New Caledonia's GDP per capita income was $15,000, while in neighboring Vanuatu it was $2,900, and in the Solomon Islands, $1,700.[72] In the Northern Mariana Islands, a U.S. territory, the per capita income was $12,500, while in the Republic of the Marshall Islands it was $1,600, and in Kiribati, $800.[73]

Accompanying these figures are poor health statistics and limited educational and economic opportunities. In addition, Pacific islanders are experiencing the drastic impact of environmental change upon their health and cultures. The economic plight of the poorer Pacific communities has led to a diaspora that has created dislocated and urbanized Pacific communities on the west coast of the United States and in Honolulu, Auckland, and Sydney that have disproportionately high rates of imprisonment and violent death.[74]

5.10 Greenpeace anti-French nuclear testing poster, 1995.
With permission from Greenpeace.

The problems for peoples that remain on the islands are also substantial. Security concerns in the new era of the War on Terror have prompted a reengagement with the islands that are deemed to present a potential site for terrorist operations, especially money laundering. The 2003 Australian-led operation Helpem Fren in the Solomon Islands was the beginning of a campaign to rectify the "failed" or

5.11 Andrew Meares, *Papeete*. *Sydney Morning Herald*,
8 September 1995. With permission of John Fairfax Publications.

"failing states" of the western Pacific.[75] Former Guam delegate to
the U.S. Congress Robert A. Underwood wrote in 2004 that "nearly
everywhere we go in the Pacific questions arise about the capacity
of Pacific Islanders to run their own governments . . . some see this
as a kind of 'recolonization' of the Pacific psyche."[76]

Indigenous peoples in Australia, New Zealand, and Hawai'i
reflect similar economic, educational, and health statistics despite
having been actively involved in political struggles since the 1970s.

A number of significant gains in material terms have been made in addition to a heightened awareness of colonial history and its enduring legacies for these people. In 1993 President Bill Clinton signed an Apology Bill for U.S. actions one century earlier in the overthrow of the Hawaiian government.[77] Currently indigenous Hawaiians are seeking Federal recognition as indigenous peoples of the United States. Australia was transformed during the Reconciliation Movement that followed the landmark *Mabo* decision in the High Court in 1992. Maori have gained large concessions in land, money, and land use rights. Yet these indigenous movements in Australia and New Zealand faltered due to the political unpopularity of indigenous issues and the perception of corruption in indigenous bureaucracies. The Australian government disbanded the once "peak" indigenous body ATSIC in April 2004 following revelations of widespread misconduct and financial mismanagement by its leaders. Political party support for Maori rights was an election issue in New Zealand in 2005.[78]

Despite the myriad troubles in the Pacific region, it is still configured in many instances as the Pacific muse. The realities of many young indigenous women's lives in the Pacific region are light years away from the ideal of soft primitivism, untouched by the negative effects of the modern world. The stereotype continues to overshadow realities, as it always has, through trivializing Pacific women. The trial and conviction of six men on Pitcairn Island in October 2004 revealed an endemic culture of sexual abuse of girls on the island from as young as twelve years of age. Some reports on this sensational trial of descendants of the *Bounty* mutiny suggested that "a non-Western code of sexual morality prevailed on the island" where girls were regularly initiated into sex at the age of eleven or twelve. While this island community has been exposed for this practice, endemic sexual abuse of girls is also a problem in many other indigenous communities throughout the region. The reasons for this dysfunction are unclear. Given the history of misrepresentation presented in this book, we could ask how much has the stereotype contributed to this situation? Has it licensed a male sexuality that is premised upon a belief in a utopian past of free access to indigenous women and girls who were willing to embrace all?[79] The limitation of economic opportunities for many indigenous women facilitates prostitution when populations of tourists or military or shipping personnel encounter the islands. Like so many travelers to the Pacific before them, many would read women's current participation in sex work as natural and desired, as opposed to being driven by less romantic reasons, such as poverty or the lack of economic alternatives.[80]

Pacific peoples have not let the stereotype prevail without challenge. Indeed, many have assailed it. The anticolonial movements across the Pacific created a new generation of indigenous artists and scholars who have targeted the feminine emblem of the Pacific. Many have taken the familiar colonial icon and recontextualized it, giving emphasis to its underlying ideologies. Nuiean artist John Pule, in a performance piece titled "Pacific Holiday," demonstrated this practice effectively in a way most germane to this book. While Pule read sexually explicit poetry about white women, a filmed series of record covers portraying intensely voyeuristic versions of the Pacific muse stereotype played behind him. In juxtaposing the two categories of women, white and indigenous, and the two categories of the male gaze, Pule challenged his audience to *re*view the racial and sexualized colonial gaze inherent within the Pacific muse.[81]

Other visual and performance artists have represented the "vahine pasifika" in ways that directly grapple with the long colonial heritage by reclaiming indigenous traditions and ridiculing the excesses of the colonial stereotypes. "The Pacific Sisters" used performance to comment upon the stereotype, as did the academic performers Teresia Teaiwa and Katerina Teaiwa through poetry and dance. The *fa'afafine* ("like a woman") performers Pasifika Divas opened the 2002 *Asia Pacific Triennial of Contemporary Art* at the Queensland Art Gallery, mocking the standard stereotypes of the Pacific through drag. In a similar vein, the art and video installation *Coming of Age in Amelika* juxtaposed Mead's anthropological classic with *fa'afafine* culture in Los Angeles.[82]

A more subtle though effective filmic engagement with the Pacific muse icon was Sima Urale's *Velvet Dreams*. As Tahitian academic Karen Stevenson wrote of Urale's film, it succeeded in using the "icon to destroy the myth," as she exaggerates artist Charles McPhee's search for his ideal island girl and his representations of "dusky maidens" on his velvet canvases. Artist Sophia Tekela-Smith likewise parodied the most excessive forms of voyeuristic images of Pacific women by placing them on T-shirts, though the anticolonial message inherent in this artistic statement could be missed. Tekela-Smith's other artworks of Pacific-inspired jewelry are representative of another important stream of young indigenous artists who are, as Stevenson writes, "trying to position themselves as versed in their culture . . . they are learning language, their history, their beliefs, in an attempt to understand the pre-Christian ideology of their ancestors."[83] Other artists, such as Jim Vivieare, quote Gauguin's *Vision of Tahiti* as a means to cut through the colonial "idiom" of the Pacific.[84]

Intellectual production by Pacific scholars has targeted the stereotype with equal verve. Haunani-Kay Trask and Mililani Trask's work has exposed the eroticism of Hawaiian women's culture and its commodification in the tourist industry. Caroline Vercoe has targeted the postcard as a conduit of feminized Pacific stereotypes. Tamasailau M. Suaali has examined exotic female beauty and white male desire. Teresia Teaiwa has also directly engaged with this icon, as we have seen, through her examination of the bikini and its relationship to atomic tests in the Pacific, while Karen Stevenson continues to bring indigenous artistic developments to the attention of a wider audience. Most recently, the Lisa Taouma–directed documentary *Pacific Body Language* tackles the contemporary implications of the Pacific muse stereotype on women's body image in Pacific cultures.[85]

The work of these indigenous scholars and artists has commenced a new era in the history of the Pacific muse. Their work insists upon a white audience acknowledging the colonial heritage inherent in images of the Pacific muse. That is, these images do not represent Pacific women, but rather exotic fantasies and Western preoccupations imbued with colonial desire. This has also been the premise and intent of this book. What remains to be seen is how effective the postcolonial challenges to this revered colonial icon will be.

Epilogue

This book has traced the evolution and dissemination of colonial stereotypes of Pacific women. We have seen that there have been numerous incarnations of these stereotypes that have served various purposes throughout the long history of colonial constructions of the feminized Pacific. The preceding chapter concluded with an open-ended query about whether Western culture can dispense with the archetypes of Pacific women now that they have been exposed by indigenous and nonindegenous scholars and artists for their inaccuracy, limitations, and utility within colonization. Some current trends indicate that these unreconstructed stereotypes are alive and well.

One highly visible example of the continuing circulation of Pacific stereotypes is the popular book by Tony Horwitz of 2002, *Blue Latitudes*, which aimed to recover Captain Cook and Pacific history for an American audience largely unfamiliar with the great navigator's feats and the region he revealed for Europeans. When Horwitz traveled to Tahiti with his copies of the J. C. B. Beaglehole edited journals of Cook, he marveled at how little had changed in contemporary Tahiti and how awash it was with *The Bounty*, Gauguin, and Stevenson.

Horwitz recounted for his readers the historical moment when the British men of the Wallis voyage first laid eyes upon Tahitian women that "it was a vision straight out of the Odyssey," which was followed by the coupling of sailors with Tahitian women "on the beach, on the ship's deck and in huts along the shore." But he neglected to mention to his readers, though he surely knew of it, the critical historical detail that a bombardment lasting several days preceded this legendary sexual traffic or sexual acquiescence. He noted of contemporary Tahiti that "Tahitians still sold sex as aggressively as they had to young sailors who landed here in the 1760s." His encounter with " a girl of about fifteen" only confirmed this: as "she reached for my groin" she inquired, "Je suck?" Here, Tahitian women of the twenty-first century are unaltered incarnations of their 1767 ancestors, and not a lot more.[1]

Horwitz's vision of Tahiti of the 1760s and early twenty-first century rests on the classic rendition of the Pacific muse stereotype, wherein the past and present coalesce and merge into an enduring effigy of exoticism that is ever present in popular Pacific representations despite recent efforts to decolonize them. Colonial stereotypes die hard. The opening of the National Museum of the American Indian in Washington, D.C., brought this to light in September 2004. To mark this occasion a *Washington Post* article explored the gulf of knowledge about indigenous Americans compared with the continuing currency of Tonto- and Pocahontas-type images of American Indians in American popular culture. The article argued that despite the decades of cultural revision spurred by decolonization, polarized images of benign, servile natives who assisted settlers in their colonial endeavors and bloodthirsty, scalping savages popularized in literature, film, and television programs remain largely intact.[2] A very similar argument can be made about the stereotypes of Pacific peoples, who arguably are even less understood in popular culture. The increased visibility of Pacific kitsch in which the island woman is central indicates that stereotypes of Pacific peoples retain a great deal of cultural currency. The Pacific muse remains a world-recognized figure of exotic beauty. Her nubile allure and sexual coquettishness embodies a utopian past for a troubled contemporary world.

This book has attempted to deconstruct the persistent stereotypes of the Pacific. It has done so by noting how this pervasive icon of the Pacific region has changed over time. We have seen that the earliest antecedents of this cultural phenomenon are found in the representations of exoticized primitive women in Homer's *Odyssey*. This book has delineated the Western tradition of exotic femininity from Circe, the Sirens, Aphrodite, Venus, and nymphs and has related how these images altered when they were applied within a colonial context. Classical science and philosophy likewise had an enduring impact upon ideas about sexuality and climate that were clearly discernable in the eighteenth and nineteenth centuries, when the modern era of Pacific colonization was well under way. This book has also argued that patterns of colonial experience and representations of indigenous Americans, Africans, and Asian women also fed into the Pacific icon as did the encounters with Pacific peoples prior to the Wallis voyages of 1767. Together, all these ways of treating, constructing, and rendering indigenous women naturalized the stereotypes. The preexisting colonial culture prompted a misreading of Pacific cultures from the 1760s and this had immense power in the history of Pacific colonialism.

Despite the considerable heritage of this colonial trope, I have also argued that the Pacific muse as a distinct category of exotic femininity was honed in the late eighteenth century by voyages to the region and has become increasingly narrow and sexualized since then. We have seen that far from having been an authentic embodiment of Pacific womanhood, the exotic woman was dependent upon changing constructions and debates on race, gender, class, civilization, and whiteness. Shifting structures of colonization were also imperative to the assignations of exotic femininity. Youthful Polynesian women could remain within this classification while most of their Aboriginal counterparts, who endured a more harsh colonial experience of dispossession, were cast into an opposing category of degraded colonized woman, ignoble savages, from the early years of white settlement in Australia. A similar representative history to that of Aboriginal women has applied to Melanesian women, while the representation of Micronesian women has followed the pattern of Polynesian women more closely.

The classically derived stereotype persisted when a narrow set of conditions were in place, even when these became increasingly unrelated to the women encountered in colonial history or imagined in colonial culture. This passive ideal always contended with a set of variables, that is, the age of women, their bodily type, maternity, shifting constructions of race, and women's empowerment, which affected how women were seen and treated by colonizers. By placing the stereotype at the center of this Pacific world history, it is apparent how susceptible to change this icon has been and how dependent it has been upon shifting notions of race, masculinity, and femininity.

We have seen how changing notions of white masculinity and femininity accommodated and changed stereotypes of Pacific women. The pervasive myth of universally available indigenous women fed into debates about male sexual freedoms and restraint throughout the modern period. After the first three mythic voyages—Wallis, Bougainville, and the *Endeavour*—which stamped Tahitian women as embodiments of women from classical myth, countless voyagers, actual and armchair, tried to recover this elusive moment that in turn licensed voyaging men to indulge in unprecedented sexual pleasures. These encounters gave rise to the expectation of sexual freedoms throughout the region. This book has shown that restraints upon desire were in place after these voyages, owing to the recognition that European crews were contaminating islanders with venereal diseases, and then island women were believed to be the culprits in the spread of disease. Also it became apparent that the expectation of sexual access to indigenous women endangered many crews. Missionaries and changing conceptions of proper male sexual behavior altered island societies and led to differing male colonial cultures among and within different colonizing nations in which male sexuality was problematic. Images of women were central to these tensions about colonial male sexuality. The other prevailing feature of the myth of Pacific sexual utopias was that violence often preceded sexual encounters. This was the case from Mendaña's encounter with Marquesans in 1595 and on many Pacific encounters that followed. Anxieties about race and degeneration from the late nineteenth century drastically affected the stereotype—so much so that white women mimicking Pacific cultures became cast as the more acceptable embodiments of this genera of women, or embodiments of Pacific women were suitably whitened to nullify race. The stereotype of sexually free women hides the persistent presence of violence in the story of Pacific sexual exchanges, and it also obscures myriad colonial anxieties, which this book has brought to light.

Stereotypes of Pacific women have also served differing functions in the construction of white femininity. In the Victorian era stereotypes of Pacific women were diametrically opposed to ideal white femininity, while at the end of the eighteenth century, Pacific women seemed to resemble exemplars of natural mothers that white woman should emulate. In the twentieth century, Pacific exoticism was incorporated into white feminine ideals that promoted a liberated though still submissive sexuality and appearance as embodied in the smiling island girl. The anxiety about cross-racial couplings bolstered the whitening of the stereotype that was highly visible in Hollywood films. The malleability of the stereotype, I argued, indicates the shifting values placed upon indigenous women. The adherence to classically derived notions of feminine beauty as young and prematernal, coupled with the transience of Pacific colonialism in the resource harvesting era and its overwhelmingly male character, led to the predominance of the nubile, sexually available component of the stereotype.

We have seen how the Pacific muse stereotype has been sustained over different historical epochs and generated in a number of different discourses—anthropology, philosophy, art, fiction, film, and historical writing. The diversity of sources seemingly attested to the authenticity of the stereotype. Pacific sexual cultures certainly differed from those of the Occidental world. Yet sexuality was linked to the sacred realm and was a facet of indigenous culture, not its sum, as the stereotype would have it. The colonial overemphasis upon Pacific sexual cultures that can be traced to the Wallis, Bougainville, and *Endeavour* accounts has diminished the complexity of indigenous cultures, trivialized them, and made them "profane."

By placing this colonial icon at the epicenter of this Pacific history, this book has shown the multifarious functions, both cultural and historical, that this colonial stereotype has had in Pacific history. The quest for the authentic precontact woman has dominated the vision of many Pacific representers who came to the Pacific after the first three legendary voyages of the 1760s. This book has related the changing stereotype to its colonial context and shown that such colonial representations have impacted history. We have seen that the stereotype consistently misinformed colonists who encountered women who did not comply with the narrow stereotype. This book has sought to restore Pacific women to a colonial history in which they are fuller historical entities than the vast majority of literature on the Pacific will allow. The shifting stereotype and the related historical renditions of Pacific women also provide a commentary upon colonial power. We have seen that this ideal, with all its suggestion of harmonious colonial relations and natural embodiments of sexual fantasy obscured a far more brutal and complex history.

Have the historical conditions that have fostered the proliferation of this icon become a thing of the past? Colonialism in its old forms has faded, yet new forms of power that have been dubbed "neo-colonial" have a firm grip upon the region. As the twenty-first century takes shape, there are perhaps more potent cultural conditions at play owing to new historical circumstances. The War on Terror has heightened suspicion and fear in the West of cultures seemingly diametrically opposed to "Western values." Conversely, this has increased the affection for foreigners who remain "friends." In this context of suspicion and negative representations of both "the West" and "the Islamic world" as mutually exclusive and opposed, Pacific peoples and their region have retained a contrasting meaning. The Pacific is culturally distinct, but it still embraces the West and the westerner with alacrity as it has always done, according to the South Seas tradition. In addition to these cultural conditions, geopolitical realities bind the Pacific to the United States, France, Australia, and New Zealand. Economic, cultural, and historic ties with these countries further ensure the continuation of the West's comfort with the region. The economic fragility and strategic vulnerability of the Pacific region, situated as it is at the doorstep of Asia, underpin the continued links Pacific nations and federated states and territories have with the West. Indeed, the Pacific and the West are inseparable. By still envisioning the Pacific as a pliant young beauty, the region remains superficial, safe, and consequently a sideshow in international politics.

The current global circumstances may well lead to a greater resurgence of the fantasies of utopian societies peopled by exotics who embrace the West without question. In contrast, this book strives to contribute to an expansive and attuned reading of Pacific colonial history in which trivialized stereotypes of Pacific peoples can be transcended.

Abbreviations

AHS   *Australian Historical Studies*

BPP   *British Parliamentary Papers*

HRA   *Historical Records of Australia*

HRNSW   *Historical Records of New South Wales*

HRNZ   *Historical Records of New Zealand*

HRVIC   *Historical Records of Victoria*

JPH   *Journal of Pacific History*

ML   Mitchell Library

PMB   Pacific Manuscripts Bureau

SSL   South Seas Letters

Notes

Introduction

1. M. Jolly, "Ill-Natured Comparisons: Race and Relativism in European Representations of Ni-Vanuatu from Cook's Second Voyage," *History and Anthropology* 5, no. 3–4 (1992): 331–64.

2. G. Dening, "Possessing Tahiti," in *Performances* (Melbourne: Melbourne University Press, 1996); G. Dening, *Mr. Bligh's Bad Language* (Cambridge: Cambridge University Press, 1992); G. Dening, *Islands and Beaches, Discourses on a Silent Land: Marquesas, 1774–1880* (Melbourne: Melbourne University Press, 1980); P. Grimshaw, *Paths of Duty: American Missionary Wives in Nineteenth-Century Hawaii* (Honolulu: University of Hawai'i Press, 1989); C. Ralston, *Grass Huts and Warehouses: Pacific Beach Communities of the Nineteenth Century* (Canberra: Australian University Press, 1977); C. Ralston, "Prostitution, Pollution, and Polyandry: The Problems of Eurocentrism and Androcentrism in Polynesian Studies," in *Crossing Boundaries: Feminism and the Critique of Knowledges*, ed. B. Caine et al. (Sydney: Allen & Unwin, 1988); A. McGrath, "Whiteman's Looking Glass: Aboriginal-Colonial Gender Relations at Port Jackson," *AHS* 24, no. 95 (October 1990).

3. B. Smith, *European Vision and the South Pacific* (Melbourne: Melbourne University Press, 1960); B. Smith, *Imagining the Pacific in the Wake of the Cook Voyages* (Melbourne: Melbourne University Press, 1992); E. Said, *Orientalism: Western Conceptions of the Orient* (Ringwood, Victoria: Penguin Books, 1995).

4. P. O'Brien, "The Gaze of the Ghosts: European Representations of Aboriginal Women in New South Wales and Port Phillip, 1800–1850," in *Maps Dreams History: Race and Representation in Australia*, ed. J. Kociumbas (Sydney: Braxus Publishing, 1998); P. O'Brien, "Exotic Primitivism and the Baudin Voyage to Tasmania in 1802," *Journal of Australian Studies*, no. 63 (2000).

5. M. Jolly, "From Point Venus to Bali Ha'i," in *Sites of Desire/Economies of Pleasure*, ed. M. Jolly and L. Manderson (Chicago: University of Chicago Press, 1997); M. Jolly, "White Shadows in the Darkness: Representations of Polynesian Women in Early Cinema," *Pacific Studies* 20, no. 4 (December 1997); M. Jolly, "Desire, Difference, and Disease: Sexual and Venereal Exchanges on Cook's Voyages in the Pacific," in *Exchanges: Cross-Cultural Encounters in Australia and the Pacific*, ed. R. Gibson (Sydney: Museum of Sydney Press, 1997);

T. Teaiwa, "Bikinis and other s/pacific n/oceans," *The Contemporary Pacific* 6, no.1 (spring 1994); H. Kay Trask and M. Trask, "The Aloha Industry," *Cultural Survival Quarterly*, winter 1992; H. Trask, "Lovely Hula Hands: Corporate Tourism and the Prostitution of Hawaiian Culture," in *From a Native Daughter: Colonialism and Sovereignty in Hawai'i* (Honolulu: University of Hawai'i Press, 1999); H. Guest, "Looking at Women: Forster's Observations in the South Pacific," in *Observations Made During a Voyage Round the World*, ed. J. R. Forster, N. Thomas et al. (Honolulu: University of Hawai'i Press, 1996); H. Guest, "The Great Distinction: Figures of the Exotic in the Work of William Hodges," *Oxford Art Journal* 12, no. 2 (1989): 36–58; N. Thomas, *Marquesan Societies: Inequity and Political Transformation in Eastern Polynesia* (Oxford: Clarendon Press, 1990); N. Thomas, *Colonialism's Culture: Anthropology, Travel, and Government* (Melbourne: Melbourne University Press, 1994); N. Thomas, *Entangled Objects: Exchange, Material Culture, and Colonialism in the Pacific* (Cambridge, Mass.: Harvard University Press, 1991); R. Porter, "The Exotic as Erotic: Captain Cook at Tahiti," in *Exoticism and Enlightenment*, ed. G. Rousseau and R. Porter (Manchester: Manchester University Press, 1990); J. Desmond, *Staging Tourism: Bodies on Display from Waikiki to Sea World* (Chicago: University of Chicago Press, 1999).

6. R. Edmond, *Representing the South Pacific* (Cambridge: Cambridge University Press, 1997); N. Rennie, *Far-Fetched Facts: The Literature of Travel and the Idea of the South Seas* (Oxford: Clarendon Press, 1995); B. Douglas, "Art as Ethnohistorical Text: Science, Representation, and Indigenous Presence in Eighteenth- and Nineteenth-Century Oceanic Voyage Literature," in *Double Vision: Art Histories and Colonial Histories in the Pacific*, ed. N. Thomas and D. Losche (Cambridge: Cambridge University Press, 1999); B. Douglas, "Science and the Art of Representing 'Savages': Reading 'Race' in Text and Image in South Seas Voyage Literature," *History and Anthropology* 11, no. 2–3 (1999); R. Nicole, *The Word, the Pen, and the Pistol: Literature and Power in Tahiti* (Albany: State University of New York Press, 2001); G. Pollock, *Avant-Garde Gambits, 1888–1893: Gender and the Colour of Art History* (London: Thames and Hudson, 1992); A. Soloman-Godeau, "Going Native," *Art in America*, July 1989; S. Eisenman, *Gauguin's Skirt* (London: Thames and Hudson, 1997); C. Lutz and J. Collins, *Reading National Geographic* (Chicago: University of Chicago Press, 1993); J. Williamson, "Woman Is an Island: Femininity and Colonization," in *Studies in Entertainment: Approaches to Mass Culture*, ed. T. Modleski (Bloomington: Indiana University Press, 1986); D. Forbes, *Encounters with Paradise: Views of Hawaii and Its People, 1788–1941* (Honolulu: University of Hawai'i Press, 1992; M. Minson, *Encounters with Eden: New Zealand, 1770–1870* (Wellington: National Library of New Zealand Press, 1990); L. Bell, *Colonial Constructs: European Images of Maori* (Melbourne: University of Melbourne Press, 1992); A. Stephen, ed., *Pirating the Pacific: Images of Travel, Trade, and Tourism* (Haymarket, New South Wales: Powerhouse Publishing, 1993).

7. M. Sturma, *South Sea Maidens* (Westport, Conn.: Greenwood, 2002); K. Wilson, *The Island Race: Englishness, Empire, and Gender in the Eighteenth Century* (New York: Routledge, 2003); L. Wallace, *Sexual Encounters: Pacific Texts, Modern Sexualities* (Ithaca, N.Y.: Cornell University Press, 2003), 1.

8. A. McClintock, *Imperial Leather: Race, Gender, and Sexuality in the Colonial Contest* (London: Routledge, 1995); M. L. Pratt, *Imperial Eyes: Travel Writing and Transculturation* (London: Routledge, 1992); L. Schiebinger, *Nature's Body: Gender in the Making of Modern Science* (Boston: Beacon Press, 1993); S. L. Gilman, *Difference and Pathology: Stereotypes of Sexuality, Race, and Madness* (Ithaca, N.Y.: Cornell University Press, 1985); A. Stoler, "Educating Desire in Colonial Southeast Asia: Foucault, Freud, and Imperial Sexualities," in *Sites of Desire*, ed. Manderson and Jolly; L. Manderson, "Parables of Imperialism and Fantasies of the Exotic: Western Representations of Thailand—Place and Sex," in *Sites of Desire*, ed. Manderson and Jolly.

Chapter I

1. Smith, *European Vision*.

2. O. H. K. Spate, *The Pacific Since Magellan: The Spanish Lake* (Canberra: ANU Press, 1979).

3. Smith, *Imagining the Pacific*, ch. 1.

4. J. Hale, *The Civilisation of Europe in the Renaissance* (London: HarperCollins, 1993), ch. 1; R. Blevins Faery, *Cartographies of Desire: Captivity, Race, and Sex in the Shaping of the American Nation* (Norman: Oklahoma University Press, 1999), ch. 2; P. Hulme, "Polytropic Man: Tropes of Sexuality and Mobility in Early Colonial Discourse," *Europe and Its Others*, ed. F. Barker et al. (Colchester, UK: Essex University Press, 1985).

5. McClintock, 25–26.

6. T. Todorov, *The Conquest of America: The Question of the Other* (New York: Harper & Row, 1982), 48–49; R. C. Trexler, *Sex and Conquest: Gendered Violence, Political Order and the Conquest of the Americas* (London: Polity Press, 1995).

7. Todorov, 48–49.

8. J. Gilbert, *A History of Discovery and Exploration: Eastern Islands, Southern Seas* (London: Aldus Books, 1973), 226–27; Tahuata, Mohotani, Hiva Oa, and Fatuhiva, respectively, which comprise the southern islands of the Marquesas group.

9. A. Dalrymple, *An Historical Collection of the Several Voyages and Discoveries in the South Pacific Ocean*, vol. 1 (1770; New York: Da Capo, 1967) 19, 67–68; Dening, *Islands and Beaches*.

10. Dalrymple, 71.

11. P. Snow and S. Waine, *The People from the Horizon: An Illustrated History of the Europeans Among the South Sea Islanders* (Oxford: Phaidon Press, 1979), 35.

12. Dalrymple, 92, 94. Other accounts of the Roggewein voyage contradict

this. For instance, in A. Sharp, ed., *Journal of Jacob Roggeveen* (Oxford: Clarendon Press, 1970), 17, Roggewein remarks, "But young women and lasses did
not come forward amongst the crowd, so that one must believe the jealousy
of the men had moved to hide them away in some distant place in the island."

13. M. Rediker, *Between the Devil and the Deep Blue Sea* (Cambridge: Cambridge
University Press, 1987), ch. 1.

14. W. Dampier, *A Collection of Voyages in Four Volumes* (London: James and
John Knapton, 1729), 394–95. Dampier's voyage account first appeared in 1697.

15. S. Greenblatt, *Marvelous Possessions: The Wonder of the New World* (Chicago:
University of Chicago Press, 1991), 109, 143; S. M. Socolow, *The Women of
Colonial Latin America* (Cambridge: Cambridge University Press, 2000), 34–35;
M. Navarro and V. Sánchez Korrol with K. Ali, *Women in Latin America and the
Caribbean: Restoring Women to History* (Bloomington: Indiana University Press,
1999), 24–25.

16. P. Turner Strong, "Captivity in White and Red: Convergent Practice
and Colonial Representation on the British Amerindian Frontier, 1606–1736,"
in *Crossing Cultures: Essays in the Displacement of Western Cultures*, ed. D. Segal
(Tucson: University of Arizona Press, 1992), 33; Hulme, 19–27; H. Carr,
*Inventing the American Primitive: Politics, Gender, and the Representation of Native
American Literary Traditions* (New York: New York University Press, 1996).

17. P. Barbour, ed., *The Jamestown Voyages Under the First Charter, 1606–1609*,
vol. 1 (Cambridge: Cambridge University Press, 1969), 80, 104, 206–7; R.
Tilton, *Pocahontas: The Evolution of an American Narrative* (New York: Cambridge
University Press, 1994), 13–15.

18. A. Sundquist, *Pocahontas and Co.: The Fictional American Indian Woman
in Nineteenth Century Literature: A Method of Study* (Atlantic Highlands, N.J.:
Humanities Press International, 1987), 50; V. G. Kiernan, "Noble and Ignoble
Savages," in *Exoticism and the Enlightenment*, ed. Rousseau and Porter, 105.

19. D. Fowler, *Northern Attitudes towards Interracial Marriage: Legislation and
Public Opinion in the Middle Atlantic and States of the Old Northwest, 1780–1930* (New
York: Garland Publishing, 1987), 7, 25–27; Tilton, 13–15, and see note 17,
ch. 1, for a fuller explanation of Virginian and Massachusetts laws enacted to
prevent interbreeding with and mistreatment of native women; W. J. Johnston,
Race Relations in Virginia and Miscegenation in the South, 1776–1860 (Amherst:
University of Massachusetts Press, 1970), ch. 7.

20. Peter Fontaine is quoted in Fowler, 169–70, and Tilton, 22.

21. Tilton, 63, 85.

22. R. W. Stedman, *Shadows of the Indians: Stereotypes in American Culture*
(Norman: University of Oklahoma Press, 1982), ch. 2.

23. A. Foa, "The New and the Old: The Spread of Syphilis, 1494–1530,"
in *Sex and Gender in Historical Perspective*, ed. E. Muir and G. Ruggiero (Baltimore: Johns Hopkins University Press, 1990), 26, 33.

24. Ibid., 31–33; H. K. Bhabha, "The Other Question . . . Homi K. Bhabha Reconsiders the Stereotype and Colonial Discourses," *Screen* 26, no.6 (1983): 18.

25. O. P. Dickason, "From 'One Nation' in the Northeast to 'New Nation' in the Northwest," in *The New Peoples: Being and Becoming Métis in North America*, ed. J. Peterson and J. Brown (Lincoln: University of Nebraska Press, 1985), 22–28.

26. Ibid., 22; S. Van Kirk, *Many Tender Ties: Women in the Fur-Trade, 1670–1870* (Norman: University of Oklahoma Press, 1980), 173–74.

27. Van Kirk, 7–8, 168–71; J. Brown, *Strangers in Blood: Fur Trade Families in Indian Country* (Vancouver: University of British Columbia Press, 1980), 134–37; see the film by Canadian filmmaker Christine Welsh, who is a descendant of Margaret Taylor. Welsh challenges the other historians' claim that the wives were in general provided for by their husbands. *Women in the Shadows*, video recording, Canada, 1991.

28. M. Poovey, *Uneven Developments: The Ideological Work of Gender in Mid-Victorian England* (London: Virago, 1989), chs. 1, 3.

29. Gilman, in *Difference and Pathology*, 79–81, argues that the links between blackness and concupiscence date to the twelfth-century traveler Benjamin of Tudela.

30. Ibid., 81; I. Berlin, *Many Thousands Gone: The First Two Centuries of Slavery in North America* (Cambridge, Mass.: Belknap Press, 1998), 8–10; F. Nussbaum, *Torrid Zones: Maternity, Sexuality, and Empire in Eighteenth-Century Narratives* (Baltimore: Johns Hopkins University Press, 1995), 79–83; Schiebinger, 94–98, 156–57, 167; A. Rothman, *Slave Country* (Cambridge, Mass.: Harvard University Press, 2005).

31. Schiebinger, 94–98; Buffon, *Buffon's Natural History Containing A theory of the Earth, A general History of Man, of the Brute Creation, and of Vegetable, Minerals & Co.*, vol. 9 (London, 1797), 109; Gilman, 83; A. Fausto-Sterling argues that Amerigo Vespucci wrote that "giving birth was no inconvenience" to the indigenous women of America he saw on the Columbus voyages, in *Deviant Bodies: Critical Perspectives on Difference in Science and Popular Culture*, ed. J. Terry and J. Urla (Bloomington: Indiana University Press, 1995), 21, 28.

32. Fausto-Sterling, 33.

33. Ibid., 29–33; B. Lindfors, "Circus Africans," *Journal of American Culture* 6, no. 2 (1983): 9–10.

34. Fausto-Sterling, 29, 42; Schiebinger, 169; Gilman, 85–88; L. Jordonova, *Sexual Visions: Images of Gender in Science and Medicine between the Eighteenth and Twentieth Centuries* (Madison: University of Wisconsin Press, 1989); T. Laqueur, *Making Sex: Body and Gender from the Greeks to Freud* (Cambridge, Mass.: Harvard University Press, 1990).

35. M. Alloula, *The Colonial Harem* (Manchester: Manchester University Press, 1986), ch. 1; Said, *Orientalism*; L. Lowe, *Critical Terrains: French and British Orientalisms*, (Ithaca, N.Y.: Cornell University Press, 1991), 36, and ch. 3;

J. Douthwaite, *Exotic Women: Literary Heroines and Cultural Strategies in Ancien Régime France* (Philadelphia: University of Pennsylvania Press, 1992), 49; J. De Groot, "Sex and Race: The Construction of Language and Image in the Nineteenth Century," in *Sexuality and Subordination*, ed. S. Mendus et al. (New York: Routledge, 1989), 111; L. P. Pierce, *The Imperial Harem: Women and Sovereignty in the Ottoman Empire* (New York: Oxford University Press, 1993).

36. Montagu quoted in Lowe, 38; R. Lewis, *Gendering Orientalism: Race, Femininity and Representation* (London: Routledge, 1996), 129.

37. Montagu quoted in A. Lytle Croutier, *Harem: The World Behind the Veil* (New York: Abbeville Press, 1989), 45, 89–90.

38. De Groot, 102; Lowe, 48; Nussbaum, ch. 6; Douthwaite, 80. There are innumerable examples to authorize this claim. See, for instance, C. Darwin, *Descent of Man and Selection in Relation to Sex*, vol. 11 (London: John Murray, 1871), 372–74.

39. H. Guest, "The Great Distinction," 36–58; Jolly, "From Point Venus," 100–102; M. Page, "Lascivious Contact," B.A. thesis, Fine Arts Department, University of Sydney, 1996; G. Byron, *The Poetical Works of Lord Byron* (London: Oxford University Press, 1933), 340, canto 1, stanza 2; Anon., *An Account of the Mutinous Seizure of the Bounty with the Succeeding Hardships of the Crew to which have been added secret Anecdotes of the Otaheitean Females* (London: Robert Turner, 1792), 13.

40. Smith, *Imagining the Pacific*, 213–24; J. L. Talmon, *Romanticism and Revolt: Europe 1815–1848* (London: Thames & Hudson, 1967), 136.

41. M. Torgovnik, *Gone Primitive: Savage Intellects, Modern Lives* (Chicago: University of Chicago Press, 1990), 24; E. Grosz, *Sexual Subversions: Three French Feminists* (Sydney: Allen & Unwin, 1989), 27; V. Plumwood, *Feminism and the Mastery of Nature* (London: Routledge, 1993), 41.

42. See Torgovnik, 23–26, and Rennie, 3–6 and 9–10, for discussion of this story in relation to male primitivism.

43. E. Hall, *Inventing The Barbarian: Greek Self-Definition through Tragedy* (Oxford: Clarendon Press, 1989), 51; Homer, *The Odyssey*, trans. W. Shewring (Oxford: Oxford University Press, 1980), 119, 122.

44. E. H. Blakney, ed., *The History of Herodotus* (London: J. M. Dent, 1936), ch. 94, p. 50; ch. 173, p. 88; ch. 196, pp. 100–101; ch.199, p. 102.

45. Aeschylus, *Persians*, ed. Edith Hall (Warminster: Aris & Phillips, 1996), 5–6, 45, 71, 548–50; Said, 21, 55–57; T. Harrison, *The Emptiness of Asia: Aeschylus' Persians and the History of the Fifth Century* (London: Duckworth, 2000), 13, 21, 27; E. Hall, "Asia Unmanned: Images of Victory in Classical Athens," in *War and Society in the Greek World*, ed. J. Rich and G. Shipley (London: Routledge, 1993), 21, 108–33.

46. Homer, 144; P. Grimal, *The Dictionary of Classical Mythology* (New York: Basil Blackwell, 1986), 421–22.

47. K. Theweleit, *Male Fantasies: Women, Floods, Bodies, History* (Cambridge: Polity Press, 1987), 283; P. Bade, *Femme Fatale: Images of Fascinating and Dangerous Women* (New York: Mayflower Books, c. 1979), 8.

48. S. de Rachewiltz, *De Sirenibus: An Inquiry into Sirens from Homer to Shakespeare* (New York: Garland Publishing, 1987), 95–96, 110.

49. De Rachewiltz, 110; B. G. Walker, *The Woman's Encyclopedia of Myth and Secrets* (Sydney: Harper & Row, 1983), 549; M. Spongberg, "Not Drowning, Falling: Prostitution and Images of Drowning in Great Britain, 1830–1900," *Not My Department: Journal of Interdisciplinary Gender Studies* 2 (1992): 74–75; Bade, 6, and B. Djikstra, *Idols of Perversity: Fantasies of Feminine Evil in Fin De Siècle Culture* (New York: Oxford University Press, 1986), 258–71; J. Cadden, *Meanings of Sex Difference in the Middle Ages: Medicine, Science and Culture* (Cambridge: Cambridge University Press, 1993).

50. Image reproduced in Smith, *Imagining the Pacific*, 25; Schiebinger, 1; J. Bondeson, *The Feejee Mermaid and Other Essays in Natural and Unnatural History* (Ithaca, N.Y.: Cornell University Press, 1999), ch. 3; J. W. Cook, *The Arts of Deception: Playing with Fraud in the Age of Barnum* (Cambridge, Mass.: Harvard University Press, 2001), ch. 2.

51. Grimal, 313–14.

52. E. Grosz, *Volatile Bodies: Towards a Corporeal Feminism* (Sydney: Allen & Unwin, 1994), 193–94; A. Carson, "Putting Her in Her Place: Women, Dirt, and Desire," in *Before Sexuality: The Construction of the Erotic Experience in the Ancient Greek World*, ed. D. Halperin et al. (Princeton: Princeton University Press, 1990), 137; L. Dean-Jones, *Women's Bodies in Classical Greek Science* (Oxford: Clarendon Press, 1994); E. Keuls, *The Reign of the Phallus: Sexual Politics in Ancient Athens* (New York: Harper & Row, 1985); R. Just, "Conceptions of Women in Classical Athens," *Journal of Anthropological Society of Oxford* 6, no. 3 (1975): 153–70; E. Cantarella, *Pandora's Daughters: The Role of Women in Greek and Roman Antiquity* (Baltimore: Johns Hopkins University Press, 1987).

53. *Sophrosyne* is a complex word that has alternate meanings that depend upon the context in which the word is used. It can also mean good sense and moderation and can imply discipline, modesty, and chasteness.

54. G. Grigson argues that Aphrodite originated in Sumeria in *The Goddess of Love: The Birth, Triumph, Death, and Return of Aphrodite* (London: Constable, 1976), 27, 44–45; C. Mitchell Havelock, *The Aphrodite of Knidos and Her Successors: A Historical Review of the Female Nude in Greek Art* (Ann Arbor: University of Michigan Press, 1995), 1.

55. Havelock, 31, 33; Grigson, 38; Aphrodite of Rhodes was not uncovered until the twentieth century; however, there are numerous other examples that resemble this piece that had been known for some time.

56. M. Miles, *Carnal Knowing: Female Nakedness and Religious Meaning in the Christian West* (Kent, UK: Boston and Tunbridge Wells, 1989), 85; Rennie, 1–29.

57. De Rachewiltz, 98; J. Milton, *Paradise Lost*, ed. C. Ricks (Melbourne:

Penguin Books, 1989), 87. See S. Brownmiller, *Femininity* (New York: Linden Press, 1984), on cultural meaning of hair in the West; J. R. Forster and N. Thomas et al., eds., *Observations Made During a Voyage round the World* (Honolulu: University of Hawai'i Press, 1996), 174.

58. L. Nead, *The Female Nude: Art, Obscenity, and the Gaze* (London: Routledge, 1992); Gilman, ch. 3.

59. G. Worgan, *Journal of a First Fleet Surgeon* (Sydney: Library Council of New South Wales, 1978), 6, 18–19, 40, 47–48; McGrath, "Whiteman's Looking Glass," 189–206.

60. E. J. Eyre, *Journal of Two Expeditions of Discovery into Central Australia and Overland from Adelaide to King George's Sound 1840–1841* (London: T. W. Boone, 1845), 153; P. Turner Strong, "Fathoming the Primitive: Australian Aborigines in Four Explorers' Journals," *Ethnohistory* 33, no. 2 (1986): 182; E. Shohat, "Gender and Culture of Empire: Toward a Feminist Ethnography of the Cinema," *Quarterly Review of Film and Video* 13, nos. 1–3 (1991): 75.

61. G. H. Von Langsdorff, *Voyages and Travels in Various Parts of the World during the years 1803–7*, vol. 1 (New York: Da Capo, 1968), 94–95.

62. M. Spongberg, *Feminizing Venereal Disease* (New York: Macmillan, 1997), especially the section on the child prostitute; A. Simpson, "Vulnerability and the Age of Female Consent," in *Sexual Underworlds of the Enlightenment*, ed. G. S. Rousseau and R. Porter (Chapel Hill: North Carolina University Press, 1988), 183.

63. Carson, 139–40.

64. Ibid., 139–41, 143.

65. J. Gascoigne, "The Ordering of Nature," in *Visions of Empire: Voyages, Botany, and Representations of Nature*, ed. D. Miller and P. Reill (Cambridge: Cambridge University Press, 1996), 113; R. Wokler, "From *l'homme physique* to *l'homme moral* and Back: Towards a History of Enlightenment Anthropology," *History of the Human Sciences* 6, no.1 (1993): 127; Nussbaum, 8–12.

66. W. Alexander, *The History of Women From The Earliest Antiquity to The Present Time, giving some account of almost every interesting particular concerning that sex, among all nations, ancient and modern*, vol. 1 (London: C. Dilly, 1782), 324; Tomaselli, 109; Buffon, vol. 4, 37; Montesquieu, ch. 2, bk. 16, *L'Espirit de Lois*, quoted in Mary McAlpin, "Between Men for All Eternity: Feminocentrism in Montesquieu's Lettres persanes," *Eighteenth Century Life* 24, no. 1 (2000): 52; M. Spongberg, "Written on the Body: Degeneracy, Atavism, and Congenital Syphilis: Re-Reading Child Prostitution in the Nineteenth Century," *JIGS* 1, no. 1 (1995): 81–88.

67. C. Groneman, "Nymphomania: The Historical Construction of Female Sexuality," in *Deviant Bodies*, ed. Terry and Urla, 227–28; G. S. Rousseau, "Nymphomania, Bienville, and the Rise of Erotic Sensibility," in *Sexuality in Eighteenth Century Britain*, ed. P. Boucé (Manchester: Manchester University

Press, 1982), 96; Nussbaum, 100–101; Buffon, vol. 4, 51; O. Fellows and
S. Milliken, *Buffon* (New York: Twayne, 1972), 33.

68. J. C. B. Beaglehole, ed., *The Journals of James Cook, The Voyage of the
Endeavour, 1768–1771*, (Cambridge: Cambridge University Press, 1955), 123.

69. M. Bakhtin, *Rabelais and His World* (Bloomington: Indiana University
Press, Indiana, 1984), 368–436; Smith, *European Vision*, 51; F. Cumont, *After Life
in Roman Paganism* (New Haven, Conn.: Yale University Press, 1922), 79–80;
G. A. Wood, "Ancient and Medieval Conceptions of Terra Australia," *The
Australian Historical Society Journal and Proceedings*, vol. 3, pt. 10 (1916): 454–65.

70. Pratt, *Imperial Eyes*; C. Chard, "Grand and Ghostly Tours: The Topo-
graphy of Memory," *Eighteenth Century Studies* 31, no. 1 (1997): 101; C. Brant,
"Climates of Gender," in *Romantic Geographies: Discourses of Travel, 1775–1844*, ed.
A. Gilroy (Manchester: Manchester University Press, 2000), 129; R. Gibson,
South of the West: Postcolonialism and the Narrative Construction of Australia (Bloom-
ington: Indiana University Press, 1992), ch. 5; C. Baldick, *In Frankenstein's
Shadow: Myth, Monsters and Nineteenth Century Writing* (Oxford: Oxford Univer-
sity Press, 1987), 174; D. Roberts, *The Myth of Aunt Jemima: Representations of
Race and Region* (London: Routledge, 1995), 29.

71. J. Swift, *Gulliver's Travels* (1726; Ringwood, Victoria: Penguin, 1986),
300–301, 269; Dampier, 464.

72. Swift, 300; R. Young, *Colonial Desire: Hybridity in Theory, Culture and Race*
(London: Routledge, 1995), 72–73, 84; McClintock, 52–53.

73. Smith, *Imagining the Pacific*, ch. 1; J. Black, *The British Abroad: The Grand
Tour in the Eighteenth Century* (Stroud, UK: Alan Sutton, 1992), 189, 192, 194,
200–201; C. Hibbert, *The Grand Tour* (London: Thames Methuen, 1987), 153;
R. Aldrich, *The Seduction of the Mediterranean: Writing, Art and Homosexual Fantasy*
(London: Routledge, 1993), x; A. Fletcher, *Gender, Sex, and Subordination in
England, 1500–1800* (New Haven, Conn.: Yale University Press, 1995), 344;
Chard, 114.

74. Black, 201; J. Brewer, *The Pleasures of the Imagination: English Culture
in the Eighteenth Century* (London: HarperCollins, 1997), 576; Nussbaum;
G. Newman, *The Rise of English Nationalism: A Cultural History, 1670–1830*
(London: Weidenfield and Nicholson, 1987), 123, 136–37; Wilson, *The Island Race*.

75. G. De Staël, *Corinne or Italy* (New Brunswick, N.J.: Rutgers University
Press, 1987), xii, xxxv, 101–3; Douthwaite, 74; Chard, 111, 114–15.

76. C. Meiners, *History of the Female Sex*, vol. 1 (London: Henry Colburn,
1808), 5–6.

77. J. Marra, *Journal of the Resolution Voyage in 1772, 1773, 1774, and 1775* (New
York: Da Capo, 1967), 162; Dening, 147–48.

78. J. Hawkesworth, *An Account of the Voyages of Discovery Undertaken by the
Order of His Present Majesty for making Discoveries in the Southern Hemisphere*, vol. 1
(London: W. Strathan and T. Caddell, 1773), 461, 463, 479.

79. G. Fitzgerald, *The Injured Islanders or the Influence of Art upon the Happiness of Nature: A Poetical Epistle from Oberea of Otaheite to Captain Wallis by the author of the Academick Sportsman* (Dublin: T. T. Faulkner, 1779), 7, 9, 16–17, 23; S. Rogers, "Composing Conscience: *The Injured Islanders* and English Sensibility," *The Eighteenth Century* 38, no. 3 (fall 1997): 259–65; Smith, *European Vision*, 85; J. Banks, *The* Endeavour *Journal of Joseph Banks*, ed. J. C. B. Beaglehole (Sydney: Angus and Robinson, 1962), 266; C. Roderick, "Sir Joseph Banks, Queen Oberea, and the Satirists," in *Captain James Cook: Image and Impact Discoveries and the World of Letters*, ed. W. Veit (Melbourne: Hawthorn Press, 1972), 69.

80. J. Scott-Waring, *A Second Letter from Oberea, Queen of Otaheite to Joseph Banks* (London: T. J. Carnegy, 1774), 11, 16; Banks, 275–76, 281; B. Orr, "Southern Passions mix with Northern Art: Miscegenation and the *Endeavour* Voyage," *Eighteenth-Century Life* 18 (November 1994): 222; J. Scott-Waring, *An Epistle from Oberea, Queen of Otaheite to Joseph Banks esq.* (Dublin: W. Wilson, 1774), 5. Roderick makes the point that Scott-Waring used Ovid's *Heriodes* as the basis for his satirical pieces on Banks and Oberea (Roderick, 71).

81. *An Epistle from Mr Banks, Voyager, Monster-Hunter and Amoroso to Oberea, Queen of Otaheite*, and Anon., *The Court of Apollo: An Heroic Epistle from the Injured Harriet, Mistress to Mr Banks, to Oberea, Queen of Otaheite*, both quoted in Roderick, 79–81. The latter poem appeared in the *Westminster Magazine* in 1774; "Otahiete," *Monthly Review*, April 1774, 310; Smith, *European Vision*, 47.

82. E. H. McCormick, *Omai: Pacific Envoy* (Auckland: Auckland University Press, 1977).

83. F. M. Link, ed., *The Plays of John O'Keefe*, vol. 2 (New York: Garland Publishing, 1981), n.p.; Smith, *European Vision*, 114–17; Dening, 157–58.

84. Elizabeth Inchbald wrote the plays *The Child of Nature* (1788) and *Nature and Art* (1796); L. Whitney, *Primitivism and the Idea of Progress in English Popular Literature of the Eighteenth Century* (Baltimore: John Hopkins University Press, 1934), 129–31.

85. Meiners, 86; R. Porter, "The Exotic as Erotic," 9. There is no publication date given for the *Whoremonger's Guide*.

Chapter II

1. G. Robertson, *The Discovery of Tahiti: A Journal of the 2nd Voyage of H.M.S. Dolphin round the World by George Robertson, 1766–1768* (Cambridge: Cambridge University Press, 1948), 148, and see Captain Samuel Wallis's account in Hawkesworth, 438.

2. Robertson, 154.

3. Ibid., 154–55, 164–65.

4. Ibid., 166, 177.

5. Ibid., 180. The editor notes that "cobing" means "thrashing."

6. Hawkesworth, 458, 481; Robertson, 196–97.

7. "We saw no appearance of disease amongst the inhabitants," noted Wallis in Hawkesworth, 488; J. Dowling in "Bougainville and Cook," ed. Veit, 33.

8. L. Bougainville, *A Voyage Round the World* (New York: Da Capo, 1967), 218–19; 256–57.

9. Bhabha, 23; Snow and Waine, 47.

10. Newman, ch. 6.

11. Beaglehole, *Endeavour*, 138.

12. M. Jolly "Desire, Difference, and Disease," in *Exchanges: Cross-Cultural Encounters in Australia and the Pacific*, ed. R. Gibson (Sydney: Museum of Sydney Publication, 1997), 194–205; Beaglehole, *Endeavour*, 92–93, 128–29; Banks, 266.

13. Dening, "Possessing Tahiti," 149–50.

14. J. Abbott, *John Hawkesworth: Eighteenth-Century Man of Letters* (Madison: University of Wisconsin Press, 1982), 154, 161; L. Hunt, ed., *The Invention of Pornography: Obscenity and the Origins of Modernity, 1500–1800* (New York: Zone Books, 1993), 21.

15. T. Hitchcock, "Redefining Sex in the Eighteenth-Century," *History Workshop Journal* 41 (1996): 78–79.

16. Buffon, vol. 4, 51; G. S. Rousseau, 96.

17. C. Hall, *White, Male and Middle-Class* (London: Polity Press, 1992), 78–82; M. Spongberg, *Feminizing Venereal Disease*, 9; Newman, 124–25.

18. L. Davidoff and C. Hall, *Family Fortunes: Men and Women of the English Middle Class, 1780–1850* (London: Hutchinson, 1987); Poovey, 11.

19. C. Hall, 86–87.

20. Jolly, "From Point Venus," 100.

21. Beaglehole, *Endeavour*, 123; J. C. B. Beaglehole, ed., *The Journals of James Cook, Resolution and Adventure*, vol. 2 (Cambridge: Cambridge University Press, 1955), 238; J. Williamson is quoted in *The Journals of Captain James Cook, Resolution and Discovery*, vol. 3, pt. 2, ed. J. C. B. Beaglehole (Cambridge: Cambridge University Press, 1955), 1344.

22. S. Parkinson, *The Journal of a Voyage to the South Seas in his Majesty's Ship the Endeavour: Faithfully transcribed from the Papers of the late Sidney Parkinson* (London: John Fothergill, 1784), 25–26.

23. H. C. Gratten, *The South-West Pacific to 1900* (Ann Arbor: University of Michigan Press, 1967), 193.

24. J. Gascoigne, *Joseph Banks and the English Enlightenment* (Cambridge: Cambridge University Press, 1994), 50–51; Fletcher, *Gender, Sex, and Subordination in England*, 340–46; R. Porter, 9–10.

25. Gascoigne, *Joseph Banks*, 50; Banks, 251.

26. J. P. Bérenger, *Collection de Tous les Voyages faits Autour du Monde par les Differentes Nations de L'Europe*, vol. 7 (Geneva: Lausanne, 1789).

27. Jacques Arago wrote that Pacific peoples "reminded" him of various aspects of the classical canon, in J. Arago, *A Narrative of a Voyage Round the World* (New York: Da Capo, 1967), 78.

28. P. Rose, *Jazz Cleopatra: Josephine Baker in Her Time* (London: Vintage, 1990), 27–28.

29. Webber made three renditions of Poedua; Smith, *Imagining the Pacific*, 210. See also Jolly, "From Point Venus," 102–5; Williamson and Edgar are quoted in Beaglehole, *Resolution and Discovery*, vol. 3., pt. 1, 247, n. 1.

30. H. Guest, "Curiously Marked: Tattooing, Masculinity, and Nationality in the Eighteenth-Century British Perceptions of the Pacific," in *Painting and the Politics of Culture: New Essays on British Art, 1700–1850*, ed. J. Barrell (Oxford: Oxford University Press, 1992), 128–30.

31. Cook and Bayly are quoted in Beaglehole, *Resolution and Discovery*, vol. 3, pt. 1, 246–47.

32. "Lt. William Bligh to Sir Joseph Banks," October 13, 1789, *HRNSW*, vol. 1, pt. 2, Government Printer, 1892, p. 273.

33. Clerke and Samwell are quoted in Beaglehole, *Resolution and Discovery*, vol. 3, pt. 2, 1317–18, 1074–77; Smith, *Imagining the Pacific*, 210.

34. Beaglehole, *Resolution and Adventure*, vol. 2, 450; Beaglehole, *Resolution and Discovery*, vol. 3, pt. 1, 170–71.

35. *Resolution and Discovery*, vol. 3, pt. 1, 265–66; Bayly and Edgar quotes are on 266, n. 1.

36. Samwell is quoted in Beaglehole, *Resolution and Discovery*, vol. 3, pt. 2, 1083–84, 1229; Jolly, "Desire, Difference, and Disease," 200–201; see also Spongberg, *Feminizing*, ch. 1.

37. Beaglehole, *Resolution and Adventure*, vol. 2, 174–75.

38. A. Salmond, *Two Worlds: First Meetings Between Maori and European, 1642–1772* (Auckland: Viking, 1991), 376–79.

39. Beaglehole, *Resolution and Discovery*, vol. 3, pt. 1, 55–56.

40. Ibid., 55, n. 51.

41. Ibid., 61–62.

42. Jolly, "From Point Venus," 194–205; M. Sahlins, *Islands of History* (Chicago: University of Chicago Press, 1985), 10; Hitchcock, 78–79; C. Ramazanoglu and J. Holland, "Women's Sexuality and Men's Appropriation of Desire," in *Up Against Foucault: Explorations of Some Feminist Tensions between Foucault and Feminism*, ed. C. Ramazanoglu et al. (London: Routledge, 1993), 252.

43. Spongberg, *Feminizing*, 10.

44. La Pérouse to Minister of the Marine, February 5, 1788, quoted in J. Linnekin, "Ignoble Savages and Other European Visions," *JPH* 26, no. 1 (June 1991): 9, 12.

45. M. Roe, ed., *The Journal and Letters of Captain Charles Bishop on the North-West Coast of America, in the Pacific and New South Wales in 1794–1799* (Cambridge: Cambridge University Press, 1967), 97; Bhabha, 18–36.

46. Spongberg, *Feminizing*, ch. 1.

47. Von Langsdorff, 112; A. J. von Krusenstern, *Voyage Round the World in the Years 1803, 1804, 1805 & 1806 by the Order of His Imperial Majesty Alexander the First*

on Board the Ships Nadeshda and Neva under the command of Captain A. J. von Krusen-stern of the Imperial Navy (New York: Da Capo, 1968), 116.

48. U. Lisiansky, *A Voyage Around the World in the Years 1803, 4, 5 & 6 performed by the order of his Imperial Majesty Alexander the first of Russia in the Ship Neva by Urey Lisiansky Captain of the Russian Navy* (New York: Da Capo, 1968), 101, 103.

49. J. Druett, *Petticoat Whalers: Whaling Wives at Sea, 1820–1920* (Auckland: Collins, 1991), 9, 11; Dwight Baldwin letter to Levi Chamberlain, May 22, 1833 (Honolulu: Hawaiian Mission Children's Library, manuscripts); Foa, 26.

50. Wilson is quoted in Druett, p. 9.

51. R. Porter and L. Hall, *The Facts of Life: The Creation of Sexual Knowledge in Britain, 1650–1950* (New Haven, Conn.: Yale University Press, 1995), ch. 4; A. N. Gilbert, "Buggery in the British Navy, 1700–1861," *Journal of Social History* 10 (1976); J. Kociumbas, *Oxford History of Australia*, vol. 2 (Melbourne: Oxford University Press, 1992), 15.

52. O'Brien, "Gaze of the Ghosts," 345–46; D. Collins, *An Account of the English Colony in New South Wales*, vol. 1, ed. Brian Fletcher (Sydney: A. H. & A. W. Reed, 1975), 463; Turner Strong, "Fathoming the Primitive," 182; G. Barrington, *The History Of New South Wales including Botany Bay, Port Jackson, Parramatta and Sydney* (London: M. Jones Publishers, 1802), 23, 35, 54. An illustration of "marriage by capture"' titled "Courtship" is opposite p. 35.

53. N. Péron, *Report on Maria Island Aborigines*, is quoted in N. J. B. Plomley, *The Baudin Expedition and the Tasmanian Aborigines, 1802* (Hobart: Blubber Head Press, 1983), 84–85.

54. Buffon, vol. 7, 25, 38, 40; Schiebinger, 3.

55. F. Péron, *Report on Maria Island Aborigines*, in Plomley, *Baudin*, 87–88.

56. Ibid., 84, 87, 88; M. Spongberg, "Are Small Penises Necessary for Civilisation? The Male Body and the Body Politic," *Australian Feminist Studies* 12, no. 25 (1997): 23–26.

57. Péron, *Report*, 87–88. These two images are reproduced in *Baudin in Australian Waters*, ed. J. Bonnemains et al. (Melbourne: Oxford University Press, 1988), 98–99.

58. Von Krusenstern, 156.

59. R. Lesson is quoted in *Duperry's Visit to New Zealand in 1824*, ed. A. Sharp (Wellington: Alexander Turnbull Press, 1971), 86–87.

60. C. Hall, 76–77; Davidoff and Hall, 149, 167–69; D. Coates to Lord Glenelg, October 31, 1838, cited in J. Woolmington, *Aborigines in Colonial Society, 1788–1850* (Melbourne: Cassell, 1973), 64; Grimshaw, ch. 4.

61. The first effort to save Pacific women by exposing them to the light of Christianity was attempted by the Spanish during their short occupation of Tahiti in the intervening years between Cook's second and third voyages. See B. G. Corney, ed., *Quest and Occupation of Tahiti by the Emissaries of Spain during the years 1772–1776* (London: Hakluyt Society, 1908), vol. 1, 333; vol. 2, 258.

62. J. Wilson, *A Missionary Voyage to the Southern Pacific Ocean Performed in the years 1796–1798 in the Ship Duff* (London: T. Chapman, 1799), 112.

63. Ibid., 128.

64. Ibid., 128, 135.

65. See Grimshaw, ch. 7, and M. Jolly, "'To Save the Girls for Brighter and Better Lives': Presbyterian Missions and Women in the South of Vanuatu, 1848–1870," *JPH* 36, no. 1 (June 1991): 27–48; J. Wilson, 140.

66. W. Puckey, "A journal consisting of a few remarks of a voyage from Portsmouth to the Society Islands," unpublished ms., 1794, in the Alexander Turnbull Library, Wellington, 136–37.

67. Ibid., 137; K. R. Howe, *Where the Waves Fall* (Sydney: Allen & Unwin, 1984), 118; W. Ellis, *Polynesia Researches*, vol. 1 (London: Dawsons, 1967), 94–95, 104–5.

68. Grimshaw, 6; N. Gunson, *Messengers of Grace: Evangelical Missionaries in the South Seas, 1797–1860* (Melbourne: Oxford University Press, 1978), 45; N. Easdale, *Missionary and Maori: Kerikeri 1819–1860* (Lincoln: Te Waihora Press, Lincoln, 1991), 46–50; P. O'Brien, "Taking Possession of Tahiti: British and French Masculinity, Queen Pomare, and the Annexation of Tahiti, 1837–1847," forthcoming.

69. Margaret Jolly argues that sexual commerce was not an exchange between individuals, but from the indigenous side it was a collective, community exchange; lecture, National Museum of Australia, May 2003. Caroline Ralston also made important distinctions between indigenous controlled sexual economies and the European notions of prostitution in the previously cited chapter, "Prostitution, Pollution, and Polyandry."

70. D. Porter, *Journal of a Cruise made to the Pacific Ocean by Capt. David Porter in the United States Frigate Essex in the years 1812, 1813, and 1814*, vol. 2 (1822; Upper Saddle River, New Jersey: Gregg Press, 1970), 42–43, 58, 71, 79; Thomas, *Marquesan Societies*, 133–42.

71. *Quarterly Review* 13, no. 26 (July 1815): 352–83; D. Porter, vol. 2, p. 59.

72. D. Porter, 17, 20, 22, 60. See also Thomas, *Marquesan Societies*, 80.

73. Ibid., vol. 2, 59; *Quarterly Review*, 355.

74. D. Porter, vol.1, xl, xi.

75. Ibid., xli.

76. J. Belich, *Making Peoples: A History of the New Zealanders from Polynesian Settlement to the End of the Nineteenth Century* (Auckland: Penguin Books, 1996), ch. 7.

77. C. Newbury, *Tahiti Nui: Change and Survival in French Polynesia* (Honolulu: University of Hawai'i Press, 1980), 62. Pomare II had sought baptism in 1812, but the LMS would not accept him owing to his dissolution, which included open sexual promiscuity with women, *mahu*, and drinking.

78. See Howe, 117–21, 169–76, for the political contexts that led to missionary empowerment in Tahiti and Hawai'i; P. Rolland, in *Any Port in a Storm: From Provence to Australia: Rolland's Journal of the Voyage of La Coquille, 1822–1825*, ed.

M. Riviere and T. Huynh Einam (Townsville, Queensland: James Cook University Press, 1993), 69.

79. M. Wilks, *Tahiti: Containing a Review of the ongoing characters and progress of French Roman Catholic destruction of English Protestant Missions in the South Seas* (London: John Snow, 1844), 93.

80. Reybauld is quoted in Wilks, 92.

81. Ibid., 92. After performing his deeds in Tahiti, Captain Laplace sailed for Hawai'i, where similar conditions were laid before Kamehameha III, who had not yet opened up his islands to Catholic missions to the satisfaction of the French. B. Lal and K. Fortune eds., *Encyclopedia of the Pacific Islands* (Honolulu: University of Hawai'i Press, 2000), 81.

82. P. O'Brien, "Think of Me as a Woman: Queen Pomare and Anglo-French Contest in the 1840s Pacific," *Gender and History*, forthcoming.

83. W. Ellis in *Minutes of Evidence before the Select Committee on Aborigines in British Settlements 1837*, vol. 8, British Parliamentary Papers (Shannon: Irish University Press, 1971), 449; C. S. Stewart, *Journal of a Residence in the Sandwich Islands During the Years 1823, 1824 and 1825* (1830; Honolulu: University of Hawai'i Press, 1970), 398.

84. S. Reynolds, Journals, vol. 3, Stephen Phillips Library, Peabody Essex Museum, Salem, Mass.; H. Forster, ed., *"The Cruise of the Gypsy": The Journal of John Wilson, Surgeon on a Whaling Voyage to the Pacific Ocean, 1839–1841* (Washington, D.C.: Ye Galleon Press, 1991), 233.

85. Log book of the *Achusnet*, Captain W. Rogers, 1845–1848, MS F. 6870.1 F, Houghton Collection, Houghton Library, Harvard University, Cambridge, Mass., entries for March 1846.

86. *Report from Select Committee on Aborigines in British Settlements, 1837*, BPP (Shannon: Irish University Press, 1971), 10, and Rev. John Beecham, *Minutes of Evidence*, 512; Grimshaw, ch. 7.

87. Belich, 153.

88. *HRVIC*, vol. 2B, 560, 695.

89. Alice Borden letter to Alice Vincent Brattain, August 20, 1888. In the private collection of her descendant Mimi Smith.

90. S. Reynolds in F. Howay, ed., *The Voyage of the New Hazard: To the Northwest Coast, Hawaii, and China, 1810–1813* (Salem, Mass.: Peabody Museum, 1938), vi. The editor of his journal notes in his preface that Reynolds had five children but did not count two children that Reynolds had with Winship, a Hawaiian woman he lived with in Honolulu from September 1825 until she died in May 1829. For more on Winship, see Reynolds, unpublished journals, vol. 2, May 1, 1829.

Chapter III

1. J. R. McNeill and W. H. McNeill, *The Human Web: A Bird's Eye View of World History* (New York: Norton, 2003).

2. J. Meares, *Voyages Made in the Years 1788 and 1789 From China to the North-west Coast of America* (New York: Da Capo, 1967), 10, 27–28; Chappell, 143.

3. Meares, 10.

4. The phrase "modern colonization" was used by Mr. Gladstone, *Minutes of Evidence before the Select Committee on Aborigines in British Settlements 1837*, vol. 8, BPP (Shannon: Irish University Press, 1971), 455.

5. G. Vancouver, *A Voyage of Discovery* (London: Hakluyt Society, 1984), vol. 3, 893–94.

6. Ibid., 894–95.

7. Ibid., 895.

8. She was tattooed on her left arm with "AS/1789" in Adams's honor when he was using the name Alexander Smith.

9. Teehuteatuaonoa, *Sydney Gazette*, July 17, 1819; G. Dening, *The Bounty: An Ethnographic History* (Melbourne: Melbourne University Press, 1988), 86. The second version of her account appeared in the *Bengal Hurkaru* on October 2, 1826, and her interview by Otto von Kotzebue in March 1824 was later published in his voyage account.

10. Dening, *The Bounty*, 35; J. Adams, from interview with J. A. Moerenhout in 1837, quoted in H. Maude, *Islands of Men: Studies in Pacific History* (Melbourne: Oxford University Press, 1968), 6; R. Langdon, "Dusky Damsels: Pitcairn Island's Neglected Matriarchs of the Bounty Saga," *JPH* 35 (June 2000): 29–48.

11. Maude notes that this is Adams's estimate. James Morrison recorded that nine women, eight men, eight boys, and a girl were aboard; Peter Heywood's count was twenty-four: eight men, nine women, and seven boys. Maude, *Islands of Men*, 6, 13–14.

12. Ibid., 14, 19–20; Fletcher Christian, Edward Young, John Mills, Isaac Martin, William Mickoy, Matthew Quintal, Alexander Smith (Adams), John Williams and William Brown. Mauatua was also known as Isabella or Mainmast. Dening, *The Bounty*, 81, 83; Teehuteatuaonoa in *Sydney Gazette*.

13. Teehuteatuaonoa in *Sydney Gazette*.

14. Anon., *An Account of the Mutinous Seizure of the Bounty with the Succeeding Hardships of the Crew to which have been added secret Anecdotes of the Otaheitean Females* (London: Robert Turner, 1792), 11–13.

15. M. Mitford, *Christina, Maid of the South Seas: A Poem* (London: A. J. Valpy, 1811), vi.

16. Bligh described Iddeah as the wife of the chief Tinah. Of her he wrote, "I judged her to be about twenty-four years of age: she is likewise much above the common size of the women of Otaheite, and has a very animated and intelligent countenance." W. Bligh, *A Voyage to the South Sea*, (Adelaide: Libraries Board of South Australia, 1969), 66; J. Wilson, 155; Rennie, 169–71. Christian and Mauatua did have a daughter, who was named Mary, and two sons, Charley

and Friday, according to Teehuteatuaonoa in *Sydney Gazette*; Mitford, canto 1, stanza 8.

17. Mitford, canto 1, stanzas 14, 15, and 37.

18. Captain P. Pipon, R.N., "Narrative of the State of Mutineers of H.M.S. Bounty settled on Pitcairn Island in the South Seas," 1814. Braborne Collection, vol. 1, ML ms A77, 92.

19. Ibid., 92.

20. J. Shillibeer, *Narrative of the Briton's Voyage to Pitcairn's Island*, (London: Taunton, 1817), 42–43, 94.

21. G. Byron, *The Poetical Works of Lord Byron* (London: Oxford University Press, 1933), 344, cantos 2, 7; Rennie, 172.

22. Ibid., cantos 2, 8.

23. J. Barrow, *The Eventful History of the Mutiny and Piratical Seizure of HMS Bounty: Its Causes and Consequences* (London: John Murray, 1839), 4, 24–25, 27.

24. D. Oxley, *Convict Maids: The Forced Migration of Women to Australia* (Melbourne: Cambridge University Press, 1996), 129; Young, *Colonial Desire*, ch. 3; Kociumbas, *Oxford*, ch. 1; J. Damousi, *Depravity and Disorder: The Sexuality of Convict Women* (Melbourne: Cambridge University Press, 1997).

25. Lord Sydney to the Lords Commissioners of the Treasury, August 18, 1786, *HRNSW*, vol. 1, pt. 2, p. 15; Governor Phillip to Under Secretary Nepean, March 1, 1787, *HRNSW*, vol. 1, pt. 2, p. 55; Phillip to Sydney, September, 28, 1788, *HRA* series 1, vol. 1, p. 75; McGrath, "Whiteman's," 194; Kociumbas, *Oxford*, 16.

26. J. Matra, "A Proposal for establishing a settlement in NSW," August 23, 1783, in *Founding of Australia*, ed. G. Martin (Sydney: Hale and Iremonger, 1978), 10–11; and in *HRNZ*, 36–38, 14.

27. "Phillip's Views on the Conduct of the Expedition and the Treatment of Convicts," in *HRNZ*, 68; *HRNSW*, vol. 1, pt. 2, 52–53; McGrath, "Whiteman's," 194–95; A. Phillip, *The Voyage of Governor Phillip to Botany Bay* (1798; Melbourne: Hutchinson, 1982), 68; *HRNSW*, vol. 1, pt. 2, p. 217; Kociumbas, *Oxford*, 17–18; Oxley, 129.

28. R. Hughes, *The Fatal Shore: A History of the Transportation of Convicts to Australia 1787–1868* (London: Collins and Harvill, 1987), 79–83, 251; J. White, *Journal of a voyage to New South Wales* (Sydney: Angus and Robertson, 1962), 63; P. G. Fidlon and R. J. Ryan, eds., *The Journal of Arthur Bowes Smyth: Surgeon on Lady Penrhyn, 1787–1789*, Australian Documents Library, Sydney, 1979, p. 67; P. G. Fidlon and R. J. Ryan, eds., *The Journal and Letters of Lt. Ralph Clark, 1787–1792*, Australian Documents Library, Sydney, 1981. The issue of the forced prostitution of female convicts has been a concern of feminist historians; see Kociumbas, *Oxford*, 1–7; M. Dixson, *The Real Matilda* (Ringwood, Victoria: Penguin, 1975); A. Summers, *Damned Whores and God's Police* (Ringwood, Victoria: Penguin, 1994).

29. D. Collins, *An Account of the English Colony*, vol. 1, p. 81; Kociumbas, *Oxford*, 19–20.

30. McGrath, "Whiteman's," 195; Kociumbas, 53; O'Brien, "Gaze of the Ghosts," 343.

31. W. Tench, *Sydney's First Four Years* (Sydney: Library of Australian History, 1979), 259; J. Hunter, *An Historical Journal of the transactions at Port Jackson and Norfolk Island* (London: John Stockdale, 1793), 95; Kociumbas, *Oxford*, 23.

32. D. Collins, 496; McGrath, "Whiteman's," 195.

33. Hunter to Portland, January 2, 1800, *HRA*, series 1, vol. 1, pp. 401–3; O'Brien, "Gaze of the Ghosts," 352–54.

34. Smith, *European Vision*, 172; O'Brien, "Gaze of the Ghosts," 326–54.

35. W. Ellis, *Polynesian Researches*, 100–101.

36. Macquarie, May 12, 1814, *HRNZ*, 322; Ralston, *Grasshuts*, 138.

37. Macquarie, May 12, 1814, 322; G. Bruce, *Life of a Greenwich Pensioner* [1776–1817], Mitchell Library, ms A1618–1, pp. 84, 92, 96.

38. Bruce, 100–101, 107.

39. Ibid., 107; G. Dening, ed., *The Marquesan Journal of Edward Robarts, 1797–1824* (Canberra: Australian University Press, 1974), 199; Macquarie, May 12, 1814, 322.

40. Von Krusenstern, 112; Journal of missionary proceedings, September 15, 1806, quoted in Dening, ed., 168, n. 13. Robarts had a French rival, Jean Bapiste Cabri, but he had been carried off on the Russian expedition and left at Kamatscha.

41. Dening, ed., 38; Ralston, *Grass Huts*, 56, 137.

42. Dening, ed., 186, 13; Bruce, 92.

43. Ralston, *Grass Huts*, 137.

44. By the mid-nineteenth century, one-fifth of sailors on U.S. vessels were Oceanian men; Lal and Fortune, eds., *Encyclopedia*, 109.

45. H. Morton, *The Whales Wake* (Dunedin, NZ: Otago University Press, 1982), ch. 17; H. Evison, *Te Wai Pounamu: The Greenstone Island* (Christchurch: Aoraki Press, 1993), 88; A. Crosby, *Ecological Imperialism: The Biological Expansion of Europe 900–1900* (Cambridge: Cambridge University Press, 1986); I. C. Campbell, *A History of the Pacific Islands* (St. Lucia: Queensland University Press, 1990); D. Scarr, *A History of the Pacific Islands* (Richmond, UK: Curzon, 2001); G. Daws, *Shoals of Time* (Honolulu: University of Hawai'i Press, 1968).

46. A. Sharp, ed., *Duperry's Visit to New Zealand in 1824* (Wellington: Alexander Turnbull Library Press, 1971), 55.

47. Ibid., 55, 75, 86–87.

48. Ibid., 86–87; Rolland, 121; Grosz, *Volatile Bodies*, 138–59.

49. Sharp, 108; Belich, 153.

50. M. Drabble, ed., *The Oxford Companion to English Literature* (Oxford: Oxford University Press, 1996), 646; H. Melville, *Moby Dick, or The Whale*

(Indianapolis: Bobbs-Merrill, 1976), 31, 150–55; R. Slotkin, *Regeneration Through Violence: The Mythology of the American Frontier, 1600–1800* (Middletown, Conn.: Wesleyan University Press, 1973), 546–47.

51. Dening, ed., 1; Drabble, 1021; H. Melville, *Typee: A Peep at Polynesian Life During a Four Months Residence in a Valley of the Marquesas* (1846; New York: Signet Classic, 1964), 103–104; Rennie, ch. 7.

52. Melville, *Typee*, 104.

53. Slotkin, p. 547; G. Blainey, *The Tyranny of Distance* (Melbourne: Sun Books, 1982), 101; J. Mackenzie, "The Imperial Pioneer and Hunter and the British Masculine Stereotype in Late Victorian and Edwardian Times," in *Manliness and Morality: Middle-Class Masculinity in Britain and American, 1800–1940*, ed. J. A. Mangan and J. Walvin (Manchester: Manchester University Press, 1987); H. Forster, ed., *The Cruise of the Gypsy: The Journal of John Wilson, Surgeon on a Whaling Voyage to the Pacific Ocean, 1839–1841* (Washington, D.C.: Ye Galleon Press, 1991), 281.

54. It is estimated that American whalers between 1804 and 1876 killed 225,000 sperm whales and 193,000 right whales. Lal and Fortune, 210.

55. A. Channamel, *History of Fashion in France* (London: Sampson Low, 1882), 154; M. Steven, *Trade, Tactics and Territory: Britain in the Pacific, 1783–1823* (Melbourne: Melbourne University Press, 1983), 68.

56. C. W. Cunnington, *English Women's Clothing in the Nineteenth Century* (New York: Dover Publications, 1990); K. Haltunnen, *Confidence Men and Painted Women: A Study of Middle-Class Culture in America, 1830–1870* (New Haven, Conn.: Yale University Press, 1982), 74; Blainey, 99.

57. Melville, *Moby Dick*, 61; B. McDonald, *Cinderellas of the Empire: Towards a History of Kiribati and Tuvalu* (Canberra: Australian National University Press, 1982), 18; Thomas, *Marquesan Societies*, 119.

58. Spate, *The Pacific Since Magellan*, 284–87; L. Ryan, *The Aboriginal Tasmanians* (St. Lucia: Queensland University Press, 1981), 53–65; D. R. Hainsworth, *The Sydney Traders: Simeon Lord and His Contemporaries* (Melbourne: Cassell, 1972); G. Abbott and N. B. Nairn, *Economic Growth of Australia, 1877–1821* (Melbourne: Melbourne University Press, 1978).

59. N. J. B. Plomley, ed., *The Friendly Mission: The Tasmanian Journals and Papers of George Augustus Robinson* (Hobart: Tasmanian Historical Research Association, 1966), 276; Ryan, 69–71; Kociumbas, *Oxford*, 99–102.

60. James Kelly is quoted in Plomley, *Friendly Mission*, 1008, 295, 324; W. Stewart in T. Dunbabin, "Whalers, Sealers, and Buccaneers," *Royal Australian Historical Society Journal* 11, pt. 1 (1925): 13; Ryan, 70.

61. Plomley, *Friendly Mission*, 24–25, 253, 271, 324, 966.

62. Ibid., 446, n. 107; A. Haebich, *Broken Circles: Fragmenting of Indigenous Families, 1800–2000* (Freemantle: Freemantle Arts Press, 2000).

63. Baudin is quoted in J. L. Cumpston, *Kangaroo Island, 1800–1836* (Canberra: Roebuck Books, 1970), 55–56; Plomley, *Friendly Mission*, 326;

N. J. B. Plomley and K. Henley, *The Sealers of Bass Strait and the Cape Barren Island Community* (Hobart: Blubber Head Press, 1990), 79, 83, Appendix B; H. Rosenman, ed., *An Account in Two Volumes of Two Voyages to the South Seas,* vol. 1, *Astrolabe, 1826–1829* (Melbourne: Melbourne University Press, 1987), 49.

64. Plomley, *Friendly Mission,* 256, 272, 333.

65. Belich, 131.

66. N. Gunson, ed., *The Reminiscences and Papers of L.E. Threlkeld, 1824–1859* (Canberra: Australian Institute of Aboriginal Studies, 1974), 49.

67. R. Cranston, "Aborigines and the Law: An Overview," *University of Queensland Law Journal* 8, no. 1 (Dec. 1973): 63–78; D. Philips, "Anatomy of a Rape Case, 1888," in *A Nation of Rogues,* ed. D. Philips and S. Davies (Melbourne: Melbourne University Press, 1994), 97–122; *Sydney Gazette,* January 3, 1827, quoted in M. Organ, *Illawarra and South Coast Aborigines, 1770–1850* (Wollongong: Wollongong University, Aboriginal Education Unit, 1990), 151; H. Reynolds, *The Other Side of the Frontier* (Ringwood, Victoria: Penguin Books, 1982), 71.

68. Plomley, *Friendly Mission,* 1008; This image is reproduced in *HRVIC,* vol. 2B, p. 54; J. Kerr, ed., *The Dictionary of Australian Artists, Painters, Sketchers, Photographers and Engravers to 1870* (Melbourne: Oxford University Press, 1992), 847; O'Brien, "Gaze of the Ghosts," 384–86; W. H. Breton cited in R. H. W. Reece, *Aborigines and Colonists* (Sydney: Sydney University Press, 1974), 102.

69. M. Christie, *Aborigines in Colonial Victoria, 1835–1886* (Sydney: Sydney University Press, 1979), 47–48; R. Broome, *Aboriginal Australians: Black Response to White Dominance* (Sydney: Allen & Unwin, 1982), 58; *New South Wales Legislative Council Select Committee Report on the Condition of Aborigines,* Government Printer, 1845, p. 986; O'Brien, "Gaze of the Ghosts," 386–87.

70. *The Push from the Bush: A Bulletin of Social History,* Special Myall Creek Issue, no. 20 (April 1985): 77.

71. Reece, 159; R. Milliss, *Waterloo Creek: The Australia Day Massacre of 1838, George Gipps and the British Conquest of New South Wales* (Ringwood, Victoria: McPhee Gribble, 1992).

72. Grimshaw, *Paths of Duty,* 40–45.

73. Rev. J. Williams and Rev. D. Coates in *Minutes of Evidence before the Select Committee on Aborigines in British Settlements 1836–1837,* 663, 512.

74. Revs. Williams, Coates and Yates in *Minutes of Evidence,* 190, 484, 663–65; O. Wilson, *From Honga Hika to Hone Heke: A Quarter of a Century of Upheaval* (Dunedin, NZ: John McIndoe, 1985), 96–98.

75. *Minutes of Evidence,* 85.

76. Lord Russell to Sir George Gipps, June, 19, 1840, *HRA,* series 1, vol. 20, 654; L. Poyer, *The Ngatik Massacre: History and Identity on a Micronesian Atoll* (Washington, D.C.: Smithsonian Institution Press, 1993), 1–29; Rear Admiral

Sir F. L. Maitland to Mr. C. Wood, Feb. 23, 1839, *HRA*, series 1, vol. 20, p.16; Ascension Island is present-day Ponape.

77. P. L. Blake in *HRA*, series 1, vol. 20, pp. 664, 668.

78. Forster, 83; Capt. Lawton in L. Cholmondeley, *The History of the Bonin Islands From the Years 1827 to the 1876 and of Nathaniel Savory one of the original Settlers* (London: Constable & Co., 1915), 27, 40, ch. 10; G. Ward, ed., *American Activities in the Central Pacific, 1790–1870* (Ridgewood, N.J.: Gregg Press, 1967), 16–17, 22–27.

79. C. Moore et al., eds., *Labour in the South Pacific* (Townsville: James Cook University Press, 1990); E. W. Docker, *The Blackbirders: The Recruiting of South Seas Labour for Queensland, 1863–1907* (Sydney: Angus and Robertson, 1970); Smith, *European Vision*, 5,6, 49, 50; E. Beechert, "Patterns of Resistance and the Social Relations of Production in Hawai'i," in *Plantation Workers: Resistance and Accommodation*, ed. B. V. Lal et al. (Honolulu: University of Hawai'i Press, 1993), 48.

80. D. Shineberg, *The People Trade: Pacific Island Laborers and New Caledonia, 1865–1930* (Honolulu: University of Hawai'i Press, 1999), 90; C. Moore, "A Precious Few: Melanesian and Asian Women in Northern Australia," in *Gender Relations in Australia*, ed. K. Saunders and R. Evans (Sydney: Harcourt Brace Jovanovich, 1992); K. Saunders, "Pacific Island Women in Queensland, 1863–1907," in *Worth Her Salt*, ed. K. Bevege et al. (Sydney: Hale and Iremonger, 1982); Moore, "The Counter Culture of Survival: Melanesians in the Mackay District of Queensland," in *Plantation Workers*, ed. Lal et al., 76.

81. Young, *Colonial Desire*, 99–117; I. Hannaford, *Race: The History of an Idea in the West* (Baltimore: Johns Hopkins University Press, 1996), chs. 9, 10; K. Malik, *The Meaning of Race: Race, History, and Culture in Western Society* (New York: New York University Press, 1996), 71–100.

82. S. Roberts, *Population Problems of the Pacific* (1927; New York: AMS Press, 1969), 68, 70; J. W. Burton, *Our Task in Papua* (London: Epsworth Press, 1926), 84; D. Denoon, P. Mein-Smith, and M. Wyndham, *A History of Australia, New Zealand and the Pacific* (Cambridge: Cambridge University Press, 2000), 79–80.

83. See the *Proceedings of the Pan-Pacific Science Congress*, 1923, vol. 2, for debates on this issue.

84. Fausto-Sterling, 28; J. Brunton Stephens, *Miscellaneous Poems* (Brisbane: Watson, Ferguson & Co., 1880); G. Dutton, *White on Black: The Australian Aborigine Portrayed in Art* (Melbourne: Macmillan, 1974); O'Brien, "Gaze of the Ghosts," ch. 3.

85. A. McGrath, *Born in the Cattle* (Sydney: Allen & Unwin, 1987), ch. 4; K. Darian-Smith, "'Rescuing' Barbara Thompson and Other White Women: Captivity Narratives on Australian Frontiers," in *Text, Theory, Space: Land, Literature, and History in South Africa and Australia*, ed. K. Darian-Smith et al. (London: Routledge, 1996), 99–114.

Chapter IV

1. J. M. De Gérando, *Observations of Savage Peoples*, trans F. C. T. Moore (Berkeley: University of California Press, 1969), 89; G. Stocking, *Race, Culture and Evolution* (New York: Free Press, 1968), 22, 25; O'Brien, "Exotic Primitivism," 13–14.

2. Stocking, 138–40; De Gérando, 138; S. Tomaselli, "The Enlightenment Debate on Woman," *History Workshop Journal* 20 (autumn 1985): 114.

3. D. Outram, *The Body and the French Revolution: Sex, Class, and Political Culture* (New Haven, Conn.: Yale University Press, 1989), 156; Laqueur, *Making Sex*, 125–27; L. Hunt, ed., *Eroticism and the Body Politic* (Baltimore: Johns Hopkins University Press, 1990), 124; G. Fraisse and M. Perrot, eds., *History of Women in the West*, vol. 4, (Cambridge: Harvard University Press, 1994); G. Fraisse, *Reason's Muse: Sexual Difference and the Birth of Democracy* (Chicago: University of Chicago Press, 1994); L. Schiebinger, *Does the Mind Have a Sex? Women and the Origins of Modern Science* (Cambridge: Harvard University Press, 1989).

4. Hunt, ed., 110–11; J. Collins, *The Ancien Régime and the French Revolution* (Belmont, Calif.: Wadsworth, 2002), 104–5, 155; S. Gullickson, "Unruly Women of the Paris Commune," in *Gendered Domains: Rethinking Public and Private in Women's History*, ed. D. Helly and S. Reverby (Ithaca, N.Y.: Cornell University Press, 1992).

5. J. Collins, 224–25; Laqueur, 5–8, 12, 194.

6. Schiebinger, *Nature's Body*, 143–44; Tomaselli, 112.

7. G. Coombe, *Outlines of Phrenology* (Edinburgh: Maclachlan, Stewart & Co., 1844), 8–15, 49; Smith, *European Vision*, 100; F. Moore, preface, in *Observations*, ed. De Gérando, 19.

8. M. Harris, *The Rise of Anthropological Theory* (London: Routledge, Keagan Paul, 1972), ch. 1.

9. Smith, *European Vision*, 37–42, 133–47; G. Williams, "Far Happier than We Europeans," *AHS* 19, no. 77 (1981); G. Williams, "Savages Noble and Ignoble: Concepts of the North American Indian," in *The Great Map of Mankind: British Perceptions of the World in the Enlightenment*, ed. G. Williams and P. J. Marshall (Manchester: Manchester University Press, 1990); R. Jones, "Images of Natural Man," in *Baudin*, ed. Bonnemains et al.; V. G. Kiernan, "Noble and Ignoble Savages," in *Exoticism and Enlightenment*, ed. Rousseau and Porter; M. Sankey, "The Baudin Expedition: Natural Man and the Imaginary Antipodean," in *Two Hundred Years of the French Revolution*, ed. D. Garrioch (Clayton, Victoria: Monash University Press, 1989); H. White, *Tropics of Discourse: Essays in Cultural Criticism* (Baltimore: Johns Hopkins University Press, 1978).

10. M. Bloch and J. Bloch, "Women and the Dialectics of Nature in Eighteenth-Century French Thought," in *Nature, Culture, and Gender*, ed. C. MacCormack and M. Strattern (New York: Cambridge University Press,

1980); G. Lloyd, "Rousseau on Reason, Nature, and Women," *Metaphilosophy* 14, nos. 3, 4 (July/October 1983): 308–9; Schiebinger, *Nature's Body*, chs. 1, 2.

11. A. Lovejoy and G. Boas, *"Primitivism" and Related Ideas in Antiquity* (Baltimore: Johns Hopkins University Press, 1935), 329.

12. R. Meek, *Social Science and the Ignoble Savage* (London: Cambridge University Press, 1976), 11.

13. Ibid., 12; Hannaford, *Race*, 192.

14. Meek, 5; Thomas, *Colonialism's Culture*, 100.

15. Outram, 74–76; J. J. Rousseau, *Émile* (London: Everyman's Library, 1961), 324.

16. C. Pateman, *The Sexual Contract* (Oxford: Polity Press, 1988), 2–3; J. J. Rousseau, *Discourse on the Origin of Inequality* (Indianapolis: Hackett Publishing, 1992), 9; W. Hogarth, *The Analysis of Beauty* (Menston: Scholar Press, 1971); E. Burke, *Philosophical Enquiry into the Origin of Our Ideas of the Sublime and the Beautiful* (London: Printed for R. & J. Dodsley, 1757).

17. Rousseau, *Discourse on the Origin of Inequality*, 26; Rousseau, *Émile*, 326.

18. Rousseau, *Émile*, 10, 122, 167, 25–26; L. Jordanova, "Natural Facts: A Historical Perspective on Science and Sexuality," in *Nature, Culture, and Gender*, ed. MacCormack and Strattern, p. 44.

19. Rousseau, *Discourse on Inequality*, 48.

20. J. Kuyper, *De Mensch: Zoo Als Hij Voorkomt op Den Bekenden Aardbol*, vol. 3 (Amsterdam: Johannes Allart, 1802); M. Spongberg, "Written on the Body," 82–84; Lloyd, 308–9.

21. Rousseau, *Discourse on Inequality*, 10–13, 24–27, 38; G. Sussman, *Selling Mother's Milk: The Wet-Nursing Business in France, 1715–1914* (Urbana: Illinois University Press, 1982), 19–20.

22. M. Sherif, "Fragonard's Erotic Mothers and the Politics of Reproduction," in *Eroticism*, ed. Hunt, 21; Schiebinger, *Nature's Body*, 69; M. Yalom, *A History of the Breast* (London: Harper Collins, 1997), 70; Outram, 143–44.

23. G. Keate, *An Account of the Pelaw Islands situated in the Western part of the Pacific Ocean composed from Journals and Communications of Captain Henry Wilson and some of his officers who in August 1783 were there shipwrecked in the Antelope* (London: G. Nicol, 1788). See also the depiction of Moana Islanders in St. Saveur's 1797 etching titled "Tableau des découvertes du Capne Cook et de La Perouse," reproduced in Smith, *European Vision*, color plate 17.

24. M. Gatens, *Feminism and Philosophy: Perspectives on Difference and Equality* (London: Polity Press, 1991), 10.

25. Beaglehole, *Endeavour*, vol. 1, vi.

26. J. Dunmore, "The Explorer and Philosopher," in *Captain James Cook: Image and Impact*, ed. W. Veit (Melbourne: Hawthorn Press, 1972), 58; J. Douthwaite, *Exotic Women: Literary Heroines and Cultural Strategies in Ancien Régime France* (Philadelphia: University of Pennsylvania Press, 1992), 156.

27. Rennie, 118–21; R. Goldberg, *Sex and the Enlightenment: Women in Rich-*

ardson and Diderot (Cambridge: Cambridge University Press, 1984), 164–65;
D. Diderot, "Supplement to the Bougainville Voyage," in *Dialogues*, trans.
F. Birrell (London: Routledge, 1927), 121, 131, 136, 138–39; Bloch and Bloch,
37–38; Nicole, 68.

28. Diderot, 136, 121; Tomaselli, 114–21.

29. Diderot, 128; Bougainville, 256; Wokler, "From *l'homme physique*," 132.

30. Alexander, *The History of Women*, vol. 1, preface; Tomaselli, 109–12,
118–21.

31. Alexander, 43.

32. Ibid., 430, 297–98; De Gérando, 89.

33. Alexander, 430.

34. Douthwaite, 7; Alexander, 163–79.

35. M. Wollstonecraft, *A Vindication of the Rights of Woman* (Melbourne:
Penguin Books, 1992), 121–22, 164, 172.

36. J. R. Forster, 260.

37. L. Ryan, *The Aboriginal Tasmanians*, 53–57; Salmond, "Death of the
Noble Savage," in *Two Worlds*; B. Douglas, "Art as Ethnographic Text," in *Double
Vision*, ed. Thomas and Losche.

38. J. J. La Billardière, *Voyage in Search of La Perouse, 1791–1794* (New York:
Da Capo, 1971), 134, 297, 305–6; J. Linnekin, "Ignoble Savages," 6.

39. La Billardière, 303–4, 308.

40. Ibid., 310–12.

41. Ibid., 312, 326.

42. *Letter by Nicholas Baudin to Minister of Marine and Colonies*, November 11,
1802, in Bonnemains et al., 104.

43. Schiebinger, *Nature's Body*, 53. See J. R. Forster's comments upon the
breasts of women of Tahiti, Society Islands, Friendly Islands, and Marquesas,
which he deemed as "not so flaccid and pendulous as is commonly observed
in negro-women." He argued that Blumenbach had attributed this to the particular way that they suckled their children. Forster, 181.

44. Schiebinger, *Nature's Body*, 53; Spongberg, "Written on the Body," 83;
W. Wales is quoted in Beaglehole, *Resolution and Adventure*, vol. 2, 796.

45. F. Péron, *A Voyage to the Southern Hemisphere* (London: Richard Phillips,
1809), 67–68.

46. A. Digby, "Women's Biological Straitjacket," in *Sexuality and Subordination*, ed. Mendus et al., 196.

47. Von Krusenstern, 154.

48. Tench, 184.

49. Péron, *A Voyage*, 23, 180–81; O'Brien, "*Gaze of the Ghosts*," 349.

50. Péron is quoted in Plomley, *The Baudin Expedition*, 31–32.

51. Ibid., 31–32.

52. Ibid., 31–32.

53. Ibid., 31–32.

54. P. Cunningham, *Two Years in New South Wales* (London: Henry Colburn, 1827), 46.

55. Nead, *The Female Nude*, 10.

56. J. La Billardière, 351, 353.

57. L. Kame'eleihiwa, *Native Lands, Foreign Desires* (Honolulu: Bishop Museum Press, 1992), and *Nā Wāhine Kapu: Divine Hawaiian Women* (Honolulu: 'Ai Pōhaku Press, 1999), 13.

58. M. Berry, *Extracts and Correspondence of Miss Berry from the years 1783 to 1852*, 3 vols. (London, 1865), vol. 3, pp. 352–54, in Hawaiian Historical Society/ MS B/ K122P, Appendix 1, 24; *The Journal of Mrs Arbuthnot, 1820–1832* (London: Macmillan, 1950), in Hawaiian Historical Society/ MS B/ K122P, Appendix 2, 25.

59. *The Journal of Mrs Arbuthnot*, 25, 27.

60. Von Kotzebue is quoted in D. Forbes, *Encounters with Paradise: Views of Hawaii and Its People, 1788–1941* (Honolulu: University of Hawai'i Press, 1992), 101; Kame'eleihiwa, *Nā Wāhine Kapu*, 13.

61. Kame'eleihiwa, *Native Lands*, 152–57.

62. J. Arago, *Narrative of a Voyage Round the World* (New York: Da Capo, 1971), 67–68.

63. Ibid., 92; H. Liebersohn, "Images of Monarchy: Kamehameha I and the Art of Louis Choris," in *Double Vision*, ed. Thomas and Losche, 55.

64. Arago, 94.

65. H. Bingham, *Twenty-Five Years in the Sandwich Islands* (New York: H. Huntington, 1848), 109.

66. Grimshaw, *Paths of Duty*, ch. 4; J. M. Ward, *British policy in the South Pacific* (Westport, Conn.: Greenwood, 1976); C. Orange, *The Treaty of Waitangi* (North Sydney: Allen & Unwin, 1989); R. Aldrich, *The French Presence in the South Pacific* (London: Macmillan, 1990).

67. Davidoff and Hall, 153–54.

68. O'Brien, "Think of Me as a Woman"; J. A. Moerenhout, *Travels to the Islands of the Pacific Ocean*, trans. A. Borden (Lanham, Md.: University of America Press, 1983), xi; Newbury, ch. 4; C. Haldane, *Tempest Over Tahiti* (London: Constable, 1963); P. O'Reilly and R. Tessier, *Tahitiens: Répetoire Biographique de la Polynésie Française* (Paris: La Société des Oceaniste, 1975), 448–54; P. De Deckker, ed., *The Aggressions of the French at Tahiti and other Islands of the Pacific*, (Auckland: Auckland University Press, 1983).

69. Newbury, 110–22.

70. O'Brien, "Think of Me as a Woman"; "Memorials Respecting the Occupation of Tahiti by the French," FO 58/50–58/54, British National Archives; Queen Pomare to Queen Victoria, January 1843, reproduced in De Deckker, 133; Queen Pomare was featured regularly in the LMS *Missionary Magazine* and

the *London Times* from 1842 to 1846; S. Williams, *An Appeal to British Christians and the Public Generally on Behalf of the Queen of Tahiti and her Outraged Subject* (London: W. Blanchard & Sons, 1844); Wilks, *Tahiti*; Anon., *Pomare: Queen of Tahiti: A Poem* (London: John Olivier, 1847); S. Stickney Ellis, *The Island Queen, 1846*, cited in Edmond, 118–19.

71. Gunson, 189.

72. *Missionary Magazine*, no. cx, July 1845, 109.

73. Nicole, 99–102, 133.

74. W. Crook, journal entry, January 1, 1828, South Seas Journals (SSJ), Box 6, Church World Missions (CWM), SOAS Library Special Collections; Newbury, 64; J. Orsmond, "Extracts from the Old Orsmond MS 1849," reproduced in *The History of the Tahitian Mission, 1799–1830*, ed. J. Davies and C. Newbury (London: Hakluyt Society, 1959), 353–54; Moerenhout, *Travels*; E. Caillot, *Histoire de la Polynésie Orientale* (Paris: Ernest Leroux, 1910); T. Henry, *Ancient Tahiti* (Honolulu: Bishop Museum, 1928). See discussion of this historiography in O'Brien, "Think of Me as a Woman," which includes previously cited Newbury; De Deckker; O'Reilly and Tessier; Haldane; and R. Langdon, *Tahiti: Island of Love* (London: Pacific Publications, Cassell, 1963).

75. H. Melville, *Omoo: Adventures in the South Seas*, ed. K. O'Conner (London: KIP Ltd., 1985), 309–10.

76. Ibid., 315–16.

77. V. Brooks, introduction, in H. Melville, *Omoo* (New York: Heritage Press, 1967), 166.

78. Queen Pomare to French President, August 26, 1851, ms, Societe des Etudes Oceaniennes, Musée de Pape'ete, available at *PMB* 71.

79. R. Thomson, March 30, 1847, *SSL*, Box 20, Folder 1, Jacket C.

80. J. Papa Ii, *Fragments of Hawaiian History* (Honolulu: Bishop Museum Press, 1983); H. G. Allen, *The Betrayal of Liliuokalani: Last Queen of Hawaii, 1838–1917* (Glendale, Calif.: A. H. Clark Co., 1982); M. Sinclair, *Nahi'ene'ena: Sacred Daughter of Hawai'i* (Honolulu: University of Hawai'i Press, 1976); G. S. Kanahele, *Emma: Hawaii's Remarkable Queen* (Honolulu: University of Hawai'i Press, 1999).

81. R. L. Bott, "I Know What Is Due to Me: Self-Fashioning Legitimisation within Queen Liluokalani's Hawaii," in *Remaking of Queen Victoria*, ed. M. Homans and A. Munich (Cambridge: Cambridge University Press, 1997).

82. Ibid., 148–50; T. Coffman, *Nation Within: The Story of America's Annexation of the Nation of Hawaii* (Honolulu: Epicenter, n.d.), 265; F. R. Dulles, *America in the Pacific: A Century of Expansion* (Boston: Houghton Mifflin, 1932), 166–67.

83. Bott, 148–50. Liliuokalani was born in 1838 and was fifty-three when she became queen.

84. Bott, 153; Liliuokalani, *Hawaii's Story by Hawaii's Queen* (Tokyo: Charles Tuttle, 1964), 145–46. See the discussion of William Strutt's images of Maori

chiefs in *Hare Pomare and Family* of 1863 in Minson, *Encounters*, 61, and Bell, *Colonial Constructs*, 87–91.

85. J. Desmond, ch. 2.

Chapter V

1. L. Stoddart, *The Rising Tide of Colour Against White World Supremacy* (London: Chapman and Hall, 1922), 154.

2. P. Gauguin, *Noa Noa: Voyage to Tahiti* (Oxford: Bruno Cassirer, n. d.), 8.

3. B. Danielsson, *Gauguin in the South Seas* (London: Allen & Unwin, 1965), 23, 29–30; De Groot, 110.

4. A number of scholars have explored Gauguin's exposure to the South Seas myth prior to his Tahitian arrival. See Pollock, *Avant-Garde Gambits*, 23; W. Anderson, *Gauguin's Paradise Lost* (New York: Viking, 1961); Edmond, ch. 8; Nicole, 114–28; S. Eisenman, *Gauguin's Skirt* (London: Thames & Hudson, 1997), 47–49, 53, 55; Gibson, *South of the West*, ch. 5.

5. Paul Gauguin to Mette Gauguin, Paris, February 1890, in M. Malingue, ed., *Paul Gauguin: Letters to His Wife and Friends* (London: Saturn Press, 1946), 137.

6. Gauguin to Emile Bernard, Paris, April 1890, in Malingue, 138–39; D. Sweetman, *Paul Gauguin: A Complete Life* (London: Hodder & Stoughton, 1995), 167–68.

7. R. von Krafft-Ebing, *Psychopathia sexualis: With especial reference to the antipathetic sexual instinct* (1886; London: Staples Press, 1965); S. Freud, *On Sexuality: Three Essays on the Theory of Sexuality and Other Works* (Ringwood, Victoria: Penguin Books, 1977); M. Foucault, *The History of Sexuality*, vol. 1, *An Introduction* (Ringwood, Victoria: Penguin, 1990); L. Bland and L. Doan, eds., *Sexology Uncensored: The Documents of Sexual Science* (Cambridge: Polity Press, 1998); M. Torgovnick, *Gone Primitive: Savage Intellects, Modern Lives* (Chicago: University of Chicago Press, 1990), 8; L. Stoler, "Educating Desire in Colonial Southeast Asia: Foucault, Freud, and Imperial Sexualities," in *Sites of Desire*, ed. Manderson and Jolly; A. Carden-Coyne, *Revenge of the Body: Modern Classicism in Postwar Culture, 1918–1933*, Ph.D. dissertation, University of Sydney, 2001.

8. Paul Gauguin to August Strindberg, February 5, 1895, in Malingue, 197; E. Showalter, *Sexual Anarchy: Gender and Culture at the Fin de Siècle* (New York: Viking, 1990); Djikstra, *Idols of Perversity*; P. Bade, *Femme Fatale: Images of Fascinating and Dangerous Women* (New York: Mayflower Books, 1979); Theweleit, *Male Fantasies*.

9. Gauguin, *Noa Noa*, 36–37.

10. Spongberg, *Feminizing Venereal Disease*; Gauguin, *Noa Noa*, 10, 21.

11. Pollock, 13; Danielsson, 115. See also articles by E. Childs, M. Jolly, T. Teaiwa, and S. Eisenman in *Pacific Studies* 23, nos.1–2 (March/June 2000): 75–125; N. Thomas, "Paul Gauguin," in *The Pacific Islands*, ed. Lal and Fortune, 169–70.

12. Sweetman, 562.

13. Jolly, *Pacific Studies*, 92.

14. See further discussions of this painting and Gauguin's homoeroticism in Eisenman, 130, and Wallace, ch. 5; Edmond, 251–53.

15. See further Torgovnick, 100–101; Gilman, *Difference and Pathology*, ch. 3; Malingue, 177–78; Gauguin is quoted in Anderson, 182–83; Gauguin, *Noa Noa*, 39.

16. Sweetman, 426; Y. Le Pichon, *Gauguin: Life, Art, and Inspiration* (New York: Harry Abrahms, 1987), 204.

17. Sweetman, 377, 438; D. Mannering, *The Life and Works of Gauguin* (London: Paragon, 1994), 65.

18. Malingue, 226; Sweetman, 503.

19. Le Pichon, 237.

20. E. Huntington, *Civilization and Climate* (New Haven, Conn.: Yale University Press, 1915); J. H. F. Kohlbrugge, "The Influence of a Tropical Climate on Europeans," *The Eugenics Review* 3 (April 1911–12): 23–36; D. Walker, *Anxious Nation* (St. Lucia: University of Queensland Press, 1998); R. Eves, "Going Troppo: Images of White Savagery, Degeneration, and Race in the Turn-of-the-Century Colonial Fictions of the Pacific," *History and Anthropology* 11, nos. 2–3 (1999): 351–85; Wayne Anderson, *The Cultivation of Whiteness: Science, Health, and Racial Destiny in Australia* (New York: Basic Books, 2003).

21. Walker, ch. 16. Walker's chart on p. 215 shows the dramatic increase in books cataloged by the Library of Congress on Pacific topics at this time. See also Williamson, "Woman Is an Island"; Desmond, *Staging Tourism*; A. Stephen, ed., *Pirating the Pacific: Images of Travel, Trade, and Tourism* (Haymarket, New South Wales: Powerhouse Publishing, 1993).

22. R. L. Stevenson, R. Jolly, eds., *South Seas Tales* (Melbourne: Oxford University Press, 1996), xxx; Edmond, ch. 6; L. Becke, *His Native Wife* (Sydney: Alexander Lindsay, 1895); Eves, 368.

23. Jolly, "Ill-Natured Comparisons," 331–64.

24. [Robert Fletcher], *Gone Native: A Tale of the South Seas* (London: Constable and Co., 1924); [Robert Fletcher], *Isles of Illusion: Letters from the South Seas* (London: Century, 1986), vi,160, 166–67, 175. This edition of *Isles of Illusions* uses Gauguin's *Nevermore* as the cover image.

25. T. L. Richards with S. Gurr, *White Man, Brown Woman: The Life Story of a Trader in the South Sea* (London: Hutchinson, 1932), 30, 9.

26. C. Morice, *Paul Gauguin* (London: Everyman, 1919); Torgovnick, 85–86.

27. S. Maugham, *The Moon and Sixpence* (New York: Heritage Reprints, 1941), 212.

28. Ibid., 215; C. Hansen, C. Needham, and B. Nichols, "Pornography, Ethnography, and the Discourses of Power," in *Representing Reality: Issues and Concepts in Documentary Films*, ed. B. Nichols (Bloomington: Indiana University Press, 1991), 202.

29. C. Chauvel, *In the Wake of the Bounty* (Sydney: Endeavour Press, 1933), 54.

30. L. Mulvey, "Visual Pleasure and Narrative Cinema," in *The Sexual Subject: A Screen Reader* (London: Routledge, 1992), 24; G. Deleuze, *Cinema 1: The Movement Image* (London: Athlone Press, 1986), 62; R. Stam and L. Spence, "Colonialism, Racism, and Representation: An Introduction," *Screen* 24, no.2 (March-April 1983): 4; L. Mulvey is quoted in Nichols et. al., 207–8.

31. Hansen, Needham, and Nichols, "Pornography," 204; H. Cohen, "Expedition, Exoticism, and Ethnography," *Photofile*, spring 1988, 35; R. Schmitt, *Hawai'i in the Movies, 1898–1959* (Honolulu: Hawaiian Historical Society, 1988), 4; L. Reyes, *Made in Paradise: Hollywood Films of Hawaii and the South Seas* (Honolulu: Mutual Publishing, 1995).

32. Cohen, 35.

33. Frances Flaherty is quoted in R. Barsam, *The Vision of Robert Flaherty* (Bloomington: Indiana University Press, 1988), 29, 30; R. Flaherty and F. Flaherty, *Moana: A Romance of the Golden Age* (Hollywood: Paramount, 1926).

34. R. L. Stevenson, *In the South Seas* (London: Chatto & Windus, 1908); A. Knight, ed., *Robert Louis Stevenson in the South Seas: An Intimate Photographic Record* (Edinburgh: Mainstream, 1986); Barsam, 42; M. Jolly, "White Shadows in the Darkness: Representations of Polynesian Women in Early Cinema," *Pacific Studies* 20, no. 4 (Dec. 1997): 125–49.

35. F. O'Brien, *White Shadows in the South Seas* (New York: Grosset & Dunlap, 1919). See also by O'Brien, *Mystic Isles of the South Seas* (New York: Hodder and Stoughton, 1921), and *Atolls of the Sun* (New York: Century Co., 1922); Barsam, 48; *Tabu*, directed by E. W. Murnau (Hollywood: Paramount, 1931).

36. L. Money, *The Peril of the White Race* (London: W. Collins, 1925); J. W. Gregory *The Menace of Colour* (London: Seeley Service, 1925); W. H. R. Rivers, ed., *Essays on the Depopulation of Melanesia* (Cambridge: Cambridge University Press, 1922). Numerous papers were given at the 1923 *Pan-Pacific Science Congress* in Melbourne on the impending calamity of depopulation of the islands. See J. Cumpston, "The Depopulation of the Pacific," *Proceedings of the Pan Pacific Science Congress*, vol. 2 (Melbourne: Government Printer, 1923), 1393.

37. B. Cameron, "The Flappers and the Feminists: A Study of Women's Emancipation in the 1920s," in *Worth Her Salt*, ed. Bevege et al.; A. Stephen, "Selling Soap: Domestic Work and Consumerism," *Labour History* 61 (November 1991): 57–69.

38. Barsam, 51; Desmond also makes this point, ch. 5.

39. Schmitt, 21; Shohat, "Gender and Culture of Empire," 51.

40. Schmitt, 25–26.

41. Shohat, 49.

42. Rose, *Jazz Cleopatra*, 22.

43. *Hula*, directed by Victor Fleming (Hollywood: Paramount, 1927); Schmitt, 28.

44. M. Mead, *The Coming of Age in Samoa: A Psychological Study of Primitive Youth for Western Civilization* (New York: Morrow, 1961). It has also been published with an alternative subtitle: "A Study of Adolescence and Sex in Primitive Societies" (London: Cox & Wyman, 1969); M. Mead, *Blackberry Winter: My Earlier Years* (New York: Morrow, 1972), 147; M. Mead, *Letters from the field, 1925–1975* (New York: Harper & Row, 1977), 19; L. Foerstel and A. Gilliam, *Confronting the Margaret Mead Legacy: Scholarship, Empire, and the South Pacific* (Philadelphia: Temple University Press, 1992); D. Freeman, *Margaret Mead and Samoa: The Making and Unmaking of an Anthropological Myth* (Canberra: Australian National University Press, 1983); M. Kahn, "Heterotopic Dissonance in the Museum Representation of Pacific Island Cultures," *American Anthropologist* 97, no. 2 (June 1995): 324–38.

45. B. Malinowski, *The Sexual Life of Savages* (London: George Routledge, 1939), vii, x; Torgovnick, 238.

46. S. De Beauvoir, *The Second Sex* (London: Picador Classics, 1953), 185, 192, 195, 451; G. Greer, *The Female Eunuch* (London: Paladin, 1972), 96–97, 339–40; K. Millet, *Sexual Politics* (London: Granada, 1970), 35, 224. See also C. Winick, *The New People: Desexualization in American Life* (New York: Pegasus, 1968), 337; S. Firestone, *The Dialectic of Sex* (New York: Bantam Books, 1979), 27.

47. Torgovnick, 228; Jolly, "From Point Venus," 105–11, 128–32.

48. Shohat, 66, 68–70.

49. G. Deleuze, *Cinema 2* (London: Athlone Press, 1989), 225–26.

50. *Bird of Paradise*, directed by King Vidor (Hollywood: RKO Radio Pictures, 1932); Nichols, 221–23.

51. Dorothy Lamour's Hollynesian credits include *The Hurricane*, directed by John Ford (Hollywood: Goldwyn, 1937; remade in 1979); *Aloma of the South Seas*, directed by Alfred Santell (Hollywood: Paramount, 1941; *Beyond the Blue Horizon*, directed by Alfred Santell (Hollywood: Paramount, 1942); and *Rainbow Island*, directed by Ralph Murray (Hollywood: Paramount, 1944). She also played Princess Shalmar in *Road to Morocco* in 1942 (Paramount) with Bing Crosby and Bob Hope.

52. *Son of Fury*, directed by John Cromwell (Hollywood: 20th Century Fox, 1942).

53. Charles Chauvel is quoted in S. Cunningham, *Featuring Australia: The Cinema of Charles Chauvel* (North Sydney: Allen & Unwin, 1991), 93–97; *Film Reporter*, June 1, 1933, 23, reproduced in I. Bertrand, *Cinema in Australia: A Documentary History* (Sydney: New South Wales University Press, 1989), 139.

54. Chauvel, *In the Wake of the Bounty*, 56, 58.

55. Ibid., 61.

56. Charles Chauvel's commentary during *In the Wake of the Bounty*, 1933.

57. Dening, *Mr. Bligh's Bad Language*, 340; S. Brawley and C. Dixon, "'The Hollywood Native': Hollywood's Construction of the South Seas and Wartime

Encounters with the South Pacific," *Sites*, no. 27 (1993); Desmond, 110; *Mutiny on the Bounty*, directed by Frank Lloyd (Hollywood: MGM, 1935); Sturma, *South Sea Maidens*.

58. K. S. Prichard, *Coonardoo* (North Ryde, New South Wales: Angus and Robertson, 1990).

59. A. Pike, "Aboriginals in Australian Feature Films," *Meanjin*, no. 4, (1997): 595; J. Janson, *Black Mary and Gunjies: 2 Plays* (Canberra: Aboriginal Studies Press, 1996).

60. There were exceptions to the predominating negativity of portrayals of Aboriginal women in white Australian culture. Such an exception is artist Margaret Olley's *Nude with Spider Lilies* of 1963, an image with obvious references to Manet and Gauguin that incorporates the Aboriginal model into the exotic tradition.

61. M. Lake, "Female Desires: The Meaning of World War II," *Australian Historical Studies* 24 (1990): 274; Manderson,131.

62. R. Gibson, "I Could Not See as Much as I Desired," in *Pirating the Pacific: Images of Travel, Trade, and Tourism*, ed. A. Stephen (Haymarket, New South Wales: Powerhouse Publishing, 1993), 30; Trask and Trask, "The Aloha Industry"; H. Trask, "Lovely Hula Hands"; Desmond, chs. 2–5.

63. Lutz and Collins, *Reading*, chs. 5 and 6.

64. C. Nordoff and J. Norman Hall, *The Bounty Trilogy* (Boston: Little, Brown and Co., 1948), 73–74. The first edition of this work of 1932 inspired the first Hollywood film of this story.

65. P. Manso, *Brando* (London: Wiedenfield and Nicholson, 1994), 531; M. Kahn, "Tahiti: The Ripples of a Myth on the Shores of the Imagination," *History and Anthropology* 14, no. 4 (2003): 317. *Mutiny on the Bounty*, directed by Lewis Milestone (Hollywood: MGM, 1962); *The Bounty*, directed by Roger Donaldson (Hollywood: Dino De Laurentis Productions, 1984).

66. B. Creed, "Breeding out the Black: *Jedda* and the Stolen Generations in Australia," in *Body Trade: Captivity, Cannibalism and Colonialism in the Pacific*, ed. B. Creed and J. Hoorn (Annandale, New South Wales: Pluto, 2002).

67. *South Pacific*, directed by Joshua Logan (Hollywood: 20th Century Fox, 1958), based on J. A. Michener, *Tales of the South Pacific* (London: Transworld Publishing, 1964). See Jolly, "From Point Venus," 111–15; *Hawaii*, directed by George Roy Hill (Hollywood: Mirisch Corporation, 1966), based on the novel of the same name by J. A. Michener, *Hawaii* (London: Corgi Books, 1991).

68. Teaiwa, "bikinis and other s/pacific n/oceans," 91; Jolly, "From Point Venus," 99; J. Dibblin, *Day of Two Suns: U.S. Nuclear Testing and the Pacific Islands* (New York: New Amsterdam, 1990); J. Niedental, *For the Good of Mankind* (Honolulu: Bravo, 2001); http://www.rmiembassyus.org/nuclear/chronology .html (accessed August 1, 2004).

69. Ida Ata and Philoméne Voirin in the film *Moruroa: The Big Secret*, directed by M. Daëron (France, 1993).

70. R. Betterton, ed., *Looking On: Images of Femininity in the Visual Arts and Media* (London: Pandora, 1987), 46–48, and G. Pollock, "What's Wrong with 'Images of Women'?" in *"The Sexual Subject": A Screen Reader in Sexuality*, Screen (London: Routledge, 1992), 143–45; *Sydney Morning Herald*, September 8, 1995, 1.

71. The Cook Islands gained self-government from New Zealand in 1965; Kiribati became fully independent in 1979, Tuvalu in 1978.

72. New Caledonian indigenous independence struggles against France of the 1980s were quelled in the early 1990s. Vanuatu gained independence in 1980, and the Solomon Islands in 1976.

73. See http://www.cia.gov/cia/publications/factbook/ (accessed August 12, 2004).

74. K. K. Green, "Colonialism's Daughters: Eighteenth- and Nineteenth-Century Western Perceptions of Hawaiian Women," in *Pacific Diaspora: Island Peoples in the United States and Across the Pacific*, ed. P. Spickard et al. (Honolulu: University of Hawai'i Press, 2002).

75. B. Vaughn, ed., *The Unraveling of Island Asia* (Westport, Conn.: Praeger, 2001); Australian Strategic Policy Institute (ASPI), *Our Failing Neighbour: Australia and the Future of the Solomon Islands* (Canberra: Australian Strategic Policy Institute Publications, 2003); Australian Prime Minister John Howard announced on July 22, 2003, that he favored "pooled regional governance" of Nauru, Kiribati, Cook Islands, Tonga, Fiji, and Tuvalu, nations that were "too small to be viable," "PM's New Pacific Solution," *The Australian*, July, 28, 2003; the 2004 South Pacific Forum set a more conciliatory and cooperative note between Australia and her island neighbors.

76. R. A. Underwood, "A Return to Confidence: Recolonization Is Not the Answer," *Pacific Magazine*, June 2004, 5.

77. *Papakolea: A Story of Hawaiian Land*, produced and directed by Edgy Lee and Saul Landau (USA, 1993).

78. "Maoris Put Clark on Notice," *The Australian*, January, 24, 2004.

79. C. Harvey, "A Secret, Horrific Pacific," *The Australian*, October 26, 2004, 11; Lal and Fortune, 439–40.

80. The author acknowledges Tracey Macintosh for her generous assistance in discussions about these contemporary issues.

81. J. Pule's performance piece, "Pacific Holiday," was performed at the National Library of Australia on August 2, 1996.

82. K. Stevenson, "Pacific Women: Challenging the Boundaries of Tradition," *New Zealand Women's Studies Journal*, no. 1 (2001). J. Castro and D. Taula-papa McMullin's art and video installation *Coming of Age in Amelika* was shown at the Asian/Pacific/American Studies Program, New York University, September 2001–January 2002.

83. C. Sambrani, "Austerity-Excess-Invention: The Asia-Pacific Triennial 2002," *Art Monthly Australia*, no. 155 (November 2002): 32; K. Stevenson,

"Pacific Art: Moving Beyond the Stereotype," *Art New Zealand*, no. 90 (autumn, 1999): 66, 68. S. Urale, *Velvet Dreams*, 1998.

84. J. Kerr, "Past Present: The Local Art of Colonial Quotation," in *Double Vision*, ed. Thomas and Losche. Other important artists in this movement are Gordon Bennett, Destiny Deacon, Tracey Moffatt, Anderson Lelei, and Lin Onus. See N. Thomas, *Oceanic Art* (London: Thames and Hudson, 1995), and W. Caruana, *Aboriginal Art* (London: Thames and Hudson, 1995).

85. C. Vercoe, "Postcards as Signatures of Place," *Art AsiaPacific* 3, no. 3 (1996): 84–89; T. Suaalii, "Deconstructing the Exotic Female Beauty of the Pacific Islands and White Male Desire," in *Bitter Sweet: Indigenous Women in the Pacific*, ed. A. Jones et al. (Dunedin, NZ: Otago University Press, 2000); *Pacific Body Language*, directed by Lisa Taouma (Television New Zealand, 2005).

Epilogue

1. T. Horwitz, *Blue Latitudes: Boldly Going Where Captain Cook Has Gone Before* (New York: Henry Holt, 2002), 42, 51, 61.

2. "In Tonto, the Museum comes face to face with its biggest faux," *Washington Post*, September 18, 2004, C1.

Bibliography

Official Printed Sources

Historical Records of Australia, Sydney, Library Committee of the Commonwealth Parliament, 1914

Historical Records of New South Wales, Sydney, Government Printer, 1892–1901

Historical Records of New Zealand, Wellington, Government Printer, 1908–1914

Historical Records of Victoria, Melbourne, Victorian Government Printer's Office, 1981–1998

Minutes of Evidence before the Select Committee on Aborigines in British Settlements, 1836–1837, 8 vols., BPP, Irish University Press, Shannon, 1971

New South Wales Legislative Council Select Committee Report on the Conditions of Aborigines, Government Printer, 1845.

Proceedings of the Pan-Pacific Science Congress, 1923, Melbourne, Government Printer

Periodicals

Missionary Magazine
Quarterly Review
Sydney Gazette
The Sydney Morning Herald
Times of London
The Australian
Washington Post

Unpublished Sources

Alice Borden letter to Alice Vincent Brattain, August 20, 1888; in the private collection of her descendant Mimi Smith.

Berry, M. *Extracts and Correspondence of Miss Berry from the years 1783 to 1852*. 3

vols. London, 1865. Vol. 3, pp. 352–54; in Hawaiian Historical Society/ MS B/ K122P, Appendix 1.

The Journal of Mrs. Arbuthnot 1820–1832. London: Macmillan, 1950; in Hawaiian Historical Society/ MS B/ K122P.

George Bruce. *Life of a Greenwich Pensioner* [1776–1817], Mitchell Library, Sydney, ms A1618–1.

Dwight Baldwin letter to Levi Chamberlain, May 22, 1833, Hawaiian Mission Children's Library, manuscripts, Honolulu.

Log Book of the *Achusnet*, Captain W. Rogers, 1845–1848, Houghton Collection, Houghton Library, MS F. 6870.1 F, Harvard University, Cambridge, Mass.

"Memorials Respecting the Occupation of Tahiti by the French," FO 58/50–58/54, British National Archives.

Pipon, Captain P., R.N. "Narrative of the State of Mutineers of *H.M.S. Bounty* settled on Pitcairn Island in the South Seas," Braborne Collection, Mitchell Library, Sydney, 1 ML ms A77, 1814.

Puckey, W. "A journal consisting of a few remarks of a voyage from Portsmouth to the Society Islands," Alexander Turnbull Library, ms., 1794, Wellington.

Reynolds, S. Journals, Stephens Phillips Library, Peabody Essex Museum, Salem, Mass.

Societe des Etudes Oceaniennes, Musée de Pape'ete, *Pacific Manuscripts Bureau* 71.

South Seas Journals (SSJ), Church World Missions (CWM), SOAS Library Special Collections.

South Seas Letters (SSL), Church World Missions (CWM), SOAS Library Special Collections.

Published Sources

Abbott, G., and N. B. Nairn. *Economic Growth of Australia 1877–1821*. Melbourne: Melbourne University Press, 1978.

Abbott, J. *John Hawkesworth: Eighteenth-Century Man of Letters*. Madison: University of Wisconsin Press, 1982.

Aeschylus. *Persians*, ed. Edith Hall. Warminster: Aris & Phillips, 1996.

Aldrich, R. *The French Presence in the South Pacific*. London: Macmillan, 1990.

——. *The Seduction of the Mediterranean: Writing, Art, and Homosexual Fantasy*. London: Routledge, 1993.

Alexander, W. *The History of Women From The Earliest Antiquity to The Present Time, giving some account of almost every interesting particular concerning that sex, among all nations, ancient and modern*. London: C. Dilly, 1782.

Allen, H. G. *The Betrayal of Liliuokalani: Last Queen of Hawaii, 1838–1917*. Glendale, Calif.: A. H. Clark Co., 1982.

Alloula, M. *The Colonial Harem*. Manchester: Manchester University Press, 1986.

Anderson, W. *The Cultivation of Whiteness: Science, Health, and Racial Destiny in Australia*. New York: Basic Books, 2003.

Anderson, W. *Gauguin's Paradise Lost*. New York: Viking, 1961.

Anon. *An Account of the Mutinous Seizure of the Bounty with the Succeeding Hardships of the Crew to which have been added secret Anecdotes of the Otaheitean Females*. London: Robert Turner, 1792.

Anon. "Otahiete." *Monthly Review*, April 1774.

Anon. *Pomare: Queen of Tahiti: A Poem*. London: John Ollivier, 1847.

Arago, J. *A Narrative of a Voyage Round the World*. New York: Da Capo, 1971.

Australian Strategic Policy Institute. *Our Failing Neighbour: Australia and the Future of the Solomon Islands*. Canberra: Australian Strategic Policy Institute Publications, 2003.

Bade, P. *Femme Fatale: Images of Fascinating and Dangerous Women*. New York: Mayflower Books, c. 1979.

Bakhtin, M. *Rabelais and His World*. Bloomington: Indiana University Press, 1984.

Baldick, C. *In Frankenstein's Shadow: Myth, Monsters, and Nineteenth-Century Writing*. Oxford: Oxford University Press, 1987.

Barbour, P., ed. *The Jamestown Voyages Under the First Charter, 1606–1609*. Vol. 1. Cambridge: Cambridge University Press, 1969.

Barrington, G. *The History of New South Wales including Botany Bay, Port Jackson, Parramatta, and Sydney*. London: M. Jones Publishers, 1802.

Barrow, J. *The Eventful History of the Mutiny and Piratical Seizure of H.M.S. Bounty: Its Causes and Consequences*. London: John Murray, 1839.

Barsam, R. *The Vision of Robert Flaherty*. Bloomington: Indiana University Press, 1988.

Beaglehole, J. C. B., ed. *The Journals of Captain James Cook: The Voyage of the Endeavour, 1768–1771*. Vol. 1. Cambridge: Cambridge University Press, 1955.

———. *The Journals of James Cook: Resolution and Adventure*. Vol. 2. Cambridge: Cambridge University Press, 1955.

———. *The Journals of Captain James Cook: Resolution and Discovery*. Vol. 3, pts. 1 and 2. Cambridge: Cambridge University Press, 1955.

———. *The Endeavour Journal of Joseph Banks*, ed. J. C. B. Beaglehole. Sydney: Angus and Robinson, 1962.

Becke, L. *His Native Wife*. Sydney: Alexander Lindsay, 1895.

Beechert, W. "Patterns of Resistance and the Social Relations of Production in Hawai'i." In *Plantation Workers: Resistance and Accommodation*, ed. B. V. Lal et al. Honolulu: University of Hawai'i Press, 1993.

Belich, J. *Making Peoples: A History of the New Zealanders from Polynesian Settlement to the End of the Nineteenth Century*. Auckland: Penguin Books, 1996.

Bell, L. *Colonial Constructs: European Images of Maori*. Melbourne: Melbourne University Press, 1992.

Berenger, J. P. *Collection de Tous les Voyages faits Autour du Monde par les Differentes Nations de L'Europe*. Geneva: Lausanne, 1789.

Berlin, I. *Many Thousands Gone: The First Two Centuries of Slavery in North America*. Cambridge, Mass.: Belknap Press, 1998.

Bertrand, I. *Cinema in Australia: A Documentary History*. Sydney: New South Wales Press, 1989.

Betterton, R., ed. *Looking On: Images of Femininity in the Visual Arts and Media*. London: Pandora, 1987.

Bhabha, H. K. "The Other Question . . . Homi K. Bhabha Reconsiders the Stereotype and Colonial Discourses." *Screen* 26, no.6 (1983).

Bingham, H. *Twenty-Five Years in the Sandwich Islands*. New York: H. Huntington, 1848.

Black, J. *The British Abroad: The Grand Tour in the Eighteenth Century*. Stroud, UK: Alan Sutton, 1992.

Blainey, G. *The Tyranny of Distance*. Melbourne: Sun Books, 1982.

Blakney, E. H., ed. *The History of Herodotus*. London: J. M. Dent, 1936.

Bland, L., and L. Doan, eds. *Sexology Uncensored: The Documents of Sexual Science*. Cambridge: Polity Press, 1998.

Blevins, Faery R. *Cartographies of Desire: Captivity, Race, and Sex in the Shaping of the American Nation*. Norman: Oklahoma University Press, 1999.

Bligh, W. *A Voyage to the South Sea*. Adelaide: Libraries Board of South Australia, 1969.

Bloch, M., and J. Bloch. "Women and the Dialectics of Nature in Eighteenth-Century French Thought." In *Nature, Culture, and Gender*, ed. C. MacCormack and M. Strattern. New York: Cambridge University Press, 1980.

Bondeson, J. *The Feejee Mermaid and Other Essays in Natural and Unnatural History*. Ithaca: Cornell University Press, 1999.

Bonnemains, J., et al., eds. *Baudin in Australian Waters*. Melbourne: Oxford University Press, 1988.

Bott, R. L. "I Know What Is Due to Me: Self-Fashioning Legitimisation within Liliuokalani's Hawai'i." In *Remaking of Queen Victoria*, ed. M. Homans and A. Munich. Cambridge: Cambridge University Press, 1997.

Bougainville, L. *A Voyage Round the World*. New York: Da Capo, 1967.

Brant, C. "Climates of Gender." In *Romantic Geographies: Discourses of Travel, 1775–1844*, ed. A. Gilroy. Manchester: Manchester University Press, 2000.

Brawley, S., and Dixon, C. "The Hollywood Native: Hollywood's Construction of the South Seas and Wartime Encounters with the South Pacific." *Sites*, no. 27 (1993).

Brewer, J. *The Pleasures of the Imagination: English Culture in the Eighteenth Century*. London: HarperCollins, 1997.

Broome, R. *Aboriginal Australians: Black Response to White Dominance*. Sydney: Allen & Unwin, 1982.

Brown, J. *Strangers in Blood: Fur Trade Families in Indian Country*. Vancouver: University of British Columbia Press, 1980.

Brownmiller, S. *Femininity*. New York: Linden Press, 1984.

Buffon, G. *Buffon's Natural History Containing a Theory of the Earth, a General History of Man, of the Brute Creation, and of Vegetable, Minerals & Co.* 9 vols. London: H. D. Symonds, 1797–1807.

Burke, E. *Philosophical Enquiry into the Origin of Our Ideas of the Sublime and the Beautiful.* London: Printed for R. & J. Dodsley, 1757.

Burton, J. W. *Our Task in Papua.* London: Epsworth Press, 1926.

Byron, G. G. *The Poetical Works of Lord Byron.* London: Oxford University Press, 1933.

Cadden, J. *Meanings of Sex Difference in the Middle Ages: Medicine, Science, and Culture.* Cambridge: Cambridge University Press, 1993.

Caillot, E. *Histoire de la Polynésie Orientale.* Paris: Ernest Leroux, 1910.

Cameron, B. "The Flappers and the Feminists: A Study of Women's Emancipation in the 1920s." In *Worth Her Salt*, ed. M. Bevege et al. Sydney: Hale and Iremonger, 1982.

Campbell, I. C. *A History of the Pacific Islands.* St. Lucia: Queensland University Press, 1990.

Cantarella, E. *Pandora's Daughters: The Role of Women in Greek and Roman Antiquity.* Baltimore: Johns Hopkins University Press, 1987.

Carden-Coyne, A. *Revenge of the Body: Modern Classicism in Postwar Culture, 1918–1933.* Ph.D. dissertation, University of Sydney, 2001.

Carr, H. *Inventing the American Primitive: Politics, Gender, and the Representation of Native American Literary Traditions.* New York: New York University Press, 1996.

Carson, A. "Putting Her in Her Place: Women, Dirt, and Desire." In *Before Sexuality: The Construction of the Erotic Experience in the Ancient Greek World*, ed. D. Halperin et al. Princeton: Princeton University Press, 1990.

Caruana, W. *Aboriginal Art.* London: Thames and Hudson, 1995.

Channamel, A. *History of Fashion in France.* London: Sampson Low, 1882.

Chappell, D. *Double Ghosts: Oceanian Voyagers on Euroamerican Ships.* New York: Armonk, 1997.

Chard, C. "Grand and Ghostly Tours: The Topography of Memory." *Eighteenth Century Studies* 31, no. 1 (1997): 101–8.

Chauvel, C. *In the Wake of the Bounty.* Sydney: Endeavour Press, 1933.

Childs, E. *Pacific Studies* 23, nos. 1–2 (March/June 2000): 75–125.

Cholmondeley, L. *The History of the Bonin Islands from the Year 1827 to the year 1876, and of Nathaniel Savory, One of the Original Settlers.* London: Constable & Co., 1915.

Choris, L. *Voyage Pittoresque Autour du Monde.* Paris: De L'Imprimerie de Firmin Didot, 1822.

Christie, M. *Aborigines in Colonial Victoria 1835–1886.* Sydney: Sydney University Press, 1979.

Coffman, T. *Nation Within: The Story of America's Annexation of the Nation of Hawaii.* Honolulu: Epicenter, n.d.

Cohen, H. "Expedition, Exoticism, and Ethnography." *Photofile*, spring 1988.

Collins, D. *An Account of the English Colony in New South Wales*, ed. B. Fletcher. 2 vols. Sydney: A. H. & A. W. Reed, 1975.

Collins, J. *The Ancien Régime and the French Revolution*. Belmont, Calif.: Wadsworth, 2002.

Cook, J. W. *The Arts of Deception: Playing with Fraud in the Age of Barnum*. Cambridge: Harvard University Press, 2001.

Coombe, G. *Outlines of Phrenology*. Edinburgh: Maclachlan, Stewart & Co., 1844.

Corney, B. G., ed. *Quest and Occupation of Tahiti by the Emissaries of Spain during the years 1772–1776*. 3 vols. London: Hakluyt Society, 1908.

Cranston, R. "Aborigines and the Law: An Overview." *University of Queensland Law Journal* 18, no. 1 (Dec. 1973): 63–78.

Creed, B. "Breeding Out the Black: Jedda and the Stolen Generations in Australia." In *Body Trade: Captivity, Cannibalism and Colonialism in the Pacific*, ed. B. Creed and J. Hoorn. Annandale, New South Wales: Pluto, 2002.

Crosby, A. *Ecological Imperialism: The Biological Expansion of Europe 900–1900*. Cambridge: Cambridge University Press, 1986.

Cumont, F. *After Life in Roman Paganism*. New Haven, Conn.: Yale University Press, 1922.

Cumpston, J. L. "The Depopulation of the Pacific." Presentation given at the Proceedings of the Pan Pacific Science Congress. Vol. 2. Melbourne: Government Printer, 1923.

Cumpston, J. *Kangaroo Island 1800–1836*. Canberra: Roebuck Books, 1970.

Cunningham, P. *Two Years in New South Wales*. London: Henry Colburn, 1827.

Cunningham, S. *Featuring Australia: The Cinema of Charles Chauvel*. North Sydney: Allen & Unwin, 1991.

Cunnington, C. W. *English Women's Clothing in the Nineteenth Century*. New York: Dover Publications, 1990.

Dalrymple, A. *A Historical Collection of the Several Voyages and Discoveries in the South Pacific Ocean* 1 (1770). New York: Da Capo, 1967.

Damousi, J. *Depravity and Disorder: The Sexuality of Convict Women*. Melbourne: Cambridge University Press, 1997.

Dampier, W. *A Collection of Voyages in Four Volumes*. London: James and John Knapton, 1729.

Danielsson, B. *Gauguin in the South Seas*. London: Allen & Unwin, 1965.

Darian-Smith, K. "'Rescuing' Barbara Thompson and Other White Women: Captivity Narratives on Australian Frontiers." In *Text, Theory, Space: Land, Literature, and History in South Africa and Australia*, ed. K. Darian-Smith et al. London: Routledge, 1996.

Darwin, C. *Descent of Man and Selection in Relation to Sex*. London: John Murray, 1871.

Davidoff, L., and Hall, C. *Family Fortunes: Men and Women of the English Middle Class 1780–1850*. London: Hutchinson, 1987.

Daws, G. *Shoals of Time*. Honolulu: University of Hawai'i Press, 1968.

Dean-Jones, L. *Women's Bodies in Classical Greek Science*. Oxford: Clarendon Press, 1994.

De Beauvoir, S. *The Second Sex*. London: Picador Classics, 1953.

De Deckker, P., ed. *The Aggressions of the French at Tahiti and other Islands of the Pacific*. Auckland: Auckland University Press, 1983.

De Gérando, J. M. *Observations of Savage Peoples*. Berkeley: University of California Press, 1969.

De Groot, J. "Sex and Race: The Construction of Language and Image in the Nineteenth Century." In *Sexuality and Subordination*, ed. S. Mendus et al. New York: Routledge, 1989.

Deleuze, G. *Cinema 1: The Movement Image*. London: Athlone Press, 1986.

———. *Cinema 2*. London: Athlone Press, 1989.

Dening, G. *Islands and Beaches, Discourses on a Silent Land: Marquesas, 1774–1880*. Melbourne: Melbourne University Press, 1980.

———. *The Bounty: An Ethnographic History*. Melbourne: Melbourne University Press, 1988.

———. *Mr. Bligh's Bad Language*. Cambridge: Cambridge University Press, 1992.

———. *Performances*. Melbourne: Melbourne University Press, 1996.

Dening, G., ed. *The Marquesan Journal of Edward Robarts, 1797–1824*. Canberra: Australian National University Press, 1974.

Denoon, D., and Firth, S. *The Cambridge History of the Pacific Islanders*. Cambridge: Cambridge University Press, 1997.

Denoon, D., Mein-Smith, P., and Wyndham, M. *A History of Australia, New Zealand, and the Pacific*. Cambridge: Cambridge University Press, 2000.

De Rachewiltz, S. *De Sirenibus: An Inquiry into Sirens from Homer to Shakespeare*. New York: Garland Publishing, 1987.

Desmond, J. *Staging Tourism: Bodies on Display from Waikiki to Sea World*. Chicago: University of Chicago Press, 1999.

De Staël, G. *Corinne or Italy*. New Brunswick, N.J.: Rutgers University Press, 1987.

Dibblin J. *Day of Two Suns: U.S. Nuclear Testing and the Pacific Islands*. New York: New Amsterdam, 1990.

Dickason, O. P. "From 'One Nation' in the Northeast to 'New Nation' in the Northwest." In *The New Peoples: Being and Becoming Métis in North America*, ed. J. Peterson and J. Brown. Lincoln: University of Nebraska Press, 1985.

Diderot, D. "Supplement to the Bougainville Voyage." In *Dialogues*, trans. F. Birrell. London: Routledge, 1927.

Digby, A. "Women's Biological Strait Jacket." In *Sexuality and Subordination*, ed. S. Mendus et al. New York: Routledge, 1989.

Dixon, M. *The Real Matilda*. Ringwood, Victoria: Penguin, 1975.

Djikstra, B. *Idols of Perversity: Fantasies of Feminine Evil in Fin de Siècle Culture*. New York: Oxford University Press, 1986.

Docker, E. W. *The Blackbirders: The Recruiting of South Seas Labour for Queensland, 1863–1907.* Sydney: Angus and Robertson, 1970.

Douglas, B. "Art as Ethnohistorical Text: Science, Representation, and Indigenous Presence in Eighteenth- and Nineteenth-Century Oceanic Voyage Literature." In *Double Vision: Art Histories and Colonial Histories in the Pacific*, ed. N. Thomas and D. Losche. Cambridge: Cambridge University Press, 1999.

———. "Science and the Art of Representing 'Savages': Reading 'Race' in Text and Image in South Seas Voyage Literature." *History and Anthropology* 11, nos. 2–3 (1999).

———. "Seaborne Ethnography and the Natural History of Man." *Journal of Pacific History* 38, no. 1 (June 2003).

Douthwaite, J. *Exotic Women: Literary Heroines and Cultural Strategies in Ancien Régime France.* Philadelphia: University of Pennsylvania Press, 1992.

Drabble, M., ed. *The Oxford Companion to English Literature.* Oxford: Oxford University Press, 1996.

Druett, J. *Petticoat Whalers: Whaling Wives at Sea, 1820–1920.* Auckland: Collins, 1991.

Dulles, F. R. *America in the Pacific: A Century of Expansion.* Boston: Houghton Mifflin, 1932.

Dunbabin, T. "Whalers, Sealers, and Buccaneers." *Royal Australian Historical Society Journal* 9, no. 1 (1925).

Dunmore, J. "The Explorer and Philosopher." In *Captain James Cook: Image and Impact*, ed. W. Veit. Melbourne: Hawthorn Press, 1972.

Dutton, G. *White on Black: The Australian Aborigine Portrayed in Art.* Melbourne: Macmillan, 1974.

Easdale, N. *Missionary and Maori: Kerikeri, 1819–1860.* Lincoln: Te Waihora Press, 1991.

Edmond, R. *Representing the South Pacific.* Cambridge: Cambridge University Press, 1997.

Eisenman, S. *Gauguin's Skirt.* London: Thames and Hudson, 1997.

———. "(Anti) Imperial Primitivist: Paul Gauguin in Oceania." *Pacific Studies* 23, nos. 1–2 (March/June 2000): 75–125.

Ellis, W. *Polynesia Researches.* 2 vols. London: Dawsons, 1967.

Eves, R. "Going Troppo: Images of White Savagery, Degeneration, and Race in the Turn-of-the-Century Colonial Fictions of the Pacific." *History and Anthropology* 11, nos. 2–3 (1999): 351–85.

Evison, H. *Te Wai Pounamu: The Greenstone Island.* Christchurch: Aoraki Press, 1993.

Eyre, E. J. *Journal of Two Expeditions of Discovery into Central Australia and Overland from Adelaide to King George's Sound, 1840–1841.* London: T. W. Boone, 1845.

Fausto-Sterling, A. "Gender, Race, Nation: The Comparative Anatomy of 'Hottentot' Women in Europe, 1815–1817." In *Deviant Bodies: Critical Perspectives on*

Difference in Science and Popular Culture, J. Terry and J. Urla, eds. Bloomington: Indiana University Press, 1995.

Fellows, O., and Milliken, S. *Buffon*. New York: Twayne Publishers, 1972.

Fidlon, P.G., and R. J. Ryan, eds. *The Journal of Arthur Bowes Smyth: Surgeon on Lady Penrhyn, 1787–1789*. Sydney: Australian Documents Library, 1979.

——. *The Journal and Letters of Lt. Ralph Clark, 1787–1792*. Sydney: Australian Documents Library, 1981.

Firestone, S. *The Dialectic of Sex*. New York: Bantam Books, 1979.

Fitzgerald, G. *The Injured Islanders, or the Influence of Art upon the Happiness of Nature: A Poetical Epistle from Oberea of Otaheite to Captain Wallis by the Author of the Academick Sportsman*. Dublin: T. T. Faulkner, 1779.

Fletcher, A. *Gender, Sex, and Subordination in England 1500–1800*. New Haven, Conn.: Yale University Press, 1995.

[Fletcher, Robert]. *Gone Native: A Tale of the South Seas*. London: Constable and Co., 1924.

——. *Gone Native: A Tale of the South Seas*. Boston: Small Maynard and Co., 1924.

——. *Isles of Illusion: Letters from the South Seas*. London: Century, 1986.

Foa, A. "The New and the Old: The Spread of Syphilis, 1494–1530." In *Sex and Gender in Historical Perspective*, ed. E. Muir and G. Ruggiero. Baltimore: Johns Hopkins University Press, 1990.

Foerstel, L., and A. Gilliam. *Confronting the Margaret Mead Legacy: Scholarship, Empire, and the South Pacific*. Philadelphia: Temple University Press, 1992.

Forbes, D. *Encounters with Paradise: Views of Hawaii and Its People 1788–1941*. Honolulu: University of Hawai'i Press, 1992.

Forster H., ed. *"The Cruise of the Gypsy": The Journal of John Wilson, Surgeon on a Whaling Voyage to the Pacific Ocean 1839–1841*. Washington, D.C.: Ye Galleon Press, 1991.

Forster, J. R., N. Thomas et al., eds. *Observations Made During a Voyage round the World*. Honolulu: University of Hawai'i Press, 1996.

Foucault, M. *The History of Sexuality*. Vol. 1. Ringwood, Victoria: Penguin Books, 1990.

Fowler, D. *Northern Attitudes towards Interracial Marriage: Legislation and Public Opinion in the Middle Atlantic and States of the Old Northwest, 1780–1930*. New York: Garland Publishing, 1987.

Fraisse, G. *Reason's Muse: Sexual Difference and the Birth of Democracy*. Chicago: University of Chicago Press, 1994.

Fraisse, G., and M. Perrot, eds. *History of Women in the West*. Vol. 4. Cambridge: Harvard University Press, 1994.

Freeman, D. *Margaret Mead and Samoa: The Making and Unmaking of an Anthropological Myth*. Canberra: Australian National University Press, 1983.

Freud, S. *On Sexuality: Three Essays on the Theory of Sexuality and Other Works*. Ringwood, Victoria: Penguin Books, 1977.

Gascoigne, J. *Joseph Banks and the English Enlightenment*. Cambridge: Cambridge University Press, 1994.

———. "The Ordering of Nature." In *Visions of Empire: Voyages, Botany, and Representations of Nature*, ed. D. Miller and P. Reill. Cambridge: Cambridge University Press, 1996.

Gatens, M. *Feminism and Philosophy: Perspectives on Difference and Equality*. London: Polity Press, 1991.

Gauguin, P. *Noa Noa: Voyage to Tahiti*. Oxford: Bruno Cassirer, n.d.

Gibson, R. *South of the West: Postcolonialism and the Narrative Construction of Australia*. Bloomington: University of Indiana Press, 1992.

———. "I Could Not See as Much as I Desired." In *Pirating the Pacific: Images of Travel, Trade, and Tourism*, ed. A. Stephen. Haymarket, New South Wales: Powerhouse Publishing, 1993.

Gilbert, A. "Buggery in the British Navy, 1700–1861." *Journal of Social History* 10 (1976).

Gilbert, J. *A History of Discovery and Exploration: Eastern Islands, Southern Seas*. London: Aldus Books, 1973.

Gilman, S. L. *Difference and Pathology: Stereotypes of Sexuality, Race, and Madness*. Ithaca, N.Y.: Cornell University Press, 1985.

Goldberg, R. *Sex and the Enlightenment: Women in Richardson and Diderot*. Cambridge: Cambridge University Press, 1984.

Gratten, H. C. *The South-West Pacific to 1900*. Ann Arbor: University of Michigan Press, 1967.

Green K. K. "Colonialism's Daughters: Eighteenth- and Nineteenth-Century Western Perspectives of Hawaiian Women." In *Pacific Diaspora: Island Peoples in the United States and Across the Pacific*, ed. P. Spickard et al. Honolulu: University of Hawai'i Press, 2002.

Greenblatt, S. *Marvelous Possessions: The Wonder of the New World*. Chicago: University of Chicago Press, 1991.

Greer, G. *The Female Eunuch*. London: Paladin, 1972.

Gregory, J. W. *The Menace of Colour*. London: Seeley Service, 1925.

Grigson, G. *The Goddess of Love: The Birth, Triumph, Death, and Return of Aphrodite*. London: Constable, 1976.

Grimal, P. *The Dictionary of Classical Mythology*. New York: Basil Blackwell, 1986.

Grimshaw, P. *Paths of Duty: American Missionary Wives in Nineteenth-Century Hawaii*. Honolulu: University of Hawai'i Press, 1989.

Groneman, C. "Nymphomania: The Historical Construction of Female Sexuality." In *Deviant Bodies: Critical Perspectives on Difference in Science and Popular Culture*, ed. J. Terry and J. Urla. Bloomington: Indiana University Press, 1995.

Grosz, E. *Sexual Subversions: Three French Feminists*. Sydney: Allen & Unwin, 1989.

———. *Volatile Bodies: Towards a Corporeal Feminism*. Sydney: Allen & Unwin, 1994.

Guest, H. "The Great Distinction: Figures of the Exotic in the Work of William Hodges." *Oxford Art Journal* 12, no. 2 (1989).

———. "Curiously Marked: Tattooing, Masculinity, and Nationality in the Eighteenth-Century Perceptions of the Pacific." In *Painting and the Politics of Culture: New Essays on British Art, 1700–1850*, ed. J. Barrell. Oxford: Oxford University Press, 1992.

———. "Looking at Women: Forster's Observations in the South Pacific." In *Observations Made During a Voyage Round the World*, J. R. Forster, N. Thomas et al, eds. Honolulu: University of Hawai'i Press, 1996.

Gullickson, S. "Unruly Women of the Paris Commune." In *Gendered Domains: Rethinking Public and Private in Women's History*, ed. D. Helly and S. Reverby. Ithaca, N.Y.: Cornell University Press, 1992.

Gunson, N., ed. *The Reminiscences and Papers of L. E. Threlkeld, 1824–1859*. Canberra: Australian Institute of Aboriginal Studies, 1974.

———. *Messengers of Grace: Evangelical Missionaries in the South Seas, 1797–1860*. Melbourne: Oxford University Press, 1978.

Haebich, A. *Broken Circles: Fragmenting Indigenous Families*. Freemantle: Freemantle Arts Centre Press, 2000.

Hainsworth, D. R. *The Sydney Traders: Simeon Lord and His Contemporaries*. Melbourne: Cassell, 1972.

Haldane, C. *Tempest Over Tahiti*. London: Constable, 1963.

Hale, J. *The Civilisation of Europe in the Renaissance*. London: HarperCollins, 1993.

Hall, C. *White, Male, and Middle-Class*. London: Polity Press, 1992.

Hall, E. *Inventing the Barbarian: Greek Self-Definition through Tragedy*. Oxford: Clarendon Press, 1989.

———. "Asia Unmanned: Images of Victory in Classical Athens." In *War and Society in the Greek World*, ed. J. Rich and G. Shipley. London: Routledge, 1993.

Haltunnen, K. *Confidence Men and Painted Women: A Study of Middle-Class Culture in America, 1830–1870*. New Haven, Conn.: Yale University Press, 1982.

Hannaford, I. *Race: The History of an Idea in the West*. Baltimore: Johns Hopkins University Press, 1996.

Hansen, C., C. Needham, and B. Nichols. "Pornography, Ethnography, and the Discourses of Power." In *Representing Reality: Issues and Concepts in Documentary Films*, ed. B. Nichols. Bloomington: Indiana University Press, 1991.

Harris, M. *The Rise of Anthropological Theory*. London: Routledge & Kegan Paul, 1972.

Harrison, T. *The Emptiness of Asia: Aeschylus' Persians and the History of the Fifth Century*. London: Duckworth, 2000.

Harvey, C. "A Secret, Horrific Pacific." *The Australian*, October 26, 2004, 11.

Havelock, C. M. *The Aphrodite of Knidos and Her Successors: A Historical Review of the Female Nude in Greek Art*. Ann Arbor: University of Michigan Press, 1995.

Hawkesworth, J. *An Account of the Voyages of Discovery Undertaken by the Order of*

His Present Majesty for making Discoveries in the Southern Hemisphere. Vol. 1. London: W. Strathan and T. Caddell, 1773.

Henry, T. *Ancient Tahiti.* Honolulu: Bishop Museum, 1928.

Hibbert, C. *The Grand Tour.* London: Thames Methuen, 1987.

Hitchcock, T. "Redefining Sex in the Eighteenth Century." *History Workshop Journal* 41 (1996).

Hogarth, W. *The Analysis of Beauty.* Menston, UK: Scholar Press, 1971.

Homer. *The Odyssey,* trans. W. Shewring. Oxford: Oxford University Press, 1980.

Horwitz, T. *Blue Latitudes: Boldly Going Where Captain Cook Has Gone Before.* New York: Henry Holt Co., 2002.

Howay, F., ed. *The Voyage of the New Hazard: To the Northwest Coast, Hawaii, and China 1810–1813.* Salem, Mass.: Peabody Museum, 1938.

Howe, K. R. *Where the Waves Fall.* Sydney: Allen & Unwin, 1984.

Hughes, R. *The Fatal Shore: A History of the Transportation of Convicts to Australia, 1787–1868.* London: Collins and Harvill, 1987.

Hulme, P. "Polytropic Man: Tropes of Sexuality and Mobility in Early Colonial Discourse." In *Europe and Its Others,* ed. F. Barker et al. Colchester, UK: Essex University Press, 1985.

Hunt, L., ed. *Eroticism and the Body Politic.* Baltimore: Johns Hopkins University Press, 1990.

———. *The Invention of Pornography: Obscenity and the Origins of Modernity, 1500–1800.* New York: Zone Books, 1993.

Hunter, J. *An Historical Journal of the transactions at Port Jackson and Norfolk Island.* London: John Stockdale, 1793.

Huntington, E. *Civilization and Climate.* New Haven, Conn.: Yale University Press, 1915.

Ii, J. P. *Fragments of Hawaiian History.* Honolulu: Bishop Museum Press, 1983.

Ives, C., et al. *The Lure of the Exotic: Gauguin in New York Collections.* New Haven, Conn.: Yale University Press, 2002.

Janson, J. *Black Mary and Gunjies: 2 Plays.* Canberra: Aboriginal Studies Press, 1996.

Johnston, W. J. *Race Relations in Virginia and Miscegenation in the South, 1776–1860.* Amherst: University of Massachusetts Press, 1970.

Jolly, M. "'To Save the Girls for Brighter and Better Lives': Presbyterian Missions and Women in the South of Vanuatu, 1848–1870." *Journal of Pacific History* 36, no. 1 (June 1991).

———. "Ill-Natured Comparisons: Race and Relativism in European Representations of Ni-Vanuatu from Cook's Second Voyage." *History and Anthropology* 5, no. 3–4 (1992): 331–64.

———. "Desire, Difference, and Disease: Sexual and Venereal Exchanges on Cook's Voyages in the Pacific." In *Exchanges: Cross-Cultural Encounters in Australia and the Pacific,* ed. R. Gibson. Sydney: Museum of Sydney Press, 1997.

———. "White Shadows in the Darkness: Representations of Polynesian Women in Early Cinema." *Pacific Studies* 20, no. 4 (Dec. 1997): 125–49.

———. "From Point Venus to Bali Ha'i: Eroticism and Exoticism in Representations of the Pacific." In *Sites of Desire/Economies of Pleasure: Sexualities in Asia and the Pacific*, ed. L. Manderson and M. Jolly. Chicago: University of Chicago Press, 1997.

———. "Fraying Gauguin's Skirt: Gender, Race, and Liminality." *Pacific Studies* 23, nos. 1–2 (March/June 2000): 75–125.

Jordonova, L. "Natural Facts: A Historical Perspective on Science and Sexuality." In *Nature, Culture, Gender*, ed. C. MacCormack and M. Strattern. New York: New York University Press, 1980.

———. *Sexual Visions: Images of Gender in Science and Medicine between the Eighteenth and Twentieth Centuries*. Madison: Wisconsin University Press, 1989.

Just, R. "Conceptions of Women in Classical Athens." *Journal of Anthropological Society of Oxford* 6, no. 3 (1975): 153–70.

Kahn, M. "Heterotopic Dissonance in the Museum Representation of Pacific Island Cultures." *American Anthropologist* 97, no. 2 (June 1995): 324–38.

———. "Tahiti: The Ripples of a Myth on the Shores of the Imagination." *History and Anthropology* 14, no. 4 (2003): 307–26.

Kame'eleihiwa, L. *Native Lands, Foreign Desire*. Honolulu: Bishop Museum Press, 1992.

———. *Nā Wāhine Kapu: Divine Hawaiian Women*. Honolulu: 'Ai Pōhaku Press, 1999.

Kanahele, G. S. *Emma: Hawaii's Remarkable Queen*. Honolulu: University of Hawai'i Press, 1999.

Keate, G. *An Account of the Pelaw Islands situated in the Western part of the Pacific Ocean composed from Journals and Communications of Captain Henry Wilson and some of his officers who in August 1783 were there shipwrecked in the Antelope*. London: G. Nicol, 1788.

Kerr, J. "Past Present: The Local Art of Colonial Quotation." In *Double Vision: Art Histories and Colonial Histories in the Pacific*, ed. N. Thomas and D. Losche. Cambridge: Cambridge University Press, 1999.

Kerr, J., ed. *The Dictionary of Australian Artists, Painters, Sketchers, Photographers, and Engravers to 1870*. Melbourne: Oxford University Press, 1992.

Keuls, E. *The Reign of the Phallus: Sexual Politics in Ancient Athens*. New York: Harper & Row, 1985.

Kiernan, V. G. "Noble and Ignoble Savages." In *Exoticism and the Enlightenment*, ed. G. Rousseau and R. Porter. Manchester: Manchester University Press, 1990.

Knight, A., ed. *Robert Louis Stevenson in the South Seas: An Intimate Photographic Record*. Edinburgh: Mainstream, 1986.

Kociumbas, J. *Oxford History of Australia*. Vol. 2. Melbourne: Oxford University Press, 1992.

Kohlbrugge, J. H. F. "The Influence of a Tropical Climate on Europeans." *The Eugenics Review* 3 (April 1911–12): 23–36.

von Krafft-Ebing, R. *Psychopathia Sexualis: With Especial Reference to the Antipathetic Sexual Instinct.* London: Staples Press, 1965 [1886].

von Krusenstern, A. J. *Voyage Round the World in the Years 1803, 1804, 1805, & 1806 by the Order of His Imperial Majesty Alexander the First on Board the Ships Nadeshda and Neva under the command of Captain A. J. von Krusenstern of the Imperial Navy.* New York: Da Capo, 1968.

Kuyper, J. *De Mensch: Zoo Als Hij Voorkomt op Den Bekenden Aardbol.* 3 vols. Amsterdam: Johannes Allart, 1802.

La Billardière, J. J. *Voyage in Search of La Pérouse, 1791–1794.* London: John Stockdale London, 1800; New York: Da Capo, 1971.

Lake, M. "Female Desires: The Meaning of World War II." *Australian Historical Studies* 24 (1990).

Lal, B. and K. Fortune, eds. *The Pacific Islands: An Encyclopedia.* Honolulu: University of Hawai'i Press, 2000.

Lal, B. et al., eds. *Plantation Workers: Resistance and Accommodation.* Honolulu: University of Hawai'i Press, 1993.

Langdon, R. *Tahiti: Island of Love.* London: Pacific Publications, Cassell, 1963.

———. "Dusky Damsels: Pitcairn Island's Neglected Matriarchs of the Bounty Saga." *Journal of Pacific History* 35 (June 2000): 29–48.

von Langsdorff, G. H. *Voyages and Travels in Various Parts of the World during the years 1803–7.* 2 vols. New York: Da Capo, 1968.

Laqueur, T. *Making Sex: Body and Gender from the Greeks to Freud.* Cambridge: Harvard University Press, 1990.

Le Pichon, Y. *Gauguin: Life, Art, and Inspiration.* New York: Harry Abrahms, 1987.

Lewis, R. *Gendering Orientalism: Race, Femininity, and Representation.* London: Routledge, 1996.

Liebersohn, H. "Images of Monarchy: Kamehameha I and the Art of Louis Choris." In *Double Vision: Art Histories and Colonial Histories in the Pacific,* ed. N. Thomas and D. Losche. Cambridge: Cambridge University Press, 1999.

Liliuokalani. *Hawaii's Story by Hawaii's Queen.* Tokyo: Charles E. Tuttle, 1964.

Lindfors, B. "Circus Africans." *Journal of American Culture* 6, no. 2 (1983).

Link, F. M., ed. *The Plays of John O'Keefe.* New York: Garland, 1981.

Linnekin, J. "Ignoble Savages and Other European Visions." *Journal of Pacific History* 26, no. 1 (June 1991).

Lisiansky, U. *A Voyage Around the World in the Years 1803, 4, 5 & 6 performed by the order of his Imperial Majesty Alexander the First of Russia in the Ship Neva by Urey Lisiansky Captain of the Russian Navy.* New York: Da Capo, 1968.

Lloyd, G. "Rousseau on Reason, Nature, and Women." *Metaphilosophy* 14, no. 3–4 (July/October1983).

Lovejoy, A., and G. Boas. *"Primitivism" and Related Ideas in Antiquity.* Baltimore: Johns Hopkins University Press, 1935.

Lowe, L. *Critical Terrains: French and British Orientalisms*. Ithaca, N.Y.: Cornell University Press, 1991.

Lutz, C., and Collins, J. *Reading National Geographic*. Chicago: University of Chicago Press, 1993.

Lytle, Croutier A. *Harem: The World Behind the Veil*. New York: Abbeville Press, 1989.

Mackenzie, J. "The Imperial Pioneer and Hunter and the British Masculine Stereotype in Late Victorian and Edwardian Times." In *Manliness and Morality: Middle-Class Masculinity in Britain and American, 1800–1940*, J. A. Mangan and J. Walvin, eds. Manchester: Manchester University Press, 1987.

Malik, K. *The Meaning of Race: Race, History, and Culture in Western Society*. New York: New York University Press, 1996.

Malingue, M., ed. *Paul Gauguin: Letters to His Wife and Friends*. London: Saturn Press, 1946.

Malinowski, B. *The Sexual Life of Savages*. London: George Routledge, 1939.

Manderson, L. "Parables of Imperialism and Fantasies of the Exotic: Western Representations of Thailand — Place and Sex." In *Sites of Desire/Economies of Pleasure: Sexualities in Asia and the Pacific*, L. Manderson and M. Jolly, eds. Chicago: University of Chicago Press, 1997.

Manderson, L., and M. Jolly. *Sites of Desire/Economies of Pleasure: Sexualities in Asia and the Pacific*. Chicago: University of Chicago Press, 1997.

Mannering, D. *The Life and Works of Gauguin*. London: Paragon, 1994.

Manso, P. *Brando*. London: Wiedenfield and Nicholson, 1994.

Marra, J. *Journal of the Resolution Voyage in 1772, 1773, 1774, and 1775*. New York: Da Capo, 1967.

Martin, G., ed. *Founding of Australia*. Sydney: Hale and Iremonger, 1978.

Maude, H. *Of Islands of Men: Studies in Pacific History*. Melbourne: Oxford University Press, 1968.

Maugham, S. *The Moon and Sixpence*. New York: Heritage Reprints, 1941.

McAlpin, M. "Between Men for All Eternity: Feminocentrism in Montesquieu's Lettres persanes." *Eighteenth Century Life* 24, no. 1 (2000): 45–61.

McClintock, A. *Imperial Leather: Race, Gender, and Sexuality in the Colonial Contest*. London: Routledge, 1995.

McCormick, E. H. *Omai: Pacific Envoy*. Auckland: Auckland University Press, 1977.

McDonald, B. *Cinderellas of the Empire: Towards a History of Kiribati and Tuvalu*. Canberra: Australian National University Press, 1982.

McGrath, A. *Born in the Cattle*. Sydney: Allen & Unwin, 1987.

———. "The Whiteman's Looking Glass: Aboriginal-Colonial Gender Relations at Port Jackson." *Australian Historical Studies* 24, no. 95 (Oct. 1990).

McNeill, J. R., and W. H. McNeill. *The Human Web: A Bird's Eye View of World History*. New York: Norton, 2003.

Mead, M. *The Coming of Age in Samoa: A Psychological Study of Primitive Youth for Western Civilization*. New York: Morrow, 1961.

——. *Blackberry Winter: My Earlier Years*. New York: Morrow, 1972.

——. *Letters from the field, 1925–1975*. New York: Harper & Row, 1977.

Meares, J. *Voyages Made in the Years 1788 and 1789 from China to the Northwest Coast of America*. London: Logographic Press, 1790; New York: Da Capo, 1967.

Meek, R. *Social Science and the Ignoble Savage*. London: Cambridge University Press, 1976.

Meiners, C. *History of the Female Sex*. Vol. 1. London: Henry Colburn, 1808.

Melville, H. *Typee: A Peep at Polynesian Life During a Four Months Residence in a Valley of the Marquesas*. New York: Signet Classic, 1964 [1846].

——. *Omoo*. With an introduction by V. Brooks. New York: Heritage Press, 1967.

——. *Moby Dick, or The Whale*. Indianapolis: Bobbs-Merrill, 1976.

——. *Omoo: Adventures in the South Seas*, ed. K. O'Connor. London: KIP Ltd., 1985.

Michener, J. A. *Tales of the South Pacific*. London: Transworld Publishing, 1964.

——. *Hawaii*. London: Corgi Books London, 1991.

Miles, M. *Carnal Knowing: Female Nakedness and Religious Meaning in the Christian West*. Boston: Beacon Press, 1989.

Millet, K. *Sexual Politics*. London: Granada, 1970.

Milliss, R. *Waterloo Creek: The Australia Day Massacre of 1838, George Gipps, and the British Conquest of New South Wales*. Ringwood, Victoria: McPhee Gribble, 1992.

Milton, J. *Paradise Lost*, ed. C. Ricks. Melbourne: Penguin Books, 1989.

Minson, M. *Encounter with Eden: New Zealand 1770–1870*. Wellington: National Library of New Zealand Press, 1990.

Mitford, M. *Christina, Maid of the South Seas: A Poem*. London: A. J. Valpy, 1811.

Moerenhout, J. A. *Travels to the Islands of the Pacific Ocean*, trans. A. Borden. Lanham, Md.: University of America Press, 1983.

Money, L. *The Peril of the White Race*. London: W. Collins, 1925.

Moore, C. "A Precious Few: Melanesian and Asian Women in Northern Australia." In *Gender Relations in Australia*, ed. K. Saunders and R. Evans. Sydney: Harcourt Brace Jovanovich, 1992.

——. "The Counterculture of Survival: Melanesians in the Mackay Distric of Queensland." In B. V. Lal et al., eds. Honolulu: University of Hawai'i Press, 1993.

Moore, C., et al., eds. *Labour in the South Pacific*. Townsville: James Cook University Press, 1990.

Morice, C. *Paul Gauguin*. London: Everyman, 1919.

Morton, H. *The Whales Wake Otago Up*. Dunedin, NZ: Otago University Press, 1982.

Mulvey, L. "Visual Pleasure and Narrative Cinema." In *The Sexual Subject: A Screen Reader.* London: Routledge, 1992.

Navarro, M., et. al. *Women in Latin America and the Caribbean: Restoring Women to History.* Bloomington: Indiana University Press, 1999.

Nead, L. *The Female Nude: Art, Obscenity, and the Gaze.* London: Routledge, 1992.

Newbury, C. *Tahiti Nui: Change and Survival in French Polynesia.* Honolulu: University of Hawai'i Press, 1980.

Newman, G. *The Rise of English Nationalism: A Cultural History, 1670–1830.* London: Weidenfield and Nicholson, 1987.

Nichols, B. ed. *Representing Reality: Issues and Concepts in Documentary Films.* Bloomington: Indiana University Press, 1991.

Nicole, R. *The Word, The Pen, and The Pistol: Literature and Power in Tahiti.* Albany: State University of New York Press, 2001.

Niedental, J. *For the Good of Mankind.* Honolulu: Bravo, 2001.

Nordoff, C., and J. Hall. *The Bounty Trilogy.* Boston: Little, Brown and Co., 1948.

Nussbaum, F. *Torrid Zones: Maternity, Sexuality, and Empire in Eighteenth-Century Narratives.* Baltimore: Johns Hopkins University Press, 1995.

O'Brien, F. *White Shadows in the South Seas.* New York: Grosset & Dunlap, 1919.

———. *Mystic Isles of the South Seas.* New York: Hodder and Stoughton, 1921.

———. *Atolls in the Sun.* New York: Century Co., 1922.

O'Brien, P. "The Gaze of the Ghosts: European Representations of Aboriginal Women in New South Wales and Port Phillip, 1800–1850." In *Maps Dreams History: Race and Representation in Australia*, ed. J. Kociumbas. Sydney: Braxus Publishing, 1998.

———. "Exotic Primitivism and the Baudin Voyage to Tasmania in 1802." *Journal of Australian Studies*, no. 63 (2000).

———. "Taking Possession of Tahiti: British and French Masculinity, Queen Pomare, and the Annexation of Tahiti, 1837–1847." Forthcoming.

———. "Think of Me as a Woman: Queen Pomare and Anglo-French Contest in the 1840s Pacific." *Gender and History*, forthcoming.

Orange, C. *The Treaty of Waitangi.* North Sydney: Allen & Unwin, 1989.

O'Reilly, P., and R. Tessier. *Tahitiens: Répetoire Biographique de la Polynésie Française.* Paris: La Société des Oceaniste, 1975.

Organ, M. *Illawarra and South Coast Aborigines, 1770–1850.* Wollongong: Wollongong University, Aboriginal Education Unit, 1990.

Orr, B. "Southern Passions Mix with Northern Art: Miscegenation and the Endeavour Voyage." *Eighteenth-Century Life* 18 (November 1994): 212–31.

Orsmond, J. "Extracts from the Old Orsmond MS 1849." In *The History of the Tahitian Mission, 1799–1830*, ed. J. Davies. London: Hakluyt Society, 1959.

Outram, D. *The Body and the French Revolution: Sex, Class, and Political Culture.* New Haven, Conn.: Yale University Press, 1989.

Oxley, D. *Convict Maids: The Forced Migration of Women to Australia.* Melbourne: Cambridge University Press, 1996.

Page, M. "Lascivious Contact." B.A. thesis, Fine Arts Department, University of Sydney, 1996.

Parkinson, S. *The Journal of a Voyage to the South Seas in his Majesty's Ship the Endeavour: Faithfully transcribed from the Papers of the late Sidney Parkinson*. London: John Fothergill, 1784.

Pateman, C. *The Sexual Contract*. Oxford: Polity Press, 1988.

Péron, F. *A Voyage to the Southern Hemisphere*. London: Richard Phillips, 1809.

———. "Report on the Maria Island Aborigines." In *The Baudin Expedition and the Tasmanian Aborigines*, N. J. B. Plomley, ed. Hobart: Blubber Head Press, 1983.

Philips, D. "Anatomy of a Rape Case, 1888." In *A Nation of Rogues*, ed. D. Philips and S. Davies. Melbourne: Melbourne University Press, 1994.

Phillip, A. *The Voyage of Governor Phillip to Botany Bay*. Melbourne: Hutchinson, 1982 [1798].

Pierce, L. P. *The Imperial Harem: Women and Sovereignty in the Ottoman Empire*. New York: Oxford University Press, 1993.

Pike, A. "Aboriginals in Australian Feature Films." *Meanjin*, no. 4 (1997): 595.

Plomley, N. J. B. *The Baudin Expedition and the Tasmanian Aborigines, 1802*. Hobart: Blubber Head Press, 1983.

Plomley, N. J. B., ed. *The Friendly Mission: The Tasmanian Journals and Papers of George Augustus Robinson*. Hobart: Tasmanian Historical Research Association, 1966.

Plomley, N. J. B., and K. Henley. *The Sealers of Bass Strait and the Cape Barren Island Community*. Hobart: Blubber Head Press, 1990.

Plumwood, V. *Feminism and the Mastery of Nature*. London: Routledge, 1993.

Pollock, G. *Avant-Garde Gambits, 1888–1893: Gender and the Colour of Art History*. London: Thames and Hudson, 1992.

———. "What's Wrong with 'Images of Women'?" In *"The Sexual Subject": A Screen Reader in Sexuality, Screen*. London: Routledge, 1992.

Poovey, M. *Uneven Developments: The Ideological Work of Gender in Mid-Victorian England*. London: Virago, 1989.

Porter, D. *Journal of a Cruise Made to the Pacific Ocean by Capt. David Porter in the United States Frigate Essex in the years 1812, 1813, and 1814*. 2 vols. Upper Saddle River, N. J.: Gregg Press, 1970.

Porter, R. "The Exotic as Erotic: Captain Cook at Tahiti." In *Exoticism and Enlightenment*, ed. G. Rousseau and R. Porter. Manchester: Manchester University Press, 1990.

Porter, R., and L. Hall. *The Facts of Life: The Creation of Sexual Knowledge in Britain, 1650–1950*. New Haven, Conn.: Yale University Press, 1995.

Poyer, L. *The Ngatik Massacre: History and Identity on a Micronesian Atoll*. Washington, D.C.: Smithsonian Institution Press, 1993.

Pratt, M. L. *Imperial Eyes: Travel Writing and Transculturation*. London: Routledge, 1992.

Prichard, K. S. *Coonardoo*. North Ryde, New South Wales: Angus and Robertson, 1990.

Pule, J. "Pacific Holiday." Performed at the National Library of Australia on August 2, 1996.

The Push from the Bush: A Bulletin of Social History. Special Myall Creek Issue, 20 (April 1985).

Ralston, C. *Grass Huts and Warehouses: Pacific Beach Communities of the Nineteenth Century*. Canberra: Australian National University Press, 1977.

——. "Prostitution, Pollution, and Polyandry: The Problems of Eurocentrism and Androcentrism in Polynesian Studies." In *Crossing Boundaries: Feminism and the Critique of Knowledges*, ed. B. Caine et al. Sydney: Allen & Unwin, 1988.

Ramazanoglu, C., and J. Holland. "Women's Sexuality and Men's Appropriation of Desire." In *Up Against Foucault: Explorations of Some Feminist Tensions between Foucault and Feminism*, ed. C. Ramazanoglu et al. London: Routledge, 1993.

Rediker, M. *Between the Devil and the Deep Blue Sea*. Cambridge: Cambridge University Press, 1987.

Reece, R. H. W. *Aborigines and Colonists*. Sydney: Sydney University Press, 1974.

Rennie, N. *Far-Fetched Facts: The Literature of Travel and the Idea of the South Seas*. Oxford: Clarendon Press, 1995.

Reyes, L. *Made in Paradise: Hollywood Films of Hawaii and the South Seas*. Honolulu: Mutual Publishing, 1995.

Reynolds, H. *The Other Side of the Frontier*. Ringwood, Victoria: Penguin Books, 1982.

Richards, T. L., with S. Gurr. *White Man, Brown Woman: The Life Story of a Trader in the South Sea*. London: Hutchinson, 1932.

Rickman, J. *Journal of Captain Cook's Last Voyage to the Pacific Ocean*. London: E. Newbery, 1781.

Rivers, W. H. R., ed. *Essays on the Depopulation of Melanesia*. Cambridge: Cambridge University Press, 1922.

Riviere, M., and T. Huynh Einam, eds. *Any Port in a Storm: From Provence to Australia: Rolland's Journal of the Voyage of La Coquille (1822–1825)*. Townsville, Queensland: James Cook University Press, 1993.

Roberts, D. *The Myth of Aunt Jemima: Representations of Race and Region*. London: Routledge, 1995.

Roberts, S. *Population Problems of the Pacific*. New York: AMS Press, 1969.

Robertson, G. *The Discovery of Tahiti: A Journal of the 2nd Voyage of HMS Dolphin round the World by George Robertson, 1766–1768*. Cambridge: Cambridge University Press, 1948.

Roderick, C. "Sir Joseph Banks, Queen Oberea, and the Satirists." In *Captain James Cook: Image and Impact Discoveries and the World of Letters*, ed. W. Veit. Melbourne: Hawthorn Press, 1972.

Roe, M., ed. *The Journal and Letters of Captain Charles Bishop on the North-West Coast of America, in the Pacific and New South Wales in 1794–1799*. Cambridge: Cambridge University Press, 1967.

Rogers, S. "Composing Conscience: The Injured Islanders and English Sensibility." *The Eighteenth Century* 38, no. 3 (fall 1997): 259–65.

Rose, P. *Jazz Cleopatra: Josephine Baker in Her Time*. London: Vintage, 1990.

Rosenman, H., ed. *An Account in Two Volumes of Two Voyages to the South Seas*. Vol. 1: *Astrolabe, 1826–1829*. Melbourne: Melbourne University Press, 1987.

Rothman, A. *Slave Country*. Cambridge: Harvard University Press, 2005.

Rousseau, G. S. "Nymphomania, Bienville, and the Rise of Erotic Sensibility." In *Sexuality in Eighteenth-Century Britain*, ed. P. Boucé. Manchester: Manchester University Press, 1982.

Rousseau, J. J. *Émile*. London: Everyman's Library, 1961.

———. *Discourse on the Origin of Inequality*. Indianapolis: Hackett Publishing, 1992.

Ryan, L. *The Aboriginal Tasmanians*. St. Lucia: Queensland University Press, 1981.

Sahlins, M. *Islands of History*. Chicago: University of Chicago Press, 1985.

Said, E. *Orientalism: Western Conceptions of the Orient*. Ringwood, Victoria: Penguin Books, 1995.

Salmond, A. *Two Worlds: First Meetings Between Maori and Europeans, 1642–1772*. Auckland: Viking, 1991.

Sambrani, C. "Austerity-Excess-Invention: The Asia-Pacific Triennial 2002." *Art Monthly Australia*, no. 155 (November 2002).

Sankey, M. "The Baudin Expedition: Natural Man and the Imaginary Antipodean." In *Two Hundred Years of the French Revolution*, ed. D. Garrioch. Clayton, Victoria: Monash University Press, 1989.

Saunders, K. "Pacific Islander Women in Queensland, 1863–1907." In *Worth Her Salt*, ed. M. Bevege et al. Sydney: Hale and Iremonger, 1982.

Scarr, D. *A History of the Pacific Islands*. Richmond, UK: Curzon, 2001.

Schiebinger, L. *Does the Mind Have a Sex? Women and the Origins of Modern Science*. Cambridge: Harvard University Press, 1989.

———. *Nature's Body: Gender in the Making of Modern Science*. Boston: Beacon Press, 1993.

Schmitt, R. *Hawai'i in the Movies, 1898–1959*. Honolulu: Hawaiian Historical Society, 1988.

Scott-Waring, J. A. *An Epistle from Oberea, Queen of Otaheite to Joseph Banks esq.* Dublin: W. Wilson, 1774.

———. *A Second Letter from Oberea, Queen of Otaheite, to Joseph Banks*. London: T. J. Carnegy, 1774.

Sharp, A., ed. *Journal of Jacob Roggeveen*. Oxford: Clarendon Press, 1970.

———. *Duperry's Visit to New Zealand in 1824*. Wellington: Alexander Turnbull Press, 1971.

Sherif, M. "Fragonard's Erotic Mothers and the Politics of Reproduction."
   In *Eroticism and the Body Politic*, ed. L. Hunt. Baltimore: Johns Hopkins
   University Press, 1990.

Shillibeer, J. *Narrative of the Briton's Voyage to Pitcairn's Island*. London: Taunton,
   1817.

Shineberg, D. *The People Trade: Pacific Island Laborers and New Caledonia, 1865–
   1930*. Honolulu: University of Hawai'i Press, 1999.

Shohat, E. "Gender and Culture of Empire: Toward a Feminist Ethnography
   of the Cinema." *Quarterly Review of Film and Video* 13, nos. 1–3 (1991): 45–84.

Showalter, E. *Sexual Anarchy: Gender and Culture at the Fin de Siècle*. New York:
   Viking, 1990.

Simpson, A. "Vulnerability and the Age of Female Consent." In *Sexual Underworlds of the Enlightenment*, ed. G. S. Rousseau and R. Porter. Chapel Hill:
   North Carolina University Press, 1988.

Sinclair, M. *Nahi'ene'ena: Sacred Daughter of Hawai'i*. Honolulu: University
   of Hawai'i Press, 1976.

Slotkin, R. *Regeneration Through Violence: The Mythology of the American Frontier,
   1600–1800*. Middletown, Conn.: Wesleyan University Press, 1973.

Smith, B. *European Vision and the South Pacific*. Melbourne: Melbourne University
   Press, 1960.

———. *Imagining the Pacific in the Wake of the Cook Voyages*. Melbourne: Melbourne
   University Press, 1992.

Snow, P., and S. Waine. *The People from the Horizon: An Illustrated History of the
   Europeans Among the South Sea Islanders*. Oxford: Phaidon Press, 1979.

Socolow, S. M. *The Women of Colonial Latin America*. Cambridge: Cambridge
   University Press, 2000.

Soloman-Godeau, A. "Going Native." *Art in America*, July 1989.

Spate, O. H. K. *The Pacific Since Magellan: The Spanish Lake*. Canberra: Australian
   National University Press, 1979.

Spongberg, M. "Not Drowning, Falling: Prostitution and Images of Drowning
   in Great Britain, 1830–1900." *Not My Department: Journal of Interdisciplinary
   Studies* 2 (1992).

———. "Written on the Body: Degeneracy, Atavism, and Congenital Syphilis: Re-
   Reading Child Prostitution in the Nineteenth Century." *JIGS* 1, no. 1 (1995).

———. "Are Small Penises Necessary for Civilisation? The Male Body and the
   Body Politic." *Australian Feminist Studies* 12, no. 25 (1997).

———. *Feminizing Venereal Disease*. New York: Macmillan, 1997.

Stam, R., and L. Spence. "Colonialism, Racism, and Representation: An Introduction." *Screen* 24, no. 2 (March-April 1983).

Stedman, R. W. *Shadows of the Indians: Stereotypes in American Culture*. Norman:
   University of Oklahoma Press, 1982.

Stephen, A. "Selling Soap: Domestic Work and Consumerism." *Labour History*
   61 (Nov. 1991).

Stephen, A., ed. *Pirating the Pacific: Images of Travel, Trade, and Tourism*. Haymarket, New South Wales: Powerhouse Publishing, 1993.

Stephens, J. Brunton. *Miscellaneous Poems*. Brisbane: Watson, Ferguson & Co., 1880.

Steven, M. *Trade, Tactics and Territory: Britain in the Pacific, 1783–1823*. Melbourne: Melbourne University Press, 1983.

Stevenson, K. "Pacific Art: Moving Beyond the Stereotype." *Art New Zealand*, no. 90 (autumn 1999).

———. "Pacific Women: Challenging the Boundaries of Tradition." *New Zealand Women's Studies Journal*, no. 1 (2001).

Stevenson, R. L. *In the South Seas*. London: Chatto & Windus, 1908.

Stevenson, R. L. *South Seas Tales*, ed. R. Jolly. Melbourne: Oxford University Press, 1996.

Stewart, C. S. *Journal of a Residence in the Sandwich Islands During the Years 1823, 1824, and 1825*. Honolulu: University of Hawai'i Press, 1970.

Stocking, G. *Race, Culture, and Evolution*. New York: Free Press, 1968.

Stoddart, L. *The Rising Tide of Colour Against White World Supremacy*. London: Chapman and Hall, 1922.

Stoler, A. "Educating Desire in Colonial Southeast Asia: Foucault, Freud, and Imperial Sexualities." In *Sites of Desire/Economies of Pleasure: Sexualities in Asia and the Pacific*, ed. L. Manderson and M. Jolly. Chicago: University of Chicago Press, 1997.

Sturma, M. *South Sea Maidens*. Westport, Conn.: Greenwood, 2002.

Suaalii, T. "Deconstructing the 'Exotic' Female Beauty of the Pacific Islands." In *Bitter Sweet: Indigenous Women in the Pacific*, ed. A. Jones et al. Dunedin, NZ: Otago University Press, 2000.

Summers, A. *Damned Whores and God's Police*. Ringwood, Victoria: Penguin, 1994.

Sundquist, A. *Pocahontas and Co.: The Fictional American Indian Woman in Nineteenth-Century Literature: A Method of Study*. Atlantic Highlands, N.J.: Humanities Press International, 1987.

Sussman, G. *Selling Mother's Milk: The Wet-Nursing Business in France, 1715–1914*. Urbana: Illinois University Press, 1982.

Sweetman, D. *Paul Gauguin: A Complete Life*. London: Hodder & Stoughton, 1995.

Swift, J. *Gulliver's Travels*. Ringwood, Victoria: Penguin Books, 1986.

Talmon, J. L. *Romanticism and Revolt: Europe, 1815–1848*. London: Thames and Hudson, 1967.

Teaiwa, T. "bikinis and other s/pacific n/oceans." *The Contemporary Pacific* 6, no. 1 (spring 1994): 87–109.

———. "A Preface for Natives." *Pacific Studies* 23, nos. 1–2 (March/June 2000): 75–125.

Tench, W. *Sydney's First Four Years*. Sydney: Library of Australian History, 1979.

Terry, J., and J. Urla, eds. *Deviant Bodies: Critical Perspectives on Difference in Science and Popular Culture*. Bloomington: Indiana University Press, 1995.

Theweleit, K. *Male Fantasies: Women, Floods, Bodies, History*. Cambridge: Polity Press, 1987.

Thomas, N. *Marquesan Societies: Inequity and Political Transformation in Eastern Polynesia*. Oxford: Claredon Press, 1990.

———. *Entangled Objects: Exchange, Material Culture, and Colonialism in the Pacific*. Cambridge, Mass.: Harvard University Press, 1991.

———. *Colonialism's Culture: Anthropology, Travel, and Government*. Melbourne: Melbourne University Press, 1994.

———. *Oceanic Art*. London: Thames and Hudson, 1995.

Thomas, N., and D. Losche, eds. *Double Vision: Art Histories and Colonial Histories in the Pacific*. Cambridge: Cambridge University Press, 1999.

Tilton, R. *Pocahontas: The Evolution of an American Narrative*. New York: Cambridge University Press, 1994.

Todorov, T. *The Conquest of America: The Question of the Other*. New York: Harper & Row, 1982.

Tomaselli, S. "The Enlightenment Debate on Woman." *History Workshop Journal* 20 (autumn 1985).

Torgovnik, M. *Gone Primitive: Savage Intellects, Modern Lives*. Chicago: University of Chicago Press, 1990.

Trask, H. K. *From a Native Daughter: Colonialism and Sovereignty in Hawai'i*. Honolulu: University of Hawai'i Press, 1999.

Trask, H. K., and M. Trask. "The Aloha Industry." *Cultural Survival Quarterly*, winter 1992.

Trexler, R. C. *Sex and Conquest: Gendered Violence, Political Order, and the Conquest of the Americas*. London: Polity Press, 1995.

Turner Strong, P. "Fathoming the Primitive: Australian Aborigines in Four Explorers' Journals." *Ethnohistory* 33, no. 2 (1986): 176–94.

———. "Captivity in White and Red: Convergent Practice and Colonial Representation on the British American Frontier, 1606–1736." In *Crossing Cultures: Essays in the Displacement of Western Cultures*, ed. D. Segal. Tucson: University of Arizona Press, 1992.

Underwood, R. A. "A Return to Confidence: Recolonization Is Not the Answer." *Pacific Magazine*, June 2004.

Vancouver, G. *A Voyage of Discovery*. London: Hakluyt Society, 1984.

Van Kirk, S. *Many Tender Ties: Women in the Fur Trade, 1670–1870*. Norman: University of Oklahoma Press, 1980.

Van Noort, O. *Description du pénible voyage fait entour de l'univers ou globe terrestre*. Amsterdam: Cornille Claeffz, 1602.

Vaughn, B., ed. *The Unraveling of Island Asia*. Westport, Conn.: Praeger, 2001.

Vercoe, C. "Postcards as Signatures of Place." *Art AsiaPacific* 3, no. 3 (1996): 84–89.

Walker, B. G. *The Woman's Encyclopedia of Myth and Secrets*. Sydney: Harper & Row, 1983.

Walker, D. *Anxious Nation*. St. Lucia: University of Queensland Press, 1998.

Wallace, L. *Sexual Encounters: Pacific Texts Modern Sexualities*. Ithaca, N.Y.: Cornell University Press, 2003.

Ward, G., ed. *American Activities in the Central Pacific, 1790–1870*. Ridgewood, N.J.: Gregg Press, 1967.

Ward, J. M. *British Policy in the South Pacific: A Study of British Policy in the South Pacific Islands Prior to the Establishment of Governments by the Great Powers*. Westport, Conn.: Greenwood, 1976.

White, H. *Tropics of Discourse: Essays in Cultural Criticism*. Baltimore: Johns Hopkins University Press, 1978.

White, J. *Journal of a Voyage to New South Wales*. Sydney: Angus and Robertson, 1962.

Whitney, L. *Primitivism and the Idea of Progress in English Popular Literature of the Eighteenth Century*. Baltimore: John Hopkins University Press, 1934.

Wilks, M. *Tahiti: Containing a Review of the ongoing characters and progress of French Roman Catholic destruction of English Protestant Missions in the South Seas*. London: John Snow, 1844.

Williams, G. "Far Happier than We Europeans." *Australian Historical Studies* 19, no. 77 (1981).

——. "Savages Noble and Ignoble: Concepts of the North American Indian." In *The Great Map of Mankind: British Perceptions of the World in the Enlightenment*, ed. G. Williams and P. J. Marshall. Manchester: Manchester University Press, 1990.

Williams, S. *An Appeal to British Christians and the Public Generally on Behalf of the Queen of Tahiti and her Outraged Subjects*. London: W. Blanchard & Sons, 1844.

Williamson, J. "Woman as an Island: Femininity and Colonization." In *Studies in Entertainment: Approaches to Mass Culture*, ed. T. Modleski. Bloomington: Indiana University Press, 1986.

Wilson, J. *A Missionary Voyage to the Southern Pacific Ocean Performed in the years 1796–1798 in the Ship* Duff. London: T. Chapman, 1799.

Wilson, K. *The Island Race: Englishness, Empire, and Gender in the Eighteenth Century*. New York: Routledge, 2003.

Wilson, O. *From Honga Hika to Hone Heke: A Quarter of a Century of Upheaval*. Dunedin, NZ: John McIndoe, 1985.

Winick, C. *The New People: Desexualization in American Life*. New York: Pegasus, 1968.

Wokler, R. "From *l'homme physique* to *l'homme moral* and Back: Towards a History of Enlightenment Anthropology." *History of the Human Sciences* 6, no. 1 (1993).

Wollstonecraft, M. *A Vindication of the Rights of Woman*. Melbourne: Penguin Books, 1992.

Wood, G. A. "Ancient and Medieval Conceptions of Terra Australia." *The Australian Historical Society Journal and Proceedings* 3, no. 10 (1916).

Woolmington, J. *Aborigines in Colonial Society, 1788–1850.* Melbourne: Cassell, 1973.

Worgan, G. *Journal of a First Fleet Surgeon.* Sydney: Library Council of New South Wales, 1978.

Yalom, M. *A History of the Breast.* London: HarperCollins, 1997.

Young, R. *Colonial Desire: Hybridity in Theory, Culture, and Race.* London: Routledge, 1995.

Films and Video Recordings

Aloma of the South Seas, directed by Alfred Santell, Paramount, USA, 1941.

Beyond the Blue Horizon, directed by Alfred Santell, Paramount, USA 1942.

Bird of Paradise, directed by King Vidor, RKO Radio Pictures, USA, 1932.

The Bounty, directed by Roger Donaldson, Dino De Laurentis Productions, USA, 1984.

Coming of Age in Amelika, Jewel Castro and Dan Taulapapa McMullin, art and video installation at the Asian/Pacific/American Studies Program, New York University, September 2001–January 2002.

Hawaii, directed by George Roy Hill, produced by the Mirisch Corporation, USA, 1966.

Hula, directed by Victor Fleming, Paramount, USA, 1927.

The Hurricane, directed by John Ford, Goldwyn, USA, 1937.

Moana: A Romance of the Golden Age, directed by Robert Flaherty, Paramount, USA, 1926.

Moruroa: The Big Secret, directed by M. Daëron, France, 1993.

Mutiny on the Bounty, directed by Frank Lloyd, MGM, USA, 1935.

Mutiny on the Bounty, directed by Lews Milestone, MGM, USA, 1962.

Pacific Body Language, directed by Lisa Taoma, Television New Zealand, 2005.

Papakolea: A Story of Hawaiian Land, produced and directed by Edgy Lee and Saul Landau, USA, 1993.

Rainbow Island, directed by Ralph Murray, Paramount, USA, 1944.

Son of Fury, directed by John Cromwell, 20th Century Fox, USA, 1942.

South Pacific, directed by Joshua Logan, 20th Century Fox, 1958.

Tabu, directed by F. W. Murnau, Paramount, USA, 1931.

Velvet Dreams, written and directed by Sima Urale, New Zealand, 1998.

Women in the Shadows, directed by Norma Bailey, produced by Christine Welsh, Canada, 1991.

Index

Illustrations are indicated with italic type.

Abbot, Major, 151
"Aboriginal Family of New South
    Wales" (Blake), 136, *137*
Aboriginal people: cinema represen-
    tations, 248–49, 253, 303*n*60;
    and convict settlements, 132;
    ignoble stereotype, 95–97,
    162–63, 196; literary represen-
    tations, 58; noble savage stereo-
    type, 175, 176, 177, *179*, 194;
    sealing industry, 148–53; sexual
    commerce, 111; violence against,
    134–35, 149–50, 153–59; and
    water mythology, 52–53. *See
    also* Maori people; Tasmanian
    people
Achushnet whaler, 110
Adams, Hannah, 129, *130*
Adams, John, 122, 123, 126
Adelaide, Queen, 204
Adventure voyage, 65, 87–88
advertising industry, 226, 235
Aeschylus, 43, 62
African women, 33–35, 37
Alexander, William, 55, 183–84
Algonquian people, 27–28
American imperial experience, 20–22,
    26–32, 72, 91
Americen Americus retexit of 1575 (van
    der Straet), 20–21

Amusemens des Otahitiens. . . .
    (Bérenger), 79, *80*
annexations/protectorates summarized,
    213–14
Antelope voyage, 178
anticolonial art, 261–62
Antoinette, Marie, 168
Aphrodite images, 47–51, 192
Arago, Jacques, 201, 202–3
Arbuthnot, Mrs., 200
Archer, Gabriel, 27
Aristotle, 54–55
Artémise voyage, 108–9
artists. *See* cinema representations;
    literary representations; visual
    representations
Atahoe (Mary Bruce), 138–40, 141
Atargatis of Askalon, 47, 49
atomic testing, 255–57, *258*
Australia: atomic testing, 256; indige-
    nous movements, 260. *See also*
    Aboriginal people; convict settle-
    ments; Maori people; Tasmanian
    people
availability stereotype. *See* promis-
    cuity stereotype
Aztec people, 26–27

Babylonians, in Herodotus's
    writings, 42

Baker, Johnny (in film), 241–42
Baker, Josephine, 236–37
Baker, Mr. (voyager), 120
Bangaroo, 194
Banks, Joseph, 64, 73, 78, 84
Barclay, Mrs., 116–17
Barker, Captain, 160
Barretos, Ysabel, 22, 23
Barrington, George, 95
Barrow, Sir John, 128–29, *130*
Barsam, Richard, 235
Bartmaan, Sarah, 34–35
Bass Strait sealers, 148–52
The Bath (Ingres), 36
Baudin voyage, 95–96, 151, 170, 191, 194–95
Baxter, George, 205–6, *207*
Bayley, William, 84
Bayly, T., 86, 89
Bay of Islands, 98
"Beach of Falesa" (Stevenson), 226
beauty, descriptions of: Aboriginal people, 52; in *Bounty* re-tellings, 125–29; breast appearance, 192; British voyagers, 120–21; French colonial brochure, 217; French voyagers, 71–72, 98; Melville's writings, 145–46; Middle East women, 37; missionaries, 100; Pipon's, 125–26; Russian voyagers, 53, 140; Spanish voyagers, 23; U.S. voyagers, 103–4. *See also* ugliness descriptions; visual representations
beauty ideals: Babylonian, 42; and morality, 194–96; and noble savage stereotype, 173–74, 181–82, 183; and Pacific royalty, 197–203; in political philosophies, 175, 181–82; and pregnancy, 192–93
Becke, Louis, 226
Belich, James, 111, 144
Bellefin, Monsieur, 195

Bérenger, Jean Pierre, 79, *80*
Berlin, Ira, 33
Berry, Mary, 198–200
Bienville, Dr., 56
Bikini Atoll, 255
Bingham, Sybil, 203
Bird of Paradise, 241–42
The Birth of Christ (Gauguin), 223
Bishop, Charles, 91, 149
Black, Neil, 154–55
Black Mary (Janson), 249
black women category, 33–35, 37. *See also* Aboriginal people
Blake, Ben (in film), 243–44
Blake, Captain, 159–60
Blake, William, 136
Bligh, William, 84, 129, 288–89*n*16
Bloody Mary (in film), 253, 255
Blossett, Harriet, 64
Blossom voyage, 128–29
Blue Latitudes (Horwitz), 263
Blumenbach, J. F., 169–70
Blumenbach, Johann, 34
body politic. *See* political philosophies
Bonin Islands, 160
Bontius, Jacob, 34
Bormus myth, 46
Bott, Robert, 209
Bougainville voyage, 71–72
Bounty mutiny, 38–39, 84, 120–29, 244–47, 251–53, 288*nn*11–12
The Bounty Trilogy (Nordhoff and Hall), 251
Bow, Clara, 237
Brando, Marlon, 253, *254*
breast-feeding, 175, 177
breast symbolism, 191–93, 196, 296*n*43
Brissac, Virginia, 235–36
Britain: American imperial experience, 31–32; annexations/protectorates summarized, 213; atomic testing, 256; *Dolphin* voyage, 63, 69–71, 84–85; masculinity ideas and

nationalism, 74–76; and Pacific royalty, 203–12; Renaissance period, 25–26. *See also* Aboriginal people; *Bounty* mutiny; Cook voyages; missionaries

Brodie, Walter, 208

Broomhall, Mr. (missionary), 102

Brown, Jennifer, 32

Brown, Mr. (from *Bounty*), 124

Brown, William, 288*n*12

Bruce, George, 138–40, 141

Bruce, Mary (Atahoe), 138–40

Bruny Island, 195

Buffon, Comte de, 34, 55–56, 74, 96

Burton, John Wear, 162

Byam, Roger (in novel), 251

Byron, Lord, 127–28

Cable, Joe (in film), 255

Calhoun, Hula (in film), 237

Calypso, in *The Odyssey*, 41–42

Canning, George, 198–99

Captain Thunderbolt (film), 249

Carson, Anne, 46

Casteneda, Movita, 247–48

Cavalier whaler, 93

censorship, 240–41, 244

Charlotte, 133

Charlton, Captain, 160

chastity and virtue. *See* morality ideals

Chauvel, Charles, 231, 244–47, 253

children: *Bounty* personnel, 122, 124, 125, 128–29; commodity perspective, 151; F. Christian's, 288–89*n*16; Gauguin's attitudes, 220–24; George Bruce case, 138, 140; hot climate theories, 53–54, 55–57; and morality ideals, 112–14, 128–29; Pacific royalty representations, 205–7; primitive man stereotype, 96, 98, 182; promiscuity stereotype, 133–34; and racial anxieties, 227–28; S. Reynolds',

287*n*90. *See also* noble savage stereotype

Chirac, Jacques, 256

Choris, Louis, 201–2

Christian, Fletcher, 122, 123, 124, 125, 288–89*n*16

Christianity: American imperial experience, 27–29; and classical traditions, 40; Eve metaphor, 23–24, 49–51; and harem image, 37; mermaid image, 44–45; and plantation economies, 162; Spanish voyagers, 285*n*61. *See also* missionaries

Christina Maid of the South Seas (Mitford), 125

cinema representations: anthropology's role, 231–35, 237; censorship effects, 240–41; character casting, 244–49, 252–53; Eve allusions, 243–44; Hollynesian image, 235–40, 242–43; by indigenous artists, 261–62; normalizing effects, 231–32; post-World War II, 251–55

Circe, in *The Odyssey*, 41–42

civil society. *See* political philosophies

Clark, Mamo, 247–48, 253

classical traditions, 19, 38–44, 46–49, 54, 146, 192

Clerke, Captain, 85

Clinton, Bill, 260

clothing: in cinema representations, 232, 233; Mead's uses, 240; missionary emphasis, 100, 216; Pacific royalty, 199, 200–201; and promiscuity stereotypes, 79–84, 89, 97; and sexual repression ideas, 180; and stereotype contradictions, 191; swimsuit fashion, 255

Coates, Dandeson, 99

Cock, John, 102

Cold War effects, 255–57

Collection de Tous les Voyages (Bérenger), 79, *80*

Collins, David, 95, 133–34, 135

Collins, Jane, 251

colonization, generally: complexity of, 10–12; as sexual conquest, 20–22

Columbus voyage, 21, 46

The Coming of Age in Samoa (Mead), 237, 239

Commerson, Philibert, 180

commodity perspective: American experience, 29–33; *Bounty* personnel, 122–29; convict settlements, 129, 131–36, 149–50; Cook's observations, 76–77, 87–90; marriage, 138–42; Monbart's explanation, 185; pastoral communities, 153–57; plantation economies, 161–64; and resource industries generally, 136–38; sealing industry, 148–53; servant roles, 116–19; with tourism, 250–51; and venereal disease, 93; whaling industry, 142–48, 159–60

Compson, Betty, 236

convict settlements, 94, 129, 131–34, 138–40, 149–50

Cook Islands, 257, 304*n*71

Cook voyages: in Horwitz's novel, 263–64; Omai's trip to England, 65; promiscuity perceptions, 56–57, 72–77, 88–91; Ra'iatea desertion, 84–85; venereal disease, 85–87; visual representations, 38, 79–84

Coonardoo (film), 249

Cooper, David, 151

Corinne or Italy (de Staël), 59–61

corruption portrayals, 226–31

Cortés, Don Martin, 27

Cortés, Hernando, 26–27

Cox, William, 153

craniology, 169–70

Cree people, 32

Cunningham, Peter, 196

Cunningham, Stuart, 244

Cuvier, Georges, 35, 170

Dalrymple, Captain, 139

Dampier, William, 25–26

Dance of the Friendly Islands (in La Billardière), 198–200

dances, 81–82, 198–200, 233, 236–37, 245–47, 251

Danielsson, Bengt, 215–16, 220, 252

Daniel whaler, 109

Darwin, Charles, 208

Davidhoff, Lenore, 204

Dean-Jones, Leslie, 46

de Blainville, Henri, 35

de Condorcet, Marquis, 169

de Cuneo, Michele, 21–22

De Gérando, Joseph Marie, 167

d'Eglantine, Fabre, 168

de Gouges, Olympe, 169

De Groot, Joanna, 36

Deleuze, Giles, 241

de Loutherbourg, Phillippe Jacques, *66*

Dening, Greg, 61, 122, 141, 247–48

D'Entrecasteaux voyage, 187–91, 198

de Oviedo, Fernandez, 30

de Quiros, Fernandez, 23

A Description of the Grand Signor's Serglio (Withers), 36

Desmond, James, 211

Desmond, Jane, 236, 248, 251

de Staël, Germaine, 59–60

Dexter, Captain, 93

Diaz del Castillo, Bernal, 26

Dickason, Olive, 31

Diderot, Denis, 180–82

Discourse on the Origin of Inequality
(Rousseau), 173–74
Discovery voyages, 84–87, 120–21
Dolphin voyagers, 61–62, 63, 69–71,
84–85
domestic ideal: missionary objectives,
98–101, 110–11, 157; Pitcairn
Island, 126–27; Victorian model,
204
Donaldson, George (in Fletcher's
story), 228
Douthwaite, Julia, 60, 180, 184–85
drawings and paintings. *See* visual
representations
Duff voyages, 99–103, 125
Duperry voyage, 98
D'Urville, Dumont, 152
Dutch voyagers, 18, 23–25

"Ebb Tide" (Stevenson), 226
economic conditions, modern, 257–58,
261
Eden images, 50–51. *See also* Eve
allusions
Edgar, Thomas, 82, 86
Ellis, Havelock, 239
Ellis, William, 103, 109
Émile (Rousseau), 173–74
Emma, Queen, 209
Ena-O-Ae-A-Ta, 140–42
Endeavour voyage, 63–64
Enewetak Atoll, 255
English voyages. *See* Britain
Eora people, 52, 134–35
An Epistle from Mr. Banks . . . (poem), 64
equal rights. *See* political philosophies
Essay on the History of Civil Society
(Ferguson), 55
ethnographic studies: feminism's uses,
239–40; political incentives, 166–
70. *See also* science perspectives
Evangelical movement. *See* missionaries

Eve allusions, 23–24, 50–51, 243–44
The Eventful History of . . . Bounty
(Barrow), 128–29, *130*
Eyre, Edward, 53

Fagasa Bay, 91
family, 174–75, 184, 188–91, 194–95
Fangataufa Atoll, 256
fashions, 147, 255
Fausto-Sterling, Ann, 34, 277*n*31
Fayaway (in Melville's novel), 145–46
feminine ideas: classical philosophy, 41,
43–53, 54; and English national-
ism, 74–76; geography-based,
57–61; representation diversity,
12–13. *See also* beauty, descrip-
tions of; political philosophies
feminism, 218–19, 239–40
Ferguson, Adam, 55
Fiji, 148, 162, 213
Fitzgerald, Gerald, 62–63
Flaherty, Frances, 232–33
Flaherty, Robert, 232–33
Fletcher, Robert, 227–28, *229*
Foa, Anna, 30
Fontaine, Peter, 29
Forster, George, 185, 186
Forster, Johann Reinholdt, 51
Foveaux Straits, 152–53
Fowler, David, 28, 29
France: American imperial experience,
31; annexations/protectorates
summarized, 213–14; atomic
testing, 256–57; Baudin voyage,
95–97, 170, 194–95; Bouganville
voyage, 71–72; breastfeeding
laws, 177; *La Coquille* voyages,
98, 143–44; politics and ethno-
graphic studies, 167–70; sexual
attitudes generally, 71–72, 107–9;
"Tahiti Affair," 204–5, 209. *See
also* Gauguin, Paul

Freycinet voyage, 201
Furneaux, Tobias, 65, 87–88
Fyans, Foster, 155

Gauguin, Mette, 217
Gauguin, Paul, 215–25, 230–31, 256
The Generalle Historie of Virginia
    (Smith), 28
General Wellesley, 141
geography-based representations,
    53–61
George IV, 200
Germany, annexations/protectorates
    summarized, 214
Gilman, Sander L., 33
Gone Native (Fletcher), 228, *229*
governance capacity, modern, 257–60,
    304*n*75
grand tour tradition, 19, 58–60, 75
Greenblatt, Stephen, 26–27
Greenpeace, 256–57
Grotius, Hugo, 172
Gypsy whaler, 109–10, 146

Haldane, Anthony (in film), 237
Hall, Catherine, 74, 204
Hall, Edith, 43
Hall, James (settler), 159
Hall, James Norman (author), 251
Hall, Juanita, 253
Handy, Alice Henriette, 112–13
Handy, Icabod, 112–13
Happah people, 104
Haraway, 99–100
harem images, 35–37
Harris, John, 101
Hart, Captain, 159
Hattie, Hilo, 253
Hawai'i: Cook voyages, 86–87; film
    industry, 235–36, 253, 255;
    indigenous movement, 259–60;
    kidnappings/abductions, 116–19,
    120–21, 151, 160; missionary

presence, 201, 203, 287*n*81; plan-
    tation economies, 161; royalty,
    198–203, 209–12; sexual contact/
    commerce, 92, 109–10; tourism,
    251
Hawaii (film), 253, 255
Hawaiian Love (film), 235–36
Hawaii's Story (Liliuokalani), 211
Hawkesworth, John, 62, *63*, 73–74
Hayes, Mrs., 67
health conditions, modern, 255–56,
    257–58
heiva dance, 81–82
Helpem Fren, 258–59
Heraklitos, 47
Herodotus, 42–43
Heyerdahl, Thor, 251
Hippocrates, 46–47
History of the Female Sex (Meiners),
    60, 65
History of Women . . . (Alexander),
    183–84
Hiva Oa, 223–25
Hobbes, Thomas, 172
Hodges, William, 38–39, 79
Hollynesian image, 235–40, 242–43,
    248
homosexuality, 94, 101
Horwitz, Tony, 263–64
hot climate theories, 52–57
Hottentot women, 34–35
Houyhnhnms Land (in Swift's
    writing), 58
Howard, John, 304*n*75
hula dance, 236–37, 251
Hula (film), 237
Hume, David, 55
Hunter, John, 135–36
The Hurricane, 243
Hylas myth, 46

Iddeah, 125, 288–89*n*16
ignoble savage stereotype: atomic

testing protests, 257, *259*; cinema representations, 234, 253; origins, 171, 172–73; Pacific royalty, 207–9; physical appearance, 143, 195–97; pregnant women, 192–93; and venereal disease, 30; violence stereotype, 94–95; women's passivity, 189–90

Illustrated News, 205, *206*

Imperial Eagle voyage, 116–17

Inchbald, Elizabeth, 65

independence movement, 257

indigenous movements, modern, 260–62

Ingres, Jean-Auguste Dominque, 36

interracial marriages. *See* marriage; sexual contact/commerce

In the Wake of the Bounty (film), 244

Irish women, 131, 133–34

Islamic Orient, 35–37

The Island (Byron), 38, 127–28

Islands of Love (Danielsson), 252

Isles of Illusion (Fletcher), 227–28

Italian voyagers, 30

Jamestown settlement, 27–28

Janson, Julie, 249

Japan, 214–15

Jedda (Chauvel), 253

Jenny (Teehuteatuanonoa), 122, 123, 124

Jenny voyage, 120

Jolly, Margaret, 13, 76, 255, 286*n*69

Ka'ahumanu (Tammeamaroo), 201–2, 203

Kamamalu, 198–200

Kame'eleihiwa, Lilikalā, 198

Kamehameha I, 201

Kamehameha II, 198, 200

Kamehameha III, 287*n*81

Kaou-Onoé, 202–3

Keate, George, 178

Keatonui, 104

Kelly, James, 150

Kent whaler, 160

kidnappings and abductions: of Aboriginal people, 135–36, 158; American imperial experience, 27–28; by *Bounty* personnel, 122–24; British admonitions, 138; for convict settlements, 131–32; by *Discovery* personnel, 84–85; of Hawaiian women, 116–19, 120–21, 151, 160; by *Lambton* personnel, 159; sealing industry, 150–52

King, Governor, 139

kings. *See* royalty

Kiribati, 257, 304*n*71

Kohkonne, Onéla, 227–28

Kotzebue, Otto von, 200

Krusenstern, Adam von, 92, 97–98, 193–94

Kunoth, Narla (in film), 253

Kuyper, Jacques, 175, *176*, 178, *179*

La Billardière, Jacques-Julien, 187–91, 198

labor trade. *See* commodity perspective; plantation economies

La Coquille voyage, 98, 143

La Dixmerie, Nicholas Bricaire de, 180

Lady Juliana, 133

Lady Penrhyn, 133

LaGarde, Jocelyne, 253

Lambton cutter, 159

Lamour, Dorothy, 242–43

Langsdorff, George Von, 53–54

La Nymphomanie (Bienville), 56

La Pérouse voyage, 91, 187, 188

Laplace, Captain, 108, 287*n*81

Larne, H.M.S., 159

Léon, Pauline, 169

L'Espirit des Lois (Montesquieu), 55

Lesson, René, 98, 143–44

Lettres Taïhitennes (Monbart), 184–85
Leviathan (Hobbes), 172
Lewis, Mr. (missionary), 102
Lewis, Renia, 36
Liat (in film), 255
Liliuokalani, Queen, 209–10
Linnekin, Jocelyn, 91
Lisiansky, Urey, 92
literary representations: Aboriginal
    people, 58; *Bounty* mutiny, 38,
    125, 127–28; cinema portrayals,
    233–34, 249; Cook voyages,
    263–64; of corrupted paradise,
    226–31; Middle East women,
    36–37; of Oberea, 62–63, 64, 65,
    282*n*80; of Omai, 65; post-World
    War II, 251; whaling industry,
    144–48
London, Jack, 226
London Missionary Society, 99–
    103, 204–5, 206, 286*n*77. *See also*
    missionaries
Lorelei legend, 45
Luana (in film), 241–42
Lulu (aide to Chavel), 246, 247
Lutz, Catherine, 251
Lydians, 42

Macquarie, Governor, 138, 140
Magellan's voyage, 18
Maimiti: in film, 247–48, 252–53, *254*;
    in novels, 251
Main, Mr. (from *Bounty*), 124
Malama, Queen (in film), 253, 255
Malinowski, Bronislaw, 239
Malintzin (Aztec woman), 26–27
Malthus, Thomas, 95
Manet, Edouard, 221
Maori people, 87–89, 112–14, 138–40,
    143–44, 152–53, 260
Marama (in film), 243
Marbuk (in film), 253
Mardsen, Samuel, 138

Maria, Doña (Malintzin), 26–27
Maria Island, 95–96
Mariner, William, 127
Marquesas: Gauguin's presence, 223–
    24; hot climate theory, 53–54;
    missionary arrival, 99–100, 101;
    promiscuity stereotype, 92, 126;
    Russian voyager descriptions, 92,
    97–98, 193–94; Spanish discov-
    ery, 22–23; tabua wealth, 147–
    48; U.S. attempted possession,
    103–7
marriage: Aboriginal, 95; American
    experience, 26–29, 31–33; com-
    modity perspective, 138–42;
    missionary objectives, 98–101,
    110–11, 157. *See also* sexual con-
    tact/commerce
Marshall Islands, 214, 255–56, 257
Martin, Isaac, 122, 124, 288*n*12
masculinity ideas: classical portrayals,
    40–41, 46–47; geography-based,
    57–61; morality and location,
    77–78; and nationalism, 74–76,
    103–9; about primitive man, 37,
    88–89, 94–97, 135, 184; sexual
    needs, 94–95, 131–32. *See also*
    political philosophies
Matahi (in film), 234
Matra, James, 131–32
Mauatua, 123, 253, 288*n*12
Maugham, Somerset, 230–31
Mazarro, Matthew, 160
McClintock, Anne, 20
McCormack, Eric, 65
McGrath, Ann, 136, 163
McPhee, Charles, 262
Mead, Margaret, 237, 239–40
Meares, John, 116–17
Meek, Ronald, 172
Meiners, Charles, 60, 65
Melaka, 139
Melanesians, 13, 161, 214–15

Melville, Herman, 144–45, 208–9
Mendaña, Alvaro de, 22–23
mermaid images, 44–45, 47, 51
métissage practice, 31
Michel, Citizen, 97
Michener, James, 253, 255
Mickoy, William, 288*n*12
Millar, John, 55
Mills, John, 288*n*12
Milton, John, 51
miscegenation as corruption, 226–31.
    See also cinema representations
missionaries: French objections, 107–
    9; humanitarian efforts, 155–
    57; morality objectives, 98–103,
    109–11, 203–4, 205; and Pacific
    royalty, 201, 203–12, 286*n*77;
    Robarts marriage, 140. *See also*
    Christianity
Mitford, Mary Russell, 125
mixed race perspectives. *See* commod-
    ity perspective; marriage; race
    theories
Moana (Flaherty), 232–33
Moby Dick (Melville), 145, 147
Moerenhout, Jacques Antoine, 204–
    5, 207–8
Monbart, Marie Josephine de,
    184–85
Monboddo, Lord, 169–70
Mongols, Meiner's theory, 60–61
Montagu, Lady Mary Wortley, 36
Montesquieu, Charles de Secondat, 55
The Moon and Sixpence (Maugham),
    230–31
morality ideals: classical tradition, 41;
    Cook's lament, 72–73, 87; grand
    tour tradition, 19, 58–60, 75; hot
    climate theory, 55; missionary
    objectives, 98–103, 109–11, 203–
    4, 205; and mixed-race children,
    112–14; and nationalism, 105–7;
    Nuku Hivan incident, 105–7;

Pitcairn Island, 126–27; in
    Pitcarin Island observations,
    126–27; voyager explanations,
    77–78. *See also* promiscuity
    stereotype
Morice, Charles, 230
Morrison, James, 123, 288*n*11
Moruroa Atoll, 256
motherhood and noble savage stereo-
    type, 173–78, 180–81
Mouat, Mr. (son), 84–85
Mouat, Patrick, 84
Munro, James, 150
Murnau, Fredrich, 233, 241
musicals, 236–37
Mutiny on the Bounty (films), 247–48,
    251–53, *254*
Myall Creek massacre, 156
My Little Bimbo, *238*

Nadeshda, 92
nails, *Dolphin* voyage, 71
Nāmāhana, 200
National Geographic, 251
nationalism: ethnographic purposes,
    103–9, 167–68; masculinity ideas,
    74–76
Native Americans, 20–22, 26–32, 72,
    91, 171–72, 174, 264
Native Woman Sitting Port Philip
    (Wedge), 154
Nehua (in Byron's poem), 127–28
Neva voyages, 92
Nevermore (Gauguin), 223, *224*
New Calendonia, 257, 304*n*72
New Guinea, 213
Newman, Gerald, 75
New South Wales, 95, 132–35, 138–40
New Zealand, 107, 111, 213, 260
Ngatik violence, 159–60
Nichols, John, 133
Nichols, Mrs. (in Maugham's novel),
    230–31

Noa Noa (Gauguin), 215, 220

noble savage stereotype: Aboriginal people, 136, *137*; cinema representations, 232–34; contradictions, 191–96; and ethnographic studies, 166–70; motherhood, 173–78, *179*, 180–81, 187–91; origins, 171–72; and Pacific royalty, 198–203; pregnant women images, 192–93; sexuality, 178, 180–86

Nomuka Island, 85–86

Nordhoff, Charles, 251

Northern Mariana Islands, 257, 304n72

northernness vs. southernness, 57–61, 64

nuclear bomb testing, 255–57, *258*

Nude with Spider Lilies, 303n60

nudity: cinema portrayals, 233, 241–42, 244–45; missionary teachings, 100; and primitive man stereotype, 96–97, 191; and promiscuity stereotypes, 79–84, 89, 174

Nuku Hiva, 53, 92, 97–98, 103–7

nymph images, 38, 46

nymphomania, 56–57

Oberea, Queen, 19, 61–67, 70, 73

The Odyssey, 40–45

O'Keefe, John, 65

older women, 65, 67, 196–97, 253, 255

Oldham whaler, 158

Olley, Margaret, 303n60

Omai, 64–65

Omoo (Melville), 208–9

Orientalist vision, 35–37, 43

Origins of the Distinction of Ranks (Millar), 55

Orio, 84–85

Orou, 181–82

Orsmond, John, 206

Oswald (in de Staël's novel), 59–60

Otaheite (poem), 64

Ottoman Empire, 35–37

Ourê-Ourê, 194–95

Pacific Body Language (film), 262

Pacific muse stereotype, overview, 3–16, 264–69. *See also specific topics, e.g.,* cinema representations; noble savage stereotype; sexual danger

Pahura, 220–21, 222–23

paintings and drawings. *See* visual representations

Paramount Studios, 232–33

Parker, E. S., 111, 155

Parkinson, Sidney, 77–78, 175, *176*

Pasifika Divas, 261

pastoral communities, 149–50, 153–57, 159–60

Pateman, Carole, 173

Peel Island, 160

Pelaw Island, 178

Penelope (in *The Odyssey*), 41

penises, voyager descriptions, 96–98

Péron, Francois, 95–97, 192–93, 194–96

Persians (Aeschylus), 43, 62

Peterson, Charley, 151

Philippe, Louis, 205

Phillip, Governor, 132

Pike, Andrew, 249

Pipon, Captain, 125–26

Pitcairn Island, 122–29, 260

Piteenee, 104–5

plantation economies, 33–34, 161–64, 214–15, 227–28

Pocahontas legend, 27–28, 67

Poedua (Webber), 82–85

political philosophies: and ethnographic studies, 166–70, 218–19; Victorian model, 204, 205; women's roles, 168–70, 173–75, 185–86, 218–19. *See also* royalty

Pollack, Griselda, 220, 221

Pomare, Queen, 108, 204–9, 297–98n70
Pomare, Queen of Tahiti (Baxter), 205–6, 207
Pomare II, 107, 286n77
Pomare V, 216
Porter, David, 103–7
Port Jackson colony, 52, 91, 94, 129, 131–34, 138–40
Port Philip colony, 154–55
Portuguese voyagers, 18
Powhatan (Algonquian man), 27
pregnant women, 34, 125–26, 192–93, 204–5, 277n31
Prichard, Katherine Susannah, 249
primitive female stereotype: Aboriginal women, 52–53; black women, 33–35, 37; in Bounty re-tellings, 124–25; classical portrayals, 40–45; geography-based beliefs, 27–29, 57–61, 64; hot climate theory, 53–56. See also noble savage stereotype
primitive man stereotype, 88–91, 94–98, 135. See also ignoble savage stereotype
promiscuity stereotype: African women, 33–35; American indigenous women, 30–31; convict settlements, 133; Cook voyages, 72–77, 90–91, 99; French lament, 107–9; grand tour tradition, 75; hot climate theory, 53–56; Middle East women, 35–37; missionary responses, 98–103; and modern prostitution, 261; and noble savage stereotype, 174, 178, 180–86; Pacific royalty, 201, 203; and primitive man stereotype, 88–89, 90–91, 95–96, 98; U.S. voyagers, 104–5; with visual representations, 78–84. See also sexual contact/commerce
prostitutes and prostitution: convict women, 131, 133; Cook portrayals, 76–77; in Herodotus' writings, 42–43; and hot climate theory, 54, 55; modern, 261, 264; Oberea portrayals, 64; siren comparison, 45; venereal disease blame, 91–93. See also sexual contact/commerce
protectorates/annexations summarized, 213–14
Puckey, William, 101–2
Pule, John, 261
Purea, 61

Quarterly Review, 105–6
Queen Charlotte's Sound, 87–88
queens. See royalty
Quintal, Matthew, 288n12

Race theories: American experience, 28–30; geography-based, 60–61; hot climates, 56; miscegenation, 227–28; and mixed-race children, 125–26; and slavery, 33–35, 155–56, 161–62; and World Wars, 234–35, 249–50
Rahiena, 120–21
Ra'iatea, 82–85, 158
"Raire" image, 5, 6
Ralston, Caroline, 141, 286n69
Rapa Nui, 24–25
rape. See violence
Reard, Louis, 255
Reiby, Mary, 151
Renaissance voyages, 20–26
Renard, Louis, 45
Representation of the Heiva at Otaheite (Rickman), 79, 81–82
Reri (in film), 234
Resolution, 86
Reybauld, M., 108–9
Reynolds, Stephen, 109, 113–14, 287n90

Richards, Mr. (missionary), 109
Richards, Tom (author), 228, 230
Rickman, John, 79, *81*
Robarts, Edward, 53–54, 92, 98, 140–42
Robertson, George (*Dolphin* voyager), 69–71
Robinson, George Augustus (missionary), 111, 149–51, 152, 154
Roggewein voyage, 24–25, 275–76*n*12
Rolfe, John, 28
Rolfe, Thomas, 28
Rolland, Thomas Pierre, 107–8
Ross, Captain, 139–40
Rousseau, Jean-Jacques, 173–76
royalty: Algonquian, 27–28; cinema representations, 234; and noble savage stereotype, 197–203; Tahitian, 19, 61–67, 107, 108; trade networks, 107; Victorian adaptations, 203–12
Russian voyagers, 92, 97–98, 193–94, 200

Said, Edward, 43
Samoa, 232–33, 237, 239–40
Samwell, David, 85, 86
Santos y Castro, Maria de los, 160
Savages of Van Diemen's Land (in La Billardière), 188–89
Savory, Nathaniel, 160
Schiebinger, Londa, 34, 192
Schmitt, Robert, 236
science perspectives: black woman category, 34–35; hot climate theory, 55–56; and political philosophies, 166–70; primitive man stereotype, 94–96; race ideology, 162–63
Scott-Waring, John, 64, 282*n*80
sealing industry, 148–53
Select Committee hearings (British), 155–56, 157–59

self-control, classical thought, 47, 54
servant perspective, 116–18
Sexton, Robert, 156
sexual contact/commerce: Aboriginal people, 132, 135, 163; in Aeschylus drama, 43; after violence, 23, 25, 61, 70–71; American experience, 22, 26–32, 72; as community exchange, 286*n*69; convict settlements, 132–33; Cook voyages, 72–73, 77–78, 84–90; as corruption, 226–31; *Dolphin* voyagers, 70–71; French perspectives, 71–72, 107–9; Gauguin's beliefs/experience, 216–25; grand tour tradition, 58–59; missionary responses, 100–103, 109–11, 182; modern, 261, 264; in Queen Oberea stories, 61–65; and racial fears, 234–35; Renaissance trade networks, 25–26; sealing industry, 150; U.S. voyagers, 104–7; whaling industry, 109–10, 142–48. *See also* prostitutes and prostitution; venereal disease
sexual danger: in *Bounty* retellings, 38–39, 84, 124, 129, 244–45; classical philosophy, 40–42, 43–46; and Cook voyages, 73–76, 90–91; Eve metaphor, 51; geography-based, 59–60; noble savage stereotype, 184; in Oberea portrayals, 64, 65, 67; from political participation, 168–70, 218–19; violence tales, 91. *See also* venereal disease
The Sexual Life of Savages (Malinowski), 239
sexual submission. *See* sexual contact/commerce; violence
The Shark God, 235–36
Sharp, A., 275–76*n*12
Shaw, Thomas, 84

Sherif, Mary, 177
Shillibeer, Lieutenant, 126
Shohat, Ella, 240
siren images, 41–42, 43–46, 51
Sirius voyage, 52
slavery, 28–29, 33–34, 37, 111. *See also*
    plantation economies
Smith, Alexander, 288*n*12
Smith, Bernard, 19, 40
Smith, John, 28
Smith, Lt., 128–29
Smyth, Arthur Bowes, 133
social order, European. *See* political
    philosophies
Socolow, Susan Midgen, 27
Solomon Islands, 257, 258–59, 304*n*72
Son of Fury, 243–44
sophrosyne, 47, 279*n*53
southernness, 57–60, 64
South Pacific, 253, 255
Spanish voyagers, 18, 22–23, 26–27,
    285*n*61
speech in films, 240–41
Spence, Louise, 231
Spirit of the Dead Watching (Gauguin),
    221–22
Spongberg, Mary, 192
St. Andrew, 160
St. Christina, Marquesas Islands, 22–23
Stam, Robert, 231
Stedman, Raymond, 30
Stephens, J. Brunton, 163
Stevenson, Karen, 261–62
Stevenson, Robert Louis, 226, 227, 233
Stewart, C. S., 109
Stewart, W., 150
Stockdale, John, *188, 190, 199*
Strickland, Charles (in Maugham's
    novel), 230–31
Suaali, Tamasailau M., 262
"Sunkissed" image, 5, *7*, 250
Sussman, George, 177
Sweetman, David, 222

Swift, Jonathan, 58
swimming club image, 5–6, *8*
syphilis. *See* venereal disease

Tabu (film), 233–34, 241
tabua, 147–48
Taeura, 84–85
Tahiatikaomata, 224
Tahiti: Cook voyages, 38, 72–73;
    discovery by Europeans, 9, 17;
    Dolphin voyagers, 69–71; French
    voyagers, 71–72; Gauguin's rep-
    resentations, 215–25; missionary
    arrival, 99, 107–9; royalty, 19,
    61–67, 107, 108
"Tahiti Affair," 204–5
Tahiti Revisited (Hodges), 38–39, 79
Tahuata, 99–103, 107–8
talkies, 240
Tammeamaroo (Ka'humanu), 201–2,
    203
Tanno Manoo, 99–100
Tasmanian people, 88, 95–97, 149–50,
    187–91, 194–96, 213
tattoos, 144
Taylor, George, 32
Taylor, Jane, 32
Taylor, John, 152
Taylor, Margaret, 32
Taylor, Mary, 32
Teaiwa, Teresia, 255, 262
Teehuteatuanonoa, 122, 123, 124
Teha'amana, 220–22
Tehaurana, 219
Teio, 124
Tekela-Smith, Sophia, 262
Tenae, 101
Tench, Watkin, 194
Te Pahi, 138
Teraura, 124
Teriipaia, Tarita Tumi, 252–53, *254*
terrorism age, 7–8, 258–59
Thia (in Diderot), 182

Thomas, William, 111
Thomson, R., 209
Thouars, Abel Du Petit, 204
Threlkeld, Lancelot, 153
Thunderbolt (film), 249
Tierney, Gene, 243–44
Tilton, Robert, 28, 29
Time magazine, 236
Tiné, Queen, 198
Titian, 49, *50*
Toafaiti, 124
Todorov, Tzventan, 21
Tohotaua, 220–21, 224–25
Tonga, 85–86, 189, 191, 198, 213
Tongatapu, 99–100
Torquil (in Byron's poem), 128
tortoiseshell trade, 159–60
tourism, 226, 250–51
tour tradition, 19, 58–59
trade networks, 25–26, 107. *See also* plantation economies; sealing industry; whalers
Transmigration (poem), 64
Trask, Haunani-Kay, 251, 262
Trask, Mililani, 251, 262
travel literature: northernness vs. southernness, 59–60; Orientalist vision, 36–37
Tubuai, 122–23
Turkish Embassy Letters (Montagu), 36–37
Tuvalu, 257
Two Natives Advancing to Combat (Parkinson), 175
Tymarow, 120–21
Typee (Melville), 144–46

Ugliness descriptions: Aboriginal people, 52–53, 58, 154; breast symbolism, 191–93; and ignoble savage stereotype, 195–97; Maori women, 143; Pacific royalty, 198, 200, 201–2; pregnant women, 192–93. *See also* beauty, descriptions of; ignoble savage stereotype

Underwood, Robert A., 259
United States: annexations/protectorates, 214; colonization experience, 20–22, 26–32, 72, 91; and Hawai'i, 209, 211; Nuku Hiva incident, 103–7
Urale, Sima, 261–62

Vaeoho, Marie-Rose, 220–21, 224
Vaitephiha Bay (Hodges), 38–39
Vancouver, George, 120–21
van der Straet, Jan, 20, 21
Van Diemen's Island (Tasmania), 88, 95–97, 149–50, 187–91, 194–96, 213
Van Kirk, Sylvia, 32
van Noort, Oliver, 23–24
Vanuatu, 257, 304n72
Velvet Dreams (film), 261–62
venereal disease: Aboriginal people, 135, 155; blame for, 30, 91–93; Cook voyages, 72, 85–87, 91–92; Gauguin's, 219–20, 222–23; and grand tour tradition, 59; Native Americans, 30; and siren image, 45
Venus images, 47–51, 181–82
Vercoe, Caroline, 262
Vernette, Tevaite, 253
Vespucci, Amerigo, 30, 277n31
Victorian model, 203–12
Vindication of the Rights of Women (Wollstonecraft), 185–86
violence: against Aboriginal people, 134–36, 149–50, 153–57, 158; *Bounty* personnel, 122–24; British policing efforts, 157–59; cinema representations, 241–42, 253; *Dolphin* voyagers, 61, 69–71, 84–85; Dutch voyagers, 24–25;

Gauguin's attitudes, 220, 223–24; ignoble savage stereotype, 94–97; La Pérouse voyage, 187, 188; Maori people, 87–88; against missionaries, 101, 102, 109; modern, 255–57, 260–61; on Ngatik, 159–60; plantation economies, 161–62; promiscuity stereotype, 133–34; and resource industries generally, 137–38; and slavery, 33; Spanish voyagers, 21–22, 23; Tahiti Affair, 205; U.S. voyagers, 104, 105

virtue and chastity. *See* morality ideals

visual representations: Aboriginal people, 136, *137*, 154, 175; American experience, 20–21; classical, *48*, 49; Cook voyages, 38–39, 79–82, 85; corrupted paradise, *229*; Dutch voyagers, 23–24; Gauguin's, 215–25, 230–31; harem images, 36; noble savage, 188–91, 198; Oberea, *66*; Pacific royalty, 198, 205–8, *210*; Tasmanian people, 188–91; Wallis voyage, 62; Winee, 117, *118*

Vivieare, Jim, 262

Voltaire, 180

Wales, William, 192

Wallis, Samuel, 9, 17, 61–62, 63, 69–71

Wallis in Conversation with Oberea (Hawkesworth), 62, *63*

Ward, Mary Anne, 249

War on Terror, 7–8, 258–59

water and feminine, 41, 43–53, 54, 79

Webber, John, 82–84

Wedge, John Herder, 154

Westpac Bank, 256–57

whalers, 93, 109, 112–14, 142–48, 158, 160

White, John, 133

The White Flower (film), 236

White Man, Brown Woman (Richards), 228, 230

White Shadows in the South Seas (Flaherty), 233

white women: appropriation of Pacific stereotype, 5–6, 235–40, 248, 250, 261; convict settlements, 94–95, 131, 132–33; and English nationalism, 74; and grand tour tradition, 59; and marriage, 78; missionaries, 102–3; whale products, 147

William, John, 124

William IV, King, 204

Williams, John, 124, 288*n*12

Williams, Rev. John, 158

Williamson, John, 77, 82

Wilson, James, 99–100, 125

Wilson, John, 109–10, 146

Wilson, William, 93

Winee, 116–19

Winship, 287*n*90

Withers, Robert, 36

wives. *See* marriage

Wollstonecraft, Mary, 185–86

Woman of Van Diemen's Land (in La Billardière), 189, *190*

Woman with a Fan (Gauguin), 224–25

Women with Mango Blossoms (Gauguin), 256–57

Worgan, George, 52

World War I, 234–35

World War II, 249–50

Wright, Henry, 133–34

Yahoos (in Swift's writing), 58

Young, Edward, 124, 288*n*12

Young, George, 129, *130*

Young, Hannah (Hannah Adams), 129, *130*

Zeïr (in Monbart's novel), 185

Zulica (in Monbart's novel), 185

www.ingramcontent.com/pod-product-compliance
Lightning Source LLC
Chambersburg PA
CBHW030637270326
41929CB00007B/107